THE AMERICAN DICTIONARY OF ECONOMICS

THE AMERICAN DICTIONARY OF ECONOMICS

Douglas A. L. Auld,
Graham Bannock,
R. E. Baxter and Ray Rees

Facts On File, Inc.
460 Park Avenue South
New York, N.Y. 10016

THE AMERICAN DICTIONARY OF ECONOMICS

Portions of this book were originally published in *The Penguin Dictionary of Economics* (first edition, 1972; second edition, 1978).

Library of Congress Cataloging in Publication Data

Auld, Douglas A.L.
American dictionary of economics.

Rev. ed. of: The Penguin dictionary of economics/G. Bannock, R. E. Baxter and R. Rees. 2nd ed. 1978.
1. Economics—Dictionaries. I. Bannock, Graham. Penguin dictionary of economics. II. Title. HB61.B38 1982 330'.03'21 81-22052 ISBN 0-87196-532-1 AACR2

Printed in the United States of America

10 9 8 7 6 5 4 3 2 1

PREFACE

This book is intended as a companion and guide for college students of economics, for the general reader who wants to follow economic discussion in the media and as a professional tool for the growing number of readers who need a knowledge of the subject in their daily work.

Modern economics is to a surprisingly large extent the achievement of English-speaking scholars and since World War II, increasingly of Americans. This is not to belittle the contributions of the early French economists, others such as Warias (Switzerland) or the members of the Austrian School and distinguished contemporaries such as Myrdal (Sweden). But in contrast to other social sciences, such as psychology, in any list of internationally respected economists such as those included in this book, British and Americans heavily predominate. Even among the many distinguished economists born and long resident in continental Europe, it is striking that many of them, for example Marx, Schumpeter, Hayek and Leontieff, did most of their work in Britain or America.

There are, of course, several dictionaries of economics on both sides of the Atlantic. We have tried to make ours a distinctive combination of micro-encyclopedic treatment with extensive cross-referencing, up-to-date institutional material and a level approach that combines academic rigor with brevity and practical utility. This formula was pioneered in the *Penguin Dictionary of Economics,* first published in Britain in 1972. The authors are grateful to Penguin Books for agreeing to withdraw our book from sale in the United States and allowing us to adapt the basic concept for our American publishers, Facts On File, Inc. While there is less difference in British and American terminology in economics than in many other subjects, it was necessary to rewrite the book completely so as to give coverage to American institutions, statistical and other illustrative material, as well as to adopt American usage and spelling.

Economics is a big subject and we have necessarily been selective in our treatment of it. Words in everyday use are not included unless they have a specialized meaning in economics. Economic theory, including international, monetary and welfare economics, has been treated fairly comprehensively, and we have devoted a considerable amount of space to economic history. Individual economists are included only where, in our judgement, they have made a definable contribution to the body of economic thought as it exists today; their entries concentrate upon that contribution rather than upon biographical information. We have been particularly sparing in the inclusion of contemporary economists and acknowledge that many distinguished living members of our profession are omitted. We have included all the key terms used by econometricians and statisticians that have practical relevance as well as those used in business finance. Our treatment of financial and business economics, public finance, international trade and payments has been more selective still but, institutions apart, we hope that nothing important has been omitted. Elaborate cross-referencing has been incorporated to avoid repetition and to make the book more useful as an educational aid.

We gratefully acknowledge the help of our publishers in preparing a complex manuscript and seeing it through the press. The authors would welcome comments from readers on errors or omissions for incorporation in future editions. We would like to thank Eveline van Sleightenhorst for her most capable and cheerful assistance.

September 1982

DA
GB
REB
RR

A Note on Cross-references

Cross-references appear frequently both within and after the entries in this book. Cross-references are set in small capital letters; those that appear in parentheses are of two types: A reference preceded by one arrow indicates *direct* amplification of the given entry. Double arrow cross-references simply complement the entry they appear under. Any reference that appears without parentheses in the text indicates that the dictionary contains an entry on the particular concept, person, theory, etc.

The Editor

THE AMERICAN DICTIONARY OF ECONOMICS

A

Above the line. Promotional expenditure incurred by a firm on selling its products or services by means of direct ADVERTISING, such as through television commercials, newspaper advertisements and posters. Below-the-line expenditure includes all other promotional sales expenditure, such as that incurred by special offers, free gifts and in-store displays.

Abstinence theory of interest. ⇛ INTEREST, ABSTINENCE THEORY OF

Accelerated depreciation. ⇛ CAPITAL ALLOWANCES

Acceleration principle. The hypothesis that the level of INVESTMENT varies directly with the rate of change of output. Given technological conditions, and the relative prices of CAPITAL and LABOR, a certain size of CAPITAL STOCK will be chosen to produce a particular rate of output. If this rate of output should change, then, other things being equal, the desired size of the capital stock will also change. Since net investment is, by definition, the amount by which capital stock changes, it follows that the amount of investment depends on the size of the change in output. At its simplest, the hypothesis asserts that investment will be proportional to the rate of change of output, at all levels of output. However, under more realistic assumptions the relationship may cease to be a simple proportional one. There may, for example, be spare capacity over some range of increasing output, so that the capital stock does not have to be increased until full capacity is reached; or the capital intensity (⇛ CAPITAL INTENSIVE) of production may vary as the level of output varies. In addition, the relation will be influenced by EXPECTATIONS, time lags, etc. As well as being very important in explaining the determination of investment expenditure in the economy, the acceleration principle also plays an important part in theories of the TRADE CYCLE, e.g. the ACCELERATOR-MULTIPLIER MODEL, and the theory of ECONOMIC GROWTH, e.g. in the HARROD-DOMAR MODEL. (⇛⇛ ACCELERATOR COEFFICIENT; CLARK, JOHN MAURICE; INVENTORY INVESTMENT CYCLE).

Accelerator coefficient. The amount of additional CAPITAL STOCK required to produce a unit increase in sales. A key element in the ACCELERATION PRINCIPLE, this is the coefficient which relates the level of INVESTMENT to the change in sales. Thus, if I_t is investment in time period $_t$, and Y_t and Y_{t-1} are output in times $_t$ and $_{t-1}$ respectively, then we have: $I_t = V(Y_t - Y_{t-1})$, where V is the accelerator coefficient. Thus, the value of V tells us the strength of the effect that a change in output or sales will have on the level of investment. The simplest form of the theory takes V as a constant determined basically by technology. However, we might also expect V to be affected by interest rates, wage rates and the CAPACITY UTILIZATION RATE. (⇛ CAPITAL-OUTPUT RATIO, INCREMENTAL).

Accelerator-multiplier model. A MODEL of the TRADE CYCLE based on the interaction of the ACCELERATION PRINCIPLE and the MULTIPLIER. A change in INVESTMENT causes, through the multiplier, change in NATIONAL

INCOME. This change in national income determines, through the acceleration principle, a level of INVESTMENT. If this level is different from the level previously attained, there is a further change in investment, a further change in income and so on. It is possible to show by a mathematical analysis of this process that it may cause national income to vary cyclically over time. (⇛ SAMUELSON, PAUL ANTHONY).

Accelerator theory of investment. ⇛ ACCELERATION PRINCIPLE

Account. A record of financial transactions in the form of STOCKS or flows. (⇛⇛ BALANCE OF PAYMENTS; BALANCE SHEET; CURRENT ACCOUNT; SOCIAL ACCOUNTING).

Accounting equation. ⇛ BALANCE SHEET

Accounting Principles Board (A.P.B.). ⇛ INFLATION ACCOUNTING

Accounts payable. ⇛ TRADE CREDIT

Accruals. ⇛ ACCRUED EXPENSES

Accrued expenses. The cost of services utilized in advance of payment and written into a company's accounts as LIABILITIES.

Accrued income taxes. Liabilities for CORPORATION INCOME TAX on profits earned. Since the government does not require payment of taxes until some time after the profits upon which they are levied arise, these tax reserves provide a continuing source of funds for profitable companies.

Acid test ratio. ⇛ "QUICK" RATIO

Activism. An explicit government policy changing tax rates or tax laws in an attempt to stimulate AGGREGATE DEMAND in a RECESSION and curtail it in a period of boom. (⇛ STABILIZATION POLICY).

Adaptive expectations. The hypothesis that future expected events are based on actual events of the past. The concept is most widely used in terms of price expectations.

Administered prices. Prices which are set consciously by a single decision-making body, e.g. a MONOPOLY firm, a CARTEL or a government agency, rather than being determined by the free play of MARKET forces.

Ad valorem tax. ⇛ TAX, AD VALOREM

Advance. Loan. ⇛ BANK LOAN

Advanced country. A state with high levels of income per person. Unlike a DEVELOPING COUNTRY, an advanced country is highly industrialized.

Advertising. The publicizing of goods and services, in the attempt to provide potential buyers with information about prices, availability and qualities of products in as persuasive a way as possible. It is clear that for a given MARKET to work effectively, buyers must be well-informed, and advertising has an important role to play in the information process. However, some economists argue that advertising, because it is supplied by the sellers of products, leads to distortions. There is likely to be an oversupply of advertising in that more advertising messages are produced than consumers would be prepared to pay for if they were sold separately; but since consumers are forced to pay for advertising in the form of higher-priced goods, they have no choice. Opponents of this view point to the failure of lower-priced, non-advertised products, e.g., supermarkets' "own brands," to replace the more expensive advertised products as evidence that consumers prefer advertised goods, and suggest that opposition to advertising stems, therefore, from paternalistic disapproval of the "irrationality" of consumers. There may also, of course, be biases in the information presented to buyers, and the true information content of advertising messages may be low, with a preponderance of devices to exploit consumer psychology in ways favorable to the product. This may explain the growth of new information sources such as magazines providing objective information on a wide range of products. The effects of advertising on the degree of competition (⇒ PERFECT COMPETITION) in a market have also been extensively analyzed. It has been suggested that advertising may lead to greater concentration in an industry, partly because it is an instrument of *product differentiation* (⇒ DIFFERENTIATION, PRODUCT) and also partly because it may enable a firm to achieve ECONOMIES OF SCALE and so undercut its rivals. Advertising may also increase the BARRIERS TO ENTRY into an industry, since a new firm may have to incur heavy expenditures to overcome existing brand loyalties. There is a strong presumption among many economists that advertising tends to be excessive in consumer-oriented oligopolistic industries (⇒ OLIGOPOLY), such as household detergents, drink and tobacco. In some respects, advertising can be thought of as a system, organized by businessmen, whereby consumption of the outputs of the mass media is subsidized from the proceeds of a tax (the advertising appropriation) on the consumption of goods.

Agency for International Development (AID). A U.S. Government Agency that carries out programs designed to assist DEVELOPING COUNTRIES make optimum use of their human and economic resources. The Foreign Assistance Act of 1961 directed the Secretary of State to establish the agency. Its functions are carried out under the direction of an administrator who reports to the President and the Secretary of State. The central office is in Washington, D.C., with missions and offices in several countries overseas. The aid programs involve food supply and storage facilities, population and health planning, educational programs and a variety of forms of technical assistance.

Aggregate demand. The total DEMAND for goods and services in the economy. It is conventionally broken down into: (a) the demands of HOUSEHOLDS for consumer goods and services; (b) the demands of firms and the government for investment goods (⇒ CAPITAL); (c) the demands of both federal and state governments for goods and services; and (d) the demands of consumers and firms in other countries for goods and services in the form of EXPORTS. Since aggregate demand determines the level of production and hence employment, analysis of the determinants of these components of aggregate demand is the core of the Keynesian (⇒ KEYNES, JOHN MAYNARD) analysis of NATIONAL INCOME and employment determination. (⇒ EMPLOYMENT, FULL; ⇒⇒ SOCIAL ACCOUNTING).

Aggregate supply. The total SUPPLY of goods and SERVICES in the economy available to meet AGGREGATE DEMAND. It consists of domestically produced goods and services plus IMPORTS.

Aggregation problem. ⇛ CAMBRIDGE SCHOOL

Allen, Sir Roy George Douglas (1906–). Educated at Sidney Sussex College, Cambridge, England, Sir R. G. D. Allen began lecturing at the London School of Economics in 1928. During the Second World War he moved from the U.K. TREASURY to Washington as Director of Records and Statistics of the British Supply Council and of the combined Production and Resources Board. In 1944 he was appointed Professor of Statistics at London University, a position he held until 1973. His publications include *Mathematical Analysis for Economists* (1938), *Statistics for Economists* (1949), *Mathematical Economics* (1956) and *Macro-Economic Theory—A Mathematical Treatment* (1967). In 1934 he published an article in *Economica* with Sir JOHN RICHARD HICKS which demonstrated the use of the INDIFFERENCE CURVE based on ORDINAL UTILITY as an analytical tool in the theory of consumer behavior. (⇛⇛ SLUTSKY, EUGEN).

Amalgamation. Synonym for COMBINATION.

American banking systems. ⇛ FEDERAL RESERVE SYSTEM

American Federation of Labor (AFL). The basis for craft unions in the United States whereby workers are joined in association or union based on their skills, not their employer or place of work. It was founded by Samuel Gompers in 1886 and reached a peak membership of 10 percent of the labor force in 1920. In the 1930s the industrial unions in steel and automobiles split from the AFL and formed the CONGRESS OF INDUSTRIAL ORGANIZATIONS (CIO).

American selling price. ⇛ GENERAL AGREEMENT ON TARIFFS AND TRADE

American Stock Exchange. One of two major U.S. STOCK EXCHANGES where STOCKS and BONDS are bought and sold publicly. The other major exchange is the New York Stock Exchange.

Amortization. Provision for the repayment of DEBT by means of accumulating a "sinking fund" through regular payments which, with accumulated INTEREST, may be used to settle the debt in installments over time. A sinking fund may be required by law, as in the case of some public utilities bond issues, or it may be set up by the borrower as a matter of financial prudence. The term is also used to refer to regular capital repayments on loans as in a house MORTGAGE and as a synonym for DEPRECIATION.

Andean Pact. A common market established, by the Cartagena Agreement in 1969, among Chile, Peru, Colombia, Bolivia and Ecuador. Venezuela joined the Pact in 1973, but Chile terminated its agreements in 1976. The aims of the group include the establishment of a common external tariff (⇛ TARIFFS, IMPORT), the freeing of trade among member countries and a policy for the rational development of specific industries on a regional basis. Tariffs on manufactured goods have been virtually eliminated among member countries, except for Ecuador and Bolivia, which have been given a further 10 years to adjust. (⇛ LATIN AMERICAN FREE TRADE ASSOCIATION).

Annuity. 1. A constant annual payment. 2. A guaranteed series of payments in the future purchased immediately for a lump sum. Annuities are described as "certain" where payment is specified for a fixed number of years. A "life" annuity payment continues until the death of the person for whom it was purchased. Annuities may be "immediate," where payment commences on purchase, or "deferred," where payment starts at a specified future date. Annuities are available from insurance companies, whose pension schemes (⇛ PENSION FUNDS) are often annuities purchased with accumulated contributions and EARNINGS on the funds in which they are invested. The price of an annuity is based on the PRESENT VALUE of the stream of income payments it provides, and it varies with RATES OF INTEREST and, in the case of life annuities, the age and sex of the person who will draw the annuity.

Anti Inflation Board (A.I.B.). In order to combat rising wage and price inflation, the Canadian government established a comprehensive PRICES AND INCOMES POLICY in October 1975. The A.I.B. was the agency established to conduct the policies laid down in Parliament. The major instrument assigned to the Board was the power to roll back wage settlements, although there was some control over profits as well. The Board was disbanded in the fall of 1978 without having achieved its specific goal. The evidence suggests, however, that the Board was successful in reducing wage inflation.

Anti-Merger Act. ⇛ CELLER-KEFAUVER ACT

Antitrust Division. The division within the U.S. Department of Justice that initiates court action against companies that are believed to have violated laws with respect to MERGER, MONOPOLY and PRICE DISCRIMINATION.

Antitrust policy. The foundation blocks of U.S. antitrust policy are the SHERMAN ANTITRUST ACT, CLAYTON ANTITRUST ACT and the FEDERAL TRADE COMMISSION. The two acts of Congress and subsequent amendments such as the CELLER-KEFAUVER ACT provide the legal basis for public policy against trusts, cartels and other forms of the abuse of monopoly power (⇛ CARTEL; TRUST), such as PRICE DISCRIMINATION, EXCLUSIVE DEALING and TYING CONTRACTS.

Prior to 1914, it was generally recognized that an agency was needed to oversee antitrust policy. This concern led to the creation of the Federal Trade Commission. Today, the Commission and the Antitrust Division of the Department of Justice share the responsibility for enforcement of the laws governing business behavior. The Antitrust Division is almost exclusively an investigative and enforcement board. If it proceeds with an antitrust charge, the case is heard before a federal district court. While the Federal Trade Commission does research, it can prosecute cases and issue cease-and-desist orders against corporations when their business policies are found by administrative law judges to violate antitrust laws.

Over the years, the interpretations by the courts with respect to violations against the Sherman and Clayton Acts have led to the conclusion that both the Justice Department and the Federal Trade Commission may bring civil actions against those suspected of violating the Acts. In either case, appeal is to the Supreme Court. The success of U.S. antitrust policy is impossible to measure because of the lack of any specific criteria of optimal business behavior. There seems little doubt that without the ghost of Senator Sherman at the board table, the degree of monopoly and the abuse of that power would be more widespread than it is at present.

Appreciation. Increase in the value of an ASSET; the opposite of DEPRECIATION. Appreciation may occur through rising PRICES as a result of INFLATION, increased scarcity or increased earning power. (⇛ CURRENCY APPRECIATION).

Arbitrage. 1. The practice of switching short-term funds from one INVESTMENT to another in order to obtain the best return. An arbitrage flow of funds will take place between two financial centers if the difference in their RATES OF INTEREST is greater than the cost of covering against the currency exchange RISK. The latter is reflected in the difference between the spot exchange rate and the forward exchange rate (⇛ FORWARD EXCHANGE MARKET; SPOT MARKET). The source of these arbitrage flows may come from dealers who specialize in this business. Arbitrage may also take place between BONDS or NOTES with different maturity dates when interest rates diverge. Arbitrage in itself is not speculative. For instance, there are two alternative methods for the holder of U.S. dollars to speculate on an appreciation (⇛ EXCHANGE RATE) of the French franc. The first is to buy francs spot in Paris and invest in bonds on the Paris market; the second is to buy forward francs and invest dollars in the New York market. The choice will depend on the actual interest rates prevailing in each market. 2. When price differences exist within any MARKET, the act of buying at the lower price and reselling at the higher price is known as arbitrage. The effect is to eliminate the price difference, and so arbitrage forms part of the process by which EQUILIBRIUM is reached. (⇛ PERFECT COMPETITION; PRICE DISCRIMINATION).

Arithmetic progression. A series of numbers in which each value differs by a constant from that of the preceding value, e.g., $x, (a+x), (2a+x), \ldots (an+x)$. (⇛⇛ GEOMETRIC PROGRESSION).

Arrow, Kenneth, J. (1921–). Professor Arrow received his M.A. and Ph.D. from Columbia University. From 1947 to 1949 he was a research associate at the Cowles Commission. He went to Stanford University in 1949 and remained there until his move to Harvard in 1968. Much of Arrow's scientific research has been concerned with proofs of the existence and stability of GENERAL EQUILIBRIUM and with how the economic system operates to achieve optimal resource allocation (⇛ ECONOMIC EFFICIENCY). He has applied to economic theory modern mathematical concepts, and helped transform the nature of mathematical economics. The research of Arrow has stressed the role of decentralization as a means of achieving optimal resource allocation. Professor Arrow's work has also encompassed the subject of the SOCIAL WELFARE FUNCTION and he is widely known for his IMPOSSIBILITY THEOREM. Among his many publications are *Social Choice and Individual Values,* 1951, 1963, (based on his doctoral dissertation); *Public Investment, The Rate of Return and Optimal Fiscal Policy* (with M. Kurz), 1972; *Essays in the Theory of Risk-Bearing,* 1971. Professor Arrow received the Nobel Prize (⇛ NOBEL PRIZES) in Economics in 1972.

Arusha Agreement. ⇛ LOME CONVENTION

Asian Development Bank (A.D.B.). The Bank was set up in November 1966 following the recommendations of the United Nations Economic Commission for Asia and the Far East. It was formed "to foster economic growth and cooperation in the region of Asia and the Far East and to contribute to the acceleration of economic development of the DEVELOPING COUNTRIES of the region." It encourages economic and financial cooperation among the regional members. Membership carries the right to contract for projects supported by bank loans. About 60 percent of the total subscribed CAPITAL of $1,100 million was contributed by the 19 countries within the United Nations commission region, which include the developed countries of Japan, Australia and New Zealand. The remaining non-regional members include the United States, which subscribed $200 million (as did Japan), West Germany, Canada, the United Kingdom and Switzerland. In 1976, by which year subscribed capital had increased to $3,700 million, agreement was reached which raised this figure to $8,800 million. The bank operates as a viable BANKING institution, charging realistic RATES OF INTEREST, and encouraging a flow of capital to the region from outside sources. (⇛ COLOMBO PLAN; INTER-AMERICAN DEVELOPMENT BANK).

Assets. An accounting term. On a company's BALANCE SHEET, everything it owns or leases and which has a money value is classified as an asset, total assets being equal to total LIABILITIES. Assets fall into the following categories, roughly in the order of degree to which realizing their money value would disrupt the company's business: (a) *Current assets:* CASH, bank deposits and other items that can readily be turned into cash, e.g., accounts receivable (⇛ TRADE CREDIT), marketable SECURITIES, INVENTORIES, PREPAYMENTS. (b) INVESTMENT in subsidiary or associated companies and other not readily marketable securities, or securities being held for long term gain. (c) *Fixed assets:* LAND, buildings, plant and machinery, vehicles, furniture and equipment. With the exception of land these assets are called *depreciable assets* and are usually written in at cost, less DEPRECIATION. (d) *Intangible* assets: goodwill, patents, etc. The assets of an individual are those possessions or the liabilities of others which to him have a positive money value.

Association of South East Asian Nations (A.S.E.A.N.). An association of five DEVELOPING COUNTRIES in Southeast Asia, and comprising Indonesia, Malaysia, the Philippines, Singapore and Thailand. In 1976, the Association agreed to cooperate on industrial projects in petrochemicals, fertilizers, steel, soda ash, newsprint and rubber, and to assist one another in the construction of major plants. The Association also set up a permanent secretariat. Progress in developing joint projects has been slow but, in 1980, it was agreed to relax the rule that all the countries must participate in each project. The Association has an emergency oil sharing scheme to assist any member country whose supplies fall significantly short of requirement.

Assurance. That branch of insurance under which a contract is made to pay a CAPITAL sum on a specified date or on the death of the person assured.

Atomistic competition. The type of MARKET STRUCTURE in which very large numbers of small firms compete independently. (⇛⇛ PERFECT COMPETITION).

Austrian school. A tradition of economic thought originating in the work of CARL MENGER (1840–1921), who was Professor of Economics at Vienna until 1903. He was succeeded in the Chair by F. VON WIESER (1851–1926) and E. BÖHM-BAWERK (1851–1914). Menger's principal achievement was the construction of a marginal utility theory of value (⇛ VALUE, THEORIES OF). His work was developed by Von Wieser, who, in addition, clearly formulated the important concept of opportunity COST. Böhm-Bawerk's main contributions were in the fields of CAPITAL and interest rate theory (⇛ RATE OF INTEREST). The Austrian tradition was followed in the work of L. E. VON MISES, F. A. HAYEK, and J. R. HICKS. (⇛⇛ JEVONS, WILLIAM STANLEY; LONGFIELD, SAMUEL MOUNTIFORT).

Auto-correlation. CORRELATION between the error terms in a regression model (⇛ REGRESSION ANALYSIS). Its effect is to invalidate one of the assumptions underlying the ordinary least squares procedure (⇛ LEAST SQUARES REGRESSION), and thus to make it necessary to modify that procedure. It is often called serial correlation.

Automatic stabilizer. ⇛ BUILT-IN STABILIZERS

Automatic transfer service (ATS). An arrangement permitting a depositor to transfer funds from TIME DEPOSITS to DEMAND DEPOSITS in order to honor checks written on the account. (⇛ BANKING; NOW ACCOUNT).

Autonomous investment. The portion of total INVESTMENT that is not determined by economic factors such as the RATE OF INTEREST, the rate of change of sales, or the profitability of investment, but rather by factors that are considered outside the economic system (⇛ EXOGENOUS VARIABLE). An example would be investment made to take advantage of some INNOVATION or technical discovery. The importance of autonomous investment in economic theory is that changes in it may spark economic fluctuations, and may influence the behavior of the TRADE CYCLE in ways that are not explained by MODELS based on investments understood in terms of endogenous factors (rate of interest, rate of change of sales, etc.).

Average. A single number meant to represent a set of numbers, by showing a "central" value around which the other numbers are grouped. The average wage of a group of workers, for example, suggests the wage those workers typically tend to earn. Necessarily, some or even all the numbers may differ from the average—a worker may never earn his "average" wage (cf. the statement, the average number of persons per HOUSEHOLD in the United States is 2⅓). Nevertheless, the average is useful; it reveals the value about which the actual numbers are closely grouped, or, as statisticians say, a measurement of the "central tendency" of the data.

There are in fact several ways to calculate an average from a set of numbers, and the different ways frequently yield different values. It is misleading to say "the average . . . is" without specifying the type of average being used. The types of average in common use are:

(a) *The arithmetic mean:* This is the "average" most often seen in everyday use: a set of numbers is summed, and the answer divided by the number of numbers. The "mean" wage of a group of 500 workers, for example, is found by summing their individual wages, and dividing by 500. The mean gives a good representation of the typical values of the numbers when the numbers are somewhat closely clustered and there are no values very much greater or very much smaller than the rest. If such extreme values are present, the mean tends to give an inaccurate representation of the numbers' typical values. As an example: the mean weekly wage of five men, earning respectively, \$150, \$170, \$180, \$200 and \$200 is given by:

$$\left(\frac{150 + 170 + 180 + 200 + 200}{5}\right) = \$180 \text{ p.w.}$$

However, if the fifth man earned \$550 per week, the mean wage would be \$250 per week, which is much less representative of the set of numbers as almost all the other wages were considerably less. Hence, in this case the mean would not be very useful.

Certain types of data frequently exhibit such extreme values—wages and incomes (⇛ INCOME DISTRIBUTION), size of firms in an industry (⇛ SIZE DISTRIBUTION OF FIRMS), size of cities in a country, etc.—that the mean is often rejected as the appropriate measurement, and other methods of averaging are used.

Note also that the usefulness of the mean depends on how *closely* the numbers are grouped around it. In the example given above, the actual wages approximate the mean of \$180. However, suppose the wages of the five men were \$80, \$110, \$180, \$260 and \$270. The mean is again \$180 per week, but it is a less typical value because the numbers are more widely dispersed. In fact, whenever a mean value is given, it should be accompanied by a measure of how closely or widely the surrounding numbers are dispersed (⇛ STANDARD DEVIATION; VARIANCE).

(b) *The median:* A type of average often used when the mean is inappropriate. The median of a set of numbers is that number which is surrounded by an equal number of values that are less than it is and greater than it is. To find the median, the set of numbers is first arranged in ascending order of size. If the number of values in the set is odd, the median is immediately established as the middle number. (In the five values in the set of wage rates given above, the middle value is the third number, i.e., \$180.) On the other hand, if the number of values is even, none of those values is the "middle number." The solution then is to take the mean of the adjacent central values (the second and third when there are four numbers, the 10th and 11th when there are 20 numbers, and so on), as the median. To illustrate: suppose the set of wage rates contains the four numbers \$150, \$170, \$180 and \$200. The two middle numbers are \$170 and \$180. Their mean is $\$\left(\frac{170 + 180}{2}\right) = \$175$. Hence, \$175 is the median wage rate, with two numbers below it (\$150 and \$170) and two above it (\$180 and \$200). In short, the middle value of the set is taken as typical or representative of the whole set. Unlike the mean, the median ignores extreme values. Thus, in the case where the fifth wage rate was \$550 per week, the median would still be $180 per week, whereas the mean would rise to $250 per week. In fact, we could make the two values above the median as high as we liked, or the values below the median as low as we liked: as long as the number of values is five, the median is $180 and remains unchanged. It follows that, when there are extreme values among the higher values in the set, the mean tends to pull above the median; when there are extreme values among the lower values in the set, the mean tends to pull below the median. In each of these cases, the median is apt to give a more accurate representation of the data.

(c) *The mode:* This is the value in the set of numbers that occurs most frequently. Thus, in the set $150, $170, $180, $200 and $200, the mode is $200. If the last $200 was deleted, the set would have no mode. If, however, the set of numbers was increased to six by adding a value of $150, it would have two modes (it would be "bi-modal"), one of $150 and one of $200. The mode can be of interest for its own sake: it may be interesting to know what wage is earned most frequently, the size of family encountered most often, etc.

(d) *The geometric mean:* This is calculated as the nth root of the product of n numbers. Thus, the geometric mean of 1 and 4 is $\sqrt{1 \times 4} = \sqrt{4} = 2$. Similarly, the geometric mean of 1, 2, 3, 13.5 is $\sqrt[4]{1 \times 2 \times 3 \times 13.5} = \sqrt[4]{81} = 3$. The geometric mean is chiefly used in calculating average growth rates over a period of time. Although this method of calculating the geometric mean could be cumbersome when the number of growth rates is large, the procedure is simplified by noting that the logarithm of the geometric mean is found by taking the arithmetic mean of the logarithms of the growth rates. (⇛⇛ WEIGHTED AVERAGE).

Average cost. Production COST per unit of output produced. It is calculated by dividing total cost of production by the number of units of output. SHORT-RUN average cost relates to the cost of production during a time period when at least one FACTOR OF PRODUCTION is fixed in quantity. For example, it may take a year for a firm to plan, order and install new machinery; during this period the firm will be constrained to use only its existing stock of machines. LONG-RUN average cost relates to the cost of production during a time when all factors of production can be treated as variable. For example if the firm, by planning now, can determine the amount of each factor of production it will have available in one year's time, it can plan its future production on the basis that all inputs are variable in quantity. It follows that when planning production for the long run the firm can choose the most efficient set of input quantities, i.e., that set which minimizes production cost. In the short run, however, the firm may be unable to attain these least-cost input quantities because of the constraint that at least one input cannot be changed. As a result average cost in the short run will be higher than average cost in the long run, *unless* the fixed input quantities are in fact the ones the firm would have chosen had it been free to do so.

Average cost pricing. The method of establishing prices in which PRICE is set equal to AVERAGE COST. Since total revenue is equal to price multiplied by quantity, and total cost is equal to average cost multiplied by quantity, average cost pricing ensures that total costs are covered by revenue. (⇛⇛ MARGINAL COST PRICING).

Average productivity. The output of a good divided by the number of units of a particular FACTOR OF PRODUCTION required to produce it. The commonly sought measure is the average productivity of LABOR which is found by dividing output by the number employed or by man-hours. Measures of average productivity are used as indicators of productive efficiency. They suffer from the limitation that interfirm productivity comparisons may be misleading if the firms have different labor and CAPITAL intensities. (⇛ CAPITAL-INTENSIVE).

Average propensity to consume (A.P.C.). When referring to the economy, this is the total value of expenditure on consumption goods and SERVICES divided by the value of NATIONAL INCOME. It is, therefore, the proportion of national income devoted to CONSUMPTION. Similarly, for an individual the A.P.C. is that proportion of INCOME devoted to consumption. Since income can either be spent or saved, the lowest value the A.P.C. can take is zero (all income is saved) and the highest is one (all income is spent). It is generally asserted that the higher the level of income of either an economy or an individual, the lower the A.P.C., and the greater the proportion that will be saved. (⇛⇛ CONSUMPTION FUNCTION; MARGINAL PROPENSITY TO CONSUME).

Average propensity to save (A.P.S.). The complement of the AVERAGE PROPENSITY TO CONSUME. The A.P.S. is defined as the proportion of INCOME of an individual or an economy which is not spent on consumption goods and services, rather it is saved (see SAVING). It is therefore measured as 1—A.P.C. It is asserted that as the income of an individual or an economy rises, a higher proportion of that income is saved, i.e., the A.P.S. rises. (⇛⇛ CONSUMPTION FUNCTION).

Average revenue. The total revenue received from the sale of a given number of units of output, divided by the number of units. Since total revenue is defined as PRICE multiplied by the number of units sold, average revenue and price are necessarily identical.

Avoidable costs. Those COSTS of production that would not be incurred if a given output were not produced. They are closely related to VARIABLE COSTS or PRIME COSTS. However, total avoidable costs need not equal total variable costs; if a firm ceases production of a good altogether, it may "avoid" costs which must be incurred if any output is to be produced, but which do not vary with output, e.g., lump-sum royalty payments on a particular process. (⇛⇛ MARGINAL COST PRICING).

B

"Bad money drives out good." Before paper MONEY (⇛ BANK NOTE) became universally accepted as a means for settling DEBTS, precious metals were the most common forms of money. Gold and silver coins were struck bearing a FACE VALUE equivalent to the value of their metal content. Debasement of the coinage occurred when the face value was kept above the value of the metal content of the coinage. The holders of the correctly valued coinage became unwilling to exchange for the debased coinage because they would obtain less metal in exchange than if they bought direct. The result was that the "good," undebased coinage did not circulate. The process is referred to as GRESHAM'S LAW.

Bagehot, Walter (1826–77). Bagehot graduated in mathematics at University College, London, England, and was called to the Bar in 1852. After a period as a banker in his father's business, he succeeded his father-in-law as editor of *The Economist* newspaper in 1860, a post he held until 1877. He was an influential commentator on current economic affairs and a prolific writer who is often quoted today. His publications include *Universal Money* (1869), *Physics and Politics* (1872), *Lombard Street. A Description of the Money Market* (1873) and *Postulates of English Political Economy* (1876).

Balanced budget. The government's BUDGET is said to balance when total receipts from taxation, investment income and other charges equal its total expenditure. During the 1970s, the federal budget was in a deficit position each year, fluctuating between a deficit of $6.7 billion and $70.6 billion. On a FULL EMPLOYMENT SURPLUS basis, the budget has fluctuated between a deficit of $21.5 billion and a surplus of $9.9 billion. It was J.M. KEYNES who showed how the budget surpluses and deficits could be used to regulate the economy. It should be remembered that a balanced budget does not necessarily have a neutral effect on the economy. For instance, if the government raised taxes on the rich to give assistance to the poor, the budget would have a MULTIPLIER effect and generate additional incomes overall. This is because the propensity to save of the rich is higher than it is of the poor (⇛ AVERAGE PROPENSITY TO SAVE). Lately, much has been said about establishing rules to force governments to produce a balanced budget each year. Since a large proportion of tax receipts respond relatively quickly to changes in economic conditions while expenditures are far more inflexible, an annual balanced budget would be rather difficult. If it was enforced by Congress, it would probably require tax cuts during INFLATION and tax increases during a RECESSION. (⇛ BUILT-IN STABILIZERS; FISCAL POLICY; STABILIZATION POLICY).

Balanced growth. A particular form of an economy's growth process in which all the main economic aggregates—NATIONAL INCOME, CONSUMPTION, the stock of CAPITAL, and EMPLOYMENT (⇛ EMPLOYMENT, FULL)—grow at the same percentage rate. Although actual economies rarely, if ever, achieve balanced growth paths, the analysis of such paths has played an important role in GROWTH THEORY, analogous to the role in static economic theory of the concept of long-run static equilibrium. (⇛ LONG RUN; STATIC EQUILIBRIUM).

Balance of payments. A tabulation of the CREDIT and debit transactions of a country with foreign countries and international institutions, prepared and published in a form similar to the INCOME STATEMENT of companies. These transactions are divided into two broad groups: current account and capital account. The current account is made up of visible trade (i.e., merchandise EXPORTS and IMPORTS) and invisible trade (i.e., income and expenditure for SERVICES such as tourism and shipping, together with profits earned overseas and interest payments). The balance on current account is the difference between the NATIONAL INCOME and national expenditure in the period. An abbreviated balance of payments account for 1979 is shown below.

U.S. BALANCE OF PAYMENTS SUMMARY 1979
($ billion)

CURRENT ACCOUNT		
Export of Goods and Services	+182.7	
Import of Goods and Services	−241.4	
Transfers and Other Items	+ 58.4	
Balance on Current Account		−0.3
CAPITAL ACCOUNT		
Inflow of Private Financial Capital	+ 48.9	
Outflow of Private Financial Capital	− 58.6	
Balance on Capital Account		−9.7
METHOD OF FINANCING		
Increase in Foreign Official Assets in U.S. (+)	− 16.3	
Reduction in U.S. Official Reserves and Increase in S.D.R.	+ 26.3	

(Adopted from U.S. Dept. of Commerce: *Survey of Current Business.)*

The capital account is composed of inward and outward flows of money for INVESTMENT by the private sector and receipts from the sale of BONDS by the public sector. Throughout the 1960s, exports tended to equal or exceed imports but the combination of foreign aid, U.S. tourist spending overseas, military aid and the FOREIGN INVESTMENT of U.S. corporations has resulted in a deficit on the balance of payments. The problem became more acute in the 1970s, especially as a result of the impact of the OPEC (⇛ ORGANIZATION OF PETROLEUM EXPORTING COUNTRIES) oil price increase which resulted in an excess of the cost of imports over the value of exports along with the capital outflows.

A balance of payments surplus means there is a net demand for dollars, an imbalance that is corrected by an appreciation in the value of the dollar. If EXCHANGE RATES are fixed, or if the authorities do not wish to see a change in the value of the currency, they must buy foreign currency. In 1979, the balance of payments deficit in the United States resulting in a net demand for foreign currency, placed downward pressure on the value of the dollar. The U.S. authorities did not wish to see the dollar decline and thus sold foreign currency to stabilize the price. The success of this policy depends on the size of the gold and foreign currency reserves (⇛ RESERVE CURRENCY) and whether the deficit/surplus is persistent or temporary. A deficit in the balance of payments is not necessarily bad, any more than a surplus need be good. It is a form of borrowing which could be used to enhance domestic savings to boost investment and stimulate future growth. On the other hand, if the deficit is occasioned, for instance, by an excess of AGGREGATE DEMAND over supply in the domestic market, it will persist until the home market has reached EQUILIBRIUM and, if the overseas borrowing is used to finance immediate consumption rather than investment, it will yield little benefit in the form of higher rates of growth in the future. There are many measures that can be taken to correct a DISEQUILIBRIUM in the balance of payments. If the imbalance is expected to be temporary, borrowing (or lending) from other countries or international institutions, either through direct arrangements or through adjustments in the level of interest rates, may be possible (⇛ INTERNATIONAL MONETARY FUND). Import tariffs, (⇛ TARIFFS, IMPORT) import QUOTAS, IMPORT DEPOSITS and EXPORT INCENTIVES could be applied in order to affect the visible trade balance quickly, but such measures are subject to the GENERAL AGREEMENT ON TARIFFS AND TRADE. Other measures include EXCHANGE CONTROL, and operations designed to ease the strain on the balance of payments by adjusting the level of aggregate demand in the home economy. In order partly to offset a balance of payments deficit and currency depreciation, the U.S. government in 1981 persuaded the Japanese to limit the sales of automobiles in the United States. Changes in the exchange rate, under the fixed system operating from the BRETTON WOODS agreement of 1944 until the exchange rate adjustments of 1971, were regarded as the final long-term solution. (⇛ SMITHSONIAN AGREEMENT).

Balance of trade. The BALANCE OF PAYMENTS on current account.

Balance sheet. A statement of the WEALTH of a business, other organization or individual on a given date; not to be confused with the INCOME STATEMENT that records changes in wealth during a given period. A balance sheet is in two parts: (a) on the left side, or at the top, ASSETS and (b) on the right side, or at the bottom, LIABILITIES. The assets of the company: DEBTORS, cash, investments and property, are set out against the claims, or liabilities, of the persons or organizations owning them: CREDITORS, lenders and stockholders, to make the two sides of the balance sheet equal. This is the principle of DOUBLE-ENTRY BOOKKEEPING. The fact that the assets and liabilities are equal does not mean the shareholders owe as much as they own—they are included among the claimants. According to the *basic accounting equation:*

Assets = Liabilities + EQUITY.

Therefore: Assets − Liabilities = Equity.

Equity, or what is the same thing, *net worth,* or *shareholders' interest* calculated from the balance sheet in this way may not reflect its true market value since assets are normally written into the balance sheet at historic cost (⇛ BOOK VALUE) without any adjustment for APPRECIATION.

Balance sheet total. The sum of ASSETS or LIABILITIES shown on the BALANCE SHEET. (⇛⇛ CAPITAL EMPLOYED).

Bancor. The term J. M. KEYNES applied to the CURRENCY which he proposed a new central international bank should create and put into circulation for the payment of DEBTS between countries (⇛⇛ KEYNES PLAN). His proposal was rejected at the 1944 BRETTON WOODS Conference, which established the INTERNATIONAL MONETARY FUND. However, the beginning of 1970 saw the introduction of a similar international currency in the allocation of SPECIAL DRAWING RIGHTS through the I.M.F.

Bank. ⇛ BANKING

Bank advances. ⇛ BANK LOAN

Bank, commercial. ⇛ COMMERCIAL BANK

Bank deposit. ⇛ DEPOSIT

Bankers' acceptances. ⇛ MONEY MARKET

Bank for International Settlements (B.I.S.). An institution, with head offices in Basle, set up on the basis of a proposal by the Young Committee in 1930. The original purpose was to enable the various national CENTRAL BANKS to coordinate through their own central bank the receipts and payments arising mainly from German war reparations. It was hoped, however, that it would develop beyond this, but many of the functions which it might have performed were, in fact, taken over by the INTERNATIONAL MONETARY FUND after the Second World War. Since then, the B.I.S. has acted like a bank for the central banks by accepting deposits and making short-term loans. It has, however, in recent years played a more active part in attempting to mitigate the effects of international financial SPECULATION and acts as a trustee for international government loans. In addition, the bank has carried out financial transactions for the ORGANIZATION FOR EUROPEAN ECONOMIC COOPERATION, ORGANIZATION FOR ECONOMIC COOPERATION AND DEVELOPMENT, EUROPEAN PAYMENTS UNION, European monetary agreement, EUROPEAN COAL AND STEEL COMMUNITY and the I.M.F. Although the major functions of a central bank for central banks are performed by the I.M.F., the monthly meetings of the directors of the B.I.S. held in Basle have been a useful means of central-bank cooperation, especially in the field of off-setting short-term monetary movements of a speculative kind. The board is made up of the representatives of the central banks of the United Kingdom, France, West Germany, Belgium, Italy, Switzerland, Netherlands and Sweden. Other countries' representatives, e.g., from the United States, Canada, Japan, however, attend meetings regularly. (⇛⇛ BRUSSELS CONFERENCE).

Bank Holding Company Act. Administered by the FEDERAL RESERVE, this act circumscribes the activities of BANKS as far as the use of a HOLDING COMPANY status to expand activities is concerned. The Act was introduced and passed in 1956 at a time when there was new bank merger activity. The purpose was to control the expansion of HOLDING COMPANIES which could exercise control over several seemingly independent banks. The Act defined a bank holding company as one with 25 percent or more control in two or more banks. These companies are required under the act to register with the FEDERAL RESERVE SYSTEM and submit to examination by the Federal Reserve. The Act was amended in 1966 to bring it in line with the CLAYTON ANTITRUST ACT and SHERMAN ANTITRUST ACT. (⇛ BANKING; EXPORT TRADING COMPANY).

Banking. The business of accepting DEPOSITS and lending MONEY. When banking is defined this way, it is carried out by some FINANCIAL INTERMEDIARIES, other than COMMERCIAL BANKS, that perform the functions of safeguarding deposits and making loans, e.g., SAVINGS AND LOAN ASSOCIATIONS. THRIFTS are not normally referred to as banks and are not regarded as part of the banking system in the traditional sense. The distinction between *banking* and the *banking system* is that the latter, chiefly the COMMERCIAL BANKS, with the CENTRAL BANK, is the principal mechanism through which the MONEY SUPPLY of the country is created and controlled. Since the early 1970's, however, the role of banks (in the broadest sense) in the determination of the money supply has been increasingly recognized, and since 1980, the DEPOSITORY INSTITUTIONS DEREGULATION AND MONETARY CONTROL ACT has extended reserve requirements to all deposit taking institutions. Banks create money in the following way. When the manager of a bank grants a LOAN to a customer, the loan creates a deposit that can be used to settle debts by the use of checks or transfers. A book debt has been incurred by the customer in return for a promise to repay it. Whether or not the loan is secured by COLLATERAL SECURITY, such as an insurance policy, or some other ASSET, the bank has added to the total money supply. In BALANCE SHEET terms, the deposit is a claim on the bank—that is a LIABILITY—while the customer's promise to repay it, or the collateral security, is an asset to the bank. In the absence of government control on lending, the limitation on the bank's ability to create deposits is their obligation, if they are to remain in business, to pay out CHECKING ACCOUNT deposits in cash on demand. Since the bank's customers meet most of their needs for money by writing checks on their deposits, the cash holdings the banks need are only a small fraction of their total deposits. This ratio between their deposit liabilities and cash holdings is called the CASH HOLDING RATIO. The authorities (⇛ FEDERAL RESERVE SYSTEM) can influence the money supply through the banking system by the use of OPEN-MARKET OPERATIONS and the DISCOUNT RATE as well as the cash holding ratio (⇛ CREDIT SQUEEZE). The objective of the banker is, of course, to keep his reserves as near to the minimum as possible, since no return is earned on holdings of cash and only a low return on other *liquid* assets (LIQUIDITY). The banking system is based on confidence in the system's ability to meet its obligations. In the short run, no bank is able to meet all its obligations in cash; should demands upon it exhaust its cash reserves, the bank would be obliged to close. Bank failures, which were widespread in the 1930's, are now rare in developed countries where the banking system is heavily regulated both by federal and state governments. National banks are supervised by the U.S. COMPTROLLER OF THE CURRENCY and must also be members of the Federal Reserve System. A bank which chooses to incorporate as a state bank is supervised by the appropriate state banking department; examiners visit the bank at least once a year to verify its compliance with banking laws and regulations. State banks may apply for membership in the Federal Reserve System and many have done so. All national banks and almost all state commercial banks have a portion of their deposits guaranteed by another government agency, the FEDERAL DEPOSIT INSURANCE CORPORATION. The F.D.I.C. also has a field staff of examiners. Government regulation of the banking system is extremely complex. In the face of rapid change in the economic, and competitive environment and in banking technology, it is now generally agreed that the system requires extensive revision if the ability of the monetary authorities to control the money supply and the development of the financial system are not to be seriously impaired. The authorities have already been forced to take action to protect the savings and loan associations from the damaging effects of interest rate ceilings (⇛ REGULATION Q) and to widening the scope of reserve control. The development of the commercial banking system has been profoundly affected by the MCFADDEN ACT for example. The GLASS-STEAGALL ACT, 1933, which forced banks to divest security trading affiliates and severed commercial from investment banking, the INTERNATIONAL BANKING ACT and the EDGE ACT are other examples of government banking regulation. (⇛ BRANCH BANKING; FREE TRADE ZONE).

Banking and Currency Schools. The representatives of the two sides of opinion in a controversy of the early 19th century. The Banking school argued that, as bank notes were convertible into gold, there was no need to regulate the note issue because the fact of convertibility would prevent any serious over-issue. Moreover, it was pointless to try to regulate the issue of bank-notes because the demand for currency would be met by an expansion of BANK DEPOSITS, which would have the same effect as an expansion of the note issue. The Currency school, on the other hand, argued that the check offered by convertibility would not operate in time to prevent serious commercial disruption. Bank notes should be regarded as though they were the gold specie they in fact represented, and consequently the quantity at issue should fluctuate in sympathy with the BALANCE OF PAYMENTS. (⇛⇛ BANKING; FIDUCIARY ISSUE; GOLD STANDARD; QUANTITY THEORY OF MONEY).

Bank loan. Funds advanced by a bank to a customer and repayable with interest. Much of bank lending consists of short-term SELF-LIQUIDATING advances, for example to producers making goods for INVENTORIES ahead of a peak sales season. The bank loan is used to pay for raw materials and the loan is repaid when the finished goods are sold. Longer-term loans may be repaid in regular instalments (⇛ TERM LOAN). Business credit accounts for the majority of bank lending although loans to private individuals are also important. SMALL BUSINESS is particularly dependent upon bank finance since unlike larger firms they cannot issue BONDS or SHARES on the CAPITAL MARKET. In the interests of minimizing bank failures following the inability of large customers to repay loans, banks are generally prohibited from lending more than 10 percent of their capital and reserves to any single borrower. Syndicated loans where a number of banks participate in lending to a single large borrower are now commonplace. Loans may be secured or unsecured (⇛ COLLATERAL SECURITY). Many banks require borrowers to maintain DEPOSIT balances as part of an arrangement for bank loans. These *compensating balances* may amount to 20 percent of the amount of the loan and effectively raise the cost of the loan to the borrower.

Bank, national. ⇛ BANKING

Bank note. A note, issued by a bank, whose FACE VALUE is payable to the bearer on demand. A bank note is, in fact, a BILL payable on sight, and in England had its origin in receipts issued by London goldsmiths in the 17th century for gold deposited with them for safekeeping. The whole practice of BANKING had its origin in the activities of those goldsmiths, who began lending money, and whose deposit receipts came to be used as money. Later the goldsmiths issued bank notes, and so did the banks that developed later still. In the United States currency is issued only by the TREASURY, but in the U.K. the Scottish and Irish Banks as well as the Bank of England are allowed to issue bank notes.

Bank of Canada. Established as a crown corporation in 1935, the Bank of Canada is Canada's CENTRAL BANK. The Bank has a board of 12 directors chaired by the governor of the Bank. The Deputy Minister of Finance is a member of the board.

Bank rate. ⇛ DISCOUNT RATE

Bankruptcy. A legal condition in which an individual's or business entity's ASSETS are transferred to an official and used to pay off creditors. Declaration of bankruptcy by a court under the Federal Bankruptcy Act may follow a petition to the court by the debtor, in which event it is known as voluntary, or by creditors (involuntary bankruptcy). When assets of a business are disposed of in this way it is because the business is *insolvent,* i.e., *its liabilities exceed its assets;* all creditors cannot be paid in full and an orderly liquidation is necessary if unsecured creditors are to be treated equitably. Certain claims have priority in law: these include tax liabilities and the legal costs of the bankruptcy procedure. The Act also provides for corporate reorganization as an alternative to bankruptcy.

Bank, state. ⇛ BANKING

Bargaining theory of wages. A theory of the determination of wages which sees them as the outcome of a bargaining process between management and LABOR. It places primary emphasis on the analysis of the bargaining process, rather than on the general analysis of SUPPLY and DEMAND FOR LABOR. Nevertheless, these two approaches are not incompatible, since we can regard demand/supply conditions as establishing the general context within which bargaining takes place, and the bargaining process itself as the means by which the EQUILIBRIUM is attained. (⇛⇛ COST-PUSH INFLATION).

Barriers to entry. Those technological or economic conditions of a MARKET that raise the costs for firms wanting to enter the market above the costs of firms already in the market, or otherwise make new entry difficult. For example, a high degree of product differentiation (⇛ DIFFERENTIATION, PRODUCT) creates a barrier to entry as a new entrant might need to spend a great deal on advertising and sales promotion in order to overcome consumers' loyalty to existing brands. Similarly, the existence of marked ECONOMIES OF SCALE in the industry may require the new firm to enter at a large scale of output, if it is not to suffer a cost disadvantage. But the need to capture a large part of the market may cause a fall in PRICES and PROFITS, and make the entry unprofitable. We would expect the nature of barriers to entry of an industry to be an important determinant of the profits earned in the industry. Hence, with low barriers, we would expect profits in the long run to approach normal profits. On the other hand, high entry barriers strengthen MONOPOLY power and may permit high profits to be earned. Other important sources of entry barriers are patents, EXCLUSIVE DEALING contracts with suppliers or distributors, and VERTICAL INTEGRATION. When there is rapid expansion in demand, or technological change, entry barriers will be less effective.

Barter. Direct exchange of goods and services without use of MONEY. In a barter system, if you have a particular quantity of some good, and require another good, you either find someone with matching requirements (who wants what you have, and has what you want), or you make one or more intermediate transactions to obtain the good sought by the person who owns the good you want. Such a system is obviously cumbersome, particularly in a highly specialized economy, (⇛ DIVISION OF LABOR) as specialization increases the need for an EXCHANGE ECONOMY to satisfy the broad range of requirements. Some form of money, in terms of which the VALUE of each good is expressed, and which can be exchanged for any COMMODITY, is therefore essential to a highly developed economy. (⇛ COUNTER DEAL).

Base period. The time period used as the base from which to calculate an INDEX NUMBER, or a growth rate. Thus, currently, the *Index of Industrial Production* is calculated with 1972 as its base year: industrial output in each year is expressed as a percentage of that in 1972; the growth rates of NATIONAL INCOME of the Western industrial economies could be compared on the basis of the annual average rate of growth between 1950 and 1976, in which case 1950 is the base period for the comparison. The main consideration in choosing a base period for any particular measurement is that it should be a fairly typical or normal period in respect of the forces which influence the numbers under consideration. If the base-period value is unusually low, subsequent growth rates will be exaggerated, and the converse will be true for an unusually high base-period value.

Basing-point pricing system. A type of price system used in industries and characterized by: (a) a relatively small number of sellers; (b) marked differences in location between buyers and sellers; (c) a product with high weight and bulk relative to its value, making transport costs an important proportion of the final price; (d) high capital intensity (⇛ CAPITAL-INTENSIVE); and (e) a tendency for marked cyclical and regional fluctuations in DEMAND. Perfect examples of industries with these characteristics are cement, and iron and steel; both industries have used a basing-point pricing system. The system works in the following way: a certain number (varying from one to all) of the plants in an industry are designated "bases," and a base PRICE is set, which is price "at the factory gate." A standard system of freight charges is then established; the charges may vary with distance from the base, e.g., $10 per ton-mile for deliveries within a five-mile radius, $8 per ton-mile for deliveries of between five and 10 miles, $7 per ton-mile for deliveries of between 10 and 15 miles, etc. All base prices, and the standard freight charges, are known to each seller. Hence, a seller calculates the price he quotes to a buyer as the base price at the location nearest to the buyer, plus standard freight charges from that base to the buyer. Prices are always delivered prices, i.e., the buyer always pays delivery charges as part of the price. Effectively the buyer does not have the option of arranging his own transport and paying the price exclusive of transport costs. The inevitable result of the system is that all sellers quote identical delivered prices to a buyer at any given location. A major advantage of the system is that it makes certain prices will be uniform in an unstable environment, and thus restricts both deliberate and accidental price competition. This may be particularly important in an industry with high overheads (⇛ FIXED COSTS) and one prone to the occasional development of EXCESS CAPACITY. It also permits firms to obtain business outside their main MARKET areas, without having to reduce prices within their main market areas, which implies, in effect, PRICE DISCRIMINATION between nearer and more remote customers. To illustrate: suppose a firm is 40 miles further away from a customer than the base closest to the customer. Freight charges included in the delivered price are calculated from the base to the customer, hence the firm's actual transport costs are likely to be much higher. In effect, the firm is reducing its price to the new customers. This ability to gain new business, while not losing profits on on-going business, is considered by some economists to be the major attraction of the system.

Bear. A STOCK EXCHANGE speculator who sells SECURITIES that he may or may not possess because he expects a fall in prices and, therefore, expects he will be able to buy (back) later at a PROFIT; the opposite of BULL. A bear who sells securities he does not possess is described as having "sold short." If he does possess the securities he sells, he is described as a "covered" or "protected" bear. The terms bull and bear originated in the London Stock Exchange in the early eighteenth century.

Bearer bonds. BONDS, the legal ownership of which is vested in the holder rather than in the name of the registered owner. Current practice is for the name of the owner to be registered with the issuer of the bond, as has always been the practice with SHARES. Bearer bonds normally have dated interest COUPONS attached to them which can be presented to the issuer of the security for payment.

Bearer securities. ⇛ BEARER BONDS

"Beggar-my-neighbor" policy. ⇛ RECIPROCITY

Behavioral assumption. An assumption about the way individual economic agents—consumers and firms—behave, their motivations, and the ways in which they respond to differences between expected and actual outcomes. Examples of such assumptions are the PROFIT-maximizing assumption in the theory of the firm (⇛ FIRM, THEORY OF), the UTILITY maximization assumption in the theory of consumer demand, and the assumption that firms respond to unexpected INVENTORY accumulation by cutting back production in the macroeconomic theory of income determination. (⇛ MACROECONOMICS; ⇛⇛ BEHAVIORAL THEORY OF THE FIRM).

Behavioral theory of the firm. A theory that attempts to improve upon the standard economic theory of the firm (⇛ FIRM, THEORY OF) by recognizing that many of today's firms are large, complex organizations, with hierarchical managerial BUREAUCRACIES. The theory rejects the classical assumption that firms wish to maximize PROFIT, and indeed rejects the idea that firms wish to maximize *anything*. Rather, it sees the firm as composed of a number of sub-groups—managers, workers, shareholders, customers, suppliers—each group with its own set of goals, which might well prove to be in conflict with the goals of other groups (higher wages mean higher PRICES, lower profits, etc.). As a result, the goals actually adopted by the organization will represent a compromise sought to resolve the conflict; hence the goals cannot maximize *any* one thing. The theory also considers the processes by which these goals are revised over time, and, again unlike the traditional theory of the firm, makes uncertainty and the search for information important determinants of the firm's behavior. Thus, the theory stresses the effects the processes of decision-taking and the organization of the firm have on the firm's final decisions. The development of the theory owes a great deal to the insights provided by organization theorists, industrial psychologists and sociologists, and is associated primarily with the work of Herbert A. Simon, J.G. March and R. Cyert, and the Carnegie Institute of Technology. Although the theory is accepted as descriptively realistic, it has not replaced the traditional theory of the firm. (⇛ SATISFICING).

Below-the line. ⇛ ABOVE THE LINE

Benelux. The CUSTOMS UNION between Belgium and Luxembourg on the one hand and the Netherlands on the other, accepted in principle before the end of the Second World War and set up in 1948. The union abolished internal TARIFFS (⇛ TARIFFS, IMPORT) and with some difficulty reduced import QUOTAS between the three countries, which adopted a common external tariff. The aim of the union, reiterated in a final treaty which was ratified in 1960, was the eventual merging of the fiscal and monetary systems of the member countries. There is free movement of LABOR and CAPITAL within the union and a common policy with other countries. In 1958, Benelux joined the EUROPEAN ECONOMIC COMMUNITY.

Bentham, Jeremy (1748–1832). The leading philosopher of UTILITARIANISM. Self-interest was deemed the sole stimulus to human endeavor and the pursuit of happiness an individual's prime concern. The purpose of government should be to maximize the happiness of the greatest number of individuals.

Bernoulli, Daniel (1700–1782) Bernoulli's hypothesis. A hypothesis, first formulated by D. Bernoulli, stating that the decision whether or not to accept a particular gamble depends on the utility an individual attaches to the sums of MONEY involved, and not just the sums themselves. For example, consider the following gamble: We toss a coin; if it comes up heads, I pay you $10, if tails, you pay me $9. The PROBABILITY of getting a head is $\frac{1}{2}$, as is the probability of getting a tail. Hence, the "expected value" to you of the gamble is given by: $\frac{1}{2}(\$10) - \frac{1}{2}(\$9) = \$0.50$. The interpretation is that if we played the game a large number of times, on average you would end up winning $0.50 per game. Hence, we would expect you to accept the gamble, and, indeed, be prepared to pay anything up to $0.50 per game for the right to be allowed to play. However, Bernoulli observed several paradoxes arising from this view, and it was also refuted by experience—people did reject gambles whose expected values were positive. This could be rationalized in the following way. Suppose the MARGINAL UTILITY of INCOME is diminishing, making it quite possible that the gain in utility from winning $10 is smaller than the loss in utility from losing $9. For example, suppose we could measure these utilities as a gain of 4 units and a loss of 5 units respectively. In deciding whether to accept the gamble, our individual would find that the utility he can expect from the gamble is negative, i.e., that $\frac{1}{2}(4) - \frac{1}{2}(5) = -\frac{1}{2}$; hence he would reject the gamble.

This emphasis on utility values rather than the absolute money values now plays an extremely important role in the economic theory of RISK and UNCERTAINTY, and the Bernoulli hypothesis has become of fundamental importance.

Bilateral flow. An expression referring to a flow of funds from the government to the PRIVATE SECTOR of the economy in exchange for goods or SERVICES; as opposed to a unilateral flow, such as pension payments or taxes (⇛ TAXATION), in which there is no corresponding flow of goods or services in exchange.

Bilateralism. The agreement between two countries to extend each other specific privileges in INTERNATIONAL TRADE which are not extended to others. These privileges may take the form of generous import QUOTAS or favorable import duties (⇛ TARIFFS, IMPORT). In so far as such agreements tend to proliferate, and in that they impose artificial restraints on the free movements of goods between countries, in the long run they could have an unfavorable effect on INTERNATIONAL TRADE compared with MULTILATERALISM, under which there is no discrimination by origin or destination. Bilateralism became widespread in the inter-war period as countries tried to protect themselves from the fall in international trade during the depression. After the Second World War, there was a fear that a restrictionist policy would be followed by the Commonwealth and Western European countries in order to protect themselves from the influence of the United States, which had emerged from the war in a relatively strong position. However, the GENERAL AGREEMENT ON TARIFFS AND TRADE was established in 1947 on multilateral principles, and has since been pursuing a policy designed to eliminate bilateralism and other restrictions on international trade. The success of this policy has been somewhat constrained by the setting up of a number of trading areas (⇛ CUSTOMS UNION; FREE-TRADE AREA). The U.S.S.R. and the Communist countries of Eastern Europe conduct their international trade predominantly in terms of bilateral agreements in which quotas are set on both sides. Exchange agreements of this kind enable these countries to set their international trade requirements into their national plan objectives (⇛ PLANNED ECONOMY).

Bilateral monopoly. A MARKET situation in which a single seller, a MONOPOLY, is faced with a single buyer, a MONOPSONY. In such a market, it is only possible to determine the EQUILIBRIUM PRICE and quantity traded as a set of possible outcomes, in the absence of further analysis of the bargaining process itself. This bargaining process will determine the precise point in the set of possible outcomes—which vary of course in their attractiveness to the parties—that will finally be achieved.

Bill. A document giving evidence of indebtedness of one party to another. A bill can be a written order for goods which is used as security for a loan to the supplier from a bank, or it can be a SECURITY such as a TREASURY BILL. The term is also used to refer to paper CURRENCY or bank notes.

Bill of lading. A document giving details of goods shipped, the ship on which the goods are consigned and the names of the consignor and consignee. Bills of lading are normally sent ahead of the ship and give proof of title to the consigner. Copies of the documents are held on the ship and by the exporter.

Birthrate. The crude birthrate is the average number of live births occurring in a year for every 1,000 population. The birthrate of the United States fell from 30.1 per 1,000 population in 1910 to a low of 18.7 in 1935. It increased thereafter until reaching the peak of 25.8 in 1947. Following a period of stability in the 1950s at about 24 or 25 per 1,000 population, it has declined, falling to a current level of about 15 per 1,000 population. Other statistical measurements which are computed for the study of population trends include: (a) the *fertility rate,* which measures the average number of live births per 1,000 for all women between the ages of 15 and 44, a statistic which has in fact exhibited similar trends in the United States as the crude birthrate (it reached a level of 66 in 1978); and (b) the rate specific for age of mother in which the number of live births per 1,000 is given for different age groups of mother. There has been growing anxiety about the social and economic consequences of the rapidly expanding size of the world population. At the present rate of growth, the current world population of four billion, 700 million people will be doubled in less than 40 years. A major factor in this growth has been the extension of life expectancy achieved by modern medicine, but high birthrates have also played an important part. Measures of family control are being taken, particularly in critical DEVELOPING COUNTRIES such as India, in order to try to achieve a growth in population more in line with available economic and social resources (⇛ MALTHUS, THOMAS ROBERT). It has been suggested that the recent decline of the birthrate in the United States is associated with the growth in *per capita* REAL INCOME, combined with the ability of parents to control family size. In DEVELOPING COUNTRIES, children are looked upon as producer goods (⇛ INTERMEDIATE PRODUCTS) in that they are required to augment HOUSEHOLD incomes and support the old; as countries develop their wealth, children come to be regarded as CONSUMPTION GOODS and this is reflected in the smaller size of families. If this interpretation is correct, the birthrate in the United States is unlikely to return to a high level, although it will fluctuate more, in accordance with the cyclical changes in real incomes and expectations. The inference for the world population problem is that the route to a solution is through permanent increases in the *per capita* real wealth of the developing countries.

Blue chip. A first-class common STOCK, the purchase of which hopefully entails little RISK, even of a sharp decline in EARNINGS, in an economic RECESSION (⇛ DEPRESSION). The term is applied as a matter of subjective judgment, of course. In the United States, General Motors, IBM and Exxon, for example, are commonly regarded as blue chip.

Böhm-Bawerk, Eugen von (1851–1914). A member of the AUSTRIAN SCHOOL, who took over the Chair of Economics at Vienna from F. VON WIESER. His analyses of the rate of INTEREST and CAPITAL have had an important influence on the development of these aspects of economic theory. His major publications include *Capital and Interest* (1884) and the *Positive Theory of Capital* (1889). The nature of the rate of interest could be found, he argued, in the three propositions: (a) people expect to be better off in the future; (b) people put a lower valuation on future goods than on present goods—"jam today is better than jam tomorrow"—these two "psychological" factors make people willing to pay to borrow against their future income to spend on consumption goods now (⇛ TIME PREFERENCE); and (c) the proposition that goods in existence today are technically superior to goods coming into existence at some future date because today's goods could be capable of producing more goods during the interval. (⇛ FISHER, IRVING; INTEREST, PRODUCTIVITY THEORIES OF). Capital is associated with roundabout methods of production. In order to reap a harvest, you could send workers into the fields to pluck the ears of corn. A more efficient method is to spend capital on making scythes and then use these to cut the corn. An even more efficient method is to spend even more capital manufacturing reaping machinery and use this to harvest your corn. Progress is achieved through the use of LABOR in more roundabout methods of production; a widening of the gap between INPUTS and outputs (⇛ INPUT-OUTPUT ANALYSIS). Capital supplies the necessary subsistence to labor during the "waiting time" before new consumer goods are produced (⇛ WAGE FUND THEORY). This waiting time is extended to yield increased productivity until, in equilibrium, productivity is equated with the RATE OF INTEREST. This theory was later developed into a theory of the TRADE CYCLE by members of the Austrian school. (⇛ HAYEK, FRIEDRICH AUGUST VON; HICKS, SIR JOHN RICHARD; MISES, LUDWIG ELDER VON; WICKSELL, KNUT).

Bond. 1. A fixed interest SECURITY issued by governments, companies and other institutions. *Secured bonds,* or *mortgage bonds* are secured by a charge upon a specific ASSET. *Unsecured bonds* are called DEBENTURES. *Convertible bonds* may be converted into STOCKS or other forms of SECURITIES after a specified date at the option of the bondholder. *Callable bonds* may be redeemed at the option of the issuing company prior to the maturity date. *Registered bonds* for which the holder's name is registered with the issuer and to whom interest is paid constitute the vast majority of bonds but some BEARER BONDS have been issued from which the holder can detach a COUPON to claim payment of interest. 2. A relatively recent innovation is the *Euro-bond* which has been defined as "a bond underwritten by an international syndicate and sold in countries other than the country of the currency in which the issue is denominated." (⇛⇛ EURO-DOLLARS). 3. A cash deposit (or sometimes a mortgage on property) to guarantee performance which is forfeited if, for example, a construction company does not complete a contract. 4. A term also used to describe goods in a warehouse on which customs duty (⇛ TARIFFS, IMPORT) has not yet been paid.

Book value. The value of ASSETS in the BALANCE SHEET of a firm. This is usually at their *historical cost,* i.e., their purchase price less DEPRECIATION, and may be less, or more than their market value.

Branch banking. A BANKING system that is most highly developed in Britain where the small number of COMMERCIAL BANKS have multiple branches around the country. In the United Kingdom, 5 banks control the majority of deposits and have some 13,000 branches, an average of 2,600 each. In the United States there are over 14,600 commercial banks but none has a really extensive branch network because state banking regulations limit the number of branches and in some states prohibit them altogether. The MCFADDEN ACT prohibits interstate banking in principle although later legislation permits a measure of interstate banking. In Arizona the average number of branches per bank is 19 and in North Carolina it is 21 but in most central states from Montana to Texas branch banking is effectively prohibited. Only 2 banks, Citicorp and Bank of America, operate in 40 states.

Brandt Report. In 1977, the President of the World Bank (INTERNATIONAL BANK FOR RECONSTRUCTION AND DEVELOPMENT (IBRD)) suggested the setting up of a Commission of inquiry into the problems of the DEVELOPING COUNTRIES. This Commission, subsequently established under the Chairmanship of Herr Willy Brandt, the former Chancellor of West Germany, published its report in 1980, entitled "North-South: A Program for Survival." The Commission emphasized the dangers inherent in the growing gap between the rich (North) and the poor (South) countries. The North, including Eastern Europe, has one-quarter of the world's population but produces four-fifths of its income. In contrast, the South, including China, has three-quarters of the world's population but produces only one-fifth of its income. The Commission proposed:

a) Increased aid to the South, rising to 0.7 percent of the Gross National Product of the rich countries by 1985 and to 1.0 percent by the year 2,000.

b) The doubling of the lending by the I.B.R.D.

c) The creation of a World Development Fund, financed automatically by an international tax.

d) The formation of an INTERNATIONAL TRADE ORGANIZATION.

e) Increased INTERNATIONAL LIQUIDITY for the South, through the use of the International Monetary Fund's SPECIAL DRAWING RIGHTS (SDR) and gold holding.

The publication of the report was followed in 1981 by the "International Meeting on Co-operation and Development," attended by 22 heads of state in Cancun, Mexico.

Bretton Woods. An international conference was held at Bretton Woods, New Hampshire, in the United States in July 1944 to discuss alternative proposals relating to postwar international payments problems put forward by the U.S., Canadian and U.K. governments. The agreement resulting from this conference led to the establishment of the INTERNATIONAL MONETARY FUND and the INTERNATIONAL BANK FOR RECONSTRUCTION AND DEVELOPMENT. (⇛ KEYNES PLAN; SMITHSONIAN AGREEMENT).

Broker. The intermediary between a buyer and seller in an organized market, e.g., a stockbroker, or a market operator working independently.

Brokerage. The fee or commission charged by a BROKER. It is characteristic of the profession that brokers operate only in highly organized markets where margins are relatively small.

Brussels Conference (1920). An international conference at Brussels which with that at Genoa in 1922 obtained agreement that every country should have a CENTRAL BANK through which to control its financial affairs. This was a necessary preliminary to the establishment of the BANK FOR INTERNATIONAL SETTLEMENTS at Basle.

Budget. An estimate of INCOME and expenditure for a future period as opposed to an account that records past financial transactions. Budgets are an essential element in the planning and control of the financial affairs of a nation or business, and are made necessary essentially because income and expenditure do not occur simultaneously. In modern large-scale business, the annual budget, normally broken down into monthly and weekly periods, is a complex document that may take several months to prepare. The starting point is an estimate of sales and income for the period, balanced by budgets for purchasing, administration, production, distribution and research costs. There are also detailed budgets of CASH FLOWS and CAPITAL expenditure. These are often made for periods of more than one year ahead, so that borrowing and capacity requirements can be assessed (⇒ CAPITAL

BUDGETING). A *flexible* budget is one based on different assumed levels of plant activity.

The national or federal government budget sets out government expenditure and revenue plans for the fiscal year.

The fiscal year for purposes of the federal budget is from July 1 to June 30. Fiscal year 1982 is the year ending June 30, 1982. The preparation of the budget for fiscal 1982 began in early 1980 and went to Congress in January of 1981. The central responsibility for preparing the budget is in the Office of Management and Budget (OMB) which requests government departments and agencies to submit their expenditure plans. After review and consultation, a tentative budget is sent to the President together with an economic outlook from the COUNCIL OF ECONOMIC ADVISORS and a revenue outlook for the Treasury. After further deliberations and analysis, the President reviews and approves a final budget in late Fall.

The annual budget is an important statement of the President's economic policy particularly as it relates to FISCAL POLICY. Whether or not the overall fiscal plan results in a budget DEFICIT has important consequences for MONETARY POLICY. (⇛ BALANCED BUDGET).

Budgetary control. A system of budgetary control, checks actual INCOME and expenditure against a BUDGET so progress toward set objectives may be measured and remedial action taken if necessary. Budget control statements comparing actual and estimated expenditure are issued weekly or monthly. These statements will be issued in considerable detail to departmental heads and in less detail to higher management. Budget control statements must, if any necessary remedial action is to be taken in time, be issued as soon as possible after the close of the period to which they relate, and for this reason they need not be as accurate as accounting statements and may be based partly on estimated data. The development of computerized accounting procedures has greatly facilitated budgetary control. The principles of budgetary control are similar for all types of administration but special problems arise in nonprofit organizations. (⇛ PROGRAM, PLANNING, BUDGETING SYSTEM).

Buffer stocks. Inventories of agricultural products (usually), resulting from the purchase of excess farm output by a government agency or marketing board in good years for resale in periods of poor harvest. The purpose is to stabilize prices and the availability of specific commodities. (⇛ INTERNATIONAL COMMODITY AGREEMENTS).

Built-in stabilizers. Institutional features of the economy which, without explicit government intervention, automatically act to reduce fluctuations in unemployment (⇛ EMPLOYMENT, FULL) and NATIONAL INCOME. Examples of these are: (a) unemployment benefits and welfare payments automatically increase in total when unemployment increases, and fall in total when unemployment falls, hence this part of government expenditure adjusts automatically in the desired directions to offset in part changes in other components of AGGREGATE DEMAND; and (b) government taxation falls in total as national income falls, and rises as national income rises, because both the incidence of INCOME TAXES changes and, with changes in CONSUMPTION expenditures, sales taxes change also. Since an increase in taxation tends to restrain expenditure, while a fall in taxation stimulates it, we again have "automatic" factors counteracting inflationary and deflationary pressures in the economy (⇛ DEFLATION; INFLATION). The effectiveness of these built-in stabilizers must not be exaggerated, however. They rarely have sufficient force to render positive corrective policies unnecessary.

Bull. A STOCK EXCHANGE speculator who purchases STOCKS and other SECURITIES in the belief that prices will rise and he will be able to sell them later at a profit (⇛ SPECULATION); opposite of BEAR. The market is said to be *bullish* when it is generally anticipated that prices will rise.

Bullion. Gold, silver or other precious metal in bulk, i.e., in the form of ingots or bars rather than in coin. Gold bullion is used in international monetary transactions between CENTRAL BANKS and forms partial backing for many CURRENCIES (⇛ GOLD STANDARD). A *bullion market* is a gold market.

Bureaucracy. The phenomenon of large-scale administrative organization involving a rigid hierarchy of authority, the use of committees to coordinate and make decisions, and the adoption of standard operating rules and procedures to classify problems and find solutions. The nature and growth of bureaucracy has been of considerable interest to sociologists and social psychologists due to its importance as a form of social organization, and the types of social behavior it tends to develop. Economists have been less concerned with the study of bureaucracy as such, and regard it merely as an aspect of the problem of diseconomies of scale (⇛ DISECONOMY): as the scale of activities increases, so the administrative superstructure expands, presenting difficulties of maintaining efficiency of operation. The critical connotations of "bureaucracy" in everyday speech—often implying inefficiency, unwieldiness, lack of humanity and inertia—are not part of its express definition; rather, the word is used simply to describe a particular form of organization. Moreover, bureaucracy is not regarded as unique to government. Although government organizations were the first to reach the size at which bureaucratic features are marked, it is increasingly the case that industrial companies too, as a result of growth, are encountering similar problems of large-scale organization and control. This is, in fact, becoming recognized in economics, and is largely responsible for the interest in organization theory and the development of the BEHAVIORAL THEORY OF THE FIRM.

Bureau of Labor Statistics. A U.S. government agency, and probably best known for its regular publication of the CONSUMER PRICE INDEX.

Bureau of the Census. Established by Congress in 1902; the major function of the Bureau is to undertake a CENSUS of the POPULATION every 10 years. It also acts as a general statistical agency, and collects, publishes and analyzes a wide variety of data about the people and economy of the United States. Regular censuses of manufacturing, mining, transportation and other subsections of the economy are also carried out.

Business cycle. ⇛ TRADE CYCLE

Business finance. The provision of MONEY for commercial use. The CAPITAL requirements of business may be divided into short-term and medium-term, or long-term. Short-term capital consists of the current LIABILITIES of a business plus medium-term capital. The main sources of short-term and medium-term capital (for a company) can be further divided into internal and external:

Internal: Retained earnings (⇛ SELF-FINANCING), including ACCRUED EXPENSES and ACCRUED INCOME TAXES. (⇛ CASH FLOW).

External: Temporary LOANS from sister companies, directors and others; FACTORING; PROMISSORY NOTES; TRADE CREDIT and short-term PORTFOLIO investments. Strictly speaking, short-term capital should only be used for investment in relatively liquid ASSETS (⇛ LIQUIDITY) so it is readily available to discharge the liability if necessary. Thus, these sources of short-term capital may be used for finished goods in INVENTORIES, work in process, trade debtors, prepaid expenses (⇛ PREPAYMENTS), cash in hand, and at the bank.

Correspondingly, the main sources of long-term liabilities or capital can be subdivided in the same way:

Internal: Reserves, retained earnings and DEPRECIATION provisions.

External: Share capital, i.e., COMMON STOCKS, PREFERRED STOCKS, long-term loans including MORTGAGES, LEASE-BACK arrangements and BONDS. Long-term capital may be used for long-term investment in fixed assets—land, buildings, plant, equipment and machinery etc.; in goodwill, patents and trademarks; in WORKING CAPITAL and in long-term portfolio investment. The main institutional sources of business finance are the commercial banks, investment banks and the institutions concerned with new issues (⇛ NEW ISSUE MARKET). A number of specialized institutions provide venture capital. (⇛ RISK CAPITAL; SMALL BUSINESS INVESTMENT COMPANIES).

Business saving. That part of the net revenue of a firm that is not paid out as INTEREST, DIVIDENDS or TAXATION, but kept in the business as reserves and DEPRECIATION allowances or to finance new INVESTMENT. Sometimes called *retentions.* (⇛⇛ SELF-FINANCING).

Business taxation. ⇛ CORPORATION INCOME TAX

Buyer's market. A MARKET in a situation of EXCESS SUPPLY. Buyers are relatively scarce and can obtain favorable terms as sellers compete with each other. Therefore, we would expect to see prices falling in a buyer's market.

C

Callable bonds. ⇛ BOND

Call option. ⇛ OPTION

Cambridge school. A system of economic thought influenced by economists at the University of Cambridge, England. ALFRED MARSHALL (1842–1924) held the Chair of Political Economy until 1908 and A. C. PIGOU (1877–1959) until 1944, and during this period the school was characterized by the theory of late CLASSICAL ECONOMICS. After the end of the Second World War, the school refuted what became known as NEO-CLASSICAL ECONOMICS and developed ideas based on those of J. M. KEYNES (1883–1946), although linked also with the early CLASSICAL (⇛ CLASSICAL ECONOMICS) period. The leading figures in the postwar debate were J. V. ROBINSON (1903–) and N. Kaldor (1908–). The Cambridge school emphasized a MACROECONOMIC approach compared with the MICROECONOMIC approach of the neo-classical school. The Cambridge school denied that there was a direct functional relationship between the rate of PROFIT and the capital intensity of an economy. They have demonstrated the possibility of CAPITAL RESWITCHING and have criticized the neo-classical school for leaping to conclusions about the aggregates derived from micro-analysis. For instance, they argue that the aggregate production function of the COBB-DOUGLAS (⇛ COBB DOUGLAS PRODUCTION FUNCTION) type is not compatible in practice with the micro-functions from which it is derived, and they dispute that it is possible to measure capital in the aggregate. The neo-classical theory of DISTRIBUTION (⇛ DISTRIBUTION, THEORY OF) which relates relative factor prices to relative MARGINAL REVENUE productivities is deficient in throwing light on aggregate factor distributed shares of product (⇛ EULER, LEONHARD). *Per contra,* they themselves are criticized for neglecting MICROECONOMIC THEORY. The Cambridge school has attempted to develop GROWTH THEORY, following J. M. KEYNES but assuming full employment, (⇛ EMPLOYMENT, FULL) from which the distributed shares of profits and wages may be determined. Generally, however, the Keynesian approach assumes under-employment of resources, with investment as the motive force.

Cantillon, Richard (1680(?)–1734). An Irish international banker, who wrote *Essai sur la nature du commerce en général,* which was not published until 1755 but had circulated from about 1730. This work was one of the first synoptic descriptions and analyses of the economic process. His views on the importance of agriculture, based on its receipt of pure RENT, and his analysis of the circulation of wealth foreshadowed the PHYSIOCRATS and the TABLEAU ECONOMIQUE.

Capacity utilization rate. The ratio of actual output of a plant, firm or economy to its full-capacity output. (⇛ EXCESS CAPACITY).

Capital. The stock of goods that are used in production and that have themselves been produced. A distinction is normally made between *fixed capital,* consisting of durable goods such as buildings, plant and machinery, and *circulating capital,* consisting of stocks of raw materials and semi-finished goods, components, etc., which are used up very rapidly (⇛ CIRCULATING CAPITAL). The word capital in economics generally means *real capital*—that is, physical goods. In everyday usage, however, *capital* can mean money capital, i.e., stocks of MONEY that are the result of saving. Two important features of capital are: (a) its creation entails a sacrifice, since resources are devoted to making non-consumable capital goods instead of goods for immediate consumption, and (b) it enhances the PRODUCTIVITY of the other FACTORS OF PRODUCTION, LAND, and LABOR. It is this enhanced productivity that represents the reward for the sacrifice involved in creating capital. We can surmise that new capital is only created as long as its productivity is at least sufficient to compensate those who make the sacrifice involved in its creation. (⇛⇛ HUMAN CAPITAL; INVESTMENT).

Capital account. ⇛ BALANCE OF PAYMENTS

Capital allowances. Reductions in TAX liability that are related to a firm's CAPITAL expenditure. In most countries expenditure on new capital assets is encouraged by various kinds of allowances and annual DEPRECIATION is recognized as an expense of the business in calculating tax liability. In the United States INVESTMENT CREDITS are also available.

Capital budgeting. The process by which CAPITAL expenditure is planned and evaluated. (⇛ INVESTMENT APPRAISAL).

Capital charges. Charges in the ACCOUNTS of a company or individual for interest paid on CAPITAL, DEPRECIATION or repayment of LOANS.

Capital, circulating. ⇛ CIRCULATING CAPITAL

Capital consumption. 1. The using up of CAPITAL in the production of new goods. 2. The sale or LIQUIDATION of capital ASSETS in order to increase current consumption. Both methods result in a diminishing stock of capital for an economy, firm or individual. In the first case, capital consumption corresponds to what is loosely termed "DEPRECIATION"—the wear and tear on machines, and their resulting loss of VALUE which occurs in the process of production. In the NATIONAL INCOME accounts, capital consumption is a category of expenditure that is based on depreciation allowances made by firms in their accounting records (⇛ CAPITAL ALLOWANCES), and is then subtracted from gross national income or product to obtain net national income or product. Conceptually, it represents an allowance for replacing capital used up in the process of production, but in practice, it is strongly influenced by accounting conventions for setting aside funds for the replacement of capital. These conventions may not accurately reflect actual capital consumption. For example, under the system known as "straightline depreciation," a fixed sum is set aside each year, even though the actual use of the capital equipment and the consequential wear and tear and loss of value may vary from year to year.

Capital, cost of. 1. The cost, measured as a RATE OF INTEREST, of the CAPITAL employed by a business weighted according to the proportions of different sources of capital used. 2. The marginal cost of capital, i.e., the cost of raising new capital. 3. In INVESTMENT APPRAISAL, the cost of capital is used in DISCOUNTED CASH FLOW calculations, either directly in the discounting procedure (⇛ PRESENT VALUE), or as a standard of comparison with the INTERNAL RATE OF RETURN. That is to say, it is the minimum rate of return which a firm would consider on a new INVESTMENT project, and ideally, it would be equal to the rate of return the firm's shareholders could obtain on comparable investments outside the company.

Capital employed. The CAPITAL in use in a business. There is no universally agreed definition of the term. The crude equivalent is total ASSETS, i.e., *the balance sheet total,* but more commonly NET ASSETS is taken to mean the capital employed in a business. For analytical purposes, calculating a RATE OF RETURN, for example, it is necessary to adjust the net asset figure by adding in BANK LOANS, excluding intangible assets and revaluing portfolio investments at market prices. (⇛ INVESTMENT APPRAISAL).

Capital expenditure. The purchase of fixed ASSETS (e.g., plant and equipment including expenditure on increases in capacity or efficiency, but not including repairs or maintenance), PORTFOLIO investment or acquisitions of other businesses and expenditure on current assets (e.g., INVENTORIES); to be distinguished from REVENUE EXPENDITURES and CAPITAL FORMATION.

Capital formation. NET INVESTMENT in fixed ASSETS, i.e., additions to the stock of real CAPITAL. *Gross fixed capital formation* includes DEPRECIATION, repairs and maintenance expenditure; *net capital formation* excludes them.

Capital gains. A realized increase in the value of a capital ASSET, as when a share is sold for more than the price at which it was purchased. Strictly speaking, the term refers to CAPITAL appreciation outside the normal course of business. In the United States, capital gains are taxed but at rates which depend on the type of asset and length of ownership (⇛ INCOME TAX). For most individual taxpayers, capital gains taxation arises from the sale of STOCK EXCHANGE securities. Capital gains arise from changes in the supply and demand for capital assets, but also from INFLATION, and it can be argued that it is inequitable to tax the latter element. Capital gains are taxed in a similar way in other countries, (although in the United Kingdom the inflation element was excluded from the tax from 1982/3), and companies as well as individuals are liable. (⇛ CORPORATION INCOME TAX).

Capital-intensive. A capital-intensive process of production is one that uses proportionately more CAPITAL relative to the quantities of other INPUTS. A nuclear power plant is a capital-intensive method of producing electricity, compared with a conventional coal-burning plant, because the cost of LABOR and fuel is a smaller proportion of total costs. (⇛ FACTORS OF PRODUCTION).

Capital issued. ⇛ ISSUED STOCK

Capitalization. 1. The amount and structure of the CAPITAL of a company. 2. The conversion of accumulated PROFITS and reserves into ISSUED STOCK. 3. *Market capitalization* is the market value of a corporation's issued stock, i.e., the quoted price of its shares multiplied by the number of shares outstanding.

Capitalized ratios. Ratios which describe the CAPITAL STRUCTURE of a corporation by indicating the proportion of each type of SECURITY issued.

Capitalized value. The CAPITAL sum at current RATES OF INTEREST required to yield the current earnings of an ASSET. For example, if the earnings of an asset were $10 per annum and the appropriate rate of interest were 10 percent, its capitalized value would be $100. Capitalized value does not represent a satisfactory means for the valuation of most capital assets, since the capitalized value of an asset would not necessarily compensate an owner for the loss of the asset.

Capital loss. A reduction in the MONEY value of an ASSET; opposite of CAPITAL GAIN.

Capital market. The market for longer-term lendable funds as distinct from the MONEY MARKET, which deals in short-term funds. There is no clear-cut distinction between the two MARKETS, although in principle capital market LOANS are used by industry and commerce mainly for fixed INVESTMENT. The capital market in any country is not one institution, but all those institutions that canalize the SUPPLY and DEMAND for long-term capital and claims on capital, e.g., the STOCK EXCHANGE, banks (⇛ BANKING) and insurance companies. The capital market, of course, is not concerned solely with the issue of new claims on capital (⇛ NEW ISSUE MARKET), but also with dealings in existing claims (SECONDARY MARKET). The marketability of SECURITIES is an important element in the efficient working of the capital market, since investors would be more reluctant to make loans to industry if their claims could not easily be traded. All advanced countries have highly developed capital markets, but in DEVELOPING COUNTRIES the absence of a capital market is often as much an obstacle to the growth of investment as a shortage of savings. Governments and industrialists in these countries are obliged to raise capital in the international capital market, i.e., that composed of the national capital markets in the advanced countries. (⇛⇛ BUSINESS FINANCE, FINANCIAL INTERMEDIARIES, PUBLIC FINANCE).

Capital-output ratio, incremental (I.C.O.R.). The increase in the CAPITAL STOCK of a firm, industry or economy, over a certain period, divided by the increase in output over that period. It is the ratio of NET INVESTMENT to change in output. For a given increase in output, the size of the change in capital stock will be determined by technological conditions and relative prices of the FACTORS OF PRODUCTION, e.g., the higher the wages and the lower the RATE OF INTEREST, the greater the net investment for a given increase in output. If the I.C.O.R. can be taken as roughly constant over a particular period, then multiplying it by the expected change in output gives the expected level of net investment; this leads to the accelerator theory of investment (⇛ ACCELERATION PRINCIPLE), with the I.C.O.R. identified as the ACCELERATOR COEFFICIENT. Accordingly, I.C.O.R.s play an important part in the theories of the TRADE CYCLE and ECONOMIC GROWTH. I.C.O.R.s are frequently used by economists in analyzing the relative growth experience of different countries. In such cases, figures of percentage increases in GROSS INVESTMENT from national accounts data are used and divided by the percentage increase in GROSS NATIONAL PRODUCT. Such a ratio is more properly called a *gross incremental capital-output ratio.* One other related ratio is the *average capital-output ratio,* in which the total depreciated capital stock (⇛ DEPRECIATION) is divided by total output.

Capital reswitching. A phenomenon which played an important part in the CAPITAL THEORY controversy between a group of economists led by Professor Joan Violet Robinson (⇛ ROBINSON, JOAN VIOLET), at Cambridge, England and a group at Cambridge, Mass. led by Professor P.A. SAMUELSON and R. Solow. Specifically, it can be shown that the proposition that INVESTMENT increases as the required RATE OF RETURN (⇛ INTERNAL RATE OF RETURN) falls may not in fact be valid. We could imagine that, as the required rate of return falls, firms would switch from less to more CAPITAL-INTENSIVE methods of production, thus increasing the rate of investment. However, it is possible to show that under quite plausible circumstances, the rate of return could reach a level at which firms would switch back, i.e., reswitch, from more to less capital-intensive production methods, thus causing investment to fall as the required rate of return falls. This possibility undermines the NEO-CLASSICAL (⇛ NEO-CLASSICAL ECONOMICS) model on which the Cambridge, Mass. argument was based.

Capital, sources of. ⇛ BUSINESS FINANCE

Capital stock. The total amount of physical CAPITAL existing at any one time, in a firm, industry or economy. In practice, it is extremely difficult to obtain a satisfactory measure of this. Clearly, it is impossible to add up the physical amounts of different types of capital. This then raises the problem of defining a useful MONEY measure. Strictly, the VALUE of the current capital stock is the PRESENT VALUE of the stream of INCOME that it will generate in the future, but it is impossible to measure this with any real precision. Hence, we are often thrown back on the valuations of ASSETS shown in firms' BALANCE SHEETS (which need bear little relationship to any economically meaningful value), or valuations made for insurance purposes.

Capital structure. The sources of long-term CAPITAL of a company. A company's capital structure is determined by the numbers and types of SHARES it issues and its reliance on fixed-interest debt (⇛ LEVERAGE). The choice between different sources of finance will be determined by their cost, the type and size of the business, its past and expected future earnings, TAXATION and other considerations. (⇛⇛ BUSINESS FINANCE; CAPITAL, COST OF).

Capital theory. That part of economic theory concerned with analysis of the consequences of the fact that production generally involves INPUTS which have themselves been produced. The existence of these "produced means of production," or CAPITAL, has profound implications for the nature of the economic system. A central element is the role of time, and intertemporal planning. The production of capital requires the sacrifice of current consumption in exchange for future, possibly uncertain, consumption, and the mechanisms by which this process is organized influence the growth and stability of the economy in important ways. The existence of capital is also central to the analysis of the INCOME DISTRIBUTION. A major and controversial question has been: What determines the income derived by the owners of capital relative to that of suppliers of labor power, and can the owners' share be justified in terms of their contribution to the production of output? An understanding of the nature and implications of capital is fundamental to an understanding of our economic system, and indeed, as one leading contributor to the subject remarked, the problem in attempting to define capital theory is to do it in such a way "as to embrace something less than the whole of economics" (C.J. Bliss, in *Capital Theory and the Distribution of Income*). (⇛⇛ BÖHM-BAWERK, EUGEN VON).

Capital, working. ⇛ WORKING CAPITAL

Cartagena Agreement. ⇛ ANDEAN PACT

Cartel. A group of firms that enter into an agreement to set mutually acceptable PRICES for their products, and often to set output and INVESTMENT quotas. The rules of the cartel are embodied in a formal document, which can be legally enforceable, and penalties are laid down for firms violating it. The essence of a cartel is that it is a formal system of collusion, as opposed to a set of informal or tacit agreements to follow certain pricing policies. Currently, cartels are illegal in the United States, it being held that their general effect is to restrict output, raise prices, and, in general, create MONOPOLY conditions in industry. On the other hand, cartels have been legalized at certain times, especially in Germany in the interwar period, when they were seen as a means of achieving gradual "rationalization" of an industry suffering from EXCESS CAPACITY, or of achieving sufficient strength to compete more effectively in INTERNATIONAL TRADE.

Cash. 1. Currency and coins. 2. LEGAL TENDER in the settlement of DEBT.

Cash flow. The flow of MONEY payments to or from a firm. Expenditure is sometimes referred to as a "negative" cash flow. The *gross cash flow* of a business is the net income (⇛ INCOME STATEMENT) or PROFIT after payment of fixed interest (⇛ RATE OF INTEREST) with the DEPRECIATION provisions added back, in any trading period, i.e., that sum of money which is available for INVESTMENT, DIVIDENDS or payment of taxes. The *net cash flow* is retained EARNINGS and depreciation provisions before or after TAXATION. Net cash flows of a particular project are usually defined as those arising after taxes have been paid, expenditure on repairs and maintenance carried out, any necessary adjustments made to WORKING CAPITAL and account is taken of any residual ASSETS at the end of the project life. This term is important in INVESTMENT APPRAISAL. "Cash flow statement" is often used synonymously with "statement of sources and uses of cash." (⇛ BUDGET).

Cash holding ratio. The fraction of bank deposits held as cash, i.e., notes and coins, by individuals (⇛⇛ BANKING).

Cash ratio. 1. The ratio of a bank's CASH holdings to its total deposit LIABILITIES (⇛⇛ BANKING, CASH HOLDING RATIO). 2. For an individual firm, the proportion of its current liabilities accounted for by cash in hand, including bank deposits, and sometimes payments due from customers.

Cash reserve ratio (CANADA). The proportion of a chartered bank's demand and savings deposits held as cash reserves. The requirement is 4 percent of savings deposits plus 12 percent of demand deposits. (⇛ REQUIRED RESERVES).

Cassel, Gustav (1866–1945). ⇛ PURCHASING POWER PARITY THEORY

Celler-Kefauver Act. An amendment in 1950 to the CLAYTON ANTITRUST ACT making a merger of two or more companies illegal when it would substantially lessen competition or create MONOPOLY.

Census. An official count or enumeration, usually providing social, demographic (⇛ POPULATION) or economic information. The first censuses were probably made to assess the TAX BASE, and date at least from Roman times.

Central American Common Market (C.A.C.M.). A common market of the five Central American states—Guatemala, El Salvador, Honduras, Nicaragua and Costa Rica—agreed to under the General Treaty of Central American Economic Integration signed in December 1960. This treaty came into operation in June 1961, and a headquarters was established in San Salvador. There is also an economic secretariat, an economic council and an executive council. FREE TRADE between the member countries was expected to be established by June 1966. Duties have been eliminated on about 9 percent of products. An agreement on the Equalization of Import Duties and Charges was made in September 1959, and subsequent agreements have established a common external tariff (⇛ TARIFFS, IMPORT) on all but a small number of products. The member countries agreed to harmonize fiscal incentives granted to industries, if they effectively contributed to the growth of the region. In 1961, the Central American Bank for Economic Integration was formed to finance industrial projects, housing and hotels in the region. In 1964, the five CENTRAL BANKS agreed to establish, in the long term, a common CURRENCY. However, C.A.C.M. suffered a set-back at the end of 1970 when Honduras suspended membership after the war with El Salvador, and after the imposition of import duties on a number of commodities by Costa Rica in 1971. A draft treaty for a revised Central American Economic Community was prepared in 1972 and was designed to extend the areas of cooperation. (⇛⇛ CUSTOMS UNION; INTER-AMERICAN DEVELOPMENT BANK).

Central bank. An instrument of government with four major functions: to be a bank for COMMERCIAL BANKS; to be a bank for government; to control the MONEY SUPPLY and to support financial markets. In carrying out these last two functions, central banks have a major influence on *interest rates* (⇛ RATE OF INTEREST). In the United States, the FEDERAL RESERVE is the central bank. Central banks play an important role in regulating the BALANCE OF PAYMENTS through their intervention in FOREIGN EXCHANGE MARKETS.

Central bank of central banks. ⇛ BANK FOR INTERNATIONAL SETTLEMENTS; INTERNATIONAL MONETARY FUND; KEYNES PLAN

Certificate of deposit (C.D.) A negotiable claim issued by a bank in return for a time DEPOSIT. Also referred to as *negotiable* CERTIFICATE OF DEPOSIT (N.C.D.) C.D.'s were introduced by the First National City Bank of New

York in 1961 and for the larger COMMERCIAL BANKS now account for over 70 percent of time deposits in accounts of $100,000 or more. Where a depositor knows that he can, if necessary, sell his C.D. he will be willing to place his funds with a bank for longer periods. He will also enjoy a higher interest rate since C.D.'s are not now subject to interest rate ceilings which apply to time deposits under federal law and regulation. Most C.D.'s are purchased by corporations and these SECURITIES enable banks to compete for corporate funds, that would otherwise be invested in TREASURY BILLS and other financial instruments.

Certificate of incorporation. ⇛ INCORPORATION

Certificate of origin. A certificate required by a customs authority to accompany imported goods that can claim preferential TARIFF (⇛ TARIFF, IMPORT) rates by virtue of their country of origin.

Chamberlin, Edward Hastings (1899–). After a period at the University of Michigan, Professor Chamberlin joined Harvard as a tutor in 1922 and became a full Professor of Economics there in 1937. His publications include *Theory of Monopolistic Competition* (1933), *Towards a More General Theory of Value* (1957) and *The Economic Analysis of Labor Union Power* (1958). In *Theory of Monopolistic Competition* he proposed a new approach for economic theory which broke away from the old concepts of pure or PERFECT COMPETITION or pure MONOPOLY. These two cases he saw as special limiting ones. In between was "monopolistic competition," which was the condition under which most industries, in fact, operated. Each firm pursued a policy of product differentiation (⇛ DIFFERENTIATION, PRODUCT) by special packaging or advertising so that it created a "penumbra" of monopoly around its product. He also analyzed the problem of selling costs, e.g., advertising. (⇛⇛ MONOPOLISTIC COMPETITION; ROBINSON, JOAN VIOLET).

Charge account. 1. An account against which purchases may be made and paid monthly. 2. A form of revolving INSTALLMENT CREDIT offered by some retail stores in which the consumer makes fixed regular monthly payments into an account and receives in return credit to purchase merchandise up to the limit of a certain multiple of the monthly payments, normally eight or twelve. A service charge, in effect an interest charge (⇛ RATE OF INTEREST), is normally made as a percentage of the value of each purchase. Purchasers usually have to identify themselves with a card which is used to provide an imprint of the account address on the bill of sale. 3. Credit cards are issued by gasoline companies, banks, travel organizations and others to enable consumers to purchase goods and services and pay for them against a monthly billing. When the bill is paid within a stated period (usually one month) no charge is made to the purchaser although a commission is deducted by the credit card company from payment to the seller. (⇛ CREDIT ACCOUNT).

Chartist. A stock-market analyst who predicts share-price movements solely from a study of graphs on which individual SHARE prices and price indices are plotted. (⇛ DOW JONES).

Check. An order written by the drawer to a COMMERCIAL BANK or CENTRAL BANK to pay on demand a specified sum to the bearer, a named person or corporation.

Checkbook money. ⇛ DEMAND DEPOSIT

Checking account. An account in a financial institution whereby money can be transferred by a check. (⇛ DEMAND DEPOSIT).

Chicago Mercantile Exchange (C.M.E.). Organized in 1919, the exchange dealt in cash and FUTURES contracts in a variety of agricultural products. Under a reorganization in 1976, the list of items for trade was expanded and now includes U.S. TREASURY BILLS, coins and some metals. The C.M.E. is the second largest COMMODITY EXCHANGE in the world. It is governed by a 21-member board and operates under Federal regulation.

Chicago school. ⇛ FRIEDMAN, MILTON; QUANTITY THEORY OF MONEY

CIF. Cost, insurance and freight, or charged in full. In 1979, Congress legislated that trade figures should be reported each month on a CIF basis as well as the FAS (free-alongside-ship) basis previously adopted. Because of the inclusion of additional costs in the IMPORT figures, the effect is to increase substantially the reported VISIBLE TRADE deficit. (⇛ INVISIBLES).

Circulating capital. Funds embodied in INVENTORIES and work in progress or other current, as opposed to fixed, ASSETS. A rarely used synonym for WORKING CAPITAL.

Clark, John Bates (1847–1938). Educated at Amherst College, and Heidelberg and Zürich Universities, Clark taught at Amherst until, in 1895, he was appointed Professor of Economics at Columbia University. He held this post until his retirement in 1923. His major publications include *Philosophy of Wealth* (1885), *Distribution of Wealth* (1899), *Essentials of Economic Theory* (1907), *The Control of Trusts* (1901) and *The Problems of Monopoly* (1904). He is regarded as the founder of the marginal productivity theory of distribution in the United States. (⇛ DISTRIBUTION, THEORY OF).

Clark, John Maurice (1884–1963). The son of JOHN BATES CLARK. He succeeded his father to the Chair of Economics at Columbia University in 1926. His publications include *Economics of Overhead Costs* (1923) and *Essays in Preface to Social Economics* (1963). In an article, "Business Acceleration and the Law of Demand," in the *Journal of Political Economy* in 1917, he formulated the ACCELERATION PRINCIPLE, one of the basic theories upon which modern dynamic macroeconomic theory has been constructed. (⇛ MACROECONOMICS).

Classical economics. The classical period of economics ranges from ADAM SMITH'S *Wealth of Nations,* which was published in 1776, to JOHN STUART MILL'S *Principles of Political Economy* of 1848, and was dominated by the work of DAVID RICARDO. The French PHYSIOCRATS had stressed the position of agriculture in the economy, claiming that this sector was the source of all economic wealth. Smith rejected this view and drew attention to the development of manufacturing and the importance of labor PRODUCTIVITY. Ultimately LABOR was the true measure of VALUE. Ricardo took up this idea and propounded a theory of relative prices based on costs of production in which labor cost played the dominant role, although he accepted that CAPITAL costs were an additional element. Capital played an important role, not only by improving labor productivity, but also by enabling labor to be sustained over the period of waiting before work bore fruit in consumable output. This was the idea of the wages fund (⇛ WAGE FUND THEORY). Wages were dependent on two forces: (a) the demand for labor, derived from the availability of capital, or savings, to finance the wage bill; and (b) the supply of labor, which was fixed in the short run, but in the long run was dependent on the standard of living. The latter was related to the level of subsistence. This was not regarded as merely the basic necessities required to keep the workers alive and to reproduce themselves. It was determined by custom, and was accepted to be increasing as real living standards improved. T. R. MALTHUS, in his theory of population, pointed to the need for restraint because of the presumption that there was a natural tendency for the growth of population to outstrip agricultural output. Ricardo analyzed the implications of the productivity of land at the margin of cultivation. The Physiocrats and Adam Smith had attributed agricultural RENT to the natural fertility of the soil, but Ricardo refuted this. Rent existed because of the poor fertility of the final increment of land taken under cultivation. Because of competition, PROFITS and labor costs must be the same everywhere and therefore a surplus must accrue to all land that was more fertile than that on the margin. This surplus was rent. The presumption that competition existed was the foundation of classical thought. The classical economists believed that, although individuals were each motivated by self-love and personal ambition, free competition ensured that the community as a whole benefited. As Adam Smith put it, "It is not from the benevolence of the butcher that we expect our dinner, but from regard to [his] own interest." As a consequence, they concluded government interference should be kept to a minimum. The classical economists gave little attention to macroeconomic problems (⇛ MACROECONOMICS), such as the TRADE CYCLE. Most of the classicists accepted J. B. SAY'S Law of Markets, the gist of which purported to maintain the impossibility of any severe economic recession (⇛ DEPRESSION) arising from an overall deficiency in AGGREGATE DEMAND. Malthus disputed this. He argued that increased savings would not only lower consumption but would also increase output, through increased investment. However, his view was not accepted. The classical economists, including Malthus, held a theory in which savings were equated with investment through changes in the RATE OF INTEREST (⇛ TURGOT, ANNE ROBERT JACQUES). J.S. Mill's book was used as a school text until the end of the nineteenth century. ALFRED MARSHALL in his *Principles of Economics* of 1890 assimilated the old classical economics with the new marginalism (⇛ MARGINAL ANALYSIS) of JEVONS, C. MENGER and M.E.L. WALRAS. The great controversy which raged in the years of the Great Depression of the 1930s, between the late classical economists and the advocates of deficit spending on public works, was resolved at the time when the classical macroeconomic theory gave way to the new economic revolution set in train by J.M. KEYNES. Classical economists continue to influence economists to this day. (⇛ NEO-CLASSICAL ECONOMICS).

Classical school. The tradition of economic thought that originated with ADAM SMITH and was developed through the work of DAVID RICARDO, T.R. MALTHUS, J.S. MILL down to A. MARSHALL and A.C. PIGOU. (⇛ CLASSICAL ECONOMICS; NEO-CLASSICAL ECONOMICS).

Clayton Antitrust Act. This act was passed in 1914 and attempted to strengthen the SHERMAN ANTITRUST ACT by allowing prosecutors to bring charges with respect to potential anti-competitive business practices. Its most important provisions regulated EXCLUSIVE DEALINGS and PRICE DISCRIMINATION and the acquisition of the stock of one company by another. (⇛ CELLER-KEFAUVER ACT; INTERLOCKING DIRECTORATE).

Clean Air Act. ⇛ ENVIRONMENTAL PROTECTION AGENCY

Clearing house. An institution that settles mutual indebtedness between a number of organizations. Bank clearing houses are the best known but other bodies, such as airlines, which accept each other's tickets, or members of a stock exchange which buy and sell SHARES among themselves, also need clearing facilities. The New York Clearing House Association has 12 member banks. The Clearing House matches groups of CHECKS to be presented to each of the other banks and offsets them, so that at the end of the day each bank has a net surplus or deficit with the others, that is with the Clearing House. A memorandum of these balances is sent to the Federal Reserve Bank of New York (⇛ FEDERAL RESERVE SYSTEM) which debits or credits the reserves of the member banks according to the totals shown on the memorandum. During the First World War the New York Clearing House kept the banking system functioning by issuing clearing house certificates in settlement of members' balances. In some parts of the country clearing houses are organized the same way as is the New York Clearing House; in other sections participating banks carry out the work on a rotation basis.

Clip coupons. ⇛ COUPON

Closed corporation. A corporation in which all the stock is owned by a small number of persons, usually including one or more of the executive officers. Most closed corporations are family businesses or SMALL BUSINESSES. Also referred to as private corporations, and closely held corporations. (⇛⇛ SEPARATION OF OWNERSHIP FROM CONTROL).

Closed-end investment company. ⇛ INVESTMENT TRUST

Closed-end trust. ⇛ INVESTMENT TRUST

Closed shop. An arrangement whereby only union members can be employed in a particular company, industry or occupation, and the union controls the membership. Since the TAFT-HARTLEY LABOR ACT such an arrangement is almost nonexistent. (⇛ OPEN SHOP; UNION SHOP).

Closing prices. Prices of a commodity, e.g., SECURITIES on the STOCK EXCHANGE, at the end of a day's trading in a MARKET.

Cobb-Douglas production function. A particular type of production function of the form:

$$q = a_o x_1^{a_1} x_2^{a_2} \ldots x_n^{a_n}$$

where $x_1\ x_2 \ldots x_n$ are quantities of the n factors of production and $a_o\ a_1 \ldots a_n$ are PARAMETERS. It was used by the economists Cobb and Douglas in a path-breaking 1928 paper which sought to explain the relative constancy of the shares of CAPITAL and LABOR in the NATIONAL INCOME, hence its name. This function, particularly in the special case where $n = 2$ and $a_1 + a_2 = 1$, has some very useful properties and has been used extensively in economics, not only in the theory of INCOME DISTRIBUTION, but also in the theory of the firm (⇛ FIRM, THEORY OF) and the theory of ECONOMIC GROWTH.

Cobweb theorem. An analysis of whether the stability of EQUILIBRIUM in markets in which the amount of output currently supplied depends on what the price was in some previous period. The purpose of this analysis is to define the conditions under which price will tend to converge to an EQUILIBRIUM, or diverge from equilibrium, if it is out of it. The analysis was first developed in the context of certain agricultural markets (it was for some time referred to as the "hog cycle" phenomenon). Suppose farmers plant an acreage of a particular crop, which, given climatic conditions and the absence of stocks, determines the supply of the crop after the harvest. At time period 1, the price will be at a particular level, farmers will plant accordingly, and in a single period's time will put the resulting crop on the market. Suppose, however, that at that time demand is higher than it was previously and the available supply is insufficient to meet the demand at the old price; price must then rise to "ration off" available supply among buyers. At time period 2, therefore, farmers will plant a larger acreage of the crop, because price is now higher; hence, one period later, a larger supply will reach the market. This supply will be more than that required to satisfy demand at the price prevailing at period 2, and so price will fall to induce buyers to take up the extra supply. Less will therefore be sown at time period 3, and less will be put on the market at time period 4, thus price must again rise. And so the process continues. The important question is: do the price changes become smaller, or larger each time? If the former, the market will converge to equilibrium—eventually, the amount put on the market will equal the amount buyers are prepared to take at the price existing in the last period. If the latter, the price fluctuations grow steadily larger. It is possible to formulate in precise terms the conditions under which each occur. The importance of the Cobweb theorem is as one of the earliest and easiest examples of dynamic analysis, which raises in sharp but relatively simple form many of the basic problems of dynamic analysis. Also, despite its assumptions that individual producers act in an uncoordinated way (no longer true even of agricultural markets), form their expectations naïvely (by considering only the price prevailing at the time of planting), and do not learn as their expectations are continually proved wrong, the analysis does shed light on the reasons for price fluctuations in certain markets. It is called the "cobweb" theorem because, if the movements of prices and quantities are plotted on a conventional SUPPLY and DEMAND diagram, the pattern is similar to a cobweb. (⇛ STABILITY ANALYSIS).

COLA (cost of living adjustment). A COLA clause in a wage contract calls for wages to rise during the life of the contract in response to changes in prices usually as measured by the CONSUMER PRICE INDEX. The adjustment is usually triggered when inflation exceeds a predetermined level. The adjustment may not always fully offset the rise in the rate of inflation. COLA clauses tend to be popular in wage agreements where there is uncertainty concerning labor's ability to be compensated for unexpected inflation over the life of a contract (⇛ INDEXATION).

Collateral security. A second security (in addition to the personal surety of the borrower) for a LOAN. BANK LOANS are normally made against the security of STOCKS, real estate or insurance policies.

Collusion. Overt cooperation between oligopolists (⇛ OLIGOPOLY) to establish common policies. These policies generally involve setting PRICES, and may also involve assigning market QUOTAS and coordinating INVESTMENT plans. Since collusion precludes price competition, and tends to promote inefficiency and a low rate of innovation, it has been criticized by economists. (⇛⇛ CARTEL).

Colombo Plan for Cooperative Economic and Social Development in Asia and the Pacific. A plan for economic assistance for the DEVELOPING COUNTRIES of Asia and the Pacific agreed in 1950 with special concern originally for the reestablishment of economic activity on a sound basis in the aftermath of the Second World War. The member countries include the United States, United Kingdom, Australia, Canada, New Zealand and Japan as well as developing Asian and Pacific countries. The consultative committee publishes an annual report describing the economic progress and aims of the developing countries in the plan and the nature and level of assistance received. (⇛⇛ ASIAN DEVELOPMENT BANK).

Combination. The joining together of two or more hitherto independent firms. It may take the form of a MERGER or a controlling stockholding. (⇛ HOLDING COMPANY).

Comecon. ⇛ COUNCIL FOR MUTUAL ECONOMIC AID

Commercial banks. Privately owned banks operating CHECKING ACCOUNTS, receiving DEPOSITS and making LOANS. There are over 14,600 commercial banks in the United States in addition to SAVINGS AND LOAN ASSOCIATIONS, MUTUAL SAVINGS BANKS, and CREDIT UNIONS which, although deposit-taking institutions, are not normally referred to as banks (⇛ BANKING). The commercial banks, some of which provide a number of other services such as credit cards, savings accounts and other financial services, have tended, nonetheless, to lose market share in the financial services industry mainly because of the effects of government regulation of the banking system.

Commercial paper. ⇛ PROMISSORY NOTE

Commission. A percentage of the VALUE of a transaction taken by an intermediary as payment for his services, e.g., BROKER's commission, realtor's commission.

Commodity. 1. A particular type of raw material or primary product such as tea, coffee, wool, cotton, rubber, tin, jute, and furs (⇛ COMMODITY EXCHANGE).

2. In PRICE THEORY, "commodity" is the general name given to goods and services, the basic objects of production and exchange. Thus coal, ice cream, and the services of an automobile mechanic would all be regarded as "commodities." There are three essential characteristics which distinguish one commodity from another:

(a) the *physical attributes* of the commodity which determine its characteristics in production and consumption. Thus coal clearly differs from ice cream which differs from a mechanic's services.

(b) The *date* at which a commodity will be made available. For example coal available to be bought and sold today is a different commodity from coal available in a year's time.

(c) The *place* at which a commodity will be made available. Coal available at the mine in the Alleghenies is a different commodity from coal available in Pittsburgh, Pa.

The reason to distinguish these three aspects is that even if commodities were identical in two aspects, they could not be regarded as perfect SUBSTITUTES if they differed in respect to the third.

Commodity agreements. ⇛ INTERNATIONAL COMMODITY AGREEMENTS

Commodity control schemes. ⇛ INTERNATIONAL COMMODITY AGREEMENTS

Commodity exchange. A MARKET in which COMMODITIES are bought and sold. It is not necessary for the commodities to be physically exchanged; only rights to ownership need be. New York and Chicago have important commodity markets such as the CHICAGO MERCANTILE EXCHANGE. These exchanges deal in a wide variety of products such as coffee, cocoa, sugar, concentrated juices, wool, rubber, corn, soybeans and metals.

The old practice of auctioning commodities from warehouses in which samples could be inspected beforehand has become less important. An efficient system of grading and modern systems of communication have enabled the practice of "CIF trading" to develop. A buyer can buy a commodity in the country of origin for delivery CIF to a specified port at which he can off-load for direct delivery to his own premises. This method saves warehouse costs and auction charges. The market not only enables commodities to be sold "spot" or for delivery at some specified time and place (⇛ SPOT MARKET), but it also includes a market in FUTURES. This latter enables merchants to avoid the effect of price fluctuations by buying for foward delivery at an agreed price, which will not be affected by intervening changes in the "spot" rate.

Commodity stabilization agreements. ⇛ INTERNATIONAL COMMODITY AGREEMENTS

Common agricultural policy (C.A.P.). The system of agricultural support adopted by the EUROPEAN ECONOMIC COMMUNITY. The central feature of the policy is that it raises the incomes of farmers by keeping agricultural prices to the consumer at a high level. The subsidy to farmers is therefore financed by the consumer as well as the taxpayer. "Target" prices are fixed by the E.E.C. Commission for specified commodities. Import prices are kept above the target prices by the imposition of levies. "Intervention" prices for domestic supplies are set somewhat below the "target" prices. If sales can only be made on the market below the "intervention" price, the Community buys into store in order to drive the price up. The "intervention" price may vary from place to place in the Community in order to induce "surplus" areas to transport to "deficit" areas and the Community may also subsidize exports in order to keep prices above the "intervention" level. Criticism has been made of the high cost of C.A.P. About 75 percent of the Community budget is absorbed by agriculture and, of that, only about 10 percent is used for agricultural reform.

Common Fund. Discussions were initiated in 1976 by the UNITED NATIONS CONFERENCE ON TRADE AND DEVELOPMENT for the setting up of a Common Fund to support INTERNATIONAL COMMODITY AGREEMENTS and primary producers. By 1980, agreement had been reached to set up the Fund in two parts. The first part would contain a capital of $400 million and would offer banking facilities to the ICAs to help them finance the operations of their BUFFER STOCKS. The second part would have a capital of $350 million and would be used to give direct assistance to producers. The ICAs would also deposit some of their own assets with the Fund. The 1980 UNCTAD program covered 18 primary commodities. In June 1982, the deadline for the ratification of the agreement to the Fund by the required 90 member states was extended to September 1983.

Common market. ⇛ CUSTOMS UNION; EUROPEAN ECONOMIC COMMUNITY

Common-property resource. A resource for which there are no private *property rights*. For example, all citizens may be allowed access to a lake, for fishing, bathing, etc., and so the lake would be regarded as a common property resource. Similarly, anyone can fish the high seas outside territorial waters, hence the high seas are a common-property resource on a world-wide scale. Economics predicts that PROFIT-seeking behavior, which may be beneficial in many contexts, can have an undesirable outcome in the case of common-property resources. First, the resource tends to be overused, so we would predict over-fishing in the above examples. This is because each individual tends to ignore the effect his own use of the resource may have on the returns to other individuals (⇛ EXTERNALITIES). For example, the individual fisherman on a lake considers only the catch he is likely to take, and ignores its effect on the catch available to others. If *all* fishermen behave this way, the lake will be over-fished. Secondly, it does not pay an individual to invest in improving or conserving the resource, as the benefits are not appropriable by him: they are available to all others who have access to the resource. For these reasons there is said to be MARKET FAILURE in the case of common property resources.

Common stocks. Shares in the EQUITY capital of a corporation entitling the holders to all distributed profits after the holders of DEBENTURES and PREFERRED STOCK have been paid. Because YIELDS and prices of common stocks, although fluctuating, have risen as the value of money has fallen, they have proved better long-term INVESTMENTS since the Second World War, than fixed-interest STOCKS.

Company taxation. ⇛ CORPORATION INCOME TAX

Comparative advantage. ⇛ INTERNATIONAL TRADE; DAVID RICARDO for the law of comparative costs.

Comparative static equilibrium analysis. A method of analysis in economics. We begin by examining the EQUILIBRIUM of the particular subject—the individual consumer, the MARKET, the economy, etc. One of the underlying determinants of this equilibrium is then changed and the resulting new equilibrium examined. The new equilibrium position is then compared to the previous equilibrium position, and from this the effects of the change are deduced.

For example: in a study of the market for a particular good, the initial EQUILIBRIUM PRICE and quantity traded are determined by the equality of SUPPLY and DEMAND. The underlying determinants of this equilibrium are such factors as the level of buyers' INCOME, their tastes, PRICES of other products, technology and prices of FACTORS OF PRODUCTION; if one of these changes, the SUPPLY CURVE or the DEMAND CURVE will shift. Suppose there is a rise in buyers' incomes. This will (unless the good is an INFERIOR GOOD) lead to an increase in demand at every price. This causes the price to rise, and the quantity supplied to increase, until the market is again in equilibrium. By comparing the new equilibrium with the initial one, we can predict that the effect of an increase in buyers' incomes is to raise the price and increase the quantity bought and sold. The same technique could have been used for a change in any other underlying determinant.

The word "comparative" is due to the comparison of two equilibrium positions. The word "static" is due to the fact that they are static equilibrium positions, i.e., in the absence of any change in the underlying determinants, the equilibrium positions would be maintained for all time—there is no built-in process of time-related change in the model.

Note that to be able to apply this kind of analysis, we first have to be assured that the system under study does move to an equilibrium position after some change. Also, the method of analysis reveals nothing about the behavior of the system between the two equilibrium positions, or how long it takes to move from one equilibrium to another—for this we need a dynamic analysis. (⇛ ECONOMIC DYNAMICS; ⇛ NEO-CLASSICAL ECONOMICS).

Comparative statics. ⇛ COMPARATIVE STATIC EQUILIBRIUM ANALYSIS

Compensating balances ⇛ BANK LOAN

Compensation principle. A criterion for the social desirability of an economic policy, which states that if those who gain from the policy could fully compensate those who lose, and still remain better off, the policy should be implemented. The fact that the compensation is hypothetical, and not actually paid, distinguishes this principle from that underlying the Pareto criterion (⇛ V.F.D. PARETO), which states that the policy is socially beneficial if no one is made worse off and someone is made better off. The compensation principle can be viewed as an attempt to deal with cases which cannot be assessed on the Pareto criterion, i.e., cases in which there are losers as well as gainers. However, there are two powerful sets of criticisms of the principle, one of which questions its logical consistency, the other its practical relevance. The first, proposed by T. Scitovsky, and termed the "Scitovsky paradox," shows that if in moving from situation A to situation B, the gainers in B can hypothetically compensate the losers, it might then be possible, in the reverse move from B to A, for the gainers (previously the losers) now to compensate the losers (the previous gainers). Scitovsky shows that this possibility arises because compensation is not actually paid, and so A and B are associated with different distributions of income. The compensation principle could "approve" a policy which moved the economy from A to B, and then one which moved it back again. The second criticism begins with the observation that as a fact of life, people, and the governments representing them, do hold VALUE JUDGMENTS about income distribution. For example, a policy making the rich richer and the poor poorer, is unlikely to gain widespread approval from the demonstration that the gainers *could* compensate the losers and still remain better off since compensation is not actually paid. Attempts to design a criterion that abstracts from distributional considerations, confronts the obstacle that economic policy-making in practice is often explicitly concerned with such considerations.

Compensatory finance. Synonym for deficit financing. (⇛ UNITED NATIONS CONFERENCE ON TRADE AND DEVELOPMENT).

Competition. ⇛ ATOMISTIC COMPETITION; PERFECT COMPETITION

Complementary demand. Two or more products are said to be complementary in DEMAND when an increase in the price of one is generally associated with a decrease in the demand for the other. Examples are: bread and butter; automobiles and gasoline; cigarettes and cigarette lighters. The complementarity stems from the nature of consumer tastes, which result in some products being habitually consumed together, or from some technical relationship that makes one necessary if the other is to be enjoyed. It follows that complementarity need not exist for all time—tastes may change, or technology may alter. Goods having such complementarity are called *complementary goods.* (⇛⇛ COMPOSITE DEMAND).

Compliance cost. Generally used today to refer to the costs imposed on the private business sector to satisfy regulatory rules and reporting practices imposed by government. (⇛ REGULATION).

Composite demand. The DEMAND for a product arising from several uses of the product. Leather, for example, may be demanded for making shoes and briefcases; sheet steel may be demanded for making automobiles and tin cans, and so forth. (⇛⇛ COMPLEMENTARY DEMAND).

Compound interest. INTEREST that is calculated not only on the original CAPITAL invested, but also on the interest earned in previous periods, e.g., a capital of $100 invested at 10 percent would yield $\frac{10}{100} \times 100 = \$10$ in the first year, $\frac{10}{100} \times (100 + 10) = \$11$ in the second year, etc. This contrasts with *simple interest,* in which the interest is calculated on the original capital only, for all years.

Comprehensive Employment and Training Act. Passed by Congress in 1973, this Act provides for widespread financial assistance, manpower training, special public service programs and the establishment of a NATIONAL COMMISSION FOR MANPOWER POLICY. Considerable financial support is made available to state and local governments to plan and operate programs such as, on-the-job training, basic education and subsidized employment programs in the public sector. (⇛ TRADE ACT).

Comptroller of the Currency. An officer of the U.S. Treasury, the Comptroller reviews applications for a bank charter. The Comptroller, in reviewing an application must be convinced there is a need for a new bank and that such a bank would not limit the business of existing banks in a serious way. The Comptroller also monitors the performance of all federally-chartered banks, visiting all banks unannounced, at least three times every two years to audit the bank's account. (⇛⇛ BANKING).

Concealed discount. ⇛ TRADE DISCOUNT

Concentration. The degree to which a relatively small number of firms account for a significant proportion of output, employment, or some other measure of size in an industry. An industry is concentrated when a small number of firms account for a high proportion of size. An industry is highly concentrated, for example, if 80 percent of employment is in the four largest firms; an industry with low concentration would be one which contained a hundred firms each of approximately the same size. The degree of concentration is therefore a characteristic of the SIZE DISTRIBUTION OF FIRMS in the industry. As such, it is one important aspect of MARKET STRUCTURE.

Interest in the degree of concentration which exists in an industry arises because it is an important determinant of the way firms behave, and of the resulting levels of prices, outputs and PROFITS. Consider three standard models of PRICE THEORY; PERFECT COMPETITION; OLIGOPOLY; and MONOPOLY. The first is characterized by a large number of small firms, i.e., by a low degree of concentration, and since each firm is so small relative to the total market, each firm takes the market price as given and adjusts to it. As a result, price is equated to MARGINAL COST, satisfying a necessary condition for an optimum allocation of resources (⇛ ECONOMIC EFFICIENCY). In oligopoly, on the other hand, there is a high degree of concentration: a small number of firms control a large percentage of sales, net ASSETS, etc. Firms may adopt policies of COLLUSION, spend large amounts on ADVERTISING and other forms of NON-PRICE COMPETITION, restrict entry of new sellers and adopt other policies that tend to run counter to the interest of consumers. Prices will tend to exceed marginal costs. Finally, in monopoly there is complete concentration. In this case, economic theory suggests that price will exceed marginal costs, that there may be a tendency to inefficiency and greater than normal profits. Hence, in each of these cases, the degree of concentration is an important determinant of the economic efficiency of the market. Attempts have also been made to measure the concentration in the economy as a whole, sometimes referred to as *aggregate concentration*. (⇛ CONCENTRATION RATIO).

Concentration ratio. A single number which attempts to indicate the degree of CONCENTRATION existing in an industry. Various forms of concentration ratio exist:

(a) The percentage of total industry sales, employment or some other measure of size, held by the largest 3, 4 or 8 firms. The greater this percentage, the more concentrated the industry.

(b) The smallest number of firms whose sales, employment or some other size measure, sum to a given percentage of the total industry sales, employment, etc.—normally 60, 75 and 80 percent. The smaller this number, the more concentrated the industry.

(c) *The Herfindahl Index,* so named after the economist, Orris C. Herfindahl, who devised it. This takes the value of sales, employment or other size measure for each firm, expresses each of these as a proportion of the industry total, squares each of these proportions, and then sums them. The formula for the index is:

$$H = \sum_{i=1}^{n} \left(\frac{X_i}{X}\right)^2$$

where H is the Herfindahl Index, X_i is the value of the size variable for the i'th firm ($i = 1, 2, \ldots n$), and X is the total value of the variable for the industry. The largest value H can take is 1, and this is when one firm has 100 percent of sales, etc., in the industry. The smallest value H can take is $1/n$ (n is the number of firms in the industry), and this occurs when the firms in the industry are all of exactly equal size. These properties of the index accord well with our intuitive ideas of concentration.

No attempt to summarize a complicated concept in a single statistic can be entirely successful, and concentration ratios are no exception. They cannot be better than the data on which they are based, and because of difficulties in data collection and industry definitions in the presence of multi-product ESTABLISHMENTS, a given concentration ratio may be somewhat inaccurate, as calculated. More importantly, the first two types of ratio listed above suffer from the conceptual weakness of not relating to the whole SIZE DISTRIBUTION OF FIRMS, but rather to a single point on it. For example, if we calculated that, in each of 2 industries, the 4 largest firms accounted for 60 percent of total sales, we may conclude that there is an "equal degree of concentration" in the industries. However, it would surely make a difference in behavior of firms in each industry, if, in a single industry 3 large firms accounted for the remaining 40 per cent, while, in the other industry, 20 firms of varying size supply this proportion. The Herfindahl Index, on the other hand, avoids this problem, as it incorporates the size of each firm; at the same time, however, the data on which to calculate the index are not usually forthcoming in sufficient quantity. Despite the limitations, of which more exist than can be mentioned here, of concentration ratios, they can be extremely useful in industrial economics, particularly in investigating relationships between such factors as PROFITS, ADVERTISING, RESEARCH AND DEVELOPMENT, on the one hand, and MARKET STRUCTURE on the other. Awareness of their limitations is, however, important in interpreting the conclusions of these studies. (⇛ GINI COEFFICIENT).

Conditional grants. Payments from the federal to local government for the provision of specific public goods and services at the city/ state level. They are made available on the condition that the funds are spent on services designated by the donor. These transfers are often on a shared-cost basis governed by an explicit formula. Such payments are also made by state to local governments.

Conference Board. An independent research organization financed by the private sector which undertakes a wide range of economic forecasting and policy analysis. It has facilities in Canada, the United States and Europe. Approximately 4,000 institutions and individuals are Associates of the Conference Board. Head offices are located in New York.

Conglomerate. A business organization generally consisting of a HOLDING COMPANY and a group of subsidiary companies engaged in dissimilar activities. Conglomerates pose especially difficult problems in ANTITRUST POLICY since their expansion by MERGER may not increase market CONCENTRATION but might affect competition in other ways. (⇛ POTENTIAL COMPETITION).

Congress of Industrial Organizations (CIO). The basis for industrial unions in the United States with workers organized according to industry. The CIO emerged in the post-1930 period when John L. Lewis, a mine worker, split his union away from the AMERICAN FEDERATION OF LABOR and fought for and won the right to represent workers as industrial groups. In 1955 the AFL and CIO joined together as a joint federation.

Consolidated accounts. ⇛ MINORITIES, MINORITY INTEREST

Conspicuous consumption. CONSUMPTION of goods which is ostentatious and intended to impress; the satisfaction derived from the consumption arises from the effect on other people, rather than from the inherent utility of the good itself. Such aspects of consumer psychology, and their implications for orthodox consumer theory, were most fully analyzed by Thorstein Veblen (1857–1929) in his book *Theory of the Leisure Class* (1899).

Constant prices. ⇛ REAL TERMS

Constant returns to scale. ⇛ RETURNS TO SCALE

Consumer credit. Short-term LOANS to the public for the purchase of specific goods. Consumer credit takes the form of CREDIT by storekeepers and other suppliers, CHARGE ACCOUNTS and INSTALMENT CREDIT. BANK LOANS, money lenders and other private sources of borrowing are not referred to as consumer credit, either because they are not tied to the purchase of specific goods or because they are long term loans, e.g., MORTGAGES. (⇛⇛ BANKING; FINANCE).

Consumer good. A commodity bought by HOUSEHOLDS for use in CONSUMPTION. (⇛ ECONOMIC GOOD).

Consumerism. The view that CORPORATIONS should be forced to serve primarily the consumer, rather than the stockholder interests. This view has manifested itself in the growth of product quality legislation, drug and auto safety regulations and truth-in-advertising codes. It is also linked with groups that try to provide independent evidence on product quality beyond what is required by law.

Consumer Price Index (CPI). An INDEX NUMBER of a series of PRICES paid by consumers for the goods they typically buy. It is also often referred to as the "cost of living index." As with any other price index number, the consumer price index is constructed by choosing a set of items, finding the current prices of those items, expressing these as percentages of their prices in some base period and then calculating a WEIGHTED AVERAGE of these "price relatives." The index is intended to provide as accurate a representation as possible of changes in the cost to HOUSEHOLDS of the range of goods which they normally buy. This involves, first of all, careful choice of which items to include, the aim being to obtain as representative a set as possible. Secondly it involves choosing an appropriate set of weights to use in calculating the weighted average of price relatives. These weights must reflect the importance of the items in the family budget. We would expect items on which households spend a relatively large proportion of their INCOMES to be weighted more heavily than items on which little is spent, since a given proportionate price rise in the former set of items will have a much bigger effect on the family's "cost of living" than the same proportionate price rise on unimportant items. The weights must also be changed to reflect significant changes in the composition of family expenditure, if the price index is to give an accurate representation of changes in the cost of living. To help decide on which items to include, and what weights to assign, the government department responsible for the index, the Bureau of Labor Statistics, conducts a family expenditure survey at regular intervals. This survey attempts to find how households typically divide their expenditure between different goods, and this information then suggests which items should be included and what weights should be attached. As with any index number, the consumer price index need not give an exact description of the changes in the cost of living of any one family. If one's expenditure pattern is significantly different from the average, or one buys from shops which sell at prices significantly above or below the average, then one's own "cost of living index" would be different. Nevertheless, the consumer price index gives a useful, concise picture of the broad movement of an important set of prices over time. (⇛⇛ GROSS NATIONAL PRODUCT DEFLATOR).

Consumers' expenditure. Total expenditure by all HOUSEHOLDS in the economy on goods and services for immediate CONSUMPTION. It constitutes about two-thirds of the NATIONAL INCOME.

Consumers' preference. A term used to denote the relative strengths of consumers' wishes to consume various goods and services. In a FREE MARKET economy, resources are said to be allocated "according to consumers' preference." The way in which consumers divide up their total expenditure among the goods and services available is determined by their relative preferences (as well as by PRICE). Total expenditure on each good or service then determines the output required from the firms producing it. This in turn determines (in conjunction with technological methods of production and prices of FACTORS OF PRODUCTION) how much of the scarce resources of the economy are used in producing each good. Thus, the greater is consumer preference for a good, the greater the demand for it, and hence the greater the amount of resources absorbed in its production. Similarly, changes in preferences will cause changes in relative demands and reallocation of RESOURCES, from goods now less preferred, as compared to the original position, to goods now more preferred. (⇛⇛ INDIFFERENCE ANALYSIS; REVEALED PREFERENCE).

Consumers' sovereignty. This is said to exist when RESOURCES are allocated in line with CONSUMER PREFERENCE, as opposed to, say, state direction. The amount of "sovereignty" possessed by each individual consumer is, of course, determined by his INCOME.

Consumer surplus. The excess of the amount a consumer is prepared to pay for a good (rather than go without it) over the amount he actually does pay for it. This term, and a rigorous analysis of the concept, was put forward by A. MARSHALL, although the French engineer A.J.E. DUPUIT first developed the idea in his analysis of the pricing of public services. The existence of consumer surplus for a good stems from the tendency of MARGINAL UTILITY to diminish as its consumption increases. Thus a consumer might pay a maximum of 50 cents for the first unit of consumption of a good, 40 cents for the second unit (given that he possesses the first), 30 cents for the third, and so on. We take this diminishing "willingness to pay" as an indication that the satisfaction he derives from the last unit of the good diminishes with the quantity consumed. If the price of the good is 30 cents, then the consumer can buy 3 units for 90 cents, whereas the total value to him of the 3 units is (50 cents + 40 cents + 30 cents) = $1.20, and so his consumer surplus is 30 cents. The fact that consumption is at the level at which the value of the last unit consumed is just equal to price, while the values of all units before this exceed the price, ensures the existence of a consumer surplus.

Marshall's analysis of consumer surplus was open to the objection, applicable to the whole of his theory of consumer demand, that it rested on the assumption that utility was a measurable quantity in the same way as profit, income and output are measurable quantities. However, J.R. HICKS was able to show that the theory of demand based on ORDINAL UTILITY and

INDIFFERENCE ANALYSIS could be used to redefine the concept of consumer surplus, although in the process the simplicity of the Marshallian concept was lost.

Consumption. 1. The total expenditure in an economy on goods and services which are used up within a specified and usually short, period of time, generally a year (plus, by convention, all expenditure on defense). This expenditure will therefore not only include consumer goods and services, but also the raw materials, etc., used in production processes. It constitutes about 80 percent of the NATIONAL INCOME. 2. The actual physical process of using a good or service: e.g., one "consumes" the services of a house by living in it; one "consumes" the services of a pair of shoes by wearing them.

Consumption function. The relationship between aggregate CONSUMPTION expenditure in an economy and aggregate consumers' DISPOSABLE INCOME. The relationship was first formulated by J.M. KEYNES and played a central role in his analysis of INCOME DETERMINATION (⇛ INCOME DETERMINATION, THEORY OF). He suggested it was a "fundamental psychological law" that as income rises, consumers' expenditure will also rise, though by less than the increase in income as some of it would be saved (⇛ AVERAGE PROPENSITY TO CONSUME; MARGINAL PROPENSITY TO CONSUME). This relationship gives rise to the MULTIPLIER. However, attempts made to quantify this relationship produced several results implying the need to refine the concept of income upon which it is based. These results were:

(a) When income and consumption were taken as averages over long periods—say 10 years—consumption was proportional to income, implying that the marginal and average propensities to consume are equal, and that the latter does not change as income changes (⇛ KUZNETS, SIMON);

(b) When *annual* consumption was related to *annual* income, the relationship was *not* proportional. The average propensity to consume exceeds the marginal, and tends to fall as income increases;

(c) The average propensity to consume tends to fluctuate widely from year to year.

To explain these results a distinction is made between the relationship of consumption and income in the SHORT-RUN on the one hand, and in the LONG-RUN on the other. Over time a consumer will try to maintain a reasonably smooth flow of consumption expenditure, and this will be geared to what he regards as his long-run income level, which could be measured as some average of his income over an entire lifetime. Moreover, consumption will also be influenced by his holding of WEALTH: the greater his wealth, the less he may need to save out of a given income. In the short-run, there may well be fluctuations in both his income and his wealth, the latter for example because of the movement of prices on the stock market. But if he is maintaining a smooth consumption pattern, this implies *short-run* variations in the proportion of income which is spent on consumption. These ideas can then be shown to reconcile the findings (a) to (c), and lead to a reformulation of Keynes' consumption function by the introduction of a wealth variable and the replacement of *current* disposable income by some measure of "long-run" or, to use M. FRIEDMAN's term, "permanent" income (⇛⇛ PERMANENT INCOME HYPOTHESIS).

Consumption goods. Goods that are bought and used by consumers for final consumption rather than by corporations for use in further production processes. For example, electricity used to light a private home is a consumption good, while electricity used to power an automobile manufacturing plant is a PRODUCER GOOD. Note therefore that the definition relates to the use to which the good is put, rather than its physical or technological characteristics.

Continuous variable. A VARIABLE that is capable of taking any fractional value. Between any two values of the variable, however close together, we can always find an infinite number of other values of the variable. For example, between the value 2.7 and 2.8, there lie an infinite number of values which can be found by writing numbers to as many decimal places as wished.

Contract curve. The graphical representation of the set of outcomes of exchange between two people, having the properties that (a) neither party is worse off than he was before the exchange; (b) neither party can be made better off without the other being made worse off. The concept was first introduced by F.Y. EDGEWORTH, who argued that if the parties to the exchange were rational, in always accepting an exchange which made at least one of them better off, then the outcome of the exchange process would in fact be a point on the contract curve. Since it can be shown that RESOURCE ALLOCATIONS on the contract curve satisfy the definition of PARETO optimality, the concept of the contract curve is also useful in that part of WELFARE ECONOMICS which is concerned with assessing the optimality of the market mechanism.

Controls on wages. ⇛ PRICES AND INCOMES POLICY

Conversion. Issue of a new STOCK to replace another. This may arise when a DEBENTURE is convertible into COMMON STOCK or where holders of government STOCK at or near redemption are offered a new stock in exchange for existing stock. (⇛ FUNDING).

Convertibility. A CURRENCY is said to be convertible when it may be freely exchanged for another currency or gold. The convertibility of the dollar into gold was suspended in 1933 but later restored. It was suspended again in 1971. (⇛ GOLD STANDARD; SMITHSONIAN AGREEMENT).

Convertible bonds. ⇛ BOND

Convertible debenture stock. ⇛ DEBENTURE

Co-ordinating Committee for Multilateral Export Controls (CoCom). A committee made up of the member countries of NATO (except Iceland) and Japan, which agrees to a list of strategic materials, the export of which, to the member countries of the Warsaw Pact, Albania, China, North Korea, Mongolia and Vietnam, should be prohibited or controlled. It was established in 1950.

Corporate law. State or federal law governing the INCORPORATION, the BANKRUPTCY and operations of companies.

Corporation. One of the three major forms of business organization in the United States. In law, it is regarded as an entity of its own, separate from those who own it through their SHARES or stock. The legal status of the corporation, large or small, means that it can be sued, but its owners cannot. Liability, in the case of bankruptcy is limited to whatever degree of ownership each shareholder possesses. There are approximately two million corporations in the United States. (⇛ PARTNERSHIP).

Corporation income tax. A tax on the income of CORPORATIONS levied, in the United States in 1981, at a rate of 22 percent on the first $25,000 of taxable income and 48 percent on the remainder. It is a tax on taxable income resulting from profits only in the corporate sector. Taxable income is defined as the gross income of a corporation less all the costs incurred in doing business to acquire that gross income. Gains from the sale of CAPITAL assets are normally included in gross income for tax purposes (⇛ TAXATION), but corporations may opt for an alternative long–term capital gains tax rate. A major problem with corporation income tax is the treatment of DIVIDENDS. If an individual has corporate income of $1000 (based on the SHARES held in the corporation), the corporate tax is, for a large corporation, $480. Profits are thus $520 after the tax; if one-half of this is paid out as a dividend, it will be taxed under the INCOME TAX at the shareholder's *marginal tax rate.* If this is 40 percent, personal income tax is $104. Total tax is $584, whereas if the individual was taxed at personal income tax rates on total corporate income, the tax would have been $400. There are those who argue that the two taxes must be integrated to remove this bias.

A second but related issue involving this tax is the question of just who bears the tax. Do corporations merely pass on or shift the tax to the price of their products? Is it shifted to labor in the form of lower wages? If shifted to product prices, the tax is basically a sales tax and the INCOME DISTRIBUTION effects would appear to be regressive. If it is shifted to labor income, it would be equivalent to some form of income tax. Empirical work has produced a wide range of estimates and the only consensus is that some portion of a corporate income tax is shifted to prices.

Correlation. A statistical technique for determining the extent to which variations in the VALUES of one VARIABLE are associated with variations in the values of another. For example, if we found that relatively high values of one variable tended to be associated with relatively high values of another, and conversely that relatively low values tended to occur together, we would say the variables were closely correlated or associated. Statisticians have made this notion precise and have devised methods of measuring the degree of association, the most frequently used of which is the *correlation coefficient* (or, strictly, the *product-moment correlation coefficient*). This coefficient measures the degree of association on a scale which varies between −1 and +1, inclusive. If the sign of the coefficient is negative, this tells us that relatively high values of one variable tend to be associated with relatively low values of the other, and *vice versa;* i.e., there is an inverse association. If the sign of the coefficient is positive, it tells us that relatively high values of both variables tend to occur together, as do relatively low values (throughout this explanation we are using "relatively high" and "relatively low" in the sense of "above average" and "below average" respectively). The actual value of the number tells us the strength of the association. A value close to ±1 indicates the variables are closely associated. On the other hand, a value close to zero, whether positive or negative, indicates that relatively high values of one variable are about as often associated with relatively high values as with relatively low values of the other. Stronger and stronger degrees of association are indicated as the coefficient varies from zero to ±1. The usefulness of correlation analysis lies in testing hypotheses about the relationships between variables. Thus, we could assert the following hypotheses: (a) the higher is household INCOME, the higher will be household expenditure; (b) the higher the rate of INTEREST, the lower the level of business INVESTMENT; (c) the greater the rate of cigarette smoking, the greater the incidence of lung cancer; and (d) the larger the size of the family, the shorter the duration of each child's full-time education. These hypotheses could be tested by measuring values of the variables and then calculating the correlation coefficients. These would show us how closely the variables were associated in practice.

Statisticians stress several limitations of correlation analysis in terms of the correlation coefficient here described, the most important of which is that the correlation coefficient does not itself prove anything about causation; it is possible for values of variables to be associated without there being a causal connection flowing from one variable to another. One reason for this may be that both variables are in fact determined by some third variable: changes in values of the latter cause changes in the former without the presence of causal relationship between them. An important instance of this is where time is the third variable: two variables may have strong time-trends which lead to their being highly correlated without there necessarily being a causal relation. Alternatively, a high correlation may arise for purely chance reasons, as, for example, the well-known high correlations between the number of storks nesting in Scandinavia and the birth rate in London, England. Thus correlation does not prove causation, and we are invariably thrown back on theoretical arguments for interpretation of the "facts." (⇛⇛ MULTIPLE CORRELATION; PARTIAL CORRELATION; REGRESSION ANALYSIS; SLUTSKY, EUGEN).

Cost. Broadly, the measure of what has to be given up in order to achieve something. Two concepts of cost can be distinguished which may, but need not, be equivalent:

(a) *Opportunity cost:* In economics, it is considered appropriate to define cost in terms of the value of the alternatives or other opportunities which have to be foregone in order to achieve a particular thing. This will coincide with outlays (see below), if and only if, the PRICES with which the outlays are calculated correctly reflect the value of alternative uses of the RESOURCES (⇛ WIESER, FRIEDRICH VON).

(b) *Outlays:* An accountant would define the cost of something as the total MONEY expenditure or outlays necessary to achieve it.

An example of the definition of opportunity cost, and the distinction between this and outlays, is the situation in which a firm is considering expanding the output of one of its products. This involves the firm in purchasing certain INPUTS—raw materials, LABOR, new machinery, etc.—and also, we assume, in diverting certain resources already possessed to the production of the good—warehouse and factory space, for example. Assume also that the FINANCE for capital expenditure is provided out of RETAINED EARNINGS. The total cost of increasing production in terms of outlays would be the sum of expenditure on materials and new machinery, the wages of the additional labor assigned to this product and the salary bill of extra managers assigned to it, plus a proportion of overheads (⇛ FIXED COSTS). The opportunity cost of the increased production, however, will consist of: (i) the outlays on the increased amounts of inputs bought; (ii) loss of PROFIT which may result from cutting down the production of other goods in order to release warehouse and factory space and divert it to the product whose output is being increased; (iii) the cost of financing the capital expenditure, which is equal to the RATE OF RETURN (⇛ RATE OF RETURN ON INVESTMENT) the firm could have obtained on the funds used to expand production if they had been used in the next most profitable opportunity open to the firm, whether internal or external.

The principle of opportunity cost involves asking what is actually foregone by choosing a particular alternative. This concept is preferred by economists, because it leads to a rational process of decision-making against which the returns from a course of action are compared to the real cost involved in undertaking it. The difference in the approach to the meaning of cost between the economist and accountant, is due to the fact that the economist is primarily interested in optimal decision-taking, while traditionally the accountant is more concerned with the ex post facto recording and presentation of money flows.

Cost accounting, costing and cost control. Procedures by which the expenditure of a firm is related to units of output. Cost accounts, while they can be directly related to financial accounts, are concerned with the detailed elements of COST in identifiable output for purposes of PRICING (⇛ PRICING POLICY), departmental budgeting and the control of manufacturing methods, material and LABOR usage for these products rather than the overall financial results of the firm's operations.

Cost-benefit analysis. A technique that attempts to set out and evaluate the SOCIAL COSTS and SOCIAL BENEFITS of INVESTMENT projects, to help determine if the projects should be undertaken. The essential difference between cost-benefit analysis and ordinary INVESTMENT APPRAISAL methods used by firms, is the stress on the *social* costs and benefits. The aim is to identify and measure the losses and gains in economic welfare that are incurred by society as a whole if the particular project in question is undertaken. In calculating the benefits of constructing a new railroad line, for example, as well as the revenues from ticket sales, we would take into account the value of reduction in traveling time to users and congestion costs to motorists, etc. Similarly, in calculating the cost of a new airport, in addition to the costs of land acquisition, construction and subsequent operation, the losses in welfare resulting from aircraft noise and denuding of areas of scenic beauty would be included. As a result of this emphasis on the taking into account all significant costs and benefits, not just the financial costs and revenues incurred and received by the agency undertaking the project, a major problem in cost-benefit analysis is the evaluation of certain types of costs and benefits.

First is the problem of measurement in physical units. We may measure traveling time savings in minutes and hours, and noise nuisance in decibels, but how do we measure the "amount of pleasure" derived from a scenic area? Next is the problem of reducing all costs and benefits to a "common unit of account" so they are comparable to one another. That is, to obtain an idea of the aggregate benefits and costs associated with a project, and to compare these for different projects whose costs and benefits are measured in different physical dimensions or none at all, it is helpful to reduce all magnitudes to some common "unit of account." Since the "unit of account" most commonly used is MONEY, this generally becomes the problem of valuing costs and benefits in monetary terms. Questions which need answers are: What is the money value of time spent in traveling? What is the money value of the loss of visual amenity in the area in which an airport is located? In some cases, economists have developed ways in principle to measure such values. Ultimately, however, many of these problems of valuation can only be resolved by political decision. Such decisions reflect society's evaluation of the costs and benefits that are not directly measurable in money terms (e.g., the value of unpolluted air, or the value placed on reducing fatal accidents along a stretch of highway).

This should not, however, be translated into the proposition that, since it is all a matter of politics anyway, the cost-benefit analysis is irrelevant and unnecessary, and is itself a waste of resources. Careful itemization of all relevant classes of costs and benefits, the exclusion of irrelevant transfer payments, quantification of what can reasonably be quantified, and a full specification of the complete set of alternatives to the project under consideration, not only provide a much sounder basis for an eventual decision, but also permit an estimate to be made of the implicit money values that must be attached to particular non-monetary benefits and costs in order to justify a particular project. At the very least, one may then consider whether these values fall within some range of "reasonableness" or are consistent with other such decisions. Thus, cost-benefit analysis should be viewed as a means of providing the best available information to governmental decision-makers, rather than as a mechanical formula for making decisions.

Cost control. ⇛ COST ACCOUNTING

Cost curves. Curves relating total COSTS, AVERAGE COSTS or MARGINAL COSTS to rate of output.

Costing. ⇛ COST ACCOUNTING

Cost of capital. ⇛ CAPITAL, COST OF

Cost of Living Council. Created by President Nixon in 1971, this Council, at cabinet level, administered Phase I of the U.S. PRICES AND INCOMES POLICY when wages and prices were frozen for 90 days. The PRICE COMMISSION assumed the major Council activities in Phase II and, by 1974, the authority of the Council lapsed. (⇛ PAY BOARD).

Cost-push inflation. INFLATION that is created and sustained by increases in production costs, independently of the state of demand. A good example of such inflation is that which took place in all Western industrial countries following the exceptional increase in oil prices of 1973. The most common source of cost-push inflation is held to be the power of trade unions to gain wage increases in excess of PRODUCTIVITY increases, leading to price rises, further wage claims, and so on, in an "inflationary spiral." Critics of this theory argue that if trade unions succeed in raising wages and prices at a time when the level of AGGREGATE DEMAND has not risen enough to justify the increase, there will be a tendency for UNEMPLOYMENT to increase, with subsequent deflationary effects in the economy (⇛ DEFLATION; STAGFLATION). Such a process could not continue indefinitely; therefore cost-push certainly could not explain the persistent inflationary processes in virtually all West European economies since the Second World War. Either the price increases must be "ratified" by stimulation of aggregate monetary demand to prevent the unemployment, or the inflation is due to EXCESS DEMAND in the first place. This latter proposition essentially argues that advocates of the cost-push theory mistake the mechanism of adjustment for a force in the process. Suppose that when firms experience increased demand for their products they do not raise prices, but instead attempt to increase output by increasing overtime, employing more workers, etc. This increased demand in the labor MARKET then leads to an increase in wage earnings and wage rates (these increases taking place in negotiations between unions and employers). As a result of these wage increases, firms are forced to raise prices. Clearly, however, the motive force for the price increase was the demand increase: the wage negotiations are simply the mechanism by which excess demand is translated into wage and price increases.

The argument that inflation is caused either by ratification of wage increases, or by excess demand, has important implications for the control of inflation. If the purely cost-push theory is accepted, then the government must either allow unemployment to develop, or try to intervene in the bargaining process with political/administrative measures to restrain unions in their demands for inflationary wage claims. On the other hand, if the theories based on excess demand are accepted (⇛ DEMAND-PULL INFLATION), then the only effective way to control inflation is through monetary and fiscal policies that restrain the level of aggregate monetary demand.

Cost schedule. A table relating total costs of production to levels of output from which schedules of MARGINAL COSTS and AVERAGE COSTS can be developed.

Costs, historical or historic. Actual costs at the time incurred. (⇛ BOOK VALUE).

Council for Mutual Economic Aid (COMECON). A council set up in 1949 consisting of the East European countries, Bulgaria, Czechoslovakia, German Democratic Republic, Hungary, Poland, Romania, and the U.S.S.R. with Outer Mongolia and, subsequently, Cuba and Vietnam (Yugoslavia, China and North Korea are observers). (Albania, an original member of the council, ceased participating in 1961.) Its aim is to develop, by means of central planning, the member countries' economies on a complementary basis, to achieve self-sufficiency. However, the East European member countries have been reluctant to allow their economic policies to be constrained by the principle of submission to the ideal of a supranational determination of economic development. A proposal for a COMECON Planning Authority put forward in 1962 was rejected, and the East European countries, particularly Romania, have pursued independent national policies. Even the U.S.S.R., because of its need for Western technology, has increased its trade with the West. The share of the group's INTERNATIONAL TRADE with the West has been increasing. COMECON's future growth is more likely to be influenced by its ability to borrow funds to finance its BALANCE OF PAYMENTS deficit with the West than by any moves to closer integration. Nevertheless, there was agreement in Bucharest in 1971 to cooperate on special projects drawn up and approved within 5-year planning periods, under which member countries would contribute funds and manpower. The International Bank for Economic Co-operation established in 1963, acts as the international clearing bank for the COMECON member countries and offers credit facilities on principles similar to those of the I.M.F. Individual projects are supported through the International Investment Bank, an institution, set up in 1970, similar in operation to the INTERNATIONAL BANK FOR RECONSTRUCTION AND DEVELOPMENT.

Council of Economic Advisors. This Council, created by the Employment Act of 1946, was set up to advise the President on the state of the economy and recommend policies for the achievement of full employment. Its influence on policy reached a pinnacle in the 1960s when, at the Council's urging, President Kennedy proposed a major tax cut to stimulate the economy. The cut was enacted in 1964 and the economic prosperity that followed was linked directly to it. With the emergence of STAGFLATION in the 1970s, and the widespread feeling that FINE TUNING was not appropriate economic policy, influence of the Council waned.

Council on Wage & Price Stability. The Council was established within the Executive Office by President Ford on August 24, 1974 to monitor the economy with special attention to wages, costs, prices, productivity and profits. It is charged with appraising government policies and programs with a view to determining their impact on inflation. The Council includes the Secretary of the Treasury, the Chairman of the COUNCIL OF ECONOMIC ADVISORS, 5 cabinet secretaries, and its 8 staff members. (⇛ PRICES AND INCOMES POLICY).

Counter deal. A form of BARTER in INTERNATIONAL TRADE in which the buyer requires the seller to accept goods (of the buyer's choosing) in lieu of currency. The seller has the task of marketing the goods. It is a popular device with the Communist Bloc countries when short of FOREIGN EXCHANGE.

Countervailing duty. A special additional import duty (⇛ TARIFFS, IMPORT) imposed on a COMMODITY to offset a reduction of its price as a result of an export subsidy in the country of origin. (⇛⇛ DUMPING; EXPORT INCENTIVES).

Countervailing power. The idea, most fully developed by J.K. GALBRAITH in his book *American Capitalism,* that excessive power held by one group can be balanced or neutralized by the power held by an opposing group, leading not to exploitation but to a workable and reasonably equitable economic or political system. Thus the power of large employers may be balanced by that of large labor unions, or of large manufacturers by retail chains.

Coupon. A piece of paper entitling the owner to MONEY payment (as in BEARER BONDS) or free goods. On a bond, CLIP COUPONS entitle the holder to claim interest at specified dates.

Cournot, Antoine Augustin (1801–77). Cournot was made Professor of Analysis and Mechanics at Lyons in 1834, and Rector of Grenoble University in 1835 and of Dijon University in 1854. His main economic work, *Recherches sur les principes mathematiques de la theorie des richesses,* was published in 1838. Other economic works were *Principes de la theorie des richesses* (1863) and *Revue sommaire des doctrines economiques* (1877). In *Recherches,* Cournot set out in mathematical form the basis for the theory of the firm (⇛ FIRM, THEORY OF) which, after being refined by A. MARSHALL, appears in elementary economic textbooks today. He was the first to set out the VARIABLES and functions facing a firm; DEMAND as a diminishing function of PRICE; COST CURVES and revenue curves. By the use of calculus, he demonstrated that a monopolist will maximize his profit at the output at which his MARGINAL COST was equal to his MARGINAL REVENUE. Cournot traced a direct logical line from the single seller (MONOPOLY) through two (DUOPOLY) or many (OLIGOPOLY) sellers to "unlimited competition." He showed how, in the latter case, "the marginal cost equals the marginal revenue relationship of the monopolist" becomes "the price equals the marginal cost relationship of the firm in PERFECT COMPETITION." In doing so, he analyzed duopoly and showed that, given each seller assumed the other's output was unaffected by his own, they would each adjust prices and output until a position of EQUILIBRIUM was reached, somewhere between that reflected by the equations for monopoly and that for unrestricted competition. Nevertheless, in spite of the undoubted significance of his work, he had no influence on the mainstream of economic thought until his ideas were adopted and developed by Marshall.

Cover. The ratio of EARNINGS per SHARE to DIVIDENDS per share. A dividend is said to be twice covered if it represents half the earnings of a company. In its inverse form this ratio is known as the *payout ratio,* i.e., the proportion of earnings which are paid out. Everything else being equal, the greater the cover or the lower the payout ratio, the less likely dividends are to be cut if PROFITS fall.

Covered bear. ⇛ BEAR

Crawling peg. ⇛ EXCHANGE RATE

Credit. Granting the use or possession of goods, services or cash without immediate payment. The opposite of DEBT. CONSUMER CREDIT enables consumers to enjoy the use of goods while they are paying for them, and is extended formally and informally by storekeepers, FINANCE COMPANIES and other financial institutions. MORTGAGE credit is a special form of credit for the purchase of property. Consumer credit is heavily supervised and regulated by government, e.g., the Consumer Credit Protection Act, 1968 (⇛ INSTALLMENT CREDIT). Business credit includes TRADE CREDIT and a wide range of LOANS (⇛ BUSINESS FINANCE). Credit enables a producer to purchase capital equipment, finance INVENTORIES and bridge the gap between the production and sale of goods. More generally credit provides the necessary link between SAVINGS and INVESTMENT, and as part of the MONEY supply it has considerable economic importance. (⇛ CREDIT CONTROL ACT; DEAR MONEY; QUANTITY THEORY OF MONEY). 2. An accounting term (⇛ DOUBLE ENTRY BOOKEEPING).

Credit account. British term for CHARGE ACCOUNT.

Credit banks. ⇛ COMMERCIAL BANKS

Credit cards. ⇛ CREDIT ACCOUNT

Credit control. ⇛ CREDIT SQUEEZE

Credit Control Act. In 1934, the FEDERAL RESERVE SYSTEM (FED), was given the power to control the use of CREDIT to purchase STOCKS listed on the STOCK EXCHANGE. It establishes the down payment or MARGIN which limits the percent of the price that can be borrowed. The Fed has the authority to raise the margin up to 100 percent in the event of a speculative stock market boom. Through REGULATION W, the FED can also control consumer credit and has done so to limit the borrowing of money to purchase consumer durables and homes during the Second World War and the Korean Conflict.

Credit guarantee. A type of insurance against default provided by the government or a credit guarantee association to a lending institution. In both the United States and Canada, government credit guarantees are given to commercial banks for loans to small businesses which, although credit-worthy do not comply with normal lending criteria, either because of an insufficiency of COLLATERAL SECURITY or some other reason. At least 10 percent of the risk remains with the lender, but in case of default he can claim the balance of the loan outstanding from the guarantor. In the United States the SMALL BUSINESS ADMINISTRATION provides Federal Government guarantees and the banks are allowed to DISCOUNT a proportion of their guaranteed small business loans in the MONEY MARKET where they have similar status to government SECURITIES and are purchased by INSURANCE companies and other financial institutions, thus providing a channel for non-bank finance to flow into SMALL BUSINESS. (⇛ EXPORT–IMPORT BANK).

Credit squeeze. Usually a deliberate policy on the part of the CENTRAL BANK to make it more difficult to borrow money. This would restrict the growth in AGGREGATE DEMAND. The DISCOUNT RATE has been raised frequently since the early 1950s to restrict member-bank borrowing, thereby limiting the availability of funds and providing a signal to the market. Credit can also be limited through the FED'S OPEN MARKET OPERATIONS (⇛ FEDERAL RESERVE SYSTEM). Credit restrictions can also be applied selectively. Until the early 1950s, the FED was in a position to legislate minimum down payments and the duration of installment loans. Federal housing agencies can impose a credit squeeze on potential home buyers by limiting the availability of mortgage funds. (⇛ BANKING; CREDIT CONTROL ACT).

Credit transfer, or Giro. A system available in Europe in which a bank or post office will transfer MONEY from one account to another on receipt of written instructions. Several accounts may be included in a list which must state the location or account numbers of the payees.

Credit unions. Consumer finance cooperatives formed to provide consumer credit, for example for automobile purchase, more widely and cheaply available than through conventional, profit-making financial intermediaries. There are some 23,000 credit unions in the United States.

Creditor. An individual or business or other organization to whom money is owed. The opposite of DEBTOR.

Creditor nation. A country with a BALANCE OF PAYMENTS surplus. The KEYNES PLAN recognized that DISEQUILIBRIUM in international payments was as much the responsibility of creditor nations as of *debtor nations*. Under the plan, the International Clearing Union or international CENTRAL BANK would have given overdrafts to debtor countries and by so doing would have created deposits for the creditor countries in terms of its special CURRENCY called BANCOR, in an operation similar to normal BANKING. However, not only would INTEREST be charged on the debtors' overdrafts but also on the creditors' deposits. Although the Keynes Plan was not accepted at the BRETTON WOODS Conference, the principle that a surplus country had "obligations" was accepted and a scarce currency clause written into the INTERNATIONAL MONETARY FUND agreement. In recent years, the eightfold increase in oil prices has fundamentally shifted the balance of creditor and debtor countries by creating large surpluses in the OPEC (⇛ ORGANIZATION OF PETROLEUM EXPORTING COUNTRIES) group and acute financing difficulties, particularly for some DEVELOPING COUNTRIES. (⇛ INTERNATIONAL LIQUIDITY; RECYCLING).

Critical-path analysis. A technique that finds the least-cost way to complete a task consisting of a number of activities, at least some of which must be done consecutively. Its main application has been in planning and controlling construction programs for large industrial projects—power stations, oil refineries, etc.—though its applications are being extended to such problems as the design of clerical systems. First it sets out the way in which activities are related and finds the length of time required by each activity. Any sequence of activities which must be carried out consecutively defines a path, and the time taken to complete all the activities in a path is simply the sum of the separate activity times. The "critical path" is the one with the longest completion time. It is "critical" in the sense that its length determines the time required by the whole task. Other paths which are not critical can be "fitted in" around the critical path in such a way as to reduce COSTS, while the main effort at reducing activity time should clearly be directed at activities which are on the critical path.

Cross-elasticity of demand. The responsiveness of the quantity demanded of one good to the changes in the PRICE of another good. It is measured by taking the proportionate change in quantity demanded of the first good and dividing this by the proportionate change in price of the second good. When this elasticity is positive, the goods are SUBSTITUTES (since a rise in price of one causes an increase in demand for the other), and when negative, they are complementary goods (⇛ COMPLEMENTARY DEMAND). As with any price-elasticity of demand, cross-elasticity can be measured either by the point-elasticity formula or the arc-elasticity formula (⇛ ELASTICITY). Finally, the numerical value of the elasticity will measure the closeness of the relationship between the two goods, a zero value denoting no relationship, a high positive or negative value denoting a close relationship.

Cross-section analysis. Statistical analysis conducted by taking data from a set of units at a particular point in time, and examining the variations in the data across the units. This is in contrast to TIME SERIES analysis. For example, we may be interested in the relationship between the size of business corporations and their profitability. We could then collect data on the size of individual corporations in terms of the number of workers they employ, their sales revenue, NET ASSETS, or whatever size measure is readily available, at a given period of time. We would also collect data on their profitability over the same period. We would then determine whether corporations which differed in size also tended to differ significantly in profitability, and, if so, in which direction the relationship went. This would be a cross-section analysis (though not a very good one, as profitability is probably determined by a number of factors and failure to take account of these in the analysis could obscure the true relationship between profitability and size).

Cross-subsidy. ⇛ SUBSIDY

Crowding out. The process whereby an increase in government spending, financed by borrowing funds domestically, raises interest rates thereby reducing private expenditure which is sensitive to higher rates of interest. One hundred percent crowding out occurs if the rise in real government spending equals the decline in interest-sensitive private spending. (⇛ KEYNES, JOHN MAYNARD).

Cum dividend. With DIVIDEND; the purchaser of a security quoted "cum" dividend is entitled to receive the next dividend due. The term "cum" meaning "with," is also used in a similar sense in relation to STOCK RIGHTS or interest (⇛ RATE OF INTEREST) attached to SECURITIES, etc.

Cum rights. ⇛ STOCK RIGHTS

Cumulative preferred stock. ⇛ PREFERRED STOCK

Currency. 1. Notes and coin that are the "current" medium of exchange in a country (⇛ MONEY SUPPLY). 2. Gold and, to a lesser extent, national currencies that act as RESERVE CURRENCIES, such as the dollar, are referred to as international currency because they are regarded as acceptable for the settlement of international DEBTS. BALANCE OF PAYMENTS problems have forced many countries to impose restrictions on the amount of currency which may be taken in and out of the country. (⇛ BANK NOTE; EXCHANGE CONTROL; EXCHANGE RATE; SOFT CURRENCY).

Currency appreciation. The increase in the EXCHANGE RATE of one CURRENCY in terms of other currencies. The term is usually applied to a currency with a floating rate of exchange; upward changes in fixed rates of exchange are called revaluations. For instance, the dollar appreciated by 7½ percent in terms of the SPECIAL DRAWING RIGHT (S.D.R.) between 1975 and 1977. (⇛ CURRENCY DEPRECIATION; DEVALUATION; EXCHANGE RATE).

Currency depreciation. The fall in the EXCHANGE RATE of one CURRENCY in terms of other currencies. Usually applied to floating exchange rates. Downward changes in fixed rates of exchange are called DEVALUATIONS. The dollar depreciated by 14 percent against the SPECIAL DRAWING RIGHT (S.D.R.) between 1973 and 1980.

Currency school. ⇛ BANKING AND CURRENCY SCHOOLS

Currency snake. ⇛ EUROPEAN CURRENCY SNAKE

Current account. That part of the BALANCE OF PAYMENTS accounts recording current, i.e., non-capital, transactions.

Current assets. ⇛ ASSETS

Current balance. The net position on the CURRENT ACCOUNT of the BALANCE OF PAYMENTS.

Current expenditure. Expenditure on recurrent, i.e., non-CAPITAL, items in business or private accounts.

Current ratio. The ratio of the current LIABILITIES to the current ASSETS of a business. Current assets normally exceed current liabilities, the difference between the two is WORKING CAPITAL. The amount of working capital required varies with the type of business and its commercial practices—e.g., on the proportion of its output sold for cash and on three months' CREDIT—so that the current ratio is not a universally useful guide to the solvency of a business. (⇛ LIQUIDITY RATIO).

Current yield. ⇛ YIELD

Customs drawback. The repayment of customs duties (⇛ TARIFFS, IMPORT) paid on imported goods which have been re-exported or used in the manufacture of exported goods.

Customs duties. ⇛ TARIFFS, IMPORT

Customs union. A customs union is established by two or more countries if all barriers (such as tariffs or QUOTAS) to the free exchange of each other's goods and services are removed and at the same time, a common external tariff is established against non-members. This contrasts with a FREE TRADE AREA in which each member-country retains its own tariffs *vis-a-vis* nonmembers (⇛ ANDEAN PACT; BENELUX; CENTRAL AMERICAN COMMON MARKET; EUROPEAN ECONOMIC COMMUNITY; EUROPEAN FREE TRADE ASSOCIATION). At one time, it was generally accepted that customs unions yielded economic benefits. Without the distortions imposed by tariffs, trade was directed in favor of the producer with advantageous costs (⇛ RICARDO, DAVID). It was believed that as FREE TRADE was beneficial in that it led to the optimal allocation of world resources, so a customs union, which was a step in that direction, must also be beneficial. However, Jacob Viner in *The Customs Union Issue* cast doubt on this belief when he pointed out that the creation of a customs union could have two effects: (a) a trade-creating effect, and (b) a trade-diverting effect. Although the former might be a gain, greater losses might be incurred by the latter. Take the example of the countries A and B, and denote the rest of the world by C. They produce a particular commodity for $50, $40 and $30 respectively. The home market for this commodity in country A is protected by a 75 percent *ad valorem* import duty. Therefore imports from C cost $52.50, those from B cost $70, and so no trade takes place. Country A is devoting $50 of resources to the production of the commodity. County A then forms a customs union with B; trade is created because it is cheaper for A to obtain the commodity from B than to produce it itself. There is a gain in so far as A is $10 better off. On the other hand, if country A's original import duty were 50 percent *ad valorem,* imports from B would cost $60 and from C would cost $45. Trade would take place with the rest of the world, C, as this would be the least–cost source for A. In this case, if A forms a customs union with B, it will switch its trade from C to B, because it can obtain the commodity for $40 from B compared with $45 from C. This, as trade-diversion, represents a move away from the optimum of RESOURCE ALLOCATION, because B is a higher real–cost source than C (⇛ SECOND BEST, THEORY OF). Therefore, whether a customs union will yield overall gains from shifts in the location of production depends on the superiority of trade-creation to trade-diversion. However, this type of analysis covers only part of the problem; many other factors must be taken into account in assessing whether a customs union is beneficial. In particular, the removal of tariff barriers between countries will change the TERMS OF TRADE and therefore the relative volumes of the different commodities demanded. It will shift the commodity pattern of trade, as well as the geographical origins of the commodities traded. Whether a community will benefit therefore, depends on the price and income-elasticities of demand for the commodities traded (⇛ ELASTICITY). An added benefit may accrue because the increase in the size of markets may enable ECONOMIES OF SCALE to be made. Finally, a protective tariff is initially imposed because home costs are high; but home costs may remain high because a protective tariff is imposed. Removal of the tariff may induce more efficient operation and lower costs.

D

Dated securities. BONDS, NOTES, or other SECURITIES which have a stated date for redemption (repayment) of their nominal value. *Short-dated securities* are those for which the REDEMPTION DATE is near; *long-dated securities* are those for which it is a long time ahead.

Dear money. High RATES OF INTEREST. A "dear money policy" carried out by a monetary authority such as the FED (FEDERAL RESERVE SYSTEM) would be one of restricting the MONEY SUPPLY, in the interests of reducing INFLATION. (⇛⇛ MONETARY POLICY; QUANTITY THEORY OF MONEY).

Death duties. Taxes imposed to limit the transfer of wealth from one generation to the next in order to promote the more equal distribution of wealth. The predominant form of death duty in the United States is the federal estate tax levied upon the total value of property owned by the deceased. Various deductions and reliefs are given which greatly reduce the base of the tax. The GIFT TAX limits the avoidance of estate duty by transfers among the living and there are special provisions to limit avoidance through the use of TRUSTS to which assets can be transferred before death; death duties have more social and political than economic importance and are not a major source of public revenue. Some states also have inheritance taxes and some have estate taxes and gift taxes. Inheritance taxes take account of the wealth of the recipient.

Death rate. The number of deaths occurring in any year for every 1,000 of the population is referred to as the crude death rate. It may be quoted for each sex and age group. The death rate has declined steadily in the United States from 14.7 recorded in 1910, to about 8.7 at the present time. (⇛ BIRTHRATE).

Debenture. Fixed-interest SECURITIES (⇛ BONDS) issued by companies in return for long-term loans. Debentures are sometimes described as unsecured bonds because they represent a claim upon the unmortgaged resources of the company and its EARNINGS rather than upon specific ASSETS. Normally the terms of a debenture limit the freedom of the issuing company to issue other bonds which might take precedence over the debenture.

Debit. ⇛ DOUBLE ENTRY BOOKEEPING

Debt. A sum of MONEY or other property owed by one person or organization to another. Debt comes into being through the granting of CREDIT or through raising LOAN CAPITAL. *Debt servicing* consists of paying interest on a debt. Debt is an essential part of all modern, capitalist economics. (⇛ CAPITALISM; NATIONAL DEBT).

Debt conversion. ⇛ CONVERSION

Debt management. The process of administering the NATIONAL DEBT or corporate borrowings, i.e., providing for the payment of interest, and arranging the refinancing of maturing BONDS.

Debtor. An individual, business or organization that owes money to another. Opposite of CREDITOR.

Debtor nation. ⇛ CREDITOR NATION

Debt ratio. ⇛ LEVERAGE

Deemed disposal. Placing a value on an ASSET as if it had been sold; an attempt to arrive at the asset's market value.

Deficit. An excess of LIABILITIES over ASSETS, or of expenditure flow over income flow, e.g., BUDGET deficit, BALANCE OF PAYMENTS deficit.

Deficit financing. A deliberate excess of expenditure over INCOME. When carried out by governments, it is also known as *compensatory finance* or *pump priming*. Such deficit financing takes the form of a budgeted deficit financed by borrowing. It has the object of stimulating economic activity and employment by injecting more purchasing power into the economy. In fact, with the growth of government expenditure, BUDGET deficits are now common even in times of full employment (⇛ EMPLOYMENT, FULL) so that deficit financing in the true sense would normally consist of increasing the deficit as a matter of policy. The use of deficit financing as a part of monetary policy was first advocated by JOHN MAYNARD KEYNES. (⇛⇛ QUANTITIY THEORY OF MONEY).

Deflation. 1. A reduction in the general level of prices. Opposite of inflation. 2. A reduction in the level of economic activity in an economy. Deflation will result in lower levels of NATIONAL INCOME, employment and IMPORTS, and lower rates of increase of wages and prices. It may be brought about by MONETARY POLICIES, such as increases in RATES OF INTEREST and contraction of the money supply, and/or by FISCAL POLICIES, such as increases in TAXATION (direct and indirect) or reductions in government expenditure. The aims of deflation may be to improve the BALANCE OF PAYMENTS, partly by reducing AGGREGATE DEMAND and thus imports, and partly by causing DISINFLATION and improving exports. 3. The adjustment of an economic variable measured in MONEY terms by a price index in order to give an estimate of the change in the variable in REAL TERMS. (⇛ INDEXATION).

Demand. The willingness and ability to pay a sum of MONEY for some amount of a particular good or SERVICE. (⇛ DEMAND, THEORY OF; ECONOMIC GOOD; MARSHALL, ALFRED).

Demand curve. A curve relating the PRICE per unit of a product to the quantity of the product the consumer wishes to buy. The demand curves of all consumers in the market can be aggregated to obtain the *market demand curve,* showing the total amount of the good which consumers will wish to buy at each price. The demand curve is usually drawn between axes, with price on the vertical and quantity demanded on the horizontal, and is generally portrayed as sloping downwards from left to right. This reflects the so-called "law of demand," which can be stated as: the lower the price, the greater the quantity of the product demanded. This "law," to which there may be exceptions, is based on an analysis of the INCOME EFFECT and the SUBSTITUTION EFFECT of price changes. Important exceptions may occur: (a) where price of the product is taken as an indicator of its quality, e.g., wine; (b) where the good is an article of ostentation, so that the higher its price the more people wish to own it, e.g., certain types of automobiles or fur coats; and (c) where there is a speculative element in the purchase of something, so that a price rise leads to the expectation of a further price rise, and more of the good will be bought (e.g., STOCKS and SHARES; GIFFEN PARADOX). In each of these cases, the demand curve will slope upwards from left to right. (⇛⇛ MARGINAL UTILITY; MARSHALL, ALFRED).

Demand deposit. Money on current account in a bank deposit that can be withdrawn without notice. Unlike TIME DEPOSITS, demand deposits do not usually earn interest; and since CHECKS can be drawn upon them they can be used to settle DEBTS and are counted in all definitions of the MONEY SUPPLY. Demand deposits are sometimes referred to as *checkbook money* (⇛ NOW ACCOUNT).

Demand for labor. The amount of a particular labor service (measured in man-hours or numbers of workers) that firms wish to employ at given wage rates. In economic theory, the demand for LABOR can be considered at two levels: (a) that of the individual firm; (b) that of the whole economy.

(a) *The firm:* the traditional economic theory of the firm's demand for labor assumes that the firm wishes to maximize PROFITS (⇛ FIRM, THEORY OF). The firm will want to employ just that quantity of labor so the contribution to revenue made by the last labor unit equals that unit's cost. The contribution to revenue made by increasing labor input by one unit depends on two things: (i) the increase in physical output; and (ii) the extra revenue received from sale of that increase in physical output. The former depends on the marginal productivity of labor (⇛ MARGINAL PRODUCTIVITY THEORY OF WAGES), which is determined by the nature of technology and the quantities of other INPUTS, especially CAPITAL, available to the firm. The latter depends on the conditions of DEMAND for the product, i.e., the level and ELASTICITY of demand. The firm's demand for labor is thus derived from the demand for its output.

(b) *The economy:* We could represent the aggregate economy-wide demand for labor as the sum of demands of individual firms, and combine this with the aggregate supply of labor to determine EQUILIBRIUM wage levels. There are several difficulties with this procedure; a major one is that since the level of labor demand derives from the demand for goods, which depends in turn on the levels of INCOME and hence wage levels, we cannot ignore the interdependence between the EQUILIBRIUM wage rate and the position of the labor demand curve. This problem is only properly resolved by integrating the supply and demand for labor with a full MACROECONOMIC model of the economy, which is necessary because, when considering the entire economy, the assumption of a given and constant level of aggregate purchasing power, made when considering the firm alone, no longer holds. (⇛⇛ WAGE FUND THEORY).

Demand function. The relationship between the quantity of a good (⇛ ECONOMIC GOOD) a consumer wants to buy, and the variables determining the demand, e.g., PRICE of the good, prices of complementary goods (⇛ COMPLEMENTARY DEMAND) and SUBSTITUTES, INCOME, consumer CREDIT conditions, etc. By holding all these variables constant except one, we can study the relationship between quantity demanded and the one variable, by observing how the former varies with changes in the latter. The DEMAND CURVE is an example of this procedure, with everything held constant in the relationship except price and quantity demanded. Tastes, needs and habits of the consumer are not explicit variables in the demand function. Rather they determine the form the function takes. (⇛⇛ SLUTSKY, EUGEN).

Demand price. The maximum PRICE a consumer would pay per unit of a good, in exchange for some specified quantity of the good.

Demand-pull inflation. INFLATION that is created and sustained by an excess of AGGREGATE DEMAND over the total flow of goods and services that can be produced by a fully employed economy. If the sum of demands for goods and services by consumers, government, and corporations exceeds available supply, prices will rise in response to this DISEQUILIBRIUM. In principle, the price increases should eliminate the excess demand and restore EQUILIBRIUM, and so some explanation must be found for the persistent tendency towards inflation which has characterized many postwar economies. A widely held explanation attributes the persistence of excess demand to government policy. Whereas consumers and corporations respond to price increases by curtailing demand, the government, because of its ability to finance its expenditure by the creation of MONEY, is able to maintain or even increase the scale of its expenditure in REAL TERMS. The result is not only a persistent tendency to inflation, but also a steady increase in the public sector's share of the total resources available to the economy. (⇛ BUDGET; COST-PUSH INFLATION).

Demand schedule. A table showing the quantities of a good (⇛ ECONOMIC GOOD) demanded at varying prices. From this information the DEMAND CURVE can be drawn.

Demand, theory of. The branch of economic theory concerned with analyzing the determinants of a consumer's choice of a particular set of purchases. The theory analyzes how the consumer's tastes and INCOME and the PRICES of the goods determine his pattern of purchases. From this analysis it is possible to predict how he will respond to such changes as increased income and reduced price of a good. In addition, it is possible to deduce the shape of the DEMAND CURVE, and clarify what determines its ELASTICITY. The analytical apparatus of choice first developed in the theory of demand, and in particular the use of INDIFFERENCE ANALYSIS, has proven applicable across the entire field of economics. The theory of demand is sometimes criticized for its apparent aridity and "unrealism," especially by those who are prepared to take its main conclusions as obvious—e.g., much of demand theory seems concerned with showing that when price goes down a consumer of that good wants to buy more of it, though actually, the theory says only that quantity demanded will rise, fall, or stay the same, following a price change! However, economists have never been content simply to take the demand curve as given, and prefer to investigate its foundations in the consumption decision of the individual consumer. (⇛⇛ MARSHALL, ALFRED).

Demography. ⇛ POPULATION

Dependent variable. A VARIABLE whose value is determined by the value(s) taken by some other variable(s). For example, in the equation $y = 2 + 3x$, once we assign a value to x, we have determined the value of y, hence y is the dependent variable. (⇛⇛ INDEPENDENT VARIABLE).

Depletion allowance. Preferential treatment accorded to extractive industries. The allowance is designed to reflect costs of exploration not yet accounted for as DEPRECIATION, and it is set as a percent of gross receipts from products mined or extracted. It is also viewed as an allowance for the using up of a finite resource which results in a lower ASSET value. Finally, it has been argued that such an allowance is needed to produce a lower rate of taxation in what is a high risk enterprise. The allowance has been criticized on the grounds that appropriate accounting procedures for depreciation would eliminate the need for the allowance; that the RENTS derived from a fixed SUPPLY are ample reward, and that RISK is appropriately reflected in the way that losses can be offset against taxable income.

Deposit. Money placed in a BANK account and constituting a claim on the bank. The term bank deposit includes deposits on all types of account. DEMAND DEPOSITS are withdrawn by writing a check giving the name of the person or institution to whom the funds are to be transferred. Federal law prohibited interest being paid on amounts in demand deposits until the enactment of the DEPOSITORY INSTITUTIONS DEREGULATION AND MONETARY CONTROL ACT, 1980. *Negotiable orders of withdrawal (NOW)* accounts are savings accounts for which a withdrawal slip is used, effectively a check, instead of an entry in a passbook. TIME DEPOSITS or savings accounts are bank accounts in which deposits earn interest and withdrawals from which require notice; the longer the period of notice, the higher the interest rate paid. (⇛ BANKING).

Deposit bank. ⇛ COMMERCIAL BANKS

Depository Institutions Deregulation and Monetary Control Act (1980). This act removed a number of regulations governing COMMERCIAL BANKS and non-bank financial institutions. Among other things, the Act allows for the elimination of interest rate ceilings and permits interest to be paid on DEMAND DEPOSITS. Prior to the Act, smaller banks were subject to lower REQUIRED RESERVES than large banks, an implicit subsidy based on size. In addition, the ceilings on interest rates were more stringently regulated in commercial banks than in other non-bank financial institutions. In a period of TIGHT MONEY, funds would flow out of banks to other institutions putting considerable stress on the system. (⇛ MONETARY POLICY; REGULATION Q).

Depreciation. 1. The reduction in VALUE of an ASSET through wear and tear. An allowance for the depreciation on a company's assets is always made before the calculation of PROFIT on the grounds that the consumption of CAPITAL assets is one of the costs of earning the revenues of the business and, according to special rules, is allowed as such by the tax authorities.

Since depreciation can only be accurately measured at the end of the life of an asset (i.e., EX POST), depreciation provisions in company accounts require an estimate both of the total amount of depreciation and the asset life. Annual depreciation provisions are normally calculated according to two methods: (a) the "straight line method" where the estimated residual (e.g., scrap) value of an asset is deducted from its original cost and the balance divided by the number of years of estimated life, to arrive at an annual depreciation expense to set against revenue; and (b) the "declining balance method." In this case the actual depreciation expense is set at a constant proportion of the depreciated cost of the asset, i.e., a diminishing annual absolute amount. There are many other methods of calculating depreciation and also of dealing with the fact that, in periods of rising prices, the replacement cost of an asset may be very much greater than its original cost (⇛ COST, HISTORIC) when the original cost of purchase is retained throughout the period. It should be noted that OBSOLESCENCE is distinct from depreciation, in that the former is an unforeseen change in the value of an asset for technological or economic reasons. If an asset becomes obsolescent, its undepreciated value is usually written off (depreciated) completely in the year of replacement. In some cases the life of an asset may be very difficult to determine because it is specific to the production of a product the demand for which is subject to rapid changes in taste or fashion, i.e., there is a high risk of product obsolescence. In these cases the life of the asset is written off over a very short period. The purpose of depreciation provisions in accounting is to ensure that the cost of the flow of services provided by capital assets is met in the price of the company's products; the purpose is not to build up funds for the replacement of these assets to be available at a certain date. In practice, depreciation provisions are treated as part of the net CASH FLOW of a business and are used to repay LOANS, to purchase other fixed assets, including of course those that are worn out, or to invest in other businesses; that is they are put to the use that will give the highest possible return. Much confusion is caused on this point, since what happens to depreciation provisions—which are, in effect, transfers of funds from fixed assets to current assets and sometimes back again—is not often clear from the BALANCE SHEET (⇛⇛ AMORTIZATION). Depreciation is accepted for tax purposes as a charge against profits. Since unrealistically accelerated depreciation can greatly reduce NET INCOME and hence tax liabilities, the INTERNAL REVENUE SERVICE needs to satisfy itself that the provisions made are reasonable in relation to the life of assets. No specific depreciation method is required by law although the IRS provides guidelines. Sometimes depreciation for tax purposes may be different from that adopted for management accounting purposes. 2. A reduction in the value of a CURRENCY in terms of gold or other currencies under FREE MARKET conditions and coming about through a decline in the DEMAND for that currency in relation to the SUPPLY. Corresponds to DEVALUATION under a fixed parity system. (⇛ CURRENCY DEPRECIATION).

Depression. A severe trough in the TRADE CYCLE where there is widespread and sustained UNEMPLOYMENT. There is no official quantitative definition of a depression as is the case with RECESSION. Only the period of the early 1930s in the United States is usually referred to as a depression.

Devaluation. The reduction of the official rate at which one CURRENCY is exchanged for another. Under the original articles of the INTERNATIONAL MONETARY FUND, its member countries agreed to the stabilization of their EXCHANGE RATES in terms of the dollar and gold fluctuations about the par rate of ±1 percent (widened to ±2.25 percent in December 1971) were permissible, but changes in the par rate itself had to be agreed to by the IMF and made only in the face of serious BALANCE OF PAYMENTS problems. Governments regarded devaluation as a means of correcting a balance of payments deficit only as a measure of last resort. They predominantly relied on DEFLATION of the home market and international borrowing. Devaluation or DEPRECIATION of the exchange rate can correct a balance of payments deficit because it lowers the price of EXPORTS in terms of foreign currencies and raises the price of IMPORTS on the home market. This does not necessarily succeed. The immediate effect is similar to an unfavorable change in the TERMS OF TRADE. For the same resources devoted to the production of exports, less foreign exchange, is earned with which to pay for imports. If the level of imports remained the same, more output would have to be diverted to exports and away from home consumption and INVESTMENT, simply to maintain the *status quo*. Devaluation or depreciation could lead to a loss of REAL INCOME without any benefit to the balance of payments. The implicit expectation in a controlled devaluation or currency depreciation therefore, is that the price ELASTICITIES of demand and supply are such that the "terms of trade" effect is more than offset by shifts of both foreign and domestic demand in favor of home production (⇛ MARSHALL-LERNER CRITERION). If, therefore, the home economy is, at the time of devaluation or depreciation, in a position of full employment (⇛ EMPLOYMENT, FULL), additional government action is required to create the spare capacity needed to meet the increased demand on home production. Unless this is carried out, the excess demand will generate INFLATION, and possibly renewed deficits in the balance of payments.

Developing country. A country that has not yet reached the stage of ECONOMIC DEVELOPMENT characterized by the growth of industrialization, and a level of NATIONAL INCOME sufficient to yield the domestic SAVINGS required to finance the INVESTMENT necessary for further growth (⇛ ROSTOW, WALT WHITMAN). The attempt by developing countries to obtain significant increases in their REAL INCOMES has been frustrated by the deterioration in their TERMS OF TRADE and the rapid expansion of their populations. Their trend growth of exports has been only about one-half that of world trade as a whole, and this has been further reduced in real terms by the fall in their terms of trade. Many ideas have been put forward to assist these countries bridge the gap between themselves and the developed countries (⇛ UNITED NATIONS CONFERENCE ON TRADE AND DEVELOPMENT). Agreement was reached in 1979 to set up a COMMON FUND through UNCTAD to finance INTERNATIONAL COMMODITY AGREEMENTS for the stabilization of the markets in primary products.

The average per annum growth in GROSS NATIONAL PRODUCT of the developing countries as a whole was about 5½ percent through the 1970s. This average, however, conceals a wide divergence between countries. For instance, the GNP of the East Asian countries grew by about 8 percent per annum, whereas developing countries in Africa south of the Sahara grew by only 3 percent per annum. Allowing for the rapid growth in population, it means the real per capita incomes of the latter countries hardly improved (⇛ LEAST-DEVELOPED COUNTRIES). In 1974, Congress passed the Trade Act which granted tariff preferences to developing countries, beginning in January 1976 for a period up to January 1985. Thousands of products exported to the United States by the developing countries are allowed free of duty. About 140 countries are eligible. (⇛ ASIAN DEVELOPMENT BANK; ASSOCIATION OF SOUTH EAST ASIAN NATIONS; COLOMBO PLAN FOR COOPERATIVE ECONOMIC AND SOCIAL DEVELOPMENT IN ASIA; GENERAL AGREEMENT ON TARIFFS AND TRADE INTERNATIONAL BANK FOR RECONSTRUCTION AND DEVELOPMENT).

Differentiation, product. The creation of real or imagined differences in essentially the same kind of product, by means of brand name, packaging, ADVERTISING, quality variation, design variation, etc. It is most prevalent in consumer goods industries, e.g., soap powders, cosmetics, automobiles, cigarettes and alcoholic beverages. The purpose of product differentiation is to build up "consumer loyalty" to one firm's product or brand. This may permit it to raise PRICE above undifferentiated versions of the same product, and make greater PROFITS. It also may ensure greater stability of sales, which facilitates production and sales planning. Some degree of product differentiation is quite likely to be in the consumer's interests since there will generally be a range of tastes and INCOMES which are best served by a range of product qualities and designs, e.g., in the automobile industry the range of "models," from expensive, high-quality, high-performance coupés to lower-priced compacts, clearly meets a wide variety of tastes and incomes. Economists' objections to product differentiation usually center on cases where it involves wasteful expenditures on advertising, packaging and design changes. It may also lead to a plethora of brands, preventing the realization of full ECONOMIES OF SCALE, and creating BARRIERS TO ENTRY of new firms while allowing established firms to make excess profits. (⇛⇛ CHAMBERLAIN, EDWARD HASTINGS; MONOPOLISTIC COMPETITION; OLIGOPOLY; ROBINSON, JOAN VIOLET).

Diminishing marginal product, law of. This is a hypothesis concerning the nature of production processes and it is of central importance in economics. It asserts that if the quantity of one FACTOR OF PRODUCTION used in a production process is increased while all others hold constant, the MARGINAL PRODUCT of that factor will at some point start to decrease. That is, successive equal increments of one factor result, after a certain point, in smaller and smaller increments in output, all other factors remaining unchanged. Loosely this can be thought of as resulting from the fact that the units of the factor that is increasing in quantity have less and less of the other factors to work with, ultimately producing something of a "saturation effect." The hypothesis is assumed to hold in all PRODUCTION FUNCTIONS used in economics. It underlies the fact that a firm's short-run demand curve (⇛ DEMAND CURVE, SHORT-RUN) for a factor of production slopes negatively from left to right; and also that a firm's short-run MARGINAL COST curve will slope upward from left to right. These in turn are important elements in ensuring a determinate short-run EQUILIBRIUM position for the firm. The hypothesis should not be confused with the assumption of diminishing RETURNS TO SCALE. The latter concerns what happens to output when *all* factors of production are allowed to increase in the same proportion, whereas the law of diminishing marginal product is concerned with an increase in the ratio of one factor to the others. One is relevant to the LONG-RUN analysis of the THEORY OF THE FIRM, the other to the short-run.

Direct taxation. Usually defined as taxes imposed on those firms or individuals who are expected to bear the burden of the tax. This is in contrast to indirect taxation where the tax is expected to be shifted from its point of imposition to someone else. Over two-thirds of total tax revenue in 1979 was derived from direct taxes: personal income tax, property tax, corporate income tax and employee contributions to payroll taxes. The arguments surrounding direct vs. indirect taxation are complex. Direct taxation on persons may decrease their work effort if the rates are too progressive. Indirect taxation such as the general sales tax, leads to higher prices and may contribute to inflation. In addition it has long been argued that SALES TAXES are REGRESSIVE. (⇛ PROGRESSIVE TAX).

Dirty float. ⇛ EXCHANGE RATE

Discount. Generally meaning a deduction from FACE VALUE, i.e., the opposite of PREMIUM. Discount has a number of specific applications in economics and commerce: (a) A *discount for cash* is a percentage deductible from a bill of sale as an incentive for the debtor to pay within a defined period. (b) A deduction from the retail price of a good (⇛ ECONOMIC GOOD) allowed to a wholesaler, retailer or other agent. A *discount store* offers goods for sale at below-normal retail prices. (c) A charge made for acquiring or cashing a SECURITY or other promissory note before its maturity date (⇛ FACTOR OF PRODUCTION). (d) The difference, where negative, between the present price of a SECURITY and its issue price. (⇛ DISCOUNTED CASH FLOW).

Discounted cash flow (DCF). A method of appraising INVESTMENTS based on the idea that the VALUE to an individual or firm of a specific sum of MONEY depends on precisely when it is to be received. Given the existence of interest rates (⇛ RATE OF INTEREST) and the possibilities of borrowing and lending, it is always better to receive money earlier rather than later; and conversely, to pay money later rather than earlier. For example, if the current annual interest rate is 10 percent and I have $100, it could be worth $110 in 1 year's time, $121 in 2 years' time, $133.10 in 3 years' time, and so on. It follows that if I am to receive $110 in 1 year's time, it is worth only $100 held today, since that is the amount that would grow to $110 if I invested it today at 10 percent. Since the value of a sum of money depends on when it is received, it follows that, in appraising investments, which typically yield PROFITS over a future period, we cannot simply add up the profits accruing at different points in time. First, it is necessary to correct for the "time-value" of money, and this is done by DISCOUNTING, i.e., dividing by a suitable factor to determine the present worth or PRESENT VALUE of a future sum. The result will be a discounted CASH FLOW, on the basis of which the true profitability of the investment can then be assessed. There are several specific procedures based on the idea of discounted cash flow. (⇛ INTERNAL RATE OF RETURN).

Discount house. 1. A "cut-rate" retail store selling goods at a DISCOUNT. 2. An institution in the London, England financial markets that purchases promissory notes and resells them or holds them until maturity. (⇛ MONEY MARKET).

Discounting. The application of a discount or RATE OF INTEREST to a CAPITAL sum, or title to such a sum. Calculations of PRESENT VALUE or the price of a bill before maturity, are made by discounting at the current appropriate rate of interest. 2. The future effects of an anticipated decline or increase in PROFITS, or some other event, on SECURITY prices, commodity prices, or EXCHANGE RATES, is said to be discounted if buying or selling leads to an adjustment of present prices in line with expected future changes in these prices. 3. The pledging of accounts receivable, i.e., sums owed by debtors, as COLLATERAL SECURITY against a LOAN. (⇛⇛ DISCOUNT).

Discount rate. The interest (⇛ RATE OF INTEREST) cost of loans by the Federal Reserve Banks to the COMMERCIAL BANKS. These loans are secured by certain eligible assets, typically government SECURITIES. The discount rate is an important tool of MONETARY POLICY, a rise in the rate being intended to discourage bank borrowing and curb credit expansion. (⇛⇛ FEDERAL RESERVE SYSTEM).

Discouraged worker. An individual who, after seeking work without success, ceases to search for a job. It has been argued that unemployment rates measured by official statistics, underestimate true unemployment because they fail to take the discouraged worker into account.

Discriminating duty. An import duty (⇛ TARIFFS) imposed at a level different from other comparable import duties, designed to favor (or discourage) the importation of a particular commodity, or imports from a particular country of origin. (⇛ GENERAL AGREEMENT ON TARIFFS AND TRADE; MOST FAVORED NATION CLAUSE).

Diseconomy. An increase in long-run AVERAGE COSTS of production which comes about when the scale of production is increased. There is an important distinction between (a) internal diseconomies and (b) external diseconomies.

Internal diseconomies arise as the result of the expansion of the individual firm. Their main source is the possibility of increased administrative costs per unit of output, which in turn is a result of increased problems of coordinating activities on a greater scale, a lengthening of the management hierarchy and a growth of BUREAUCRACY. Though, logically, we expect that there must be scales of output at which such diseconomies occur, in practice it appears that large firms may be capable of avoiding them by specialization in administrative functions, introducing electronic equipment, e.g., computers, and delegating authority and responsibility to avoid delays and bottlenecks.

External diseconomies arise as a result of the expansion of a group of firms, such expansion creating cost increases to one or more of the firms. These diseconomies are usually classified into: (i) Pecuniary: Diseconomies arising from increases in prices of inputs caused by the expansion of demand, e.g., expansion of the oil refining industry may cause the price of crude oil to rise, thus creating an external pecuniary diseconomy to any one firm buying crude oil (it is assumed that expansion by one firm alone would not cause a rise in prices). (ii) Technological: Diseconomies arising out of higher input requirements per unit of output. For example, as firms in particular areas expand, road congestion increases, due to increased deliveries, shipments, etc. This, in turn, increases the transport costs of all firms; similarly, expansion of a group of chemical firms located along a riverbank may lead to increased discharge of effluent into the river, thus increasing the cost of cleaning and using the water to firms located downstream. (⇛⇛ SOCIAL COSTS).

Disequilibrium. A state in which EQUILIBRIUM has not been attained because opposing forces that act on the system are not in balance, hence there is a tendency for at least some of its ENDOGENOUS VARIABLES to change over time. In economics disequilibrium is usually associated with the mutual inconsistency of the plans of economic decision-takers, so that some of these plans are not realized, and all of them are eventually revised. For example, a MARKET will be in disequilibrium if the total quantity that buyers plan to purchase at the going price exceeds the quantity that sellers plan to sell. In such an event, some buyers will be unable to realize their plans, price will be bid up, and all sellers and buyers will revise their plans accordingly. A question of great interest for all economic systems is whether the characteristics of the system are such that this process of plan revision will lead to or away from an equilibrium, and this is the subject matter of STABILITY ANALYSIS. Where the disequilibrium adjustment process leads toward an equilibrium, the system is called *stable;* the term *unstable* is applied to the converse case. (⇛ COBWEB THEOREM; ECONOMIC DYNAMICS).

Disguised unemployment. A potential addition to the labor force which is not revealed unless opportunities are actually available, and consequently does not show up in UNEMPLOYMENT statistics. Married women are a major element; if the opportunities existed, they might have jobs, but otherwise they are not registered as unemployed. The likely extent of disguised unemployment in a given region or area may be gauged by comparing its PARTICIPATION RATE with other areas.

Dishoarding. The running down of stocks of goods or MONEY accumulated by HOARDING.

Disinflation. The reduction or elimination of INFLATION.

Disinvestment. This occurs when items of CAPITAL equipment—machines, buildings, vehicles, etc.—are not replaced as they wear out, and hence, stock is reduced. The opposite of INVESTMENT. (⇛ AMORTIZATION).

Disposable income. Personal INCOME including TRANSFER PAYMENTS after all DIRECT TAXES have been deducted. For both the individual and the economy as a whole, this gives a measure of the amount available for expenditure on CONSUMPTION and SAVING.

Dissaving. The excess of CONSUMPTION expenditure over DISPOSABLE INCOME. Either the stock of WEALTH accumulated by past SAVING is being diminished, or borrowing against future INCOME is taking place. In either case, there is a net decrease in the ASSETS of the individual.

Distribution, theory of. The branch of economics concerned with explaining how the prices of FACTORS OF PRODUCTION (LAND, LABOR and CAPITAL), and hence the INCOMES they receive, are determined. It attempts to explain the way in which the total flow of goods and SERVICES (ECONOMIC GOOD) available for consumption is distributed among people in the economy. The traditional approach is to analyze the question of distribution in terms of market analysis: each factor of production is bought and sold in a MARKET. The conditions of the SUPPLY of and DEMAND for each factor determines its EQUILIBRIUM PRICE (RENT, wages, RATE OF INTEREST) and the EQUILIBRIUM QUANTITY utilized, and the product of these gives the total flow of income to that factor of production. Why a dentist earns more than a garbage collector, would be answered in terms of the supply and demand conditions for each type of labor, and factors such as the period of training, restrictions on entry, etc., would be seen as determining the conditions of supply and demand. Since, in the traditional theory, the DEMAND CURVE for a factor of production is determined by its MARGINAL PRODUCTIVITY, the theory is sometimes called the *marginal productivity theory of distribution* (⇛ EULER, LEONHARD).

There have, of course, been suggested alternatives to this theory. The existence of MONOPOLY and MONOPSONY in particular types of factor market has emphasized the development of BARGAINING THEORIES of factor prices (in fact, such theories have been generally directed at the determination of wages). Furthermore, in contrast to the MICROECONOMIC approach of the traditional theory of distribution, Nicholas Kaldor has put forward a macroeconomic theory of distribution which, though it does not explain the determination of the prices of factors of production, attempts to explain the relative shares of factors of production in national income, using an extension of the KEYNESIAN model of the economy. A major aim of this theory is to explain the observed constancy of the relative shares of wages and profits in national income over the past 50 years or so. Although the traditional theory is not inconsistent with such constancy, it requires some rather special assumptions to give this result. (⇛ COBB-DOUGLAS FUNCTION; FRIEDMAN, MILTON; GALBRAITH, JOHN KENNETH; RICARDO, DAVID).

Disutility. The opposite or negative of utility. Someone is paid to "consume" a good (⇛ ECONOMIC GOOD) which yields disutility, or someone pays to reduce "consumption" of such a good, e.g., people install double-glazing to reduce "consumption" of outside noise, or they pay to have garbage removed. Similarly, the fact that work tends to yield increasing marginal disutility the more one does, explains why overtime rates are usually higher than normal hourly rates of pay.

Diversification. This occurs when a firm undertakes production of a new product, without ceasing production of its existing products. Diversification may take place for one or more reasons: (a) from a desire to spread RISKS or compensate for seasonal or cyclical fluctuations in DEMAND; (b) because of the existence of spare management or productive capacity; (c) from a desire to grow faster and earn greater PROFITS than are possible in existing markets, which may be declining or expected to decline; (d) following a decision to exploit to the full an innovation or research result; or (e) as a result of some specific opportunity which, though not necessarily planned for, may seem too good to miss. Diversification often takes place by MERGER with a firm in the industry into which the firm is diversifying, though this is not always the case. Writers on diversification have stressed the fact that there are usually close links between existing products and products into which firms diversify—similarities of underlying technological characteristics, or marketing techniques, or very strong research and development expertise in the relevant areas of technology. In contrast, there is the pattern of diversification shown by HOLDING COMPANIES and financial trusts (⇛ TRUST), and some so-called CONGLOMERATES, where the only common area of expertise is in financial management and control, and there is considerable diversity of products and technologies.

Dividend. A payment by a company to its shareholders. Dividends are normally related to current PROFITS although the board of directors may decide to maintain a dividend out of its earned surplus, even if profits fall. Dividends are paid quarterly by most corporations and usually in cash although they may be in the form of a SCRIP ISSUE. (⇛ CUM DIVIDEND; EX-DIVIDEND; YIELD).

Dividend cover. The number of times the net PROFITS available for distribution to stockholders exceeds the DIVIDEND actually paid or declared. For example, if a company's net profits were $100,000 and the dividend $5,000, the dividend cover would be 20.

Dividend yield. ⇛ YIELD

Divisia index. A type of price index which, in contrast to such indexes as the PAASCHE and LASPEYRES, takes into account the continuous effects of price changes on the cost of living. While the Paasche and Laspeyres index numbers take price and expenditure values at two distinct points in time, say at intervals of one year, a Divisia index, in theory, takes price and expenditure levels at every moment of time across that period.

Division of labor. The specialization of workers in particular parts or operations of a production process. From the time of ADAM SMITH, the division of LABOR has been a recognized source of ECONOMIES OF SCALE, and a basic reason for the development of an EXCHANGE ECONOMY. The techniques of division of labor which Adam Smith noticed in a pin-making factory have perhaps reached their ultimate development in modern automobile assembly plants, where a particular worker's function can consist entirely of tightening a particular set of bolts. The advantages of division of labor were also clearly documented by Adam Smith—the increase in skill and speed of operation which comes through specialization, together with the time saved by workers not having to switch from one operation to another. In a broader sense, the division of labor has led to the modern exchange economy. Rather than an individual attempting to produce each of his needs himself, he specializes, obtaining his other requirements from other specialists through the medium of MONEY.

Dollar certificate of deposit. ⇛ EURO-DOLLARS

Dollar gap. The Second World War destroyed the productive capacity of Western Europe, and in the immediate postwar years the primary need was to replenish the devastated stock of capital ASSETS and raw materials. At the same time, consumers emerged from the war years with substantial MONEY balances which they had been prevented from spending. There was, therefore, both a high potential demand for all kinds of goods (⇛ ECONOMIC GOOD) for consumption and INVESTMENT, and at the same time an inability of the Western European countries to meet such demands from home production. European recovery had to be based on imports, and only the United States was in a position to supply the necessary goods. The BALANCE OF PAYMENTS of Western Europe plunged into deficit, primarily with the United States, and gold and dollar reserves were rapidly exhausted, in spite of restrictions on IMPORTS. American aid was necessary to carry Western Europe over the postwar recovery period (⇛ EUROPEAN RECOVERY PROGRAM). The dollar gap lasted until the mid 1950s. (⇛ CONVERTIBILITY; INTERNATIONAL LIQUIDITY).

Balance of payments of Organization for European Economic Cooperation countries ($1,000m.)

	1947	*1948*	*1949*	*1950*	*1951*	*1952*	*1953*	*1954*
Current account	−6.9	−3.6	−1.4	−0.5	−1.3	+0.8	+1.9	+2.2
Capital account	+4.9	+3.6	+2.5	+1.5	+0.4	+0.6	−0.4	−1.3
Of which economic aid	+5.8	+5.2	+4.6	+2.9	+2.3	+1.5	+1.0	+0.8

SOURCE: *Europe and the Money Muddle,* Robert Triffin, Yale University Press, 1957.

Domestic credit expansion (DCE). A measure of the change in the MONEY SUPPLY, which is adjusted to take into account the effects of changes in FOREIGN EXCHANGE reserves and government borrowing overseas. The basic definition of the money supply as notes, coins and BANK DEPOSITS, also includes holdings of foreign exchange reserves. However, if we are primarily concerned with the changes in internal CREDIT availability (deposit creation by the banks, increased availability of notes and coin by the government), it is helpful to exclude changes in foreign exchange reserves, as these simply distort the measurements and have no economic significance. Hence, the change in foreign exchange reserves, *less* the change in government overseas borrowing (which is regarded simply as a means to avoid an equal change in reserves), is subtracted from the change in money supply, as conventionally measured, to get DCE.

Domestic International Sales Corporation (DISCS). In 1972, the United States Government allowed MULTINATIONAL (⇛ MULTINATIONAL CORPORATION) firms to establish subsidiary companies called DISCS to which all overseas earnings were accounted. At the same time, it was agreed that these earnings would not be subject to United States TAXES, unless and until they were transferred to the parent firm or another domestic firm. In 1976, however, it was found that this practice contravened the GENERAL AGREEMENT ON TARIFFS AND TRADE. There is a possibility that the rules governing their taxation will be changed. (⇛ EXPORT INCENTIVES).

Double-entry bookkeeping. The accounting system in which every business transaction, whether a receipt or a payment of MONEY, gives rise to two entries: a DEBIT and a corresponding CREDIT, traditionally placed on opposite pages of a ledger. Debit entries are made on the left side of the account and credits on the right. The credit entries record the sources of finance, e.g., shareholders' CAPITAL, funds borrowed from third parties or generated through current operations; the debit entries record the use to which that finance is put, e.g., bank deposit acquisition of fixed ASSETS, INVENTORIES of raw materials, financing of debtors and current operating expenses, etc. Since every debit entry has an equal and corresponding credit entry, it follows that if the debit and credit entries are totaled they will (or should) come to the same figure, i.e., balance (⇛ BALANCE SHEET). Confusion is caused by identifying credit and debits with gains and losses. While this is basically true in the long run, the profit or loss over a short period is measured by selecting from ledger balances those items of income and expenditure which are used to produce an INCOME STATEMENT. (⇛ BUSINESS FINANCE).

Double taxation. The situation in which the same TAX BASE is taxed more than once. Double-taxation agreements between two countries, for example, are designed to avoid INCOMES of nonresidents being taxed both in the country in which they live, and in their country of origin.

Dow Jones. A daily index (⇛ INDEXATION) of prices on the STOCK EXCHANGE in New York. It is an average of the prices of 30 industrial stocks and is calculated and published every day the stock exchange is open (⇛ STANDARD AND POOR'S INDEX). It is named after the company, Dow Jones and

Co., founded by Charles H. Dow, editor of the *Wall Street Journal* at the end of the 19th century.

Drawback. ⇛ CUSTOMS DRAWBACK

Dumping. The sale of a COMMODITY on a foreign MARKET at a PRICE below MARGINAL COST. An exporting country may endure the short-run losses of this policy in order to eliminate competition and gain a MONOPOLY in the foreign market. Alternatively, it may dump in order to dispose of temporary surpluses and avoid a reduction in home prices and producers' INCOMES. The GENERAL AGREEMENT ON TARIFFS AND TRADE accepts the imposition of special import duties (⇛ TARIFFS) to counteract such a policy, if it can be established that dumping is taking place. The practice of dumping is prohibited under the terms of the EUROPEAN ECONOMIC COMMUNITY Treaty of Rome. Note that export prices that are lower than home market prices are not conclusive evidence of the existence of dumping. Rules to be followed by governments were agreed upon as part of the KENNEDY ROUND OF TRADE NEGOTIATIONS by the EEC, the United States, Canada and the EUROPEAN FREE TRADE ASSOCIATION. In 1980, the EEC imposed a temporary anti-dumping TARIFF on IMPORTS of polyester yarn from the United States, claiming "serious market interruption" under Article 19 of GATT because the U.S. manufacturers were claimed to benefit from subsidized energy costs. In the same year, U.S. steel producers complained of the dumping of foreign steel in the home market. As a result, the "trigger price" on steel was reintroduced. This price is based on Japanese steel production costs which are considered to be the world's lowest. Any imports below this price are therefore regarded as having been dumped and an investigation is "triggered off." Another factor which "triggers" a dumping enquiry is if imports exceed 15.2 percent of the U.S. home market when U.S. steel production is less than 87 percent of capacity.

Duopoly. The MARKET situation in which only two sellers of a particular good (⇛ ECONOMIC GOOD) or SERVICE exist. The essence of the situation is that the actions of one seller affect the position of the other, and induce a response from him. Hence, neither firm can predict the precise consequences of its own actions unless it can also predict the reaction of its competitor. This is the characteristic problem of OLIGOPOLY in an acute and simplified form, and so the duopoly model was often used to analyze oligopolistic situations. Without assuming something about the reactions of the two firms, it is impossible to find a determinate EQUILIBRIUM solution in the market. However, the range of possible assumptions which could be chosen, and which generally give different results, creates an additional problem. (⇛ COURNOT, ANTOINE AUGUSTIN).

Duopsony. The MARKET situation in which there are only two buyers of a particular good (⇛ ECONOMIC GOOD) or SERVICE. It is thus the analogue of DUOPOLY on the buying side.

Dupuit, Arsene Jules Etienne Juvenal (1804–66). A French civil engineer, whose main works relating to economics were *De la mesure de l'utilite des travaux publics* (1844) and *De l'influence des peages sur l'utilite des travaux publics* (1844) and *De l'influence des peages sur l'utilite des voies de commu-*

nication (1849). His studies of the pricing policy for public SERVICES such as roads and bridges led him to the idea of CONSUMERS' SURPLUSES and PRODUCERS' SURPLUSES. These terms were, in fact, invented by A. MARSHALL, but the ideas were clearly brought out by Dupuit. He realized that the prices were not the maximum that users would be willing to pay for services, except those users at the very margin who found it just worthwhile to pay. Consumers, therefore, benefited from the difference. Similarly, a producer selling the service obtains a surplus insofar as his fixed charge is related to his cost at the margin (⇛ MARGINAL COST), and that this is greater than his AVERAGE COST. These concepts were refined by Marshall. Dupuit also noted that the total yield of a tax will fall if the rate of tax is raised to a sufficiently high level: "If a tax is increased from zero up to a point where it becomes prohibitive, its yield is at first zero, then increases until it reaches a maximum, after which it declines until it becomes zero again." (⇛ LAFFER CURVE).

Durable goods. Those consumer goods such as washing machines, automobiles and TV sets, that yield SERVICES or UTILITY over a period of time, rather than being used up at the moment of CONSUMPTION. As most consumer goods are durable to some degree, the term is often used in a more restricted sense to denote relatively expensive, technologically sophisticated goods—"consumer durables"—such as the examples given above. The significance of the durability of these goods is that the conventional apparatus of demand analysis must be supplemented by the modes of analysis developed in CAPITAL THEORY. (⇛ DEMAND, THEORY OF).

Dynamic economics. ⇛ ECONOMIC DYNAMICS

Dynamic peg. ⇛ EXCHANGE RATE

E

Earnings. 1. The return for human effort, as in the earnings of LABOR and the earnings of mangement. In labor economics wage earnings are distinguished from wage rates; the former include overtime, the latter relate only to earnings per hour or standard working week. Earnings may be quoted as pre- or post-tax (gross or net) and other deductions and in REAL TERMS or money terms. 2. The INCOME of a business, part of which may be retained in the business and part distributed to the shareholders (⇛ INCOME STATEMENT; RETAINED EARNINGS). Earnings per SHARE (post-tax), which is a measure of the total return earned by a company on its COMMON STOCK (EQUITY capital), is calculated by taking gross income after DEPRECIATION, INTEREST, PREFERRED STOCK and minority interests, deducting tax and dividing the resulting figure by the number of common stocks. Note that earnings per share are normally higher than the DIVIDEND per share, since a portion of PROFITS is usually retained for INVESTMENT or to build up reserves.

Earnings yield. ⇛ YIELD

Econometrics. The application of mathematical and statistical techniques to economic problems. Econometric studies proceed by formulating a mathematical MODEL. Then, using the best data available, statistical methods are used to obtain estimates of the PARAMETERS in the model. Methods of STATISTICAL INFERENCE are then used to decide whether the hypotheses underlying the model can be rejected or not. Econometrics is thus concerned with testing the validity of economic theories and providing the means of making quantitative predictions (⇛⇛ CORRELATION; REGRESSION ANALYSIS).

In addition, side by side with the empirical application of econometric methods, a body of statistical and mathematical theory has been developed that is essentially concerned with the particular difficulties encountered in applying statistical methods to economic theory and data (⇛ AUTOCORRELATION; MULTICOLLINEARITY). Thus, it becomes possible to speak of "econometric theory" and "applied econometrics," of which the latter may still appear rather abstract to the layman.

Economic aid. Usually in the form of contributed financial capital to less developed countries (LDCs), such assistance allows a country to expand its CAPITAL STOCK and thereby enhance its PRODUCTIVITY. Most assistance from the United States is channeled through the AGENCY FOR INTERNATIONAL DEVELOPMENT.

Economic Cooperation Administration (ECA). An Act for the appropriation of $6.098 billion for foreign aid was signed by President Truman in 1948, and the ECA was set up under Paul G. Hoffman, president of the Studebaker Corporation, to administer the fund. Under the program the United Kingdom received $2.694 billion. The ECA was superseded by the Mutual Security Agency in 1951, the Foreign Operations Administration in 1953 and the International Cooperation Administration in 1955. (⇛ EUROPEAN RECOVERY PROGRAM).

Economic development. The process of growth in total and per capita income of DEVELOPING COUNTRIES, accompanied by fundamental changes in the structure of their economies. These changes generally consist of the increasing importance of industrial as opposed to agricultural activity, migration of LABOR from rural to urban industrial areas, lessening dependence on imports for the more advanced producer and consumer goods, and on agricultural or mineral products as main exports, and finally a diminishing reliance on aid from other countries to provide funds for INVESTMENT and thus a capacity to generate growth themselves. Associated with this economic process will tend to be important social and political reforms such as revisions in the system of land tenure, and a greater democratization of political systems, but the latter are by no means inevitable. The main objective of economic development is to raise the living standard and general well-being of the people in the economy. (⇛ ECONOMIC GROWTH, STAGES OF).

Economic dynamics. That part of economics that analyzes the movement of economic systems through time. Relationships are explicitly time-dependent and contain variables whose values may change over time. Appropriate mathematical methods are used to examine the time paths of the variables that emerge as solutions to the system. The three main areas of economic dynamics are STABILITY ANALYSIS, GROWTH THEORY and the theory of TRADE CYCLES. An important recent development has been the extension of the theory from the analysis of time paths of variables "mechanistically" generated by a model to the search for OPTIMUM time paths, such as the optimum growth path for the NATIONAL INCOME and CAPITAL STOCK of an economy, or the optimal time path of ADVERTISING expenditures for a company. The mathematical methods involved are advanced and draw heavily on the work of mathematicians involved in space research—the problem of choosing a trajectory for a space rocket from a point on Earth to a point on the moon can be regarded as an analogue to the problem of choosing a growth path of the economy from now to some date in the future! (⇛ COBWEB THEOREM; DISEQUILIBRIUM; OPTIMAL GROWTH THEORY; SISMONDI, JEAN CHARLES LEONARD SIMONDE DE).

Economic efficiency. Efficiency in the use and allocation of RESOURCES. In the use of resources, economic efficiency requires that any given output is produced at minimum COST, which means both that waste and technological inefficiency are avoided and that appropriate input PRICES are used to find the cost-minimizing production process. In the allocation of resources, economic efficiency requires that it must not be feasible to change the existing resource allocation in such a way that someone is made better off and no one worse off, since, if this is possible, the existing resource allocation must involve a "welfare waste." This criterion of allocative efficiency was first proposed by VILFREDO FEDERICO DAMASO PARETO and so is known as the

Pareto criterion. WELFARE ECONOMICS has been concerned with translating these conceptions of economic efficiency into concrete propositions about economic policy and with the desirability of certain kinds of economic organization, e.g., the PRICE SYSTEM.

Economic good. A physical COMMODITY that yields UTILITY and that could command a price if bought or sold on a market.

Economic growth. The steady process of increasing productive capacity of the economy and hence of increasing NATIONAL INCOME. The analysis of economic growth has played an increasingly important part in economics in the last two or three decades. On the one hand, awareness of the problems of DEVELOPING COUNTRIES and the inapplicability of conventional tools to these problems has led to the development of a whole body of theoretical and descriptive economics concerned with them. On the other hand, the shift of emphasis away from the problem of persistent UNEMPLOYMENT in advanced industrialized capitalist economies toward the problems of full employment (⇛ EMPLOYMENT, FULL) naturally led to the question of what determined the rate at which the economy grows over time. The general emphasis is on the rate of growth of the labor force, the proportion of national income saved and invested, and the rate of technological improvements (including increasing skill of the labor force and managerial efficiency) as being the main determinants of the growth rate of the economy. The economic theories of growth have been rather abstract and formalistic, and much more attention has been paid to the logical and mathematical properties of the various growth MODELS than to their empirical relevance, which is fairly low (⇛ HARROD-DOMAR MODEL). The everyday concern with economic growth arises out of the idea that the greater the rate of growth of the economy, the greater, other things being equal, the increase in the level of well-being (⇛ WELFARE ECONOMICS). Several economists, chief among whom is E. J. Mishan, have, however, pointed out the possible fallacies in this. An economy may be growing more slowly than others because its population prefers to consume more now rather than later, i.e., it has a high rate of TIME PREFERENCE. This is perfectly rational, in the sense that a high preference for current as opposed to future consumption is, on economic grounds alone, no more reprehensible than a low preference. Hence, the idea that the population should consume less in order to save and invest more and grow as fast as other countries is both crude and paternalistic. Dr. Mishan has also criticized the preoccupation with economic growth on the grounds that unless SOCIAL COSTS incurred are allowed for—e.g., the costs of environmental pollution—the welfare benefits of growth may be illusory. (⇛ TURNPIKE THEOREMS).

Economic growth, stages of. The five stages of economic growth that all economies are considered as going through in their development from fairly poor agricultural societies to highly industrialized mass-consumption economies. These five stages were defined and analyzed by WALT WHITMAN ROSTOW in his book *The Stages of Economic Growth.* The five stages in question are:

1. The traditional society, in which adherence to long-lived economic

and social systems and customs means that output per capita is low and tends not to rise.

2. The stage of the establishment of the preconditions for "takeoff" (see below). This stage is a period of transition, in which the traditional systems are overcome, and the economy is made capable of exploiting the fruits of modern science and technology.

3. The takeoff stage. "Takeoff" represents the point at which the "old blocks and the resistances to steady growth are finally overcome," and growth becomes the normal condition of the economy. The economy begins to generate its own INVESTMENT and technological improvement at sufficiently high rates so as to make growth virtually self-sustaining.

4. The "drive to maturity," which is the stage of increasing sophistication of the economy. Against the background of steady growth, new industries are developed, there is less reliance on IMPORTS and more exporting activity, and the economy "demonstrates" its capacity to move beyond the original industries that powered its takeoff and to absorb and apply efficiently the most advanced fruits of modern technology.

5. The age of "high mass consumption," where there is an affluent population, and durable and sophisticated consumers' goods (⇛ ECONOMIC GOOD) and SERVICES are the leading sectors of production.

As a broad and imaginative description of the process of economic growth, this characterization of the stages of growth is interesting and possibly useful, having much the same flavor as KARL MARX's famous theory of the evolution of society from feudalism to bourgeois CAPITALISM and finally to communism. It also leads directly to a policy conclusion that was already favored by many: Aid should be given to the economies at the pre-takeoff stages, in an attempt to get them to the takeoff stage. Once this is achieved, these economies will have their own dynamic and momentum, and hence aid becomes much less necessary. The theory has had only limited impact among professional economists concerned with the problem of ECONOMIC DEVELOPMENT. Partly this is because Rostow's analysis of exactly what factors were responsible for takeoff and subsequent self-generating growth tended to be vague, ambiguous and incomplete. Also, the theory is framed in such general terms that it can be made consistent with virtually any past growth situation. Partly, too, the broad sweep of the historian's vision, with the implication of the inexorability of the historical processes, is perhaps not very much help in trying to solve the particular development problems of particular economies.

Economic rent. The excess of total payments to a FACTOR OF PRODUCTION (LAND, LABOR OR CAPITAL) over and above its total TRANSFER EARNINGS. For example, a film star might receive an annual INCOME of $100,000. If he were not a film star, his occupation might be a shoe salesman earning $20,000 a year. If this were the only alternative, any income over $20,000 a year would be more than enough to make him stay a film star. Hence, we could calculate that his economic rent was $80,000 a year. (⇛⇛ QUASI-RENT).

Economic Report of the President. An annual report from the office of the President of the United States that summarizes the state of the economy and economic policies under consideration by the President. (⇛ COUNCIL OF ECONOMIC ADVISORS).

Economics. Economists seem never to have agreed on a definition of their subject, criticizing most suggestions, either because they do not cover all aspects of it, or because they beg questions by committing some circularity of definition. For example, Lionel Robbins's famous definition "Economics is the science which studies human behavior as a relationship between ends and scarce means which have alternative uses" seems to capture the essence of MICROECONOMICS but does not convey much of the spirit of MACROECONOMICS (the development of which, of course, the definition predated). On the other hand, the not wholly serious "Economics is what economists do" is meaningless without a definition of an "economist." We offer the following definition: "Economics is a science concerned with those aspects of social behavior, and those institutions, that are involved in the use of scarce resources to produce and distribute goods and services in the satisfaction of human wants."

It may well be that a wholly acceptable definition does not exist. The set of phenomena studied by economists, as the set of economists itself, is perhaps best defined not by a succinct definitional principle, but rather by enumeration. By reading through this book, the student will get a better idea of the content of economics than can be given in any compressed definition.

Economic sanction. A measure, taken in respect of some economic activity, that has the effect of damaging another country's economy. Examples would be a complete embargo of trade between countries and refusal to permit BANK DEPOSITS held in the country imposing the sanction to be drawn upon by the government and residents of another. A recent such sanction was the embargo on grain exports to the USSR made by the United States following the Afghan crisis.

Economic stabilization. ⇛ STABILIZATION POLICY

Economic Stabilization Act. An Act of Congress in 1970 giving the President executive power to establish an incomes policy. The Act was originally to be in force only until 1972, but it was extended to 1974, allowing the President to continue with the PRICES AND INCOMES POLICY of 1971–74. (⇛ STABILIZATION POLICY).

Economies of scale. These exist when expansion of the scale of productive capacity of a firm or industry causes total production costs to increase less than proportionately with output. As a result, LONG-RUN average costs of production fall (⇛⇛ AVERAGE COSTS). Economies of scale are generally classified as

Internal economies occur as a result of the expansion of the individual firm, independently of changes in size of the other firms in the industry. The most important of the sources of internal economies of scale are:

1. Indivisibilities. Many types of plant and machinery have, for en-

gineering reasons, a single most efficient size. Either it will be technically impossible to make the equipment at a different size, or the production costs associated with other sizes are higher. Then, as scale of output increases up to this optimum, increasing productive efficiency is achieved. Similarly, there may be indivisibilities in production processes, as well as plant. Certain types of production processes may only be viable at certain rates of output. The word *indivisibilities* is used to categorize these sources of scale economies because they would not arise if the plant and processes were capable of being increased or decreased in scale by small amounts without any change in their nature, i.e., if they were perfectly divisible.

2. Expansion in scale of activities permits greater specialization and DIVISION OF LABOR among workers (cf. ADAM SMITH's dictum that division of labor is limited by the extent of the MARKET). This, in effect, is also an "indivisibility," in that it is the result of the fixed capacity of an individual worker and the fact that this is optimally utilized when devoted exclusively to a specific task.

3. There may be certain "overhead processes" (⇛ FIXED COSTS) that must be undertaken if any output is to be produced, but that have the same scale regardless of the subsequent rate of output. Examples would be the process of designing an airplane, setting up the print for a newspaper or book, or, indeed, writing a book. Clearly, the more units produced, the lower the cost per unit of these overhead processes.

4. Area-volume relationships. As a physical fact, if the volume of some vessel or container is increased to the cube of itself (i.e., a volume x is increased to x^3), the area enclosing it is increased only to the square of itself (i.e., an area y is increased to y^2). If the output capacity therefore depends on the volume, while cost depends on the area, then cost increases less than proportionately to output. Among others, this relationship is held to account at least in part for the trend toward very large bulk-cargo ships (oil tankers, ore carriers).

5. If several interrelated processes are required to make a particular product, and each process has a different optimal scale of operation, then the overall combined optimum scale is the lowest common multiple of the individual process optima.

6. Where inventories of raw materials, components, goods or money are held in anticipation of random fluctuations in output, expenditure or receipts, then in general the size of the inventories will vary less than proportionately with the scale of output, expenditure or receipts.

The above are the main ways in which internal economies of scale arise. Some, especially 1 and 2, apply just as much to organizational and managerial activities as to production activities. In terms of the conventional theory of the firm (⇛ FIRM, THEORY OF), the effect of internal economies of scale is to cause the long-run average COST CURVE of the firm to slope downward; if such economies exist over a very large range of outputs, then it is likely that firms will be large in size, and OLIGOPOLY or MONOPOLY will tend to emerge.

External economies exist if the expansion in scale of the whole industry or group of firms results in a fall in costs of each individual firm. Analogously to external DISECONOMIES of scale, external economies are generally classified as:

1. Pecuniary economies, or savings in money outlays, technological conditions remaining unchanged. An example would be where expansion of the whole industry led to a significant increase in demand for a particular component, whose PRICE then fell because of internal economies of scale in its manufacture.

2. Technological economies, resulting from increased technological efficiency, improvement in quality of INPUTS, etc.

The effect of external economies of scale in the standard theory of the firm is to shift the whole long-run average cost curve of the firm downward. That is, long-run average cost of each firm is less at every level of output, and this requires a new curve to be drawn.

Economistes, Les. ⇛ PHYSIOCRATS

Edge Act. The legislation embodied in this Act of 1919 permits American banks to organize corporations to engage in foreign BANKING activities. Some out-of-state banks have established what are known as Edge Act Corporations in major U.S. cities, and, while legally restricted to international finance, these corporations are viewed by some as a means of breaking down the barriers of unit banking. (⇛ MCFADDEN ACT; UNIT-BRANCH STATE).

Edgeworth, Francis Ysidro (1845–1926). Edgeworth held the chair of political economy at Oxford University, England from 1891 to 1922 and edited the *Economic Journal* from 1891 to 1926. His published work includes *Mathematical Psychics* (1881), *Theory of Monopoly* (1897), *Theory of Distribution* (1904) and *Papers Relating to Political Economy* (1925). The latter includes the two reports of 1887 and 1889 of the committee on the study of INDEX NUMBERS set up by the British Association for the Advancement of Science, for which Edgeworth acted as secretary. Apart from economics, Edgeworth made valuable contributions to statistics and statistical method. In showing the inadequacy of the VALUE theory of WILLIAM STANLEY JEVONS, Edgeworth invented the analytical tools of INDIFFERENCE CURVES and CONTRACT CURVES. (⇛⇛ PARETO, VILFREDO FEDERICO DAMASO).

Elasticity. Defined in general terms as a measure of degree of responsiveness of one VARIABLE to changes in another. The *price elasticity of demand* is the degree of responsiveness of the quantity demanded of a good to changes in its price; INCOME ELASTICITY OF DEMAND refers to the responsiveness of the quantity demanded of a good to changes in INCOME of consumers; *price elasticity of supply* is the responsiveness of the quantity of a good (⇛ ECONOMIC GOOD) supplied to changes in its PRICE. Numerically, it is given by the proportionate change in the DEPENDENT VARIABLE (e.g., quantity demanded, quantity supplied) divided by the proportionate change in the INDEPENDENT VARIABLE (e.g., price, income) that brought it about. The resulting elasticity measure is a pure number, independent of units, and so its magnitude can be readily compared for things measured in different units. For example, the price elasticity of demand for cornflakes is greater than that for Rolls-Royce automobiles if the elasticity measure for the former is 2 (i.e., a 10 percent fall in price increases demand for cornflakes by 20 percent), and that for the latter is 1 (i.e., a 10 percent fall in price causes an increase of 10 percent in quantity). It obviously means more to say that the demand for cornflakes is more responsive to change in its price than is the demand for Rolls-Royce autos on the basis of this measurement than on the basis of absolute price and quantity changes. Since elasticity is a measure of responsiveness of one variable to changes in another, it is implicit in the shape of the DEMAND CURVES, SUPPLY CURVES and COST CURVES used by the economist.

Elasticity can be measured in two ways:

1. *Arc elasticity*. Let two variables, X and Y, be such that the values taken by Y depend on those taken by X. If X changes by a certain number of units—say, DX units—then Y will also change by a certain number of units—say, DY units (where D is a symbol meaning "a small, finite change in"). The proportionate change in X can be measured in three different ways, that is,

$$DX/X_1 \text{ or } DX/X_2 \text{ or } DX \Big/ \frac{X_1 + X_2}{2}$$

where X_1 is the initial value and X_2 the final value; and similarly we may measure the proportionate change in Y as

$$DY/Y_1 \text{ or } DY/Y_2 \text{ or } DY \Big/ \frac{Y_1 + Y_2}{2}$$

The elasticity of Y with respect to changes in X is:

$$\frac{\text{Proportionate change in } Y}{\text{Proportionate change in } X}$$

This measure is called an *arc elasticity* measurement because it is taking finite changes in X and Y, and so, if we imagine the relationship between X and Y being portrayed as a curve between two axes, we are measuring the proportionate change in Y as a result of a change in X over an arc of this curve. The defects of this measure are that the value of the elasticity may depend on the size of the change in X taken (which is essentially arbitrary) and will certainly differ according to which of the three methods of measuring the proportionate change is chosen. These defects are avoided by the second measure, point elasticity.

2. *Point elasticity*. Here, we take an infinitely small change in X, dX, and find the corresponding infinitely small change in Y, dY, and express these as proportions, respectively, of their initial values, X and Y (d is a symbol meaning "an infinitely small change in"; those who know some calculus will recognize it as the differential operator). We then find the point elasticity of Y with respect to changes in X as:

$$\frac{\text{Proportionate change in } Y}{\text{Proportionate change in } X} = \frac{dY/Y}{dX/X} = \frac{dY}{dX} \cdot \frac{X}{Y}$$

This measure is called a *"point" elasticity* measurement because it effectively measures elasticity at a point on the curve relating Y to X, corresponding to the values of X and Y chosen, and this is a result of taking infinitely small changes in X and Y. The above expression for point elasticity included the term dY/dX, the first derivative of Y with respect to X. In fact, point elasticity is calculated by evaluating this derivative at a particular pair of values of X and Y and inserting this into the above formula (⇛ MARSHALL, ALFRED).

With reference to price elasticity of demand (defined above), if the measured elasticity is greater than 1, it is said that the good has "elastic demand" (e.g., cornflakes in the above example); if the elasticity is equal to 1, the good is said to be of unit elasticity (e.g., Rolls-Royce autos in the above example); and if the elasticity is less than 1, the good is said to have "inelastic demand." The importance of the measure of price elasticity of demand is that it tells us what will happen to total expenditure on a good if its price should change.

Elasticity of substitution. The percentage change in the proportion in which two INPUTS are used, divided by the percentage change in the RATE OF TECHNICAL SUBSTITUTION. That is, as we move from point to point along an ISOQUANT, the rate of technical substitution between the inputs will change, as will the proportion in which inputs are used. The elasticity of substitution then measures the relationship between these changes as we move along an isoquant. The usefulness of the measure is that it summarizes the ease with which one input can be substituted for the other without changing output. A value of zero would indicate that there is no change in the proportion in which inputs must be used, i.e., they have to be used in fixed proportions and hence are not SUBSTITUTES. A value of infinity would indicate no change in the rate of substitution as factor proportions are varied, i.e., they are perfect substitutes.

Empirical testing. The confrontation of theories with facts.

Employment, full. The economy is said to be at full employment when only FRICTIONAL UNEMPLOYMENT exists. Everyone who wishes to work at the going wage rate for his type of labor is employed, but, because it takes time to switch from one job to another, there will at any one moment be a small amount of unemployment. The full employment level of GROSS DOMESTIC PRODUCT can be thought of as measuring full-capacity output, i.e., the largest output of which the economy is capable when all RESOURCES are employed to their feasible limits.

Employment, natural rate of. ⇛ UNEMPLOYMENT, NATURAL RATE OF

Endogenous variable. A VARIABLE whose VALUE is to be determined by forces operating within the MODEL under consideration. For example, in a model of the MARKET for wheat, the price of wheat is an endogenous variable because it is determined by the forces of SUPPLY and DEMAND, which are incorporated in the model. (⇛⇛ EXOGENOUS VARIABLE).

Engel, Ernst (1821–96). ⇛ ENGEL'S LAW

Engel's law. A law of economics stating that, with given tastes or preferences, the proportion of INCOME spent on food diminishes as incomes increase. The law was formulated by Ernst Engel, the director of the Bureau of Statistics in Prussia, in a paper published by him in 1857.

Enterprise zone. A designated area within which businesses enjoy very favorable tax credits and other concessions, such as exemption from planning regulations, to encourage investment. They are generally set up in derelict inner urban districts that have experienced very severe declines in employment opportunities. The U.S. government announced in 1982 plans for setting up 26 such zones. The United Kingdom has already established 11 zones for an experimental 10 years. (⇛ FREE-TRADE ZONES).

Entrepreneur. The name given in economic theory to the owner-manager of a firm. The functions of the entrepreneur are to: (1) finance the supply of the firm's CAPITAL; (2) organize production by buying and combining INPUTS; (3) decide on the rate of output, in the light of his expectations about DEMAND; and (4) bear the RISK involved in these activities, risks that inevitably arise out of the fact that RESOURCES must be committed to production before the output can be sold. PROFITS constitute the income of the entrepreneur. Like the firm itself in economic theory (⇛ FIRM, THEORY OF), the entrepreneur is a theoretical abstraction, although he does have an empirical counterpart in the many small firms in the economy. In the large JOINT-STOCK COMPANIES, which supply the great proportion of goods (⇛ ECONOMIC GOOD) and services in the economy, however, the entrepreneurial functions are divided. Finance is supplied by individuals and institutions who make fixed-interest LOANS, buy BONDS and DEBENTURES or ordinary SHARES. The firm is actually owned by its ordinary shareholders, who receive profits from operations in the form of DIVIDENDS. Since dividends fluctuate with profits and business conditions, and may be zero, ordinary shareholders also bear the risks of the enterprise. The functions of decision making in the firm, and the actual taking of risks (as opposed to risk bearing), are carried out by the board of directors and salaried executives of the company. In the most important companies of the present-day economy, there is no single entrepreneur. If it could be shown that the predictions that the standard economic theory makes about the behavior of the firm corresponded reasonably closely to what happens in practice, then its simplified "entrepreneur" would be a useful abstraction. Many economists currently working in this field, however, regard the separation of the entrepreneurial functions as having important implications for economic theory and for the behavior of the firm. (⇛⇛ SEPARATION OF OWNERSHIP FROM CONTROL).

Entry. ⇛ BARRIERS TO ENTRY; FREEDOM OF ENTRY

Environmental Protection Agency (EPA). Established in 1970, this agency serves as the focus of environmental policy in the United States. The agency enforces the Clean Air Act of 1970 through the establishment of air quality standards. It regulates industrial water pollution and conducts environmental research (which often involves a significant amount of COST-BENEFIT ANALYSIS). Administered by a director appointed by the President, the EPA is one of a number of agencies concerned with the regulation of standards of health and safety. A similar agency, for instance, is the Occupational Safety and Health Administration (OSHA), which determines such matters as the acceptable levels of lead, benzene, cotton dust, asbestos and chlorine in work environments. The budget of these two agencies together amounted to $1.58 billion in 1980. (⇛⇛ REGULATION).

Equalization grant. An unconditional payment from one level of government to a subordinate level based upon a formula that ensures that in order to raise a specific per capita level of public revenue, the subordinate government does not have to levy unduly harsh rates of taxation. This specific level of per capita revenue might be the average for all subordinate governments or the average of the two wealthiest subordinate levels of government. The basic objective is to equalize taxable capacities of jurisdictions with different per capita income and wealth conditions.

Equation of international demand. The law of comparative cost (⇛ RICARDO, DAVID) sets out the limits of the TERMS OF TRADE within which one country will exchange commodities with another. JOHN STUART MILL realized that the point at which exchange actually took place within these limits set by costs would depend on the reciprocal DEMAND of each country for the other's commodities. This "equation of international demand" will determine the EQUILIBRIUM terms of trade. It will depend, *inter alia,* on the ELASTICITIES of DEMAND and SUPPLY of the goods traded. (⇛ MARSHALL-LERNER CRITERION).

Equilibrium. A state in which forces making for change in opposing directions are perfectly in balance, so that there is no tendency to change. For example, a MARKET will be in equilibrium if the quantities of the product that buyers want to buy at the prevailing PRICE are exactly matched by the amount that sellers wish to sell. If this were not so, then the price would be changing, as buyers try to buy more of a good (⇛ ECONOMIC GOOD) than is in fact available, or sellers try to sell more of a good than buyers are prepared to accept at prevailing prices. In this case, price is the equilibrating mechanism. The concept of equilibrium is a very general one, which can be applied to any situation that is characterized by a set of interacting forces. (⇛⇛ GENERAL EQUILIBRIUM; STABILITY ANALYSIS).

Equilibrium price. The PRICE at which a MARKET is in EQUILIBRIUM. (⇛⇛ PRICE SYSTEM).

Equilibrium quantity. The quantity of a good that is bought and sold when a MARKET is in EQUILIBRIUM.

Equities. ⇛ EQUITY

Equity. The residual VALUE of a company's ASSETS after all outside LIABILITIES (other than to stockholders) have been allowed for. In a MORTGAGE or INSTALLMENT CREDIT contract, equity is the amount left for the borrower if the asset concerned is sold and the lender repaid. The equity in a company under LIQUIDATION is the property of the holders of COMMON STOCKS, the nominal value of these stocks being referred to as *equity capital. Equities* is a British synonym for common stocks.

Equity capital. ⇛ EQUITY

Escalator clause. ⇛ INDEXATION

Established program financing. This refers to a set of public expenditures in Canada whose costs are shared between the federal and provincial government, the latter government administering the programs.

Establishment. A term to describe an operating unit of business, regardless of control. For example, each McDonald's restaurant is an establishment, or place of business, although there is one central, controlling unit. Statistics related to restaurant outlets would include each establishment, while statistics related to restaurant corporations would include McDonald's as one such business.

Estate duty. ⇛ DEATH DUTIES

Estate tax. ⇛ DEATH DUTIES

Euler, Leonhard (1707–83). Economists have found that certain propositions in mathematics developed by Leonhard Euler, a Swiss mathematician, can be usefully applied to problems in economic theory. The most notable application concerns a theory of distribution based on marginal productivity. This theory states that FACTORS OF PRODUCTION (i.e., LAND, LABOR and CAPITAL) will each earn an INCOME corresponding to the VALUE of output produced by the last unit of the factor employed. For instance, if a firm employs 19 workers at an average wage of $200 per week, it will employ an additional worker as long as his output is greater than $200. Moreover, if the 20th worker yields, say, $210 per week in profit it will be worthwhile to pay him more than $200 to attract him. The firm cannot, however, pay its workers different wages if they have the same skill and therefore must pay all of them more than $200 per week. A similar argument is applied to other factors of production and for the total national output as well as for a single firm. However, total output must, by definition, equal total income (⇛ NATIONAL INCOME). National output is distributed among the three basic factors of production: land, labor and capital. No arithmetical reasons, however, could be thought of as to how the different factor incomes, derived from marginal productivities, could necessarily add up to the same as total output. Euler's Theorem solved the problem by showing what assumptions about the nature of the PRODUCTION FUNCTION (which describes how the factors of production are combined to produce outputs) had to be made in order for the equality between the sum of incomes and the sum of outputs to be achieved. These assumptions imply that RETURNS TO SCALE must be constant. (⇛ CAMBRIDGE SCHOOL; DISTRIBUTION, THEORY OF; NEOCLASSICAL ECONOMICS).

Euler's Theorem. ⇛ EULER, LEONHARD

Eurobond. ⇛ BOND

Eurocurrency. ⇛ EURODOLLARS

Eurodollars. Dollars held by individuals and institutions outside the United States. In its annual report in 1966, the BANK FOR INTERNATIONAL SETTLEMENTS described the Eurodollar phenomenon as "the acquisition of dollars by banks located outside the United States, mostly through the taking of DEPOSITS, but also to some extent through swapping other

CURRENCIES into dollars, and the relending of these dollars, often after redepositing with other banks, to non-bank borrowers anywhere in the world." It should be noted, therefore, that the market for Eurodollars is not confined to Europe. In terms of a simple example, what happens is as follows. A London bank, as a result of a commercial transaction of one of its customers, has, say, a CREDIT balance with an American bank in New York. A Belgian businessman asks his bank for dollars to finance imports from the United States. In order to meet this request, the Brussels bank accepts the dollar deposit transferred by the London bank from its account in New York. The essential point about this operation is that it creates credit. The London bank still has a claim, on Brussels instead of New York, whereas the Brussels bank now has a claim on New York, which its customer can use to finance his trade. The questions are naturally raised, why should London be willing to transfer its deposit, and why should Brussels finance its requirements in this way? The former can be answered broadly by the fact of the U.S. BALANCE OF PAYMENTS deficits supplying the means and interest rate ARBITRAGE (New York *versus* Brussels) supplying the PROFIT. On the second question, again relative RATES OF INTEREST are a factor, but, in addition, the existence of national EXCHANGE CONTROLS and credit controls encourages the practice. The Brussels bank avoids the need to exchange francs for dollars. In practice, of course, there can be many relending transactions between banks in response to differentials in interest rates. The size of the market has increased substantially in recent years, from about $59 billion in 1970 to about $500 billion in 1975 and $1,800 billion in 1982. London has obtained the major share (about 30 percent) of the transactions in this business acting as a BROKER by borrowing dollars from a country with a dollar surplus and lending it out to foreign banks or directly at favorable interest rates. The U.S. deficit is not the only source of funds; the market also attracts U.S. funds directly. Early in 1969 the deflationary policy of the U.S. government induced the overseas branches of U.S. banks to repatriate to their parent banks dollars borrowed on the Eurodollar market to such an extent as to cause European interest rates to rise sharply and European central bankers (⇛ CENTRAL BANKS) to express some concern at the volatile nature of such a large source of funds that can move outside the usual exchange control regulations. The *dollar certificate of deposit*, issued by the overseas branches of U.S. banks, which is fully transferable and negotiable, is also a source of funds. Other Eurocurrencies exist to serve similar markets in other currencies. The setting up of international banking facilities in the United States, which gives banks freedom from domestic regulations, may cause a shift in this market in favor of New York. (⇛⇛ FREE-TRADE ZONES).

European Coal and Steel Community (ECSC). The Schuman Plan (named after the French foreign minister) for the establishment of a common market in coal and steel was embodied in a treaty and ratified by the member countries—Germany, France, Italy and BENELUX—in 1952. All import duties and QUOTA restrictions on coal, iron ore, steel and scrap were eliminated on intra-community trade. The treaty also provided for the control of restrictive practices and MERGERS considered contrary to the maintenance of free competition. Overall executive responsibility is invested in the High Authority, which has power to raise finance by means of a tax on producers. This INCOME finances a readaptation fund that gives assistance to redundant or redeployed workers. The authority may make LOANS for capital INVESTMENT. It may also, at the request of the Council of Ministers, fix price levels and production and trade quotas. In addition, the treaty established a parliamentary common assembly and a court of justice, both of which were merged with the corresponding institutions of the EUROPEAN ECONOMIC COMMUNITY. Denmark, the Republic of Ireland and the United Kingdom became members in 1973. (⇛ CUSTOMS UNION).

European currency snake. The countries of the EUROPEAN ECONOMIC COMMUNITY agreed in 1972 to manage their currencies so that their EXCHANGE RATES moved in respect to one another and, within certain narrow bands, with respect to the dollar. It was considered that the management of the currencies of the Community in this way was the necessary first step to monetary union and, eventually, to the ideal of a common currency. The fluctuations in the rates of each currency were confined within a margin of ±2.25 percent. In addition, the group as a whole was also managed in respect to the dollar, with fluctuations confined within a range of ±4.45 percent. Initially, the arrangement was referred to as the "snake in the tunnel." After 1973, however, the "snake" was left to float against the dollar, and the "tunnel" vanished. The countries in the "snake" were, for varying periods of time, Belgium, Denmark, the Netherlands, Norway, Sweden, West Germany, United Kingdom, Italy and France. This method of managing European currencies was replaced in 1979 by the EUROPEAN MONETARY SYSTEM. (⇛ LOME CONVENTION).

European Currency Unit. ⇛ EUROPEAN MONETARY SYSTEM

European Development Fund (EDF). ⇛ LOME CONVENTION

European Economic Community (EEC). Six countries of Western Europe—France, West Germany, Italy, Belgium, Netherlands and Luxembourg—signed the Treaty of Rome in 1957 for the creation between them of a CUSTOMS UNION, or common market. By this treaty, the EEC came into force on January 1, 1958. The primary aims of the treaty were the elimination of all obstacles to the free movement of goods (⇛ ECONOMIC GOOD), SERVICES, CAPITAL and LABOR between the member countries and the setting up of a common external commercial policy, a common agricultural policy and a common transport policy. The treaty foresaw the prohibition of most SUBSIDIES and DUMPING and the supranational control of public MONOPOLIES and the vetting of MERGERS. The executive management of the EEC was vested in a commission whose members are appointed for periods of four years. Problems of policy are the concern of the Council of Ministers, to which the commission's proposals are submitted. Each member country is represented by one minister in the council. The treaty also established a parliamentary assembly and a court of justice. Consultative institutions include an economic and social committee and a monetary committee. The EUROPEAN INVESTMENT BANK has been formed and a European Regional Development Fund established with powers to lend and grant money for the development of backward regions of the Community. In addition, a European Social Fund has been set up to assist the redeployment of workers thrown out of work, particularly if caused by the creation of the Community, and a European Development Fund established to provide aid to countries of the LOME CONVENTION. All internal import duties were abolished and the common external tariff established by July 1, 1968. For agricultural products, all protectionist measures such as QUOTAS and import duties have been replaced by a levy that is determined by the difference between the world price and the internal (guaranteed) price (⇛ COMMON AGRICULTURAL POLICY). Workers and their families can move from one country to another without a permit, and foreign workers from within the community have the same rights to social security and are subject to the same taxation as nationals. Under a "Treaty of Fusion" the EEC institutions have been merged with those of the EUROPEAN COAL AND STEEL COMMUNITY and Euratom. As of January 1, 1973, the Republic of Ireland and two members of the EUROPEAN FREE TRADE ASSOCIATION—The United Kingdom and Denmark—became full members of the community. The elimination of tariffs between the original six and the new members and the adoption by them of the Common External Tariff was completed on January 1, 1977. At the same time, industrial FREE-TRADE agreements have been concluded with the remaining members of the European Free Trade Association. Greece became a member of the Community in 1981, and it is expected that Portugal and Spain will accede in 1983 or 1984. The commission has an association agreement with Turkey, which is also expected to become a full member at some future date. (⇛⇛ EUROPEAN MONETARY SYSTEM).

European Free Trade Area. Pressure for the formation of a FREE-TRADE AREA between the 17 countries of the ORGANIZATION FOR EUROPEAN ECONOMIC COOPERATION gathered strength in the early 1950s. Impetus was given to this idea by the conferences in 1955 and 1956, which led to the signing of the Treaty of Rome in 1957, between the 6 countries that were to establish the EUROPEAN ECONOMIC COMMUNITY. Negotiations for a free-trade area between the EEC and the other member countries of the OEEC failed. A free-trade area was, however, established in the EUROPEAN FREE TRADE ASSOCIATION.

European Free Trade Association (EFTA). The text of the convention setting up the European Free Trade Association was approved at Stockholm in November 1959 by the United Kingdom, Norway, Sweden, Denmark, Austria, Portugal and Switzerland. In April 1961 these seven concluded a trade agreement with Finland, which, in effect, brought Finland within the association. In March 1970 Iceland was also admitted as a full member, but Denmark and the United Kingdom left the association on becoming members of the EUROPEAN ECONOMIC COMMUNITY in 1973. The Stockholm

Agreement established a FREE-TRADE AREA between the member countries. While retaining their own individual tariffs on imports from nonmembers, they agreed to eliminate import duties on goods originating in any member country. As the group is in a free-trade area rather than a CUSTOMS UNION, rules are necessary to prevent products from nonmembers from being sold in a high-tariff member country via a low-tariff member. These rules were amended in 1973 following the conclusion of a number of free-trade agreements with the European Economic Community. The EFTA accepted the proposal of the EEC that goods subject to those agreements should be granted certificates of origin if they were "wholly produced" or sufficiently "processed" within the member countries. The principal test for "sufficient processing" is that the goods should be given a tariff classification different from that of the components entering into their production. (⇛⇛ GENERAL AGREEMENT ON TARIFFS AND TRADE).

European Investment Bank (EIB). A bank established by the EUROPEAN ECONOMIC COMMUNITY whose board of governors is made up of the ministers of finance of the Community. It is a nonprofit institution whose function is to make loans and give guarantees with respect to (1) projects in the underdeveloped areas of the Community and associated countries (⇛ LOME CONVENTION); (2) projects of modernization, conversion or development that are regarded as necessary for the establishment of the Common Market; and (3) projects in which member countries of the Community have a common interest. The loans, which are generally not more than 40 percent of the capital cost of the project, are for terms from 7 to 12 years and are made in a mix of foreign currencies. They have to be repaid in the currencies in which they were granted.

European Monetary Fund. ⇛ EUROPEAN MONETARY SYSTEM

European Monetary System (EMS). The European Council agreed in 1978 to the setting up of the European Monetary System, which was eventually inaugurated in 1979 for an initial period of two years, since extended. The intention was to follow this with a second phase, during which would be reestablished a strong European Monetary Fund, based on the new European Currency Unit (the ECU). The first phase of the EMS has, in fact, been a continuation of the previous EUROPEAN CURRENCY SNAKE. The currencies in the system are the West German deutsche mark, the French and Belgium francs, the Danish krone and the Irish punt. Each currency is managed so that its EXCHANGE RATE fluctuates within a specified margin around the central value of the ECU. The latter is a weighted "basket" of all the currencies of the EUROPEAN ECONOMIC COMMUNITY. The ECU is used for settling debts between the CENTRAL BANKS of the EEC.

European Payments Union (EPU). The 17 member countries of the ORGANIZATION OF EUROPEAN ECONOMIC COOPERATION established the European Payments Union between themselves in 1950. The EPU replaced the INTRA-EUROPEAN PAYMENTS AGREEMENT set up under the EUROPEAN RECOVERY PROGRAM. This was a clearing system for the multilateral international debits and credits that arose between the member countries. In addition, however, it afforded a mechanism for the extension of automatic lines of credit to any member with a BALANCE OF PAYMENTS deficit with fellow members. The BANK FOR INTERNATIONAL SETTLEMENTS acted as agent for the union. The union was replaced by the European Monetary Agreement in 1958, when the Western European countries restored currency CONVERTIBILITY. The union was an important stimulus to European unification and prevented the growth of BILATERALISM in Europe.

European Recovery Program. In June 1947 the U.S. secretary of state, General G.C. Marshall, in a speech at Harvard, made clear the willingness of the United States to extend economic assistance to countries whose productive ASSETS had been destroyed in the Second World War. This offer did not exclude the USSR and the Eastern European countries but was never accepted by them. The resultant European Recovery Program became known as MARSHALL AID. Sixteen Western European countries attended a conference in Paris in 1947 that led to the establishment of the ORGANIZATION FOR EUROPEAN ECONOMIC COOPERATION in 1948 to coordinate the recovery program in conjunction with the U.S. ECONOMIC COOPERATION ADMINISTRATION. It was established on the basis of a four-year commitment to provide Western Europe with between $15,000 million and $17,000 million.

European Units of Account. Because of the variety of national currencies, the EUROPEAN ECONOMIC COMMUNITY found it necessary to invent a common unit of account for bookkeeping purposes (⇛ MONEY, FUNCTIONS OF). Units of Account have been invented for the BUDGET, the EUROPEAN COAL AND STEEL COMMUNITY, agriculture, the EUROPEAN INVESTMENT BANK, Customs tariff (⇛ TARIFF, IMPORT) and the European Development Fund (⇛ LOME CONVENTION). Intially, all these units were defined as having the value of 0.88867088 grams of fine gold and were converted into member countries' currencies at their par rates of exchange (⇛ EXCHANGE RATE). After the international policy of fixed exchange rates was abandoned, the gap between the conversion rate of units of account and actual market rates made the system impractical. The revised unit of account is defined as the sum of amounts of each member country's currencies. These amounts are fixed at a level relating to the size of each member country's economy. The value of a unit of account in terms of any currency—say, the dollar—is calculated daily by translating each amount of currency in the "basket" into, say, dollars, according to the going rates of exchange for that currency and adding up the resultant sums (⇛ SPECIAL DRAWING RIGHTS). The original gold-based unit of account is still used for the agricultural budget. (⇛ COMMON AGRICULTURAL POLICY).

Ex ante. Intended, desired or expected before the event. Ex-ante DEMAND is the quantity that buyers wish or intend to buy at the going price; ex-ante INVESTMENT is the amount that firms plan or intend to invest. It must be distinguished from the outcome that actually occurs—that is, the actual quantity bought, the actual volume of investment—since these need not be equal to the ex-ante values, and, in fact, in DISEQUILIBRIUM situations they may well not be. (⇛⇛ EX POST; MYRDAL, GUNNAR KARL).

Excess capacity. 1. In a narrow sense refers to the proposition that, under MONOPOLISTIC COMPETITION, free entry of firms will result in only normal PROFIT being earned, but with too many firms, each producing at too low a rate of output to exploit ECONOMIES OF SCALE to the full. The difference between actual output and the output required to achieve full economies of scale is known as excess capacity. The excess capacity prediction was regarded as one of the most novel insights of the theory when it first appeared (⇛⇛ CHAMBERLIN, EDWARD HASTINGS; ROBINSON, JOAN VIOLET). 2. In general terms excess capacity exists when actual output is below the rate at which all the INPUTS of a firm, industry or economy are fully employed.

Excess cash reserves. A bank's cash reserves are in excess when the percentage of cash to DEPOSITS is higher than required by the CENTRAL BANK (⇛ FEDERAL RESERVE SYSTEM). Banks will attempt to loan out these excess reserves in order to attract interest (⇛ RATE OF INTEREST). (⇛⇛ BANKING; OPEN-MARKET OPERATIONS; REQUIRED RESERVES).

Excess demand. A situation in which the amount of a good or service that buyers wish to buy exceeds that which sellers are prepared to sell. The result is that the price is bid up, thereby inducing sellers to increase the quantity they are prepared to sell and buyers to reduce the quantity they wish to buy. Price will continue to rise until excess demand is eliminated, i.e., until DEMAND and SUPPLY are equal. Excess demand is a DISEQUILIBRIUM situation. It may also relate to an economy wide AGGREGATE DEMAND for goods and services that is greater than the capacity of the economy to meet it. This will then lead to a general price increase, i.e., to INFLATION.

Excess profit. ⇛ PROFIT

Excess supply. A situation in which the quantity of a good or service that sellers wish to sell at the prevailing price is greater than the quantity that buyers wish to buy. This causes sellers to bid down prices, thus causing an increase in the quantity demanded and a decrease in the quantity offered for sale, until SUPPLY and DEMAND are equal. Excess supply, like EXCESS DEMAND, is a DISEQUILIBRIUM situation.

Exchange control. The control by the state through the BANKING system of dealings in gold and foreign CURRENCIES. Exchange control is concerned with controlling the purchase and sale of currencies by residents alone, since governments do not have complete powers to control the activities of non-residents. This must be done through the MARKET and is a matter of exchange management. Exchange control is only required where a country wishes to influence the international VALUE of its currency. It is not willing to leave the value of its currency in terms of other currencies or gold to be determined in the FREE MARKET, as it would be under a system of floating EXCHANGE RATES, or to allow the fixed external value of its currency to be the determinant of the domestic price level as it was under the GOLD STANDARD. In its most extreme form, a country facing a balance of payments deficit may use exchange control to restrict imports to the amount earned in FOREIGN EXCHANGE by its nationals. In Brazil in the 1960s, foreign currency in the form of import licenses was auctioned to the highest bidder.

All forms of exchange control are discouraged by the ORGANIZATION FOR ECONOMIC COOPERATION AND DEVELOPMENT and other international organizations concerned with encouraging INTERNATIONAL TRADE. It should be noted that a currency is not fully convertible. (⇛ CONVERTIBILITY) when exchange control is operated.

Exchange economy. An economy in which specialization (⇛ DIVISION OF LABOR) takes place, which then creates the need for exchange, either through BARTER or through the medium of money. It is difficult to think of any economy today in which specialization has not proceeded far enough to make that economy an exchange economy.

Exchange of shares. A means of business combination that can take two forms. In form *a* the companies retain their separate identities but exchange a quantitiy of SHARES so that each company holds shares in the other, and normally some directors will sit on both boards (⇛ INTERLOCKING DIRECTORATE). In form *b* two companies will merge, shares of one company being exchanged with or without a cash adjustment for the whole of the issued share capital of the other. (⇛ MERGER).

Exchange rate. The price (rate) at which one CURRENCY is exchanged for another currency, for gold or SPECIAL DRAWING RIGHTS. These transactions are carried out spot or forward (⇛ FORWARD MARKET; SPOT MARKET) in the FOREIGN EXCHANGE MARKETS. The actual rate at any one time is determined by SUPPLY and DEMAND conditions for the relevant currencies in the market. These in turn would depend on the BALANCE OF PAYMENTS deficits or surpluses of the relevant economies and the demand for the currencies to meet obligations and expectations about the future movements in the rate. If there were no government control over the exchange market, there would be an entirely *free* or *floating exchange rate* in operation. With a freely floating system, no GOLD AND FOREIGN EXCHANGE RESERVES would be required, as the exchange rate would adjust itself until the supply and demand for the currencies were brought into balance (⇛ PURCHASING POWER PARITY THEORY). Under the rules of the INTERNATIONAL MONETARY FUND, established at the BRETTON WOODS CONFERENCE toward the end of the Second World War, exchange rates were fixed at a par value in relation to the dollar, and fluctuations around this value were confined within a ±1 percent band. The dollar itself was not subject to this restriction, because the U.S. government was committed to buying gold on demand at a fixed rate of $35.0875 per ounce. However, in August 1971 the United States suspended the CONVERTIBILITY of the dollar into gold and other currencies, imposed a 10 percent surcharge on IMPORTS and took other measures aimed at eliminating its balance of payments deficit. There followed a period during which some major currencies were allowed to float but subject to exchange-control regulations to keep the exchange-rate movements within limits (a "dirty float"). In December 1971 the "Group of Ten," in the IMF meeting at the Smithsonian Institution, Washington, agreed to a realignment of exchange rates that left the dollar devalued by about 5 percent against an average of all other currencies in exchange for a rise in the dollar price of gold to $38 per ounce and the removal of the import surcharge. In addition, it was agreed that the margin of permitted fluctuations should be ± 2.25 percent.

There has been much discussion in the past of the relative merits of floating compared with fixed exchange rates, and indeed of many hybrid systems that lie between these extremes. The floating rate has apparent attractions comparable to the advantages obtained, in terms of efficient resource allocation (⇛ RESOURCES), by a freely operating price mechanism (⇛ PRICE SYSTEM). This comparison, however, is superficial, because exchange rates are not just a PRICE; changes in exchange rates are likely to alter substantially the INCOME levels of communities. Fluctuations in the rate are inconvenient for trading, and these fluctuations could be volatile if left to move freely. Moreover, because of the pressure of short-term CAPITAL movements or SPECULATION, the exchange rate could move in a direction different from what might be required by the domestic economy as reflected in its basic balance of payments. The system of fixed rates has been criticized on the grounds of its inflexibility and the fact that it places too much of the adjustment burden on the domestic economy. A middle course has been proposed in the "moving-parity," "sliding-parity," "dynamic" or "crawling-peg" idea. In the *moving parity* the par rate is automatically adjusted according to a moving average of past rates taken over a number of months. Professor J.E. Meade has put forward a refined version of this, called the *sliding-parity* or *crawling-peg*. In this, instead of the whole amount of a revaluation or devaluation taking place at once, it is spread in small percentages over a number of months, e.g., a 10 percent devaluation may be achieved by a monthly 0.2 percent reduction for 50 months. This system has the advantage that it is known and certain, while the monthly adjustment is too small to cause excessive speculative flows. Hendrik Houthakker, in his capacity as a member of the U.S. President's Council of Economic Advisors, has put forward proposals for a crawling peg that are similar to Professor Meade's. He has suggested that gradual adjustments in the exchange rate should be allowed up to 2 percent to 3 percent per annum. These adjustments should be linked to the level of a country's reserves rather than past exchange rates. The Smithsonian System of flexible but fixed parities did not, in the event, last long. The floating of sterling in June 1972, marked the end of the fixed parity system and since 1973 all currencies have been subjected to a "managed" float. A survey, financed by the Rockefeller Foundation, among bankers and multinational corporations, was carried out in 1980 to get their views on their experience of the "managed" or "dirty" float. The research showed that these institutions were generally in favor. Even the multinationals preferred floating to fixed exchange rates, though they admitted that foreign exchange now took up more management time. (⇛⇛ EUROPEAN CURRENCY SNAKE; INTERNATIONAL LIQUIDITY).

Excise tax. ⇛ SALES TAX

Exclusive dealing. Restriction by a manufacturer of the sales of his products to particular customers or sales outlets. The CLAYTON ACT forbade exclusive dealing where this has an anti-competitive effect. Exclusive dealing is usually defended on grounds of maintaining standards of service to customers—e.g., for automobiles—although it might in certain circumstances prevent a new manufacturer from selling his products or a new retailer from competing with existing retail outlets. (⇛⇛ ANTITRUST POLICY).

Ex-dividend. Without DIVIDEND. The purchaser of a SECURITY quoted ex-dividend does not have the right to the next dividend when due. The term *ex-*, meaning excluding, is also used in a similar sense in relation to STOCK RIGHTS.

Eximbank. ⇛ EXPORT-IMPORT BANK

Exogenous variable. A VARIABLE that, although playing an important part in a MODEL, is determined by forces outside the model and is unexplained by it. For example, in a model of the market for wheat, weather conditions may play an important part in determining the supply and hence the price of wheat. But the model itself does not try to explain what determines weather conditions. (⇛⇛ ENDOGENOUS VARIABLE).

Expectation. Belief or state of mind with respect to the nature of future events. Expectations are often crucial in determining economic behavior. A firm will select a PRICE or a level of output or some other policy variable in the light of its expectations about the future. Similarly, a consumer may base his current purchases on his expectations of what the price will be over the next month. A difficulty this presents for economics is that, though expectations may determine current behavior, they cannot be directly observed, and this then makes it difficult to test the validity of hypotheses. For example, we may hypothesize that a rise in price causes a fall in quantity demanded. Yet we may observe a rise in price of, say, a company stock to be followed by an increase in the quantity demanded. We may then argue that our theory of demand is not refuted, because the buyers' *expectations* were of a further rise in price, after which they could sell at a PROFIT. But unless we can find some way of discovering what buyers' expectations really are, we cannot firmly answer the question. One possible solution is to attempt to explain how expectations are formed, e.g., by hypothesizing that they are some function of the current and past values of the relevant variables (⇛ ADAPTIVE EXPECTATIONS). Another is to attempt to find, by questionnaire, what the expectations of a particular group of decision makers are and then try to discover what determines the changes in expectations over time. (⇛⇛ RATIONAL EXPECTATIONS).

Expenditure tax. ⇛ SALES TAX

Export Control Act. Enacted in 1949, this legislation allows the government to exercise control over EXPORTS that are significant to national security. The Act was amended in 1962 to include, among other things, sanctions against exports to communist countries. In 1956 and 1966 Congress removed presidential discretion related to the sale of agricultural products to socialist countries. In addition, presidential discretion in offering EXIMBANK (⇛ EXPORT-IMPORT BANK) credit for exports to communist countries was withdrawn. (⇛⇛ CO-ORDINATING COMMITTEE FOR MULTILATERAL EXPORT CONTROLS).

Export-Import Bank (Eximbank). A Washington-based U.S. agency that, since 1934, has guaranteed export credit, provided export credit insurance and allowed credit to borrowers outside the United States. It operates in conjunction with a COMMERCIAL BANK to provide a guarantee against risk or nonpayment for an exporter, given certain conditions. The foreign buyer must pay the exporter 10 percent of the value of the transaction upon delivery and provide a PROMISSORY NOTE for the remainder. On the remainder the exporter assumes at least 10 percent and the commercial bank pays the exporter the remainder, carrying the risk on the early installments. The Eximbank guarantee covers the remaining installments and all political risk. In addition to this major service, Eximbank provides information on credit ratings, advice on export financing and assistance in developing export finance programs for U.S. businesses. The bank's loans are normally for a maximum of 10 years, which is the limit agreed by the OECD (⇛ ORGANIZATION FOR ECONOMIC COOPERATION AND DEVELOPMENT). In fiscal 1980–81 its budget was $5.4 billion. It has been forced to cut its interest rate offers to very low levels and extend the loan period because of competitive pressure from the EEC (⇛ EUROPEAN ECONOMIC COMMUNITY). Credit rates had fallen to 7.5 percent at a time when the cost of borrowing was very high. (⇛ EXPORT INCENTIVES).

Export incentives. Preferential treatment for firms that sell their products abroad, compared with firms that sell to the home market. They may take the form of direct SUBSIDIES, special CREDIT facilities, grants, concessions in the field of DIRECT TAXATION, benefits arising from the administration of indirect taxation, and export credit INSURANCE on exceptionally favorable terms. Various international associations discourage the practice of artificially stimulating exports by any of these methods. The GENERAL AGREEMENT ON TARIFFS AND TRADE lays down special provisions relating to export subsidies, direct or indirect, in an attempt to limit them. The Stockholm Convention setting up the EUROPEAN FREE TRADE ASSOCIATION lists various forms of aid to exporters that member countries are required to avoid. The Treaty of Rome, which established the EUROPEAN ECONOMIC COMMUNITY, although less specific than the Stockholm Convention, nevertheless discourages the granting of privileged aid to any economic sectors (⇛ EXPORT-IMPORT BANK; EXPORT TRADING COMPANY).

Export rebates. ⇛ CUSTOMS DRAWBACK; EXPORT INCENTIVES

Exports. The goods and SERVICES produced by one country that are sold to another in exchange for the second country's own goods and services, for gold and FOREIGN EXCHANGE, or in settlement of DEBT. Countries tend to specialize in the production of those goods and services in which they can be relatively most efficient, because of their indigenous factor endowments (⇛ FACTORS OF PRODUCTION). Countries devote home resources to exports because they can obtain more goods and services by international exchange than they would obtain from the same resources devoted to direct home production. U.S. exports are currently about 8 percent of GNP. This compares with about 10 percent in Japan and between 17 percent and 25 percent in the member countries of the EEC (⇛ EUROPEAN ECONOMIC COMMUNITY). (⇛⇛ BALANCE OF PAYMENTS; INTERNATIONAL TRADE; MERCANTILISM).

Exports, unrequited. ⇛ UNREQUITED EXPORTS

Export surplus. ⇛ BALANCE OF PAYMENTS

Export trading company. In 1982, the U.S. government passed the Export Trading Company Act that enabled small firms to form export trading companies through which to conduct their overseas business (⇛ INTERNATIONAL TRADE). The Act allows BANK HOLDING COMPANIES to invest in and extend CREDIT to the export trading companies and eases the incidence on the latter of the antitrust laws.

Ex post. The ex-post VALUE of some VARIABLE—e.g., supply, INVESTMENT, quantity bought—is the value that the variable actually takes in the event. Ex post is opposed to the EX-ANTE value, which is the expected or intended value. Ex ante, a consumer might plan to buy 10 units of a particular good (⇛ ECONOMIC GOOD) but in the event might only buy 8 units, because an insufficient quantity was on sale, or its PRICE turned out to be higher than at first expected. (⇛ MYRDAL, GUNNAR KARL).

Ex-rights. ⇛ STOCK RIGHT

External deficit. A synonym for BALANCE OF PAYMENTS deficit.

Externalities. Externalities in CONSUMPTION exist when the level of consumption of some good by one consumer has a direct effect on the welfare of another consumer, an effect that is *not* transmitted through the price mechanism; production externalities exist when the production activities of one firm directly affect the production activities of another firm. External ECONOMIES OF SCALE and DISECONOMIES of scale are therefore particular cases of externalities in production. Examples of consumption externalities are:

1. A, wanting privacy, builds a high fence, which reduces the amount of sunshine flooding in through B's window.

2. A, in making a left turn on a busy highway, causes a large traffic jam to build up behind him.

Examples of production externalities are:

1. Firm A discharges effluent into a river, which greatly increases costs of Firm B downstream.

2. Firm A sets up a training school for computer programmers, which increases the availability of programmers to Firm B.

There may also, of course, be mixed production/consumption externalities. For example:

1. Night flights by jet airliners may cause residents in areas close to an airport to lose sleep.

2. Holiday motorists may increase congestion on a highway and so increase costs of truckers.

The essence of externalities, whether in production or consumption, is that their costs or benefits are not reflected in market prices, and so the decision of the consumer or firm creating the externalities on the scale of the externality-creating activity generally does not take its effect into account. Hence, since the time of ARTHUR CECIL PIGOU, economists have argued that social welfare (⇛ SOCIAL WELFARE FUNCTION) would be increased if the private consumption or production decision were modified so as to take the external effect into account. The means of doing this were traditionally held to be the imposition of taxes on activities that created losses in welfare or increases in costs, and payment of SUBSIDIES for activities that increased welfare or lowered costs. In practice, tax-subsidy schemes are rarely adopted. More frequently, externalities are uncorrected or absolutely prohibited—left turns in certain streets, smoking in certain parts of the airplane—or PROPERTY RIGHTS are created, and redress is possible through the courts. If these property rights are well-defined and it is not too costly to do so, the parties to an externality situation may get together and bargain, thus in effect creating a MARKET, the absence of which initially gave rise to the externality.

External surplus. A synonym for BALANCE OF PAYMENTS surplus.

F

Face value. Nominal as distinct from MARKET value. The face value of a SECURITY is the price at which it will be redeemed; of COMMON STOCK, the PAR VALUE or issued price; of a coin the amount stamped on it, which might, for a silver or gold coin, be less than its market value.

Factoring. The business activity in which a company takes over the responsibility for the collecting of the DEBTS of another. It is a service primarily intended to meet the needs of small and medium-sized firms. Typically, the client debits all his sales to the factor and can draw cash up to about 80 percent of their value, thus increasing his cash flow considerably. The factor takes over the entire responsibility for retrieving the debts due from the client's customers and protects the client from bad debts. The factor, however, has some control over sales, either by imposing a maximum CREDIT limit that he is willing to meet or by vetting specific prospective clients. Through international factoring companies, the factor can offer a service to EXPORTS by protecting his customers from bad debts overseas and by giving, for instance, expert advice on FOREIGN EXCHANGE transactions.

Factor markets. MARKETS on which the FACTORS OF PRODUCTION are bought and sold. Analysis of these markets suggests how PRICES of the factors of production are determined and therefore provides an explanation of the distribution of income. (⇛ DISTRIBUTION, THEORY OF).

Factors of production. According to ALFRED MARSHALL, these are "the things required for making a commodity." In modern terminology they would be referred to as "INPUTS." Typically, they are grouped into LAND, LABOR and CAPITAL for broad purposes of analysis, but within each broad category there will be a wide diversity of types. (⇛⇛ NATURAL RESOURCES; SAY, JEAN-BAPTISTE).

Fair trade policy. ⇛ RECIPROCITY

Farm Board. A U.S. agency established in 1929 to purchase and sell agricultural produce as a means of stabilizing the marketing of commodities.

FAS (free alongside ship). ⇛ CIF (CHARGED IN FULL)

Federal Advisory Council. This is part of the FEDERAL RESERVE SYSTEM. The council advises the board of governors of the position of the commercial banks on monetary and other policies. The 12-member council has no real power.

Federal Aviation Commission. ⇛ REGULATION

Federal Communications Commission. ⇛ REGULATION

Federal Deposit Insurance. A guarantee to commercial bank depositors that their deposits are insured up to a limit even in the face of a bank failure.

Federal Energy Regulation Commission (FERC). Prior to 1977 this was the Federal Power Commission, established in 1920 by Congress to deal largely with matters of waterpower. Over time it was assigned additional functions related to energy, most notably the regulation of natural gas prices.

Through the Natural Gas Policy Act of 1978, virtually all gas pricing is under federal control, and the FERC is assigned the task of interpreting the Act and ruling on its provisions if necessary. (⇛ REGULATION).

Federal funds rate. The RATE OF INTEREST on a TREASURY BILL. (⇛ FEDERAL RESERVE SYSTEM).

Federal Home Loan Bank Board. The activities of the 12 regional Home Loan Banks are monitored by this board, which is appointed by the President. The Home Loan Banks were established in the 1930s with the failure of a large number of SAVINGS AND LOAN ASSOCIATIONS. The 12 Home Loan Banks supervise the activities of the savings and loan associations, acting, if necessary and in a limited way, as a lender of last resort.

Federal Open Market Committee (FOMC). This committee is composed of the 7 governors of the FEDERAL RESERVE SYSTEM of the United States and 12 regional bank presidents. It meets each third Tuesday of the month to decide upon the directives to be issued to the Federal Reserve's open-market manager concerning the OPEN-MARKET OPERATIONS that are to be pursued.

Federal Reserve Act. ⇛ FEDERAL RESERVE SYSTEM

Federal Reserve bank. ⇛ FEDERAL RESERVE SYSTEM

Federal Reserve Board. ⇛ FEDERAL RESERVE SYSTEM

Federal Reserve note. ⇛ FIAT MONEY

Federal Reserve System (FED). The FED was created in 1913 when President Wilson signed the Federal Reserve Act. The Act (and creation of a CENTRAL BANK) was in response to the widespread and severe financial problems of 1907, during which many banks failed. Although the idea of a central bank was opposed by many initially, it became clear that the financial system needed a lender of last resort.

The FED today, as it did in 1913, consists of 12 Federal Reserve banks, representing 12 districts of the country and a board of governors. Each of the 12 banks is controlled by part-time directors, three of whom are elected by the member COMMERCIAL BANKS and must be bankers. Three others who are not bankers are elected by the banks as well. The remaining three are appointed by the board of governors.

The Federal Reserve banks perform such functions as monitoring commercial banks, reviewing applications for mergers, clearing checks and replacing worn-out currency. Each bank can set the DISCOUNT RATE for its district. However, since the rate must be approved by the board of governors, each Federal Reserve bank only advises.

The Federal Reserve Board, or board of governors, is located in Washington and consists of seven individuals appointed by the President for a term of 14 years. The chairman of the FED has a term of only four years, allowing each President to appoint his own chairman. Until the 1960s most members of the board were bankers and businessmen. Recently, however, the majority have been professional economists, some from staff positions in the Federal Reserve System. The main functions of the board are

OPEN-MARKET OPERATIONS, changing the RESERVE requirements in the system and setting the discount rate.

When the FED was initially established, a major provision of the Act stated that commercial banks had to maintain their reserves in the Federal Reserve. This interrelationship is shown in the summary balance sheets below. In 1980 commercial bank reserves ($31.2 billion and shown as an ASSET in the banks' balance sheet) are shown as a LIABILITY in the FED. To conduct open-market operations that would restrict credit, the FED would sell government securities to those who have deposits in the commercial banks. To pay for these government securities, deposits (and cash reserves) would decline, forcing banks to restrict loans in order to meet reserve requirements.

Raising the discount rate would make it more expensive for commercial banks to acquire cash that could be loaned out, thus slowing the expansion of credit.

By using its MONETARY POLICIES to expand or restrict credit, the FED can exert a significant influence on AGGREGATE DEMAND and the rate of ECONOMIC GROWTH and UNEMPLOYMENT. (⇛ BANKING).

Federal Reserve (1980) $ Billions				**Commercial Banks (1980)** $ Billions			
ASSETS		**LIABILITIES**		**ASSETS**		**LIABILITIES**	
Gold	11.2	Banks' reserves	31.2	Reserves with Federal Reserve	31.2	Deposits	1,063.1
Govt. securities	116.3	Currency held by public	108.9	Other cash assets	135.3	Other liabilities	404.5
Other net assets	27.8	Other liabilities	15.2	Loans and investments	1,301.1		
	155.3		155.3		1,467.6		1,467.6

Source: *Federal Reserve Bulletin*

Federal Trade Commission. The commission was established by the U.S. Congress in 1914 and is independent of the Antitrust Division of the Justice Department (⇛ ANTITRUST POLICY). The commission has for the most part been concerned with the degree of CONCENTRATION in industry, especially in the manufacturing sector. It cooperates with the Justice Department in its investigations and prosecutions, especially those dealing with MERGERS and MONOPOLY power. It is charged to investigate industrial practices and police unfair trade activities. Originally, it had the power to issue "cease and desist" orders without judicial review, but this was withdrawn by the Supreme Court in 1919.

FED MIT Penn. model. A MODEL of the U.S. economy, using ECONOMETRIC techniques, developed by the FEDERAL RESERVE SYSTEM, Massachusetts Institute of Technology and the University of Pennsylvania.

Fertility rate. ⇛ BIRTHRATE

Fiat money. MONEY that is declared by the government to be legal tender for settling debts. Paper currency or Federal Reserve notes are fiat money. (⇛ FIDUCIARY ISSUE).

Fiduciary issue. Paper currency, or MONEY, not backed by gold or silver. The term has its origins in the Bank Charter Act of 1844 in Britain, which fixed the fiduciary issue limit at £14 million. Any notes issued in excess of this amount had to be fully backed by gold. The fiduciary limit has been successively raised, and the monetary authorities are now free to alter the note issue as they wish; effectively the note issue in Britain, as in the United States, is now entirely fiduciary. (⇛⇛ BANKING AND CURRENCY SCHOOLS; FIAT MONEY).

Final products. Commodities used by consumers in CONSUMPTION rather than by firms as INPUTS into processes of production, i.e., INTERMEDIATE PRODUCTS. A commodity may, of course, be both.

Finance. The provision of MONEY when and where required. Finance may be short-term (usually up to one year), medium-term (usually over one year and up to five to seven years) and long-term. Finance may be required for CONSUMPTION or for INVESTMENT. For the latter, when provided, it becomes CAPITAL. (⇛⇛ BUSINESS FINANCE; CONSUMER CREDIT; FINANCIAL INTERMEDIARIES; PUBLIC FINANCE).

Finance company. An imprecise term covering a range of FINANCIAL INTERMEDIARIES. Finance companies provide loans, usually for well-defined purposes, and obtain their own funds by borrowing or issuing SHARES. Most finance companies specialize in direct lending to individuals (⇛ CONSUMER CREDIT; INSTALLMENT CREDIT). Sales finance companies purchase installment credit receivables from retailers. Commercial finance companies lend directly to businesses for equipment purchase and make loans against assigned accounts receivable. (⇛⇛ FACTORING).

Financial Accounting Standards Board (FASB). ⇛ INFLATION ACCOUNTING

Financial futures. ⇛ FUTURES; SPECULATION

Financial intermediaries. Institutions that hold MONEY balances of, or that borrow from, individuals and other institutions in order to make LOANS or other INVESTMENTS. Hence, they serve the purpose of chaneling funds from lenders to borrowers. It is usual to distinguish between banks and non-banks among financial intermediaries (⇛ BANKING). The importance of this distinction arises from the fact that the LIABILITIES of banks are part of the MONEY SUPPLY, and this is not true of the nonbank financial intermediaries (whose liabilities may nevertheless be regarded as "NEAR" MONEY). The most important of the nonbank financial intermediaries are the SAVINGS AND LOAN ASSOCIATIONS, MUTUAL SAVINGS BANKS, FINANCE COMPANIES, the contractual savings institutions, INSURANCE companies and PENSION FUNDS, and finally MUTUAL FUNDS and TRUSTS.

Financial ratios. 1. Specifically, measures of credit worthiness. The principal measures are the CURRENT RATIO, the "QUICK" RATIO, the debt or net worth ratio (long-term debt to net worth), DIVIDEND COVER and INTEREST COVER. All these ratios are measures of the asset or income cover available to the suppliers of CAPITAL (including TRADE CREDIT) to the business (⇛ BALANCE SHEET). 2. More generally, calculations based upon company accounts and other sources, such as STOCK EXCHANGE prices, designed to indicate the profitability or other financial aspects of the business, such as the capital structure. Examples are: return on net assets (⇛ RATE OF RETURN), PRICE-EARNINGS RATIO, LEVERAGE and stock-sales ratio. (⇛ INVENTORY TURNOVER).

Financial trust. ⇛ TRUST

Financial year. Years of account for financial purposes often do not coincide with calendar years and are hence referred to as financial years. A financial year 1983–84, for example, might run from August 31, 1983 to September 1, 1984. Also referred to often as *fiscal year,* although this term should be strictly reserved for the government tax year, which runs from July 1 to June 30.

Fine tuning. Frequent but relatively small changes in taxes and/or government expenditure in order to control the path of AGGREGATE DEMAND as precisely as possible. In the 1950s and 1960s, this policy was strongly advocated by Keynesians (⇛ KEYNES, JOHN MAYNARD) as a means of achieving full employment (⇛ EMPLOYMENT, FULL) and stable prices. Because of the apparent failure of such policies to control inflation in the late 1960s and 1970s, fine tuning is not nearly as popular as in earlier years. (⇛ MONETARY POLICY; STABILIZATION POLICY).

Firm, theory of. That part of MICROECONOMICS that is concerned with explaining and predicting decisions of the firm, particularly with respect to output, PRICE, INPUTS and changes in these. The theory deals with the firm at a very high level of abstraction. It assumes away many of the characteristics of modern firms—divorce of ownership from management as represented in the JOINT-STOCK COMPANY; large, complex organizational structures; imperfections of information about the external environment the firm faces—and considers the firm as attempting to maximize PROFITS, subject to given known DEMAND and COST conditions. The nature of these demand conditions, and therefore the levels of output and inputs selected by the firm, may differ according to whether the firm sells in a perfect or imperfect market (⇛ PERFECT COMPETITION). Nevertheless, the underlying theory of the firm is the same in each case: The firm maximizes profits with full information and complete certainty, with no problems of an organizational character.

The theory is obviously unrealistic in a descriptive sense. Nevertheless, it is still a cornerstone of the accepted body of microeconomics. This is not, as some would argue, because economists are so obsessed with theoretical elegance and neat abstractions that they ignore the "real world." Rather, it is because the theory is so simple yet so powerful: It permits a wide range of predictions to be made about the behavior of firms, which are reasonably accurate and which might not be obtained so easily and unambiguously from more complicated theories. In addition, it is the essential first step in the process of building up a theory of MARKETS and, from that, a theory of the process of RESOURCE allocation in the economy as a whole, and these have given considerable insight into the workings of FREE-MARKET ECONOMIES.

Nevertheless, there has been a great deal of dissatisfaction with the traditional theory of the firm. Partly, this arises from a desire for realism for its own sake. Partly, it stems from the fact that certain predictions of the theory seem to have been refuted, e.g., that firms will not change price in response to a change in a fixed cost. Finally, the importance of oligopolistic markets (⇛ OLIGOPOLY) has created a need for revision of the theory of the firm, for two reasons: (1) The indeterminacy of the standard theory of the firm in situations of oligopoly suggests that if definite predictions are to be made, more attention must be paid to the actual behavior of firms in such situations; and (2) the fact that oligopolistic firms are to some extent shielded from competitive pressures means that they have discretion to pursue goals other than profits.

Since the early 1950s there has been a steady development of theories that attempt to improve upon the traditional theory. The most significant developments have concentrated on the objectives of the firm, i.e., the assumption of profit maximization. It was observed that stockholders, the recipients of profits and the owners of the firm, tend not to participate actively in running their firms, but instead just expect a reasonable level of DIVIDEND to be maintained, while managers actually control the decision making of the firm. This then led to a series of theories based on the hypothesis that decisions would be taken to further the objectives of the top executives, subject always to the constraint that shareholders were paid satisfactory levels of dividends. A theory put forward by W.J. Baumol in *Business Behavior, Value, and Growth* suggested that firms would try to maximize their size, as measured by sales revenue, since managerial satisfaction and rewards depended more on size than profits. This led to certain predictions of behavior that differ from those that would be made by profit maximization, e.g., firms would produce larger outputs and advertise more than under profit maximization and would respond to an increase in fixed costs by raising prices.

A MODEL on similar lines was developed by Oliver E. Williamson in *The Economics of Discretionary Behavior.* He suggested that the satisfaction of managers depended on the sizes of their departments (as measured by administrative expenditure), the amount of declared profits they could retain rather than distribute to shareholders (since this then gave them discretion to make investments that do not have to meet with the approval of shareholders), and finally the size of expense accounts and amount of other perquisites (company autos, etc.) that managers are able to get for themselves. Again, the theory gives a wide range of predictions that differ both from the classical model and the theory of Baumol just described.

A third model somewhat in this vein is that developed by R. Marris in *The Economic Theory of Managerial Capitalism,* which took the maximization of the rate of growth of the firm as being the managerial objective. The notable feature of this model is that it drops the static framework of the conventional theory (maintained in the two models discussed above) and attempts explicitly to construct an analysis of the growth rate of the firm (⇛ ECONOMIC DYNAMICS).

The common feature of these "modern" theories of the firm is that they concentrate on the objectives of the firm, tending still to ignore problems of organization and imperfections in information. They also assume that the firm attempts to maximize something, i.e., seeks the greatest value possible, rather than to achieve certain satisfactory levels of sales, profits, etc. In these respects, they are still very close to the traditional approach. The most significant departure from this had been made by the BEHAVIORAL THEORY OF THE FIRM, which drops the assumption that firms maximize something and instead concentrates on the decision processes of the firm and the way in which these are affected by the organizational environment. This last theory probably comes closer than any other to being a realistic description of real-world firms. (⇛⇛ COURNOT, ANTOINE AUGUSTIN; GALBRAITH, JOHN KENNETH; SIMON, HERBERT A.).

First in first out (FIFO). An accounting term referring to the principle on which INVENTORIES are valued. Under FIFO raw materials are assumed to be withdrawn from stock in the order in which they were put in, the oldest items being "drawn first." This traditional convention results in valuation at original rather than current prices. In a period of INFLATION, this may mean that material costs are seriously understated and current inventory values and profits overstated. Last in first out (LIFO) is an alternative procedure that has the opposite effect. A second alternative is to average the opening and closing inventory.

Fiscal drag. A term coined by Walter Heller, chairman of the COUNCIL OF ECONOMIC ADVISORS in the 1960s. With a given level of public spending, and tax revenues that increase as national income rises, there develops a budget surplus as the economy approaches full employment (⇛ EMPLOYMENT, FULL). This surplus tends to hold back the economic expansion. (⇛⇛ BUILT-IN STABILIZERS).

Fiscal federalism. The economic and financial arrangements in a decentralized fiscal system. The Constitution of the United States did not clearly specify the taxation rights of states and federal government, nor did it clearly establish areas of expenditure responsibility. The debate over whether or not the federal government should have the major fiscal powers began in the early 19th century; by the end of the century it was accepted that the federal government had the powers, and this continued into the 20th century. To a considerable extent, state governments depend upon "CONDITIONAL GRANTS" from the federal government to finance their expenditure programs. In turn, state governments provide assistance to local governments. Over one-quarter of state revenue and one-third of local revenue comes from such grants. Until the early 1970s most grants were of the conditional type. The introduction in 1972 of REVENUE SHARING led to the growth of "unconditional grants" to states and through them to local governments. Such revenue sharing is known as the Heller-Pechman plan and is very complex in terms of the factors that are taken into account when assigning these grants. A major purpose of these grants is to provide a measure of equalization (⇛ EQUALIZATION GRANT) across fiscal units.

Fiscalist. A person holding the view that fiscal policy is the only, or at least the most effective, way of raising aggregate demand to achieve full employment. A more contemporary term is NEO-KEYNESIAN, a school of thought that has opposed the views of MONETARISM.

Fiscal policy. That part of government policy which is concerned with raising revenue through TAXATION and other means and deciding on the level and pattern of expenditure. It is through the level and pattern of budgetary surpluses and their means of financing that the government can control the level of demand in the economy.

In the 1950s and 1960s, it was widely believed that fiscal policy could be used for the purpose of FINE TUNING the economy. The Kennedy-Johnson tax cut of 1964 was an example of such demand management. Lately, however, there has been very little enthusiasm for fiscal policy and "STABILIZATION POLICY" in general. (⇛⇛ FRIEDMAN, MILTON; KEYNES, JOHN MAYNARD; MONETARISM; MONETARY POLICY).

Fiscal year. ⇛ FINANCIAL YEAR

Fisher equation. ⇛ FISHER, IRVING; QUANTITY THEORY OF MONEY

Fisher, Irving (1867–1947). A mathematician by professional training, Fisher was professor of political economy at Yale University from 1898 to 1935. His main works on economics were *Mathematical Investigations in the Theory of Value and Prices* (1892), *Nature of Capital and Income* (1906), *The Rate of Interest* (1907), *Purchasing Power of Money* (1911), *The Making of Index Numbers* (1922) and *Theory of Interest* (1930). *The Rate of Interest,* which was substantially revised in 1930, progressed the theory of interest onward from EUGEN VON BOHM-BAWERK toward the modern theory of INVESTMENT APPRAISAL. The RATE OF INTEREST is governed by the interaction of two forces: (1) the "willingness or impatience" of individuals with respect to the giving up of INCOME now compared with income in the future (Fisher invented the term TIME PREFERENCE); and (2) the "investment opportunity principle," the technological ability to convert income now into income in the future. He called the latter the "rate of return over cost," which JOHN MAYNARD KEYNES said was the same as his "marginal efficiency of capital" (⇛ INTERNAL RATE OF RETURN). He defined this "rate of return over cost" as that DISCOUNT RATE which equalized the PRESENT VALUE of the possible alternative investment choices open. He showed how the ranking of investment choices depended on the rate of interest used. He clarified economists' ideas on the nature of CAPITAL, distinguishing between a stock and a flow of WEALTH. A house is capital stock, but its use is a flow of income. He was the author of the "quantity of money" (exchange) equation $MV = PT$, in which M = the stock of money, V = the velocity of circulation, P = the PRICE level and T = the output of goods (⇛ ECONOMIC GOOD) and SERVICES (⇛ QUANTITY THEORY OF MONEY). Fisher developed the theory of INDEX NUMBERS and established a set of conditions that an index should satisfy.

Fixed asset. ⇛ ASSET

Fixed capital. ⇛ CAPITAL

Fixed charge. ⇛ FLOATING CHARGE

Fixed costs. COSTS that in the short run do not vary with output. These costs are borne even if no output is produced and are consequently also called overheads (⇛ FIXED ASSETS), e.g., payment of RENT on buildings and interest payments on past borrowing. In the LONG RUN, by definition, there are no fixed costs; that is, all the costs are variable.

Fixed exchange rate. ⇛ EXCHANGE RATE

Flags of convenience. An expression relating to the practice of many shipowners of registering their vessels with countries other than that of their own home port in order to avoid taxes or stringent safety regulations. The extent of the movement can be seen from the growth of the merchant fleets of such small countries as Panama and Liberia. The DEVELOPING COUNTRIES wish to see the practice outlawed, and talks have been started up in UNCTAD (⇛ UNITED NATIONS CONFERENCE ON TRADE AND DEVELOPMENT) to see if some agreement can be reached about their future role.

Flat yield. A YIELD on a fixed-interest SECURITY calculated by expressing the annual interest payable as a proportion of the purchase price of the security. It omits any allowance for the difference between the purchase price and the redemption price. (⇛ REDEEMABLE SECURITIES).

Flexible exchange rate. ⇛ EXCHANGE RATE

Float. A balance arising from delays between receipts of cash and their credit to a bank account (deposit collection float) or from the issue of a check and the debit to the issuer's account (check payment float). The former has a negative effect upon the cash requirements of a business and the latter a positive effect.

Floating asset. ⇛ FLOATING CAPITAL

Floating capital. CAPITAL that is not invested in fixed ASSETS, such as machinery, but in work in progress, wages paid, etc. Synonomous with working capital. (⇛⇛ CURRENT RATIO).

Floating charge. An assignment of the total ASSETS of a company or individual as collateral for a DEBT, as opposed to particular assets, when such an assignment is called a fixed charge.

Floating exchange rate. ⇛ EXCHANGE RATE

Flow of funds. Social accounts (⇛ SOCIAL ACCOUNTING) of the sources and uses of finance. Data regularly published by the Federal Reserve Board show, for example, in MATRIX form, the various types of credit instrument (BONDS, MORTGAGES, etc.) and the sectors and amounts of funds supplied by the financial sector, government, business and households.

FOB (free on board). A term describing the valuation of goods including all costs up to the point of embarkation at the border. It is an alternative expression for free alongside ship. It contrasts with CIF (charged in full) which is the valuation that includes all transport costs and insurance to final overseas destination.

Food and Agricultural Organization (FAO). An organization set up in 1945 within the framework of the United Nations. Headquartered in Rome, it conducts research and offers technical assistance with the aim of improving the standards of living of agricultural areas. It is concerned with the improvement of PRODUCTIVITY and distribution networks for the agricultural, forestry and fishing industries. It conducts surveys, issues statistics, produces forecasts of the world food situation and sets minimum nutritional standards.

Food and Drug Administration. ⇛ REGULATION

Foreign balance. ⇛ BALANCE OF PAYMENTS

Foreign exchange. Claims on another country held in the form of the currency of that country or interest-bearing BONDS. (⇛⇛ GOLD AND FOREIGN EXCHANGE RESERVES).

Foreign exchange market. The MARKET in which transactions are conducted to effect the transfer of the CURRENCY of one country into that of another. The market is not located at a single center but is international, with transactions conducted by telephone and data transmitted electronically. The need to settle accounts with foreigners gave rise to the foreign bill of exchange, which was accepted by banks or other institutions of international standing. These bills were traded at discount, and in this way the foreign exchange market was established, the bills reflecting actual international trade flows. However, the market has developed in modern times and is now dominated by financial institutions that buy and sell foreign currencies, making their PROFIT from the divergences between the EXCHANGE RATES and RATES OF INTEREST between the various financial centers. (⇛ ARBITRAGE; CONVERTIBILITY; FORWARD EXCHANGE MARKET).

Foreign investment. The acquisition by institutions or individuals in one country of ASSETS in another. Foreign investment is defined to cover both direct investment and PORTFOLIO investment and includes investment by public authorities, private firms and individuals. For a country in which SAVINGS are insufficient relative to the potential demand for INVESTMENT, foreign capital can be a fruitful means of stimulating rapid growth. Canada in particular has benefited in this way, with foreign investment reaching as much as $925 million in 1971. In 1976 Canada experienced negative foreign investment after more than two decades of a positive inflow. By 1982 Canadians were making large investments in the United States, to the extent that the issue was brought before a congressional subcommittee. Some countries have passed laws limiting foreign investment. In addition, direct investment may be a means of easing the strain on the BALANCE OF PAYMENTS that might otherwise occur in response to an increase of home demand. Direct investment often involves the setting up of subsidiary companies for the production of COMMODITIES abroad that previously were imported from the parent company. Concern in Canada about U.S. ownership of Canadian companies through direct investment led to the establishment of the Foreign Investment Review Agency (FIRA), which monitors and approves or disallows takeovers of Canadian businesses. In 1980 U.S. direct investment abroad totaled $18.5 billion compared with foreign direct investment in the United States of $10.9 billion.

Foreign Operations Administration. ⇛ ECONOMIC COOPERATION ADMINISTRATION

Formula flexibility. A type of BUILT-IN STABILIZER whereby tax rates would, for example, decline when the unemployment rate exceeded a predetermined level. Tax rates would automatically rise in periods of rapid expansion and inflation. The procedure could be applied to monetary control as well: The rate of growth of the money supply could be automatically decelerated or accelerated in response to selected economic indicators.

Forward exchange market. A MARKET in which contracts are made to supply CURRENCIES at fixed dates in the future at fixed PRICES. Currencies may be bought and sold in the FOREIGN EXCHANGE MARKET either "spot" or "forward" (⇛ FORWARD MARKET; SPOT MARKET). In the former case the transaction takes place immediately, and it is in this market that EXCHANGE RATES are kept at their managed levels by government intervention. In the forward exchange market, currencies are bought and sold for transacting at some future date, i.e., in three months' or six months' time. The difference between the "spot" rate of exchange and the "forward" rate is determined by the RATE OF INTEREST and the exchange risk; that is, the possibility of APPRECIATION or DEPRECIATION of the currencies transacted. Therefore, the size of the PREMIUM or DISCOUNT of forward dollars compared with spot dollars indicates the strength of the market's expectation of an appreciation or depreciation of dollars and its extent.

Forward market. Any MARKET in FUTURES; that is to say, a market in which promises to buy or to sell SECURITIES or COMMODITIES at some future date at fixed PRICES are bought and sold. An example of a forward market is the FORWARD EXCHANGE MARKET.

Fractional reserve banking. ⇛ REQUIRED RESERVES

Freedom of entry. Ability of a new supplier to enter the MARKET for a good (⇛ ECONOMIC GOOD). Entry is free when BARRIERS TO ENTRY do not exist. (⇛⇛ PERFECT COMPETITION).

Free exchange rates. ⇛ EXCHANGE RATE

Free goods. Goods that are not relatively scarce and therefore do not have a PRICE, e.g., fresh air, seawater.

Free market. A MARKET in which the forces of SUPPLY and DEMAND are allowed to operate unhampered by government regulation or other interference.

Free-market economy. An economy in which RESOURCES are allowed to be allocated by the operation of FREE MARKETS. (⇛⇛ PRICE SYSTEM).

Free on board. ⇛ FOB

Free port. A port that will accept cargo without the imposition of any tariff (⇛ TARIFFS, IMPORT) or tax.

Free trade. The condition in which the free flow of goods (⇛ ECONOMIC GOOD) and SERVICES in international exchange is neither restricted nor encouraged by direct government intervention. Now virtually an archaism, since all governments are heavily involved today in regulating overseas trade. The most common means of affecting the distribution and level of international trade are import tariffs (⇛ TARIFFS, IMPORT), import QUOTAS and export subsidies (⇛ EXPORT INCENTIVES). It has been broadly accepted among economists that an international free-trade policy is desirable to optimize world output and INCOME levels in the long run. The ORGANIZATION FOR ECONOMIC COOPERATION AND DEVELOPMENT and the United Nations are both committed to freeing world trade, but most economists would agree that under present conditions complete freedom of trade would not be desirable. In any case, it is clear that individual countries could gain from protectionism (⇛ CUSTOMS UNION; INFANT INDUSTRY ARGUMENT; PROTECTION). Toward the end of the 18th century, there was a reaction against MERCANTILISM, which had advocated government intervention to obtain surpluses on VISIBLE TRADE. This reaction gathered strength in a new economic liberalism and the doctrine of LAISSEZ-FAIRE. The classical economists' (⇛ CLASSICAL ECONOMICS) support of a free-trade policy was not so much based on specific economic analyses of international trade as simply part of their general belief in what ADAM SMITH called the "hidden hand": The greatest good is achieved if each individual is left to seek his own PROFIT. The free-trade era lasted in England for almost a century. After the First World War, economic nationalism reached its peak, and free trade was abandoned for protectionism. However, since the end of the Second World War, there has been a general acceptance internationally of the dangers of protectionism and some reduction in INTERNATIONAL TRADE barriers, especially for manufactured goods. Progress has been slow and has paradoxically been associated with the growth of regional CUSTOMS UNIONS. (⇛⇛ GENERAL AGREEMENT ON TARIFFS AND TRADE; EUROPEAN ECONOMIC COMMUNITY).

Free-trade area. An association of a number of countries between whom all import tariffs (⇛ TARIFFS, IMPORTS) and QUOTAS and export subsidies and other similar government measures to influence trade (⇛ EXPORT INCENTIVES) have been removed. Each country, however, continues to retain its own INTERNATIONAL TRADE measures *vis-a-vis* countries outside the association. (⇛⇛ CUSTOMS UNION; EUROPEAN FREE TRADE ASSOCIATION).

Free-trade zones. A customs-defined area in which goods or SERVICES may be processed or transacted without attracting taxes (⇛ TAXATION) or duties or being subjected to certain government regulations. A special case is the free port, into which goods are imported free of customs duties. Free port zones have been approved at 56 centers in the United States, of which about 30 are operational. In these, customs duties are not paid until, and if, the goods are sold in the United States outside the zone. A plan was proposed in 1977 and approved by the Federal Reserve Bank (⇛ FEDERAL RESERVE SYSTEM) in 1980 for the setting up of free zones for banks dealing in international finance. This enables the banks to service the accounts of multinational firms without attracting city and state taxes and also to be free from the normal banking regulations, such as the FED's (⇛ FEDERAL RESERVE

SYSTEM) reserve requirements and RATE OF INTEREST ceilings. They will, however, have to insure their deposits with the Federal Deposit Insurance Corporation (⇛⇛ BANKING). The first free-trade zone ever set up in the United States was at Staten Island. The first inland zone, privately operated, is at Kansas City. There are about 350 free port zones throughout the world. (⇛ ENTERPRISE ZONE; EURODOLLAR).

Frequency distribution. A table or graph that shows how a group of items is distributed according to their values of some particular measurable attribute. It is prepared by dividing the range of values of the attribute up into classes and by counting the number of items having values in each class. For example, suppose that the heights (the attribute) of 50 people (the items) range from 5 feet 3 inches to 6 feet 5 inches. We could define five classes of 3 inches each (where 3 inches would be called the "class interval"). The classes are shown in the table below. By assigning each height to the appropriate class, the number of people falling in each class can be entered alongside the classes. The table illustrates, then, a frequency distribution of a group of people by height.

Height		Frequency
5′3″ or over, and under 5′6″		4
5′6″ or over, and under 5′9″		15
5′9″ or over, and under 6′0″		25
6′0″ or over, and under 6′3″		5
6′3″ or over, and under 6′6″		1
	Total	50

The "frequency" is the number of items falling in each class. The table shows how these frequencies are distributed over the classes of the VARIABLE.

Frequency distributions are used extensively in presenting numerical information in the social sciences. For example, the distribution of firms (the items) by some measure of size (the attribute); distribution of households by INCOME (the "INCOME DISTRIBUTION"); distribution of cities by POPULATION; distribution of people by age, height, weight, number of years spent in full-time education; and so on. The usefulness of the frequency distribution lies in the fact that it is a reasonably concise way of presenting a great deal of information while at the same time showing clearly the underlying characteristics of the data, especially the "central tendency" of the data (⇛ AVERAGE) and the extent and evenness of dispersion about the central values. (⇛ VARIANCE).

Frictional unemployment. UNEMPLOYMENT resulting from the time lags involved in the redeployment of LABOR. Even if the number of vacancies for each type of labor were exactly equal to the number seeking employment, so that in principle there should be no unemployment, in practice it takes time for the unemployed to find vacancies, be interviewed and taken on. At any one time, therefore, there will be a small pool of unemployment owing to these "frictions" in the working of the LABOR MARKET. Frictional unemployment can be reduced by improving the mechanism by which employers and unemployed are brought together—that is, by increasing the efficiency of "search"—but it cannot be eliminated altogether.

Friedman, Milton (1912–). Professor of economics at the University of Chicago and leading member of the "Chicago school." After a short period with the Natural Resources Commission in Washington, Professor Friedman joined the research staff of the National Bureau of Economic Research in 1937 and, apart from a short period, he has maintained a close association with this important research organization. During the Second World War, he served in the Tax Research Division of the U.S. Treasury. In 1946 he was appointed associate professor of economics and statistics at the University of Chicago, becoming professor of economics there in 1948. In 1976 he was awarded the Alfred NOBEL Memorial Prize in Economics by the Royal Swedish Academy of Science. His main published works in economics include *Taxing to Prevent Inflation* (1943), *Essays in Positive Economics* (1953), *A Theory of the Consumption Function* (1957), *A Program for Monetary Stability* (1960), *Price Theory* (1962), *A Monetary History of the United States 1867–1960* (1963), *Inflation Causes and Consequences* (1963), *The Great Contraction* (1965), *The Optimum Quantity of Money* (1969) and *A Theoretical Framework for Monetary Analysis* (1971).

Friedman has made contributions to the THEORY OF DISTRIBUTION, arguing for an approach in which high incomes are regarded as a reward for taking risks. He has also been a leading defender of the Marshallian tradition in MICROECONOMICS (⇛ MARSHALL, ALFRED) and made a methodological defense of classical economics that stimulated controversy for a decade. His PERMANENT INCOME HYPOTHESIS was also an important contribution to the theory of the CONSUMPTION FUNCTION.. His main work, however, has been on the development of the QUANTITY THEORY OF MONEY and its empirical testing. He has extended the Fisher equation (⇛ FISHER, IRVING) to include other VARIABLES such as WEALTH and RATES OF INTEREST, and made statistical tests to attempt to measure the factors determining the demand for money to hold. Friedman has advocated strict control of the MONEY SUPPLY as a means for cutting INFLATION. (⇛ LIQUIDITY PREFERENCE; UNEMPLOYMENT, NATURAL RATE OF).

Fringe Benefits. Compensation for employment over and above wages and salaries. They include such items as pension arrangements, medical and dental programs, paid holidays, sick leave and maternity leave. Fringe benefits plus wages and salaries constitute total labor compensation. Such benefits are attractive because they are not subject to income tax. They have become increasingly important in collective bargaining agreements. For example, in 1980 the average annual wage paid to an automobile worker was $19,800, but the average total cost to the company including fringe benefits was $31,700.

Full employment surplus (FES). This is the government's BUDGET balance that would occur if the economy were operating at full-employment capacity (⇛ EMPLOYMENT, FULL) given fixed or unchanged budget parameters (tax rates, benefit schedules). It is used to distinguish discretionary fiscal policy from BUILT-IN STABILIZERS by comparing the FES of two or more years. An increase in the FES would indicate restrictive policy, since such a change would require an increase in tax rates or a reduction in expenditures. A decline in the FES would indicate expansionary fiscal policy. In contrast, a change in the actual budget balance could be the result of either discretionary fiscal policy or budget items, e.g., taxes simply responding to a change in income. (⇛⇛ FISCAL DRAG).

Full-line forcing. The practice whereby a seller forces a buyer to take several products, rather than just one of them, and hence forces him to take a "full line." It can be used most effectively when the seller has a MONOPOLY in some of the products but has competitors in the others. The full-line force can then be used to extend the monopoly power of the firm at the expense of competing firms. An example of a full-line force would be where color film is sold "process-paid"; that is, on purchase of the film, the buyer would also pay a charge for developing the negatives. The buyer does not have the option of buying the film separately from the processing.

Funding. The refinancing of debt by retiring SECURITIES or paying off bank LOANS and issuing new securities. Generally, the process of converting short-term to long-term DEBT by the sale of long-term securities to pay off short-term debt. Funding may be carried out by a company because its CAPITAL STRUCTURE is inappropriate, i.e., to take advantage of the fact that long-term CAPITAL is normally cheaper and less likely to be withdrawn than short-term capital. Companies or governments may also take advantage of a period of low RATES OF INTEREST to repay long-term BONDS at the earliest possible date and replace them with new bonds at lower rates of interest. Funding has also been used as an instrument of MONETARY POLICY by the government as well as for NATIONAL DEBT management.

Futures. Contracts made in a "futures MARKET" for the purchase or sale of COMMODITIES on a specified future date. Futures are traded on commodity exchanges in many financial centers all over the world and especially in London, New York and Chicago. The commodities covered include wool, cotton, grains, metals, tropical foodstuffs, livestock and, more recently, petroleum products. Forward commodity markets permit manufacturers and traders to hedge against changes in PRICE of the raw materials they use or deal in. There are similar markets in SECURITIES and foreign currencies. (⇛ FORWARD EXCHANGE MARKET; SPECULATION).

G

Galbraith, John Kenneth (1908–). A leading American political economist, he was born in Canada, and after graduating at Toronto in agriculture, he took a Ph.D. at the University of California. In 1949 he became professor of economics at Harvard University and was, from 1961 to 1963, U.S. ambassador to India. His major books include *A Theory of Price Control* (1952), *American Capitalism* (1952), *The Great Crash 1929* (1955), *The Affluent Society* (1958), *The Economic Discipline* (1967), *Economics, Peace and Laughter* (1971), *Economics and the Public Purpose* (1974) and *The Nature of Mass Poverty* (1979). He has been a sharp critic of current economic theory because of its preoccupation with growth (⇛ GROWTH THEORY). He has accused advanced societies of producing waste simply to satisfy the need for growth for its own sake. He has argued that in modern advanced economies the problems of the distribution (⇛ DISTRIBUTION, THEORY OF) of the total product to the different sectors of society should be given more attention. At the same time, he believes that academic theoretical economics is too bound by its old tradition of the efficacy of competition to the extent of losing touch with the real world. In *American Capitalism* he showed how modern society breeds monopolistic power systems. MONOPOLY in industry induces a countervailing monopoly or MONOPSONY in distribution, in LABOR and even in government purchasing agencies.

In *The New Industrial State* (1967) he argued that the "technostructure" (managers) of the largest corporations in modern industrial society is motivated primarily by a desire to remain secure and to expand its corporation rather than to maximize PROFITS. The highly capitalized nature of the industrial system has required a considerable extension of planning and control, notably of the CAPITAL supply, through SELF-FINANCING, and of DEMAND, through advertising and distribution techniques. Under these conditions, the assumption of CONSUMERS' SOVEREIGNTY that underlies modern microeconomic theory (⇛ MICROECONOMICS) is invalid and the theory no longer relevant to much of the economic system. Galbraith's views have been challenged by many economists as an overstatement of monopolistic power but are nonetheless sometimes accepted as an accurate statement of tendency in the modern economy. He has been critical of the advocates of the strict control of the supply of MONEY as a means of reducing INFLATION. (⇛⇛ CONSUMPTION; FIRM, THEORY OF; KEYNES, JOHN MAYNARD; MILL, JOHN STUART; OLIGOPOLY; QUANTITY THEORY OF MONEY).

Galiani, Ferdinando (1728–87). A Neapolitan priest who wrote a number of treatises on economic subjects, in particular *Della moneta* (1751), on MONEY and exchange, and *Dialogues sur le commerce des blés* (1770), on FREE TRADE in cereals. He resolved the so-called *paradox of value*—e.g., water is useful but cheap, whereas diamonds are useless but expensive—by analyzing the PRICE of a COMMODITY in terms of SCARCITY on the one hand and its UTILITY on the other, utility being a reflection not only of a commodity's usefulness but also of its pleasure-giving potential. He explained how price both influences and is influenced by DEMAND. Much of his work in VALUE theory was original, though part of a long tradition of ecclesiastical thought. However, he was not familiar to English-speaking economists of the early 19th century, and much of the ground covered by Galiani was gone over again by them. (⇛ MARGINAL UTILITY).

Galloping inflation. Picturesque term given to very rapid INFLATION, such as that which characterized Germany and several other European countries just after the First World War. PRICES rose so rapidly that MONEY quickly lost its VALUE; people lost confidence in the monetary system; and ultimately the system broke down, and people resorted to BARTER.

Games, theory of. A theoretical analysis of two types of situation: (1) the situation of pure conflict, where the gains made by one "player" are the losses of the other or others; and (2) the situation of mixed conflict and cooperation, where "players" may cooperate to increase their joint payoff, but conflict arises over its division. The theory attempts to abstract the essential elements of a wide range of economic, political and social situations. For example, the nuclear arms race, the behavior of oligopolists (⇛ OLIGOPOLY) and people playing poker can be shown to have important similarities that permit general analysis. Game theory is essentially concerned with the question of whether, in the various situations of conflict and cooperation, self-seeking behavior by the players will lead to a determinate EQUILIBRIUM. Its originators were J. von Neumann and O. Morgenstern.

Gearing. ⇛ LEVERAGE

General Agreement on Tariffs and Trade (GATT). An international organization with a secretariat in Geneva that came into operation in January 1948 as a result of an agreement made at an international conference the previous year, which also included plans for an INTERNATIONAL TRADE ORGANIZATION. Nothing came of the latter, but GATT has proved a useful body for international tariff (⇛ TARIFFS, IMPORT) bargaining. Its articles of agreement pledge its member countries, which now number 99, to the expansion of multilateral trade (⇛ MULTILATERALISM) with the minimum of barriers to trade, reduction in import tariffs and quotas, and the abolition of preferential trade agreements. There have been successive negotiations between the contracting parties, aimed at reducing the levels of tariffs, from the first meeting in Geneva in 1947 up to the seventh, the so-called TOKYO ROUND OF TRADE NEGOTIATIONS, which began in 1974 and was concluded in 1979. The first major revision of GATT was ratified in March 1955. The provisions regarding the treatment of SUBSIDIES designed to reduce IMPORTS or increase exports were strengthened. (⇛ EXPORT INCENTIVES) Members are required to give details of any subsidies, and if these are liable to prejudice the interests of any other member, they are required to discuss the possibility of reduction or elimination. On export subsidies, in particular, member governments "should seek to avoid" the use of subsidies on the export of primary products. For exports of other products, subsidies, whether direct or indirect, should cease "as soon as practicable" if they result in export prices lower than the home prices of the product. A new code of conduct regarding protection against subsidies was agreed to in the Tokyo Round. In 1965 a revision came into force of the section of the agreement dealing with trade and development that laid emphasis on the special problems of the DEVELOPING COUNTRIES, and a committee on trade and development was given the responsibility of working toward the elimination of barriers on the trade in products of particular interest to the developing countries. This new approach enables the MOST FAVORED NATION CLAUSE to be waived in relation to agreements entered into with developing countries. Since the completion of the Kennedy Round (⇛ KENNEDY ROUND OF TRADE NEGOTIATIONS), there has been a growing tendency for countries to become more protectionist (⇛ PROTECTION) through the imposition of non-tariff barriers and for economic blocs to make preferential trade agreements with other countries. Examples of the latter are the EUROPEAN ECONOMIC COMMUNITY with respect to countries in the Mediterranean, and the United States with respect to Latin America. Examples of non-tariff barriers are government agencies that direct purchases in favor of particular countries. New codes of conduct were agreed to in the Tokyo Round on these issues.

General Agreements to Borrow. ⇛ INTERNATIONAL MONETARY FUND

General equilibrium. The simultaneous existence of EQUILIBRIUM on all the MARKETS in an economy. Economists see the economy as being composed of a system of interrelated markets for FINAL PRODUCTS, INTERMEDIATE PRODUCTS and FACTORS OF PRODUCTION. HOUSEHOLDS sell their SERVICES in FACTOR MARKETS in return for INCOME, which they spend in product markets. Firms sell in final or intermediate product markets, receiving revenue, which is then paid out to factors of production. Equilibrium exists in any one market when SUPPLY equals DEMAND. In a general equilibrium system, however, all markets are interdependent, and so general equilibrium exists only when supply equals demand in all markets in the economy. (⇛⇛ GENERAL EQUILIBRIUM ANALYSIS; WALRAS, MARIE ESPRIT LEON).

General equilibrium analysis. 1. An examination of the following questions: (*a*) In the model of GENERAL EQUILIBRIUM, under what conditions will there *exist* a set of PRICES at which the economy will be in EQUILIBRIUM, with SUPPLY equal to DEMAND in every market? (*b*) Is equilibrium in the model *stable,* in the sense that if the economy is initially not at an equilibrium, the process of change that then takes place converges to an equilibrium position over time? (⇛⇛ TATONNEMENT PROCESS).

2. The analysis of the consequences of some economic change throughout the entire economy. Suppose, for example, we sought to find the consequences for an economy of the discovery of natural gas. This would involve examining the interrelations between the market for gas and other markets (electricity, coal, oil, domestic appliances, gas engineers) and the

interrelations between these and still other markets (for coal miners, electricity generating equipment, oil tankers) and so on, until the ramifications of the initial change have been traced throughout the economy. This type of analysis is to be contrasted with PARTIAL EQUILIBRIUM ANALYSIS, which considers only the effects of the change on the initial market or small group of related markets. Clearly, general equilibrium analysis is more complicated than partial equilibrium analysis, particularly as it must take the possibility of feedback into account, i.e., the possibility that induced changes in other markets react back onto the market in which the initial change occurred. The choice of methods of analysis therefore involves weighing up the relative complexities of the methods against the scope and accuracy of their conclusions. (⇛⇛ LEONTIEF, WASSILY W.; WALRAS, MARIE ESPRIT LEON).

Geneva Conference (1947). ⇛ GENERAL AGREEMENT ON TARIFFS AND TRADE

Genoa Conference (1922). ⇛ BRUSSELS CONFERENCE

Geometric progression. A series of numbers in which each value is a constant multiple of the preceding value: x, ax, a^2x, a^3x, ... a^nx. (⇛⇛ ARITHMETIC PROGRESSION).

George, Henry (1839–97). An American economist and politician who stood for election as mayor of New York for the "single tax" party. His major publication was *Progress and Poverty* (1879). He was considerably influenced by the English classical economists, ADAM SMITH, DAVID RICARDO and JOHN STUART MILL (⇛⇛ CLASSICAL ECONOMICS). Ricardo's analysis had drawn attention to the way in which agricultural production could yield an INCOME to landowners in the form of RENT, which was surplus to all costs, including normal PROFIT. J.S. Mill had suggested that all future additions to rental income should be taxed away. This would have the merit, George claimed, of enabling the TREASURY to be financed by one tax (⇛ TAXATION) only and of avoiding the distortions caused by multiple taxation of different economic activities. This idea has some affinity with *"l'impôt unique"* of the PHYSIOCRATS.

Giffen goods. Goods that do not obey the "law of DEMAND," namely, that less is bought as PRICE rises. Rather, the quantity demanded of a Giffen good falls as its price falls, and it therefore has a positively sloped DEMAND CURVE. The expression is named after Sir Robert Giffen, to whom is attributed the observation that, among the laboring classes, when the price of bread (the main item of their diet) rose, their consumption of bread rose, and when its price fell, their consumption of bread also fell. This he saw as a refutation of the "law of demand." However, Giffen goods are nowadays seen as special cases of standard demand analysis rather than refutations of it. If the total expenditure on a particular good by a consumer is a large proportion of INCOME, then changes in price of that good have a significant effect on REAL INCOME. If a good is an INFERIOR GOOD (a rise in consumer's income causes a fall in demand, a fall in income causes a rise in demand), it is then possible that a rise in price could cause an increase in demand, and a fall in price could cause a fall in demand, via this INCOME EFFECT. For quantity demanded actually to change in the same direction as price, it is not enough that the income effect work in the way just described; it must also be strong enough to outweigh the SUBSTITUTION EFFECT. Given a change in the price of a good, if the consumer's real income is held constant (by a compensating change in money income), the quantity of the good demanded will always change in the opposite direction to the price change: If the price rises, substitute goods whose prices have stayed the same are now relatively cheaper than the good in question and so will be substituted for the latter; if price falls, substitute goods will now be relatively more expensive, and the good in question will be substituted for them. The overall change in quantity of the good demanded, following a change in its price, is the result of these two effects—the income effect and the substitution effect. If the income effect works so as to change demand in the same direction as the price change (i.e., the good is an inferior good), while the substitution effect works so as to change demand in the opposite direction to the price change (always the case), and if the former effect outweighs the latter, the net effect is that the quantity demanded changes in the same direction as price. It was this special case that was observed by Giffen.

Giffen paradox. Refers to the observation by Sir Robert Giffen that a rise in the PRICE of bread caused more of it to be bought, contrary to the general idea that DEMAND varies inversely with price. However, this possibility is seen as an extreme case in the theory of demand rather than a refutation of it. (⇛⇛ GIFFEN GOODS).

Giffen, Sir Robert (1837–1910). ⇛ GIFFEN GOODS; GIFFEN PARADOX

Gift tax. A levy on the VALUE of certain property given away to others and paid by the donor. The federal gift tax is cumulative, but an annual exclusion is allowed up to a certain sum for gifts made to any one recipient. (⇛ DEATH DUTIES).

Gilt-edged securities. Fixed-interest British government SECURITIES traded on the London STOCK EXCHANGE. They are called gilt-edged because it is certain that interest will be paid and that they will be redeemed (where appropriate) on the due date. Gilt-edged securities are not, of course, a risk-free investment because of fluctuations in their market value. (⇛ YIELD).

Gini coefficient. A measure of inequality derived from the LORENZ CURVE. As the degree of inequality increases, so does the curvature of the Lorenz curve, and thus the area between the curve and the 45° line becomes larger. The gini coefficient is measured as:

$$G = \frac{\text{Area between Lorenz curve and 45° line}}{\text{Area below the 45° line}}$$

If there is perfect equality, the Lorenz curve would coincide with the 45° line, and so $G = 0$. (⇛ CONCENTRATION RATIO).

Giro system. ⇛ CREDIT TRANSFER, OR GIRO

Glass-Steagall Act. This Act, passed in 1933, was the most comprehensive change in banking legislation since the Federal Reserve Act of 1913. The Act introduced more rigid control over the activities of COMMERCIAL BANKS that are members of the FEDERAL RESERVE SYSTEM. It paved the way for the establishment of FEDERAL DEPOSIT INSURANCE and gave statutory recognition to the FEDERAL OPEN MARKET COMMITTEE. The final bill was an amalgam of legislation proposed by Senator Glass and Representative Steagall in May of 1933 in response to the public outcry that became widespread with the collapse of several U.S. banks and the revelation of questionable practices in the financial system.

GNP gap. The difference between the actual level of GROSS NATIONAL PRODUCT and the level of GNP corresponding to the rate of unemployment that would not cause inflation to accelerate. (⇛ NATURAL RATE OF UNEMPLOYMENT).

Gold and foreign exchange reserves. The stock of gold and foreign CURRENCIES held by a country to finance any calls that may be made from its creditors for the settlement of DEBT. The extent of these requests for settlement are dependent, first, on the size of the outstanding LIABILITIES, which, in turn, is related to the BALANCE OF PAYMENTS surplus or DEFICIT; and second, on the willingness of creditors to hold the debt (currency) in question. Pressure on the reserves may therefore be either a reflection of the underlying trading problems of the country or the expectation of a fall in the EXCHANGE RATE of the country's currency. The official published figures of reserves, however, do not necessarily reflect the total amount of gold and foreign currency that could be used to meet obligations any more than an individual's CHECKING ACCOUNT at the bank represents his total assets. The reserves exclude, for instance, the CREDIT facilities available through the INTERNATIONAL MONETARY FUND and PORTFOLIO foreign investments.

Gold exchange standard. A special form of the GOLD STANDARD. In this system the CENTRAL BANK will not exchange its CURRENCY for gold on demand (as is the case under the gold standard) but will exchange it for a currency that is itself on the gold standard. The central bank holds the latter country's currency in its reserves along with gold itself. The Scandinavian countries adopted this system with respect to sterling up until 1931, when the United Kingdom came off the gold standard.

Gold points. ⇛ SPECIE POINTS

Gold standard. A country is said to be on the gold standard when its CENTRAL BANK is obliged to give gold in exchange for any of its CURRENCY presented to it. The gold standard was central to the classical economic (⇛ CLASSICAL ECONOMICS) view of the equilibrating processes in INTERNATIONAL TRADE. The fact that each currency was freely convertible into gold fixed the EXCHANGE RATES between currencies (⇛ SPECIE POINTS), and all international debts were settled in gold. A BALANCE OF PAYMENTS surplus caused an inflow of gold into the central bank's reserves. This enabled the central bank to expand the money supply without fear of having insufficient gold to meet its LIABILITIES. The increase in the quantity of money (⇛ MONEY SUPPLY) raised prices, resulting in a fall in the demand for EXPORTS and therefore a reduction in the balance of payments surplus. The reverse happened in the event of a DEFICIT.

Most of the important trading nations maintained a gold standard of some kind until the 1930s, with the exception of the period of disruption caused by World War I. The system finally collapsed in the slump of the 1930s. The United States suspended dollar CONVERTIBILITY in 1933 and banned exports of gold. However, convertibility was subsequently restored, and gold was fixed at $35 per ounce at BRETTON WOODS. It was raised by the SMITHSONIAN AGREEMENT in 1971 to $38 per ounce and again in 1973 to $42 per ounce. This official price was finally abandoned in 1976, and gold was removed from the articles of the INTERNATIONAL MONETARY FUND. (⇛⇛ BANKING AND CURRENCY SCHOOLS; GOLD EXCHANGE STANDARD).

Gossen, Hermann Heinrich (1810–58). Born in Duren, near Aachen, in Germany, Gossen studied law and went into government service in deference to his father's wishes. It was not until after his father's death in 1847 that he dedicated himself to the study of economics. His major economic work is *Entwicklung der Gesetze des menschlichen Verkehrs und der daraus fliessenden Regeln für menschliches Handeln* (1854). In this book Gossen set out a theory of consumer behavior based on ideas that were subsequently to be independently rediscovered in their work on MARGINAL UTILITY by WILLIAM STANLEY JEVONS, CARL MENGER and MARIE ESPRIT LEON WALRAS. The first edition of his book was completely ignored, and Gossen's recognition had to wait until after his death. It was Jevons who, in the preface to his own *Theory of Political Economy* (1891), drew attention to the significance of Gossen's achievement, admitting that Gossen had "completely anticipated him as regards the general principles and methods of economics." Gossen's first law states that the pleasure obtained from each additional amount consumed of the same COMMODITY diminishes until satiety is reached. Gossen's second law states that once a person had spent his entire INCOME, he would have maximized his total pleasure from it only if the satisfaction gained from the last item of each commodity bought was the same for each commodity. Gossen's third law, derived from the first two, states that a commodity has a subjective VALUE, and the subjective value of each additional unit owned diminishes and eventually reaches zero. (⇛ BERNOULLI'S HYPOTHESIS).

Government expenditure. ⇛ BUDGET

Government National Mortgage Association. A federal agency that guarantees securities backed by federally insured MORTGAGES. The securities are issued by THRIFTS, which initiate the mortgages, and these are sold to PENSION FUNDS or INSURANCE companies. Roughly 20 percent of household-financed assets are held in such institutions.

Gresham's Law. If two coins are in circulation whose relative FACE VALUES differ from their relative BULLION content, the "dearer" coin will be extracted from circulation for melting down. "BAD MONEY DRIVES OUT GOOD." The law is named after Sir Thomas Gresham (1519–79), a leading Elizabethan businessman and financial adviser to Queen Elizabeth I.

Gross cash flow. ⇛ CASH FLOW

Gross domestic product (GDP). A measure of the total flow of goods and services produced by the economy over a specified time period, normally a year. It is obtained by valuing outputs of goods and services at MARKET prices and then aggregating. Note that all INTERMEDIATE PRODUCTS are excluded, and only goods used for final CONSUMPTION or investment goods (⇛ CAPITAL) are included. This is because the VALUES of intermediate goods are already implicitly included in the PRICES of the final goods. The word *gross* means that no deduction for the value of expenditure on capital goods for replacement purposes is made. Because the INCOME arising from INVESTMENTS and possessions owned abroad is not included, only the value of the flow of goods and services produced in the country is estimated; hence, the word *domestic* to distinguish it from the GROSS NATIONAL PRODUCT. Since no adjustment is made for indirect taxes (⇛ DIRECT TAXATION) and SUBSIDIES, the measure here defined is often referred to as "Gross domestic product at market prices." (⇛⇛ GROSS DOMESTIC PRODUCT AT FACTOR COST).

Gross domestic product at factor cost. In measuring GROSS DOMESTIC PRODUCT, MARKET prices are used to value outputs so that they can be aggregated. This implies that, to the extent that market prices include indirect taxes, i.e., SALES TAX and SUBSIDIES, the VALUE of output will not equal the value of INCOMES paid out to FACTORS OF PRODUCTION. This is because it is the revenue received by firms after indirect taxes (⇛ DIRECT TAXATION) that is distributed as factor incomes. Thus, by subtracting the total of indirect taxes (and, since subsidies have the opposite effect of taxes, by adding in subsidies) from the GDP, we arrive at the estimate of the GDP at factor cost, which is consistent with the value of incomes paid to factors of production.

Gross investment. INVESTMENT expenditure inclusive of replacement of worn-out and obsolescent plant and equipment, i.e., inclusive of DEPRECIATION. (⇛ NET INVESTMENT).

Gross margin. In a retail business the margin on a sale that is the difference between the purchase PRICE and the price paid by the retailer, i.e., it makes no allowance for overheads or tax (⇛ FIXED ASSETS; TAXATION). The gross margin is often referred to as *gross profit*. (⇛ PROFIT).

Gross national expenditure. ⇛ NATIONAL INCOME

Gross national product (GNP). GROSS DOMESTIC PRODUCT plus the INCOME accruing to domestic residents arising from INVESTMENT abroad less income earned in the domestic market accruing to foreigners abroad.

Gross national product at factor cost. GROSS NATIONAL PRODUCT at MARKET prices minus all indirect taxes (⇛ DIRECT TAXATION) and SUBSIDIES. (⇛⇛ GROSS DOMESTIC PRODUCT AT FACTOR COST).

Gross national product at market prices. GROSS NATIONAL PRODUCT with all flows valued at MARKET prices. Since market prices include indirect taxes (⇛ DIRECT TAXATION) and SUBSIDIES, and since taxes and subsidies are regarded simply as TRANSFER PAYMENTS, it is often preferable to measure national output excluding these. This gives the measure of national output, net of TAXATION and subsidies, known as GROSS NATIONAL PRODUCT AT FACTOR COST.

Gross national product deflator. A price INDEX NUMBER used to correct MONEY values of GROSS NATIONAL PRODUCT for PRICE changes, so as to isolate the changes that have taken place in the physical output of goods (⇛ ECONOMIC GOOD) and services.

Gross profit. ⇛ GROSS MARGIN; PROFIT

Group of Ten. ⇛ INTERNATIONAL MONETARY FUND

Growth theory. That part of economics which is concerned with analyzing the determinants of the rate at which an economy will grow over time. By the growth of an economy, we mean the growth in its major economic aggregates: NATIONAL INCOME, CONSUMPTION, total employment and stock of CAPITAL. (⇛⇛ ECONOMIC GROWTH; HARROD-DOMAR MODEL; OPTIMAL GROWTH THEORY; TURNPIKE THEOREMS).

H

Hard currency. A CURRENCY traded in a FOREIGN EXCHANGE MARKET for which DEMAND is persistently high relative to the SUPPLY. (⇛ SOFT CURRENCY).

Harrod-Domar model. A model that analyzes the determinants of the rate of growth of NATIONAL INCOME in an economy. It was first formulated independently by the English economist Sir R. F. Harrod and the American Evsey D. Domar. It is based upon JOHN MAYNARD KEYNES' model of national income determination and is generally regarded as the starting point for all modern analyses of the process of economic growth in developed economies.

The model assumes first a very rigid form of technology: Total national output in any period is produced with CAPITAL and LABOR, which must be used in a *fixed proportion.* Let us say, for example, that 1 unit of output requires 2 units of labor and 1 unit of capital. If the economy possesses, say, 10 units of labor and 5 of capital, it can produce 5 units of output (which reflects a constant RETURNS TO SCALE assumption). Moreover, because of the fixed-proportions requirement, still only 5 units of output could be produced with 15 units of labor and 5 units of capital, or 10 units of labor and 10 units of capital—the labor or capital in excess of that implied by the fixed-proportions requirement would simply be surplus or unemployed. It follows that the growth rate of output must be the *lower* of the growth rate of capital and the growth rate of labor, e.g., if labor doubled to 20 units while capital increased by only 50 percent to 7.5 units, then output can increase by only 50 percent to 15 units, and 5 units of labor will be unnecessary or unemployed. But if capital doubled while labor increased by 50 percent, output could again only grow to 7.5 units, and there would be surplus capital. Clearly, only if capital and labor are growing at the same rate, which will also be the rate at which output grows, can there be full employment of *both* inputs.

The model then proceeds by considering, first, the rate of growth of output that would be determined by growth in capital, ignoring labor; and second, the rate of growth of output that would be determined by growth in labor, ignoring capital. It is assumed that households save a fixed proportion of their income—say, 20 percent—and that this is then all invested by business. If each extra unit of capital provided by this investment adds 1 unit of output, it follows that output must also grow by 20 percent. More generally, if the proportion of income saved by households is s, and 1 unit of output requires v units of capital to produce it, then the growth rate in output is s/v. Harrod called this the "warranted growth rate," since it is the growth in output made possible by the savings behavior of households and investment decisions of corporations. s is in fact Keynes' MARGINAL PROPENSITY TO SAVE, while v is the inverse of the incremental CAPITAL OUTPUT RATIO. (⇛ ACCELERATION PRINCIPLE).

On the side of labor input, it is assumed that the labor force is growing at some rate n, for reasons that are exogenous (⇛ EXOGENOUS VARIABLE) to the model. Moreover, labor productivity is growing at the rate p. Hence, assuming capital imposes no constraints, output would grow at the rate $n + p$, due to the effective growth in labor input. This Harrod called the "natural growth rate."

In general, there is no reason for the warranted and natural growth rates to coincide—each is determined independently of the other. But if the warranted rate were below the natural rate, output would not be growing fast enough to absorb all the labor that is becoming available, and increasing UNEMPLOYMENT would result. If the warranted rate were above the natural rate, actual output could not grow fast enough to use to capacity all the capital corporations are installing, thus falsifying their expectations. Only if the two rates *happen* to be equal would BALANCED GROWTH be possible. The conclusions of the model are therefore very pessimistic: Only by an improbable accident would there not be growing unemployment of one input or the other. This result, however, follows from the extreme rigidities of the model: fixed input proportions in production, a fixed propensity to save and exogenously given growth rates of labor and productivity. Much of the rest of GROWTH THEORY is concerned with showing that, by introducing a reasonable degree of flexibility in one of these respects, balanced growth becomes much more probable, if not certain.

Hawley-Smoot Act. An Act of the U.S. Congress in 1928 that imposed tariffs on the value of IMPORTS in an attempt to protect domestic industry. (⇛⇛ PROTECTION).

Hayek, Friedrich August von (1899–). Born in Vienna, Hayek was director of the Austrian Institute for Economic Research from 1927 to 1931 and lectured at Vienna University. In 1931 he was appointed Tooke Professor of Economic Science and Statistics at the London School of Economics, a post he held until 1950. From 1950 until 1962 he was professor of social and moral science at Chicago University. He was professor of economics at the University of Freiburg until 1969, when he was appointed visiting professor of economics at the University of Salzburg. In 1974 he received the Alfred Nobel Memorial Prize (⇛ NOBEL PRIZES) in Economics jointly with GUNNAR KARL MYRDAL. His published works include *Monetary Theory and the Trade Cycle* (1929), *Prices and Production* (1931), *Profits, Interest, Investment* (1939), *The Pure Theory of Capital* (1941), *Individualism and Economic Order* (1948), *The Constitution of Liberty* (1961), *Studies in Philosophy, Politics and Economics* (1967), *Law, Legislation and Liberty,* 3 volumes (1973–79), *Denationalization of Money* (1976) and *New Studies in Philosophy, Politics, Economics and the History of Ideas* (1978).

A member of the AUSTRIAN SCHOOL, Hayek elaborated the TRADE CYCLE theory of LUDWIG EDLER VON MISES by integrating it with EUGEN VON BOHM-BAWERK'S theory of CAPITAL. In a boom REAL WAGES fall because of the rise in prices, and firms therefore switch to less "roundabout" (CAPITAL-INTENSIVE) methods of production. In consequence, INVESTMENT in total is reduced. In RECESSION, the reverse situation induces "roundabout" production methods, and investment is stimulated. (⇛⇛ ACCELERATION PRINCIPLE; KEYNES, JOHN MAYNARD; RICARDO EFFECT).

Heckscher-Ohlin principle. The law of comparative advantage (⇛ DAVID RICARDO) had been established by economists as an explanation for the existence and pattern of international trade based on the relative COST advantages between different countries of producing different commodities. The law says nothing about why or how a comparative advantage exists. The Heckscher-Ohlin principle states that advantage arises from the different relative factor (⇛ FACTORS OF PRODUCTION) endowments of the countries trading. A country will export those commodities that are intensive (⇛ CAPITAL-INTENSIVE; LABOR INTENSIVE) in the factor in which it is most well endowed. The principle was first put forward by Eli F. Heckscher (1879–1952) in an article published in 1919 and reprinted in *Readings in the Theory of International Trade* (1949). It was refined by BERTIL OHLIN in his *Interregional and International Trade* (1933). The principle has been developed further by Professor PAUL ANTHONY SAMUELSON in his factor price equalization theorem.

Heller-Pechman plan. ⇛ FISCAL FEDERALISM

Hicks, Sir John Richard (1904–). Educated at Balliol College, Oxford, England, Hicks lectured at the London School of Economics from 1926 until 1935, when he became a fellow of Gonville and Caius College, Cambridge. In 1938 he was appointed to the chair of political economy at the University of Manchester. In 1946 he was made official fellow of Nuffield College, Oxford and in 1952 Drummond Professor of Political Economy at Oxford, a post he held until 1965. In 1972 he was awarded the Alfred Nobel Memorial Prize (⇛ NOBEL PRIZES) in Economics jointly with Professor KENNETH ARROW. His major published works include *The Theory of Wages* (1932), *Value and Capital* (1939), *The Social Framework* (1942), *A Contribution to the Theory of the Trade Cycle* (1950), *A Revision of Demand Theory* (1956), *Capital and Growth* (1965), *Critical Essays in Monetary Theory* (1967), *A Theory of Economic History* (1969), *Capital and Time: A Neo-Austrian Theory* (1976), *Economic Perspectives: Further Essays on Money and Growth* (1977) and *Causality in Economics* (1979).

In an article in *Economica* in 1934, Hicks and Professor R.G.D. Allen showed how the INDIFFERENCE CURVE could be used to analyze consumer behavior on the basis of ORDINAL UTILITY. Their exposition did give an important impetus to the development of this tool of analysis in economic theory (⇛⇛ SLUTSKY, EUGEN). In his work on the TRADE CYCLE, Hicks demonstrated by means of mathematical MODELS how the accelerator could induce several types of fluctuation in total output. (⇛ ACCELERATION PRINCIPLE).

Hidden economy. A term that refers to income flows that are not recorded in the GROSS NATIONAL PRODUCT (GNP) but nevertheless involve the production of goods and services and/or receipt of money for services rendered. Examples of transactions in the hidden economy would be the labor value in owner-builder homes, "moonlighting" or working for a cash-only fee that is not declared as income for tax or other purposes.

Peter Gutman, writing in *Challenge* (1979), estimated that the hidden or irregular economy was currently $200 billion, or 10 percent of GNP. Edward Feige, writing in the same publication, argued that the number could well be higher and has grown significantly in the 1960s and 1970s.

There is considerable controversy over the methods used to measure the hidden economy, since by its nature this is a difficult task. The Gutman method involves the following steps:

1. Calculate the ratio of CURRENCY to DEMAND DEPOSITS for the benchmark period 1937–41. Let this be X percent.

2. Estimate the currency required for legal transactions in 1976 as X percent of demand deposits in 1976. Call this Y.

3. Then actual currency in 1976 minus Y = cash for irregular or hidden transactions. Call this Z.

4. Hidden income generated by Z is then found by multiplying Z by the following ratio: Actual GNP/*Legal* currency + deposits.

Feige's method, which is more complex, involves analyzing how the relationship between total transactions and income changes. The change, he states, can be attributed to the relative prices of total to new goods, structural change and changes in the irregular or hidden economy. The first two factors can be calculated, leaving the residual as an estimate of the hidden economy.

Hidden hand. ⇛ INVISIBLE HAND; SMITH, ADAM

High powered money: The quantity of money held as reserves by the commercial banks (⇛⇛ BANKING). It is an ASSET for the commercial bank and held by the FEDERAL RESERVE SYSTEM as a liability. Reserves beyond those needed to fulfill the REQUIRED RESERVES can be loaned out and lead to an expansion of the MONEY SUPPLY.

Hoarding. The withdrawal of MONEY from active circulation by accumulating it rather than spending it on CONSUMPTION or buying ASSETS. It can be thought of as a withdrawal of money from the MARKET for borrowing and lending in order to hold it in idle balances. It represents, therefore, the net change in stocks of idle balances.

"Hog-cycle" phenomenon. ⇛ COBWEB THEOREM

Holding company. A company that controls one or more other companies, normally by holding a majority of the STOCK of these SUBSIDIARIES. Unlike an INVESTMENT TRUST, a holding company is concerned with control, and not with INVESTMENT, and may be economically justifiable where one holding company can perform financial, managerial or marketing functions for a number of subsidiaries. In its pure form a holding company performs no functions other than control or the provision of services to its subsidiaries, but most large corporations have large numbers of subsidiaries. The holding company form of organization has a number of practical advantages, e.g., it is a simpler and less expensive way of acquiring control of another company than by purchasing its ASSETS or by outright MERGER, and the original company can retain its name and goodwill. However, legal and fiscal considerations will also affect the choice of corporate structure. (⇛⇛ CORPORATE LAW).

Home loan banks. ⇛ FEDERAL HOME LOAN BANK BOARD

Homogeneous products. When the outputs of different firms are undifferentiated and perfect SUBSTITUTES in the eyes of consumers, then the product is said to be homogeneous. (⇛⇛ PERFECT COMPETITION; PRODUCT DIFFERENTIATION).

Horizontal merger. ⇛ MERGER; VERTICAL INTEGRATION

Hotelling, Harold (1895–). Associate professor of mathematics at Stanford University from 1927, Hotelling became professor of economics at Columbia University in 1931. He held this post until 1946, when he was appointed professor of mathematical statistics of the University of North Carolina. His article "The General Welfare in Relation to Problems of Taxation and of Railway and Utility Rates," published in *Econometrica* in 1938, put forward the case for MARGINAL COST PRICING by public utilities. He argued that even if, by so doing, such industries ran at a loss that had to be financed by lump-sum payments by the state, total economic welfare would be increased by such a pricing policy. (⇛ WELFARE ECONOMICS).

Household. An economic unit that is defined for the purpose of the CENSUS of POPULATION as a single person living alone or a group voluntarily living together, having meals prepared together and benefiting from housekeeping shared in common. Because of the fact of shared use, which is a household's characteristic, it is an important economic statistic when considering the MARKET potential for certain consumer products. The percentage of households owning consumer durables is critical to the growth of the future sales. In the initial introductory period, sales grow fast as households buy for the first time, but they slow down rapidly when a high proportion of the households own the product (⇛ LOGISTIC CURVE). Thereafter, sales can only be for replacement. The number of households in the United States in 1980 was about 80 million.

Housing and Home Finance Agency (HHFA). A U.S. government agency that supervises a number of other agencies concerned with providing housing MORTGAGES, federal assistance for low-rent public housing and technical assistance for urban planning.

Human capital. The skills, capacities and abilities possessed by an individual, which permit him to earn INCOME. We can thus regard income he derives from supplying labor SERVICES (as opposed to lending MONEY, letting property) as the return on the human capital he possesses. We can regard a period of formal or informal training and acquisition of these skills as a process of creating human capital, just as the construction of machinery, buildings, etc., creates physical CAPITAL.

Hume, David (1711–76). Scottish philosopher whose systematic treatment of economics is contained in several chapters of his *Political Discourses* (1752). He exposed as unwarranted the mercantilist fear (⇛ MERCANTILISM) of a chronic imbalance of trade and loss of gold. He argued that the international movement of BULLION and specie responded to the rise and fall of prices and in so doing kept national price differences within limits and prevented permanent BALANCE OF PAYMENTS surpluses or deficits. He also foresaw how this mechanism could be distorted by the growth of domestic BANKING and of paper money. He accepted a QUANTITY THEORY OF MONEY but distinguished between SHORT-RUN and LONG-RUN effects. By tracing the course of the effects of a rise in the quantity of MONEY, he came to the conclusion that money was not neutral but could affect employment, although only in the short run. His belief that the level of the RATE OF INTEREST depended on the rate of business profits became the basis of ADAM SMITH'S interest-rate theory. (⇛ INTEREST, CLASSICAL THEORY OF).

Hutcheson, Francis (1694–1746). The teacher of ADAM SMITH at Glasgow University, Scotland, Smith succeeded him to the Chair of Moral Philosophy.

Hyperinflation. A situation in a country where the rate of INFLATION rises at ever-increasing rates until the MONEY in that country ceases to be a reasonable store or measure of value between short-term periods. For example, a 100-mark note in Germany in September 1923 was worth ⅓ of a mark in October 1923.

Hypothesis. A statement about any set of phenomena that is capable of being refuted by confrontation with facts. A hypothesis is therefore a theoretical proposition, which may be right or wrong, as opposed to a *tautology,* which is always true by definition. Examples of hypotheses in economics are: (*a*) The quantity of a good (⇛ ECONOMIC GOOD) demanded depends on its PRICE; (*b*) consumers' expenditure is positively related to total DISPOSABLE INCOME; (*c*) firms attempt to maximize PROFITS; (*d*) the quantity of MONEY that individuals in the economy wish to hold depends on the level of NATIONAL INCOME, the general price level and the RATE OF INTEREST. Examples of tautologies in economics, on the other hand, are: (*a*) National income is equal to the sum of consumers' expenditure, INVESTMENT expenditure, government expenditure and EXPORTS minus IMPORTS; (*b*) the amount of a good bought is equal to the amount sold. Any field of study that adopts a scientific method proceeds by formulating hypotheses, testing them against facts, rejecting those that appear to be refuted, or reformulating and amending as the feedback of information from the testing deems appropriate. The procedure of formulating and testing hypotheses is the essence of the scientific method.

I

Impact effect. The immediate effect of some change or policy measure, in contrast to longer-term effects. The ultimate effect of the change will differ from the impact effect if certain forces are set in motion that take time to work themselves out but that gradually modify the initial change. The impact effect of a rise in DEMAND in a particular MARKET might be a sharp rise in PRICE. However, if this creates excess PROFITS, and if there are no BARRIERS TO ENTRY, new entrants will be attracted into the industry. The effect of this is to increase SUPPLY and reduce price as compared to the level resulting from the impact effect, and the ultimate effect might be a very small price rise. There is a close similarity here with the analysis of the SHORT RUN and LONG RUN in economics: The impact effect may be looked upon as the effect in the shortest of all runs.

Imperfect competition. ⇛ MONOPOLISTIC COMPETITION

Imperfect market. A MARKET in which the theoretical assumptions of PERFECT COMPETITION are not fulfilled. This may be because there are few buyers, few sellers, a non-HOMOGENEOUS PRODUCT, an inadequate flow of information or BARRIERS TO ENTRY. There are three types of imperfect markets that are separately analyzed, namely, MONOPOLY, OLIGOPOLY and MONOPOLISTIC COMPETITION.

Import deposits. A system of IMPORT RESTRICTION under which importers are required to deposit with a government insitution a percentage of the VALUE of their IMPORTS. This DEPOSIT is held by the government for a period of time, after which it is then repaid to the importer. The system restricts imports because it reduces the LIQUIDITY of importers and also imposes an extra charge on them, inasmuch as they are, in effect, forced to give an interest-free loan to the government. However, the impact of import deposits may be weakened if there is sufficient liquidity generally in the economy to enable importers to obtain loans at favorable RATES OF INTEREST against the COLLATERAL SECURITY of their import-deposit receipts. Again, foreign exporting companies may be willing to finance the deposits themselves rather than lose their market position, especially if it is expected that the scheme is only a temporary one.

Italy introduced a temporary import deposit scheme in 1981. Under this scheme importers had to deposit 30 percent of the value of the commodities they were importing. These deposits were lodged with the CENTRAL BANK for three months without earning a RATE OF INTEREST. A similar measure was also introduced in Italy in 1976 but at a 50 percent deposit rate and lodged for six months without interest.

Import duties. ⇛ TARIFFS, IMPORT

Import license. A document that gives the importer authority to import the commodity to which the license applies. It is a device to enable the government to regulate and supervise the flow of IMPORTS for instance, under its import QUOTA regulations.

Import quotas. ⇛ QUOTAS

Import restrictions. Restrictions on the importation of products into a country may be effected by means of TARIFFS, QUOTAS or IMPORT DEPOSITS and are generally imposed to correct a BALANCE OF PAYMENTS deficit. Their purpose, as with DEVALUATION, is to divert expenditure away from foreign-produced goods in favor of goods produced at home. The magnitude of this diversionary effect will depend on the ELASTICITY of demand for the IMPORTS in question; that is to say, the degree to which acceptable SUBSTITUTES are available on the home market. In addition, import restrictions could be used to increase a country's economic welfare (⇛ WELFARE ECONOMICS) at the expense of foreign countries to the extent that it has power to exploit its foreign suppliers, e.g., as a monopolist (⇛ MONOPOLY), without fear of retaliation. Import duties may be applied to protect the market of domestic industry while it is being established (⇛ FREE TRADE; INFANT INDUSTRY ARGUMENT; PROTECTION). Finally, restrictions on imports may be imposed as a countermeasure against unfair trading (⇛ DUMPING). The U.S. International Trade Commission may investigate complaints from domestic producers concerning unfair imports and make recommendations for action to the President. Non-tariff BARRIERS TO TRADE include revenue duties, such as value-added tax, which, being imposed as a percentage on landed, i.e., duty-paid, value, increase the cost of imported goods more than locally produced goods and thus discriminate in favor of the latter. Other examples are domestic taxes applied according to the technical characteristics of goods, e.g., on engine capacity, which may subtly discriminate against imports. (⇛⇛ GENERAL AGREEMENT ON TARIFFS AND TRADE).

Imports. The flow of goods and SERVICES that enter for consumption into one country and that are the products of another country. In the United States goods currently account for about 75 percent of total goods and services, compared with just over 60 percent 20 years ago. The United States accounts for about 15 percent of total world (excluding the USSR and China) imports, importing about 40 percent more than the next largest importer, West Germany (in 1979). Imports of goods and services amount to about 10 percent of the GROSS NATIONAL PRODUCT in the United States, compared with about 25 percent in West Germany. The commodity composition of U.S. imports has changed dramatically over the last 20 years. The increasing dependence on foreign supplies of fuel and the escalation in fuel prices has meant that fuel now accounts for about 25 percent of total imports of commodities, compared with only 10 percent in 1960. However, there has been an equally major expansion in imports of machinery and vehicles. These also accounted for only 10 percent of the total in 1960 but now claim as much as 30 percent of the total. This is partly a reflection of the change in world trade generally. With the growth of DEVELOPING COUNTRIES, the traditional raw materials are no longer coming to the industrialized countries in that form but as semimanufactured and finished goods. At the same time, the growth in technology and the advantage of specialization (⇛ DIVI-

SION OF LABOR) have stimulated trade in manufactures between the advanced nations. (⇛⇛ BALANCE OF PAYMENTS, INTERNATIONAL TRADE).

Import specie point ⇛ SPECIE POINTS

Import surcharge. A temporary increase in import tariffs (⇛ TARIFFS, IMPORT) designed to correct a short-term BALANCE OF PAYMENTS deficit and to stabilize the EXCHANGE RATE. In August 1971 the U.S. government imposed a 10 percent surcharge on about 50 percent of imports. It was lifted in December 1971 at the time of the SMITHSONIAN AGREEMENT.

Import tariffs. ⇛ TARIFFS, IMPORT

Impossibility theorem. In a general sense, a theorem that proves that some proposition cannot logically be true. However, in economics the term is used specifically to refer to a theorem by KENNETH J. ARROW, which shows that it is impossible to have a set of rules or procedures (i.e., a constitution) that possesses certain minimal desirable properties and that converts the preferences of individual members of a group into a consistent set of group preferences. (⇛⇛ PARADOX OF VOTING; SOCIAL WELFARE FUNCTION).

Imputed cost. The opportunity cost of INPUTS owned by a firm that it "supplies" to itself and that have alternative uses. The owner of a firm may supply certain FACTORS OF PRODUCTION—the use of a site he owns, finance for investment, managerial services, etc. In practice, he may not be paid the "PRICE" of each of these inputs but rather will take the residual of revenues after all payments have been made to factors of production "bought in." However, any input supplied by the owner may have an alternative use, with a corresponding price, and this represents the effective cost of using that input in the firm in question. Hence, we could attribute a price to each input supplied by the owner of the firm, even if no explicit price is in fact paid. Such a price is called the "imputed cost" of the input. For example, if the firm owns the land it uses and pays no explicit RENT, we can impute a rent for that land, equal to what the firm could obtain for it in some alternative use. A similar interpretation could be given to imputed interest (⇛ RATE OF INTEREST) (finance supplied by the owner) and imputed salary (managerial services supplied by the owner). The important corollary to the doctrine of imputed costs is the idea that if sales revenues are insufficient to cover actual outlays and imputed costs, then, in the long run, the firm should not stay in business. If it does stay in business, it must mean that the factors owned by the firm are receiving less than their imputed costs and hence could be more profitably employed elsewhere. On the other hand, if the revenues remaining after payment of all actual outlays exceed the imputed costs, then the firm is earning excess or supernormal PROFIT.

Imputed income. IMPUTED COSTS to the firm represent imputed income to the FACTORS OF PRODUCTION being supplied.

Inactive money. That portion of the total stock or MONEY or MONEY SUPPLY (CURRENCY plus BANK DEPOSITS) in existence at any one time, which is not being used to finance current transactions, or being lent out on the MONEY MARKET. It may also be referred to as *idle money*. It need not remain constant in amount over time, since part of it is meeting the demand for money arising out of the SPECULATIVE MOTIVE, and so will vary with changes in RATES OF INTEREST and prices of other financial ASSETS—BONDS, STOCKS, SHARES, etc. Inactive money can be represented as resulting from what JOHN MAYNARD KEYNES called LIQUIDITY PREFERENCE, i.e. the desire to hold money rather than interest-earning assets, and goods.

Income. In general terms, income is the flow of MONEY or goods accruing to an individual, group of individuals, a firm or the economy over some time period. It may originate from the sale of productive services (as wages, INTEREST, PROFITS, RENT, NATIONAL INCOME); it may represent a gift (e.g., a legacy from a will or income of a TRUST fund) or a TRANSFER PAYMENT (e.g., a welfare check). Income may be in money but can also be "in kind," e.g., use of a company automobile by a business executive. Its essential feature is that it is a flow accruing to the wealth of a particular economic unit. Income is an extremely important concept in economics. The analysis of the behavior of FACTORS OF PRODUCTION and firms is carried out on the assumption that they choose between alternatives in such a way as to maximize income (where the income to the owners of the firm is, of course, profit). Income appears in the theory of consumer choice as the factor that constrains the consumer in his choice of consumption pattern; he cannot spend more on consumption that his total income and therefore must allocate his fixed income among goods in a way that maximizes his UTILITY. Finally, the question of what determines the aggregate flow of income in the economy as a whole forms an important part of the subject matter of MACROECONOMICS, the implication being that national income is an important determinant of social welfare (⇛ SOCIAL WELFARE FUNCTION). For the accounting definition see NET INCOME.

Income and earned surplus statement. ⇛ DOUBLE-ENTRY BOOKKEEPING; INCOME STATEMENT

Income, circular flow of. INCOME, in the form of factor (⇛ FACTORS OF PRODUCTION) payments, is paid by firms to HOUSEHOLDS that supply INPUTS. Households in turn spend part of their income on goods and services, this expenditure then accruing to firms as revenue and being again paid out by them to factors of production, and so on. It is this process of a flow of income from firms to households and a flow of expenditure from households to firms that is known as the circular flow of income. It is, in fact, a very simplified MODEL of the working of the economy. Viewed in one way, it shows the interrelationship between product and factor MARKETS, with firms alternately in the roles of sellers and buyers, and households alternately in the roles of buyers and sellers. Viewed in another way, it is the basic prototype of the MACROECONOMIC model of income determination (⇛ INCOME DETERMINATION, THEORY OF), since it shows that NATIONAL INCOME will remain at the same level as long as households' "withdrawals" from the circular flow, in the form of SAVING, TAXATION or expenditure on IMPORTS, are counteracted by "injections" into the flow, such as government expenditures (⇛ BUDGET), INVESTMENT expenditure and EXPORT demand. If this is the case, the payments by firms to households, which become consumption, saving and taxes, will be equal to the receipts of firms, which consist of consumers' expenditure, investment expenditure, government expenditure and exports; and so firms will have no reason to vary their production levels. (⇛ MULTIPLIER; TABLEAU ECONOMIQUE).

Income determination, theory of. The theory that attempts to explain the determinants of the level of NATIONAL INCOME at a particular point in time and of the changes in national income over time. In its modern form the theory was first developed by JOHN MAYNARD KEYNES in his *General Theory of Employment, Interest and Money,* but this drew on much earlier work and has been considerably added to and amended since then. Briefly, the rate of production of goods and services, and hence the level of national income, depends on the level of AGGREGATE DEMAND. The level of aggregate demand itself depends partly on income (via the CONSUMPTION and possibly the INVESTMENT and government expenditure components) and partly on the RATE OF INTEREST (via consumption and investment). The rate of interest in turn is determined partly by the flows of SAVINGS and investment (since interest is the price that borrowers have to pay lenders) and partly by conditions on the MARKET for existing ASSETS, especially the extent to which individuals wish to hold assets in each of the various forms of MONEY, BONDS (short- and long-term), STOCKS, etc. The total MONEY SUPPLY that the government and BANKING system make available is held by households and firms partly to finance normal transactions and partly as an asset (that is, as a way of storing WEALTH), and the total demand for money to hold in each of these forms must be consistent with the total supply available. EQUILIBRIUM in the level of national income can then occur only if the levels of national income and interest rates are such that there is simultaneous equilibrium on the markets for goods and services, for new borrowing and lending, and for existing assets. Keynes emphasized that an equilibrium level of income could occur at a level of employment that was below the full employment level, and therefore that persistent unemployment, such as that which characterized most industrial economies during the 1930s, could be generated by the "normal" workings of the economy.

Much academic debate centered on this last proposition. It is possible to show that the economy would in fact tend to return to full employment equilibrium if it were ever out of it (PIGOU, ARTHUR CECIL). But this process could take a very long time, and so many economists would argue that the Keynesian policy prescriptions retain their validity. The major contribution of the theory of income determination is that it is a considerable simplification of the complex reality that at the same time retains the important causal relationships.

Income distribution. The way in which total NATIONAL INCOME is divided among HOUSEHOLDS in the economy. It is measured statistically first by dividing annual household income into size classes, e.g.:

less than \$1,000	per annum
\$1,000–\$1,999	per annum
\$2,000–\$2,999	per annum

and so on. Then, on the basis of a SAMPLE survey, the numbers of households whose annual incomes fall within each size class are found. The resulting tabulation of numbers of households against income classes gives the distribution of income by households (⇛ FREQUENCY DISTRIBUTION). A characteristic of the income distribution of virtually all economies is that a high proportion of households have incomes falling within the lower-income classes, while a very small proportion of households fall within the high-income classes. This feature remains remarkably stable over time, the main changes being a general upward shift in the whole distribution rather than a greater compression of it. (⇛ LORENZ CURVE; PARETO, VILFREDO FEDERICO DAMASO).

Income effect. The effect that a change in the PRICE of a good has on a consumer's DEMAND for the good via the change it induces in his REAL INCOME. Suppose a consumer has a given money income, which he spends on a range of products, one of which, product *X*, costs 50 cents per unit. Assume the consumer initially buys 10 units of *X*. If its price now falls to 30 cents, the real income of the consumer has increased, since with his money income unchanged, he can consume the same quantities of goods as before and have 10×20 cents = \$2 left over to spend on more goods. This change in real income will have the effect of increasing the consumer's demand for certain goods. If *X* is one of them, then the change in real income has contributed to the overall increase in quantity demanded of *X* resulting from its price fall. If no more of *X* is bought as a result of the real income change alone, then the change in the quantity of *X* is due entirely to the fact that, because *X* is now cheaper relative to its substitutes than it was previously, it will tend to be substituted for them (hence this is called the SUBSTITUTION EFFECT of the price change). Finally, if the increase in real income would actually tend, other things being equal, to decrease the quantity of *X* bought (i.e., *X* is an INFERIOR GOOD), then the income effect will tend to offset the substitution effect, and we may observe only a small increase in the quantity of *X*, or even a decrease. This case of a good being so strongly inferior that its income effect outweighs its substitution effect and causes a fall in quantity demanded of a good whose price has fallen is the theoretical explanation of the "GIFFEN GOODS" case.

Income elasticity of demand. The responsiveness of the DEMAND for a good to changes in the buyers' INCOME. It is measured as the proportionate change in quantity demanded, divided by the proportionate change in income that brought it about. As with other ELASTICITY concepts—e.g., price elasticity of demand—income elasticity of demand may be measured by the point elasticity formula or the arc elasticity formula. Normally, we would expect the income elasticity of demand for a good to be positive (increase in income causes increase in demand) or zero (increase in income causes no change in demand). However, in some cases, the elasticity may be negative, at least for some levels of income, and in such cases the goods are termed INFERIOR GOODS.

Income from operations. The profit earned from the normal activities of a business and calculated in the INCOME STATEMENT by deducting the cost of goods sold and operating expenses from sales revenue.

Income statement. A financial statement of the amount of revenues earned by a business less the expenses incurred in earning these revenues, thus a statement of PROFIT or loss. Revenues consist of cash or other assets received. Expenses will include *operating expenses* such as DEPRECIATION, salaries and advertising. The form of the statement will vary with the type of business; for example, in a retailing business it will be necessary to deduct sales returns and allowances from gross sales revenue and to deduct the cost of goods sold to arrive at a gross profit on sales, from which operating expenses are deducted to arrive at income from operations. Where the business has investments and/or borrowings, it will be necessary to include revenue from investments and interest paid in the computation. Finally, income taxes are deducted to give *net income,* the "bottom line" as it is often referred to. CORPORATION INCOME TAX rates are not levied upon income exactly as defined in the income statement. Taxable income differs in several ways from that shown in financial statements; for example, depreciation may be calculated differently, while dividends received from U.S. PORTFOLIO investments are subject to an 85 percent deduction for tax purposes. Also known as the *profit and loss statement* or a *statement of operations.*

Income tax. A tax paid by individuals each year based upon the amount of taxable income received during the year. In the United States income from all sources, such as wages, rent, salaries and dividends, is combined to produce what is called adjusted gross income (AGI). It is not a global concept, since some forms of income are excluded and others receive special treatment. From AGI the taxpayer makes a variety of deductions—e.g., mortgage interest—and is permitted a series of exemptions, such as those for dependent children. After allowing for deductions and exemptions, taxable income is taxed, for joint returns (married couples) at rates ranging from 14 percent on the first $1,000 of joint taxable income to 70 percent on joint income over $200,000. CAPITAL GAINS are realized when the sale of an asset not associated with carrying on a registered business takes place. If the asset has been held for less than six months, it is considered as ordinary income, and the gain is part of AGI. Only one-half of longer-term gains is included in ordinary income. In addition, the first $20,000 of capital gains is taxed at a maximum rate of 25 percent. U.S. legislation allows for only a small portion of a capital loss to be claimed as a deduction. Revenue from personal income taxation accounts for roughly 40 percent of total tax revenue. (⇛⇛ INDEXATION).

Income velocity of circulation. The rate at which MONEY circulates through the economy in order to finance transactions. It is measured as $\nu = \frac{Y}{M}$, where M is the MONEY SUPPLY available in the economy for a specified period (generally a year), Y is the money value of NATIONAL INCOME over that period, and v is the income velocity of circulation. In general, v is greater than 1, indicating that the quantity of money circulates more than once through the economy to finance the total volume of transactions. v was at one time regarded as an "institutional constant," determined by factors such as the intervals at which wages and salaries are paid (weekly, monthly, etc.); the extent to which payments and receipts of income earners, firms, etc., are synchronized; and so on. As such, it played an important role in both classical (⇛ CLASSICAL ECONOMICS) and Keynesian (⇛ KEYNES, JOHN MAYNARD) theories of the demand for money (⇛ QUANTITY THEORY OF MONEY). However, more recently it has been suggested that v may in fact be influenced by the RATE OF INTEREST. When interest rates are high, people will try to economize on the CASH balances they hold (since the interest rate is the opportunity COST of holding money), and hence a given volume of transactions can be financed with a smaller stock of money—i.e., v increases. The converse applies when interest rates are low.

Incorporation. The formation of a company as a legal entity. Corporations are chartered by state governments and are subject to state regulations. The charter takes the form of a *certificate of incorporation,* which is filed with the state by the promoters of the company and which becomes a matter of public record. The certificate will list the purposes of the corporation, the number and type of shares to be authorized, the names of the incorporators and other matters. Once a year the company is required to file an annual report giving details of its share capital, the names of officers and directors, etc. The owners of the corporation are the holders of STOCK, but their liabilities are limited to the paid-up cost of their shares. (⇛ LIMITED LIABILITY). Companies are required to establish bylaws governing such matters as voting procedures, the timing of the annual shareholders' meeting and the election of officers. It is usual for candidates for directorships to be nominated by existing or outgoing directors, but such nominations must be approved by the shareholders. Some states provide special regulations for CLOSED CORPORATIONS and for *professional corporations.* Professional corporations allow doctors, lawyers, and accountants to take advantage of certain provisions affecting corporations in the tax code but do not confer limited liability. The corporation is the principal business organization for large enterprises, and there are no limits to the number of shareholders or the total CAPITAL that they can raise. (⇛⇛ LIQUIDATION; CORPORATION INCOME TAX; STOCK EXCHANGE).

Incremental capital output ratio ⇛ CAPITAL-OUTPUT RATIO

Independent variable. A VARIABLE whose VALUE we are free to choose, which then determines the value taken by another variable. (⇛ DEPENDENT VARIABLE).

Indexation. The introduction of automatic linkage between monetary obligations and the price level. In practice, this would mean, for example, that the money value of a long-term loan would be increased in line with the CONSUMER PRICE INDEX so that the borrower would have to repay the loan in REAL TERMS. In the absence of indexation, INFLATION, by eroding the real value of loans, shifts resources from lenders to borrowers and therefore disrupts the credit mechanism and the CAPITAL MARKET. Some economists consider that indexation helps to reduce inflationary expectations and thus contributes to the control of inflation. In the United States there has been considerable pressure on government to introduce indexed bonds. The purchaser of such a bond is guaranteed a real rate of interest, since the nominal interest rate is automatically adjusted to compensate for inflation. Such bonds were introduced in the United Kingdom for the first time in 1981. Such a move would have to go hand in hand with a change in REGULATION Q, which limits nominal interest rates in the banks. In both the United States and Canada, the INCOME TAX has been indexed such that exemptions and tax brackets are adjusted each year to the rate of inflation in the previous year. Many workers today are now fully or partly protected from unexpected inflation through a COLA clause in their wage contract, which automatically adjusts wages to the cost of living.

Index number. A single number that gives the AVERAGE value of a set of related items, expressed as a percentage of their average value at some base period. The statement "The Wholesale Price Index is currently 140" means that the average value of current wholesale prices is 140 percent of the average value in, say, 1970—i.e., that they have on average increased by 40 percent between 1970 (or whenever the base period is) and now. A whole series of index numbers attempts to give a concise summary of the broad movement in the values of a set of items over time. Index numbers can be classified into three groups on the basis of the types of items they are calculated for: (a) price index numbers, e.g., the Consumer Price Index, the Wholesale Price Index, DOW JONES index of share prices, etc.; (b) volume index numbers, e.g., Index of Industrial Production; (c) value index numbers.

A *price index number* takes the price of a given quantity of each item in the current period, expresses this as a percentage of the price of the same quantity in the base period and then takes a WEIGHTED AVERAGE of these percentages (or "price relatives") to give the overall price index.

A *volume index* takes the weighted average of the percentage changes in the physical volumes of the items, abstracting from price changes. In general, the basic data may not initially be available in volume terms but only in value (price times quantity) terms. This could be because of the way in which the data are collected or, more importantly, because a particular item (e.g., chemicals) may in fact be an aggregation of several sub-items (e.g., plastics, pharmaceuticals, organic chemicals, inorganic chemicals), which may be measured in different physical units—tons, gallons, cubic feet—and so cannot be summed. The money values of outputs must be found and aggregated. These money values will, however, be influenced by price changes, and so to isolate the change in values due purely to volume changes, it is necessary to "deflate" the money values, removing the influence of price changes by, in effect, valuing the physical quantities in each year at the prices that prevailed at one particular year. Hence, there is obtained a series of money values of the items "at constant prices," and these values reflect only the changes in physical volumes of the items. By expressing the value of each item as a percentage of the value at the base period, a set of "quantity relatives" is obtained, and these are then averaged to give the overall volume index number for the set of items.

A *value index* takes the money value of each item at a particular period, expresses each money value as a percentage of the money value of the item at the base period and averages these percentages. A value index thus shows the (net) effects of price *and* quantity changes.

When the price, volume or value percentages for the items are averaged to obtain the overall index number, a weighted average is normally taken. The weights may relate to the base period, in which case we have a "base-weighted index," or to the current period, in which case we have a "current-weighted index." A current-weighted index still has a "base period," in the sense that all values are expressed as percentages of their values in some past year; however, the weights used in calculating the average percentage change will be chosen on the basis of information in the current year. For a further discussion of the weighting procedure, see CONSUMER PRICE INDEX.

Index numbers are a very concise and efficient way of providing information. They have the usual property of averages in summarizing the values of a large number of items. Also, by the device of relating all values to a single base period, they make comparison of values at different periods very easy—the relation between 138 and 120 is much more quickly seen than the relation between $17,618 million and $15,320 million. Finally, they highlight the aspects of TIME SERIES in which we are most often interested, namely, the proportionate rate of change through time. The fact that index numbers are averages necessarily means that all the information about the underlying items is not presented—particular components will necessarily move in ways different from the average. Similarly, the fact that they are generally *weighted* averages means that there is a difficult problem of choice of appropriate weights, and that there may be an element of distortion as weights become inappropriate (⇛ INDEX NUMBER PROBLEM). Despite these limitations, however, index numbers remain very useful summary statistics. (⇛⇛ DIVISA INDEX; EDGEWORTH, FRANCIS YSIDRO; LASPEYRES INDEX; PAASCHE INDEX).

Index-number problem. In general terms, this is the problem of obtaining a satisfactory measure of the changes in some attribute of a group of items by using a single summary measure, or INDEX NUMBER. Specifically, however, it is used in economics to denote the difficulty of measuring differences in the standard of living or well-being of communities at different times or at different places.

Consider the problem of measuring the change over time in the standard of living of a group of people. A reasonable approach might be to take some standard set of commodities purchased, in fixed quantities, and then find how the cost of these changes over time; i.e., we would construct a

LASPEYRES INDEX of prices. Naturally, the actual quantities of commodities purchased over time will change in response to relative PRICE changes (more of goods that become cheaper and less of goods that become dearer, will be bought). However, if we find that the cost of the actual purchases which were made exceeds the cost of the base-year (⇛ BASE PERIOD) quantities, when both sets are valued at current prices, we can conclude that the standard of living must have risen. This is so because, since they cost less, the base-year quantities could have been bought, but instead people preferred another set of quantities which previously were not available to them, and so they must be better off.

In addition, we might take the current-year quantities purchased, value them at base-year prices and then see how the cost of the current consumption has changed over time. This is called a PAASCHE INDEX of prices. If we find that the current quantities would have cost less in the base year than they do in the current year, we can conclude that the standard of living has gone down. This is because, since current quantities cost less at base-year prices, they could have been bought then, but were not; hence the previous set of quantities must have been preferred. However, if we find that the cost of base-year purchases at current prices is greater than the value of current purchases at current prices, while the cost of current purchases at base-year prices is also greater than the cost of base-year purchases at base-year prices, then we are unable to say whether the standard of living has increased or not, since the current quantities were not available in the base year, and the base-year quanitites are not available now. This is the index number problem. The problem becomes even more intractable if we wish to make comparisons over time periods long enough for tastes to have changed significantly, since the above discussion assumes constancy of tastes.

Indifference analysis. The analysis of consumer DEMAND based on the notion of ORDINAL UTILITY. The consumer is thought of as having a given amount of money available to him to spend and as being faced with given PRICES of all the goods he might consume. He will then decide on some set of quantities of the goods to buy, given his tastes, the money available and their prices. The basic problem of consumer demand analysis is then (*a*) to clarify how these factors interrelate to determine the consumer's pattern of purchases; (*b*) to see what can be said about the nature of the EQUILIBRIUM position; and (*c*) to predict the effects on his purchases of various kinds of changes in prices, INCOMES and tastes. In doing this, indifference analysis rejects the idea that the consumer's tastes can be represented by measurements of the "amounts of utility" various quantities of the different goods yield him. Indeed, it shows that such measurements are unnecessary for the purpose. It assumes instead that, faced with a set of alternative baskets of goods (where one basket differs from another in having different amounts of the same collection of goods), the individual is able to rank them all in order of preference. That is, given any two baskets, he is able to tell us whether he prefers one to the other, or whether he is indifferent between them. Indifference means that he regards them as equally desirable, or equivalent. On the basis of this very mild assumption, together with the further assumption that his preference ordering possesses a certain kind of consistency, a model of the consumer is constructed, which is then used to analyze the problems described above. (⇛⇛ DEMAND, THEORY OF; INDIFFERENCE CURVE; MARGINAL UTILITY; TRANSITIVITY).

Indifference curve. A curve showing a series of baskets of two goods among which a consumer is indifferent. For example, if a basket of goods consisting of 5 pounds of sugar and 2 pounds of potatoes were regarded by a consumer as neither more nor less preferable than 4 pounds of sugar and 2½ pounds of potatoes, then these two pairs of values would lie on an indifference curve, drawn between axes on which were measured quantities of potatoes and sugar, respectively. The figure illustrates a typical indifference curve. In constructing it, we assume we have confronted the consumer with a large number of choices between pairs of alternative consumption baskets, and in each case he has indicated whether he prefers one basket over the other or is indifferent between them. The properties we ascribe to the curve follow from specific assumptions we make about the psychology of the consumer. These properties, and the assumptions that give rise to them, are as follows:

(*a*) The set of baskets among which the consumer is indifferent lie along a line and not in an area or band. This follows from the assumption that the consumer will always prefer more of a good to less. For example, given point *B* in the figure, corresponding to 5 pounds of sugar and 2 pounds of potatoes, the consumer would prefer any basket with at least 5 pounds of sugar and more than 2 pounds of potatoes, or at least 2 pounds of potatoes and more than 5 pounds of sugar. Similarly, *B* would be preferred to any basket with less of one good and no more of the other. It follows that all points due north or due east of *B*, or in between, must be preferred to it; while *B* must be preferred to all points south and west of it, or in between. If we apply that argument to every point on the indifference curve, it is clear that the graph of the set of baskets indifferent to each other cannot be "thicker" than a line.

(*b*) It is continuous, having no gaps or breaks. This follows from an assumption that could be expressed as a "willingness by the consumer always to accept some quantity of one good in 'exact compensation' for a reduction, however small or large, in the amount he has of the other." In the figure, at point *B*, if we were to make a reduction in the amount of sugar in the basket by any amount, however small or large, we could always find a corresponding increase in potatoes that would get the consumer back on the indifference curve (which is what we mean by "exact compensation"). This would not be so if, for example, the curve had a gap between points *B* and *C*—all points southeast of *B* and northwest of *C* either preferred or inferior to them. It would then follow that a reduction from *B* of, say, 1 pound of sugar could not be exactly compensated—there would be no quantity of potatoes that, in conjunction with 4 pounds of sugar, yield a bundle indifferent to *B* and *C*.

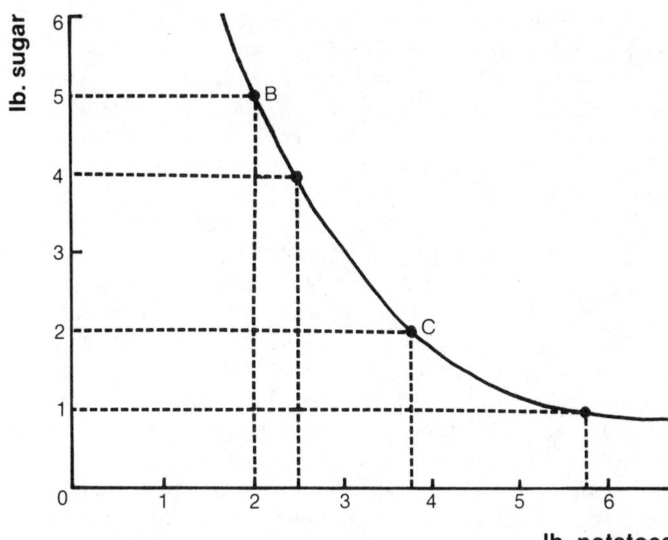

Although this continuity assumption may seem esoteric, it plays an important part in ensuring that certain mathematical conditions are met that guarantee an optimal choice of consumption basket by the consumer, given his income and the prices of the goods.

(*c*) It is drawn sloping downward from left to right. This expresses the idea that if we subtract some of one of the goods from the consumer's basket, we would have to increase the quantity of the other to compensate, in order to leave him with a new basket equivalent to the first. This again rests on the assumption that a consumer will always prefer to have a combination containing more of at least one good and no less of the other. This then rules out indifference curves that are horizontal, vertical or sloping upward from left to right. If, on the other hand, one of the "goods" was something like garbage, aircraft noise, work, then we would expect the indifference curve to slope upward from left to right.

(*d*) It is drawn convex to the origin, i.e., it bulges outward when looked at from below. This curvature of the indifference curve expresses the idea that, as one good becomes more plentiful relative to the other, further increases in it are worth less in terms of the other. This can be illustrated as follows: Beginning at point *B* in the figure, we could imagine "moving" the consumer along his indifference curve by reducing the amount of sugar in the basket and increasing the amount of potatoes. We substitute potatoes for sugar in such a way as to leave him always with baskets that he regards as equivalent to *B*. Now, at *B*, the consumer has a lot of sugar and not many potatoes. If we subtract 1 pound of sugar from his basket, we have to compensate by giving roughly ½ pound of potatoes, leaving him with a new basket that is equivalent to *B*. At *C*, on the other hand, he has a lot of potatoes and little sugar. If we now subtract one pound of sugar from his basket, we find we have to give him about 2 pounds of potatoes in order to give him a basket that is equivalent to *C*. The quantity of potatoes required to compensate the individual for the loss of one pound of sugar gets steadily greater as potatoes become plentiful and sugar scarce, and this is reflected in the shape of the curve.

The concept of the indifference curve is used extensively in the theory of consumer DEMAND, in WELFARE ECONOMICS and indeed in any area of economics concerned with problems of choice between alternative combinations of variables. It is a way of representing the preferences of a decision maker on the basis of information on rankings alone, and no assumption of the measurability of UTILITY is involved. Since the decision maker can rank all possible baskets, there can be drawn a set of indifference curves that completely fill the space between the two axes, and this set is known as the *indifference map*. As a result of assumption (*a*), baskets on higher indifference curves are preferred to those on lower curves. Also, two indifference curves cannot intersect without logical contradiction. If, for example, *X* and *Y* are points on two intersecting indifference curves, with *X* having more of both goods than *Y*, then, because of assumption (*a*), *X* must be preferred to *Y*. But both *X* and *Y* are indifferent to the point *Z*, at which the two indifference curves intersect, and so should be indifferent to each other. Since *X* cannot at the same time be both preferred and indifferent to *Y*, avoidance of logical contradiction implies that indifference curves cannot intersect.

The overall result of the theory of indifference curves is that the decision maker's preferences over alternatives can be represented by a set of continuous, nonintersecting, convex-to-the-origin indifference curves, which then form the basis for further analysis of choice. (⇛ EDGEWORTH, FRANCIS YSIDRO; INDIFFERENCE ANALYSIS; MARGINAL RATE OF SUBSTITUTION; ORDINAL UTILITY; PARETO, VILFREDO FEDERICO DAMASO).

Indirect taxation. ⇛ DIRECT TAXATION

Individual Retirement Account. A tax provision that permits individuals to claim up to $2,000 per year (1981) as a tax deduction if funds are placed in an account for retirement purposes. If an individual's spouse is not working, the amount is $2,250 per year. If the money is withdrawn before age 59½, there is a 10 percent tax penalty on the sum withdrawn. The funds may be left to the beneficiary in an estate without taxation.

Infant industry argument. An argument in support of the retention of a protective import tariff (⇛ TARIFFS, IMPORT). An industry does not operate at an optimum least-cost output until it has reached a sufficient size to obtain significant ECONOMIES OF SCALE. Therefore, a new industry, in, say, a DEVELOPING COUNTRY, will always be in a competitively vulnerable position *vis-à-vis* an established industry in an advanced country. It follows that the stage of growth at which the industry (or country) can "take off"

(⇒ ROSTOW, WALT WHITMAN) industrially will be postponed indefinitely. The argument concludes that protection is necessary until the industry has reached its optimum size.

Inferior good. A good the DEMAND for which falls when its consumers' INCOMES rise. For example, as people become richer, they may buy fewer bicycles, and so bicycles would be defined as an inferior good. It follows that an inferior good has a negative INCOME ELASTICITY OF DEMAND. (⇒⇒ INCOME EFFECT).

Inflation. A process of steadily rising prices, resulting in diminishing purchasing power of a given nominal sum of MONEY. Inflation has been a marked characteristic of most economies since World War II and has received considerable attention from economists. Theories of its causes are often classified as cost-push (⇒ COST-PUSH INFLATION) theories and demand-pull (⇒ DEMAND-PULL INFLATION) theories, the latter of which would include the issue of the influence of the MONEY SUPPLY on the price level (⇒⇒ QUANTITY THEORY OF MONEY). Solutions to the problem of inflation most often suggested include: (*a*) to use MONETARY POLICIES and FISCAL POLICIES to restrain AGGREGATE DEMAND, increase UNEMPLOYMENT and hence reduce inflationary pressure; and (*b*) to make a direct intervention in the MARKETS for goods and FACTORS OF PRODUCTION to restrain price and wage increases (⇒⇒ PRICES AND INCOMES POLICY). There have also been proposals that taxes related to the size of wage increases granted should be imposed on firms, to "stiffen employers' resistance" to wage claims. However, apart from distorting the operation of the price mechanism (⇒ PRICE SYSTEM) in its allocative role, it is unlikely that measures of administrative intervention would restrain inflation completely in the absence of restraint on aggregate monetary demand, since the administrative task of preventing implicit wage and price increases would be enormous (⇒ WAGE DRIFT). Many economists who would usually be classed as "Keynesians" (⇒ KEYNES, JOHN MAYNARD) see the real difficulty as one of balancing the costs of inflation against the costs of avoiding it, in terms of higher unemployment against lower output of real goods and services. A low rate of inflation (perhaps about 2 percent to 3 percent per annum) may not in general be considered objectionable and, indeed, might be considered an inevitable consequence of an expanding economy. The "evils" of inflation, however, are generally held to result from:

(*a*) The possibility that a slow rate of inflation may accelerate and become GALLOPING INFLATION, the consequences of which could be a breakdown of the monetary system.

(*b*) The fact that there may be undesirable redistributions of real INCOME, since those whose money incomes rise at a slower rate than the rate of inflation clearly lose, while the real incomes of those whose money incomes rise faster than the rate of inflation increase. At the extreme, those whose money incomes change infrequently—e.g., senior citizens—may become very badly off. Clearly, the difficulty arises here because the rate of inflation is not fully anticipated. If it were, then contracts could be made in

REAL TERMS, and these redistributive effects might not take place (⇛ INDEXATION).

(*c*) Inflation may discourage SAVING, since the real value of the sum saved falls through time. However, RATES OF INTEREST will tend to rise to offset this, and also many forms of saving exist that provide a hedge against inflation, because their money values rise accordingly, e.g., real estate. Therefore, *unanticipated* inflation is again what creates the problem.

(*d*) Where an economy engages extensively in INTERNATIONAL TRADE, with a fixed EXCHANGE RATE, inflation may cause its prices to rise relative to those of other countries. This will cause EXPORTS to fall, IMPORTS to rise, and BALANCE OF PAYMENTS deficits may develop. Note, however, that the relevant thing here is the rate of that country's inflation relative to the others. If all countries were inflating at the same rate, relativities would remain unchanged. There would then be a redistribution of world wealth, since the real value of the liabilities of debtor nations would fall as would the real value of assets of the creditor nations. When exchange rates are floating rather than fixed, the changes in the balance of exports and imports caused by differential rates of inflation will bring about movements in exchange rates, so that, other things being equal, we expect the currency of a country inflating faster than other countries to depreciate (⇛ DEPRECIATION).

The emphasis on policies to counter inflation has strengthened considerably throughout the Western industrial nations during the 1970s and early 1980s, following the very rapid acceleration in inflation rates that has been experienced over that period.

Inflation accounting. Methods of keeping a record of financial transactions and analyzing them in a way that allows for changes in the purchasing power of money over time. Until quite recently, *historic cost accounting* methods had been used, that is to say, accounts were derived more or less directly from bookkeeping records of actual expenditures and receipts. Fixed ASSETS, for example, such as machinery, were recorded in the balance sheet at their actual (depreciated) cost. (⇛ DEPRECIATION) In a period of rapidly rising prices, the replacement cost of these assets is likely to be much higher than their recorded cost, and historic cost accounting may therefore understate depreciation and costs in REAL TERMS and overstate profits. Over a period of time, this may lead to a situation where CAPITAL is not being maintained in real terms at all but distributed as "illusory" money profit in dividends and tax payments.

The problem of the effects of INFLATION on accounts has been under discussion since the 1930s and has become increasingly urgent with the speeding up of inflation rates and the slowing of economic growth since the early 1970s. The *general purchasing power* (GPP) method, or *current purchasing power* (CPP) method, which retain historic cost accounting conventions but express accounts in terms of "purchasing units" using a general price index (⇛ CONSUMER PRICE INDEX) rather than money data, have received the support of professional accounting bodies in the United States. In 1969 the Accounting Principles Board (APB) issued voluntary guidelines for GPP accounting, although these were not, in practice, followed by many companies. The GPP method may still result in overstated profits where, as is frequently the case, the replacement cost of assets has risen faster than the general price level. In 1976 the SECURITIES AND EXCHANGE COMMISSION issued a regulation requiring large companies to publish replacement cost information in notes to their accounts. In 1979 the Financial Accounting Standards Board (FASB), which superseded the APB in 1973, issued Statement Number 33, *Financial Reporting and Changing Prices,* requiring the 1,500 largest companies to publish supplementary accounting information both on a GPP basis and on a *current cost accounting* basis. Current cost accounting, which involves the use of specific indices to revalue BALANCE SHEET items, is open to the objection that it allows too much scope for individual discretion in valuation. Controversy therefore continues, although for major companies inflation accounting information now appears alongside conventional accounting statements. The FASB Statement Number 33 has been issued for a five-year experimental period, ending in 1984.

Inflationary gap. The excess of AGGREGATE DEMAND in the economy over the AGGREGATE SUPPLY of resources coming forward to meet the demand. The consequences are persistently rising PRICES. (⇛⇛ INFLATION).

Inflationary spiral. ⇛ GALLOPING INFLATION; INFLATION

Inflation tax. During a period of inflation and rising nominal incomes, government revenue will rise faster than real GNP due largely to PROGRESSIVE TAXES, which tax increments of taxable income at higher rates. This results in the ratio of government revenue to GNP increasing over time without the need to change tax rates.

Inheritance tax. ⇛ DEATH DUTIES

Innovation. The introduction of new products or production processes. Innovation is therefore the last stage in the important process of (*a*) *invention:* the discovery or devising of new products and processes; and (*b*) *development:* the process by which the ideas and principles generated at the stage of invention are embodied in concrete products and techniques of production leading to innovation. In one sense, innovation is economically the most important of these stages, since it is only when this stage is completed that the fruits of invention and development are gained.

Input. A FACTOR OF PRODUCTION. In the traditional economics literature, *factor of production* was the term used, but increasingly the more modern and concise term *input* is used for the same concept—some commodity or service that is used in technological processes to produce output.

Input-output analysis. A branch of economics concerned with the structure of the production relationships in an economy and in particular with the relation between a given set of demands for final goods and services and the implied amounts of manufactured INPUTS, raw materials and LABOR this requires. The first step is to draw up a list of basic commodity groups and then to find, from empirical data, the amount of the output of any one group that is required to produce one unit of output of each other group, including itself. These latter are referred to as the "input-output" coefficients. Given these coefficients, it is then possible to trace through the effects on the whole production pattern of the economy of some initial set of output requirements. Input-output analysis has been very widely applied in economics. Its originator was the economist WASSILY W. LEONTIEF.

Input-output matrix. ⇛ INPUT-OUTPUT ANALYSIS; LEONTIEF, WASSILY W.; MATRIX

Inputs. Goods and services used in production. (⇛⇛ FACTORS OF PRODUCTION).

In rem tax. A tax "on things," independent of the owner of an item or party to a transaction. The description is used to distinguish personal taxes from taxes on goods, property or employment. (⇛ DIRECT TAXATION; INCOME TAX; SALES TAX).

Insolvency. A condition where an individual or other legal entity is unable to meet its LIABILITIES with available resources. A firm is insolvent if its liabilities, excluding EQUITY capital, exceed its total ASSETS. (⇛⇛ BANKRUPTCY).

Installment credit. A form of CONSUMER CREDIT in which the purchaser pays a DEPOSIT on an article and pays the balance of the purchase price plus a RATE OF INTEREST in regular installments over periods of six months to two years or more. In a hire purchase contract, unlike a credit sale, ownership of the goods does not pass from the seller to the buyer until the final payment is made, i.e., the goods are security for the LOAN. Until that time the seller is entitled to repossess the goods under law. Because interest charges are calculated on the total loan and not the amount outstanding, hire purchase is a more expensive form of CREDIT than it often seems to be. Installment credit originated with retailers in the United States during the 19th century, and the development of PERSONAL LOANS and other forms of credit do not appear to have affected this type of business very much. The control of the volume of installment credit has, in the past, been an important object of monetary policy, whereby the Federal Reserve (⇛ FEDERAL RESERVE SYSTEM) could select certain areas of the economy for control. Minimum down payments and maximum periods for repayment are controls of this kind. Such controls, however, have not been used since the early post-World War II period. (⇛ CREDIT SQUEEZE).

Institutional economics. A school of economic thought that flourished in the 1920s in the United States. Economists holding institutional views criticize orthodox economists for relying on theoretical and mathematical models that not only distort and oversimplify even strictly economic phenomena but, more importantly, ignore their noneconomic, institutional environment. The political and social structure of a country may block or distort the normal economic processes. Institutionalists believe that there is a need for economists to recognize the relevance of other disciplines—e.g., sociology, politics, law—to the solution of economic problems. T.B. Veblen (1857–1929), W.C. Mitchell (1874–1948) and GUNNAR KARL MYRDAL (1898–) have been the leading economists sympathetic to institutionalism.

Institutional investor. An organization, as opposed to an individual, that invests funds arising from its receipts from the sale of SECURITIES, from DEPOSITS and other forms of SAVING, i.e., INSURANCE companies, corporate PENSION FUNDS, INVESTMENT TRUSTS and mutual stock funds, and trustees (⇛ TRUST). These funds are invested in SECURITIES, real estate and other property, including works of art. Most personal savings are now contractual in insurance plans and mutual funds plans, and much of them are also involuntary, as in contributions to corporate pension funds. The investment of these steadily increasing savings is gradually altering the structure of ownership of national ASSETS. More than 30 percent of LISTED SECURITIES are now owned by FINANCIAL INTERMEDIARIES on behalf of widely dispersed owners, giving rise to what Peter Drucker has called *Pension Fund Socialism* in a book of that title. The economic implications of the growth of institutional investment are attracting increasing attention by economists. One is that large financial institutions tend to invest in real estate, government securities, and the STOCKS and BONDS of large corporations rather than in SMALL BUSINESS, because of the cost of investing in small parcels, risk aversion and legal restrictions. (⇛⇛ SEPARATION OF OWNERSHIP FROM CONTROL).

Insurance. A contract to pay a PREMIUM in return for which the insurer will pay compensation in certain eventualities, e.g., fire, theft, automobile accident. The premiums are so calculated that, on average in total, they are sufficient to pay compensation for the policyholders who will make a claim, together with a margin to cover administrative costs and profit (⇛⇛ UNDERWRITING). In effect, insurance spreads risk, so that loss by an individual is compensated for at the expense of all those who insure against it, and as such it has an important economic function. Insurance companies invest their very substantial reserves against policyholders' claims and other ASSETS in MORTGAGES, real estate and financial SECURITIES. There are important income tax concessions on insurance premiums (including medical insurance), and life insurance is a popular way of providing for old age as well as protecting the financial position of dependants. (⇛⇛ PENSION FUNDS).

Intangible assets. ⇛ ASSETS

Inter-American Development Bank (IDB). The bank was established in 1959 to give financial assistance to the developing countries of Latin America and the Caribbean. Until 1974 membership was limited to the United States and 22 Latin American and Caribbean countries. However, membership now covers 25 countries in Latin America and the Caribbean, 15 countries in Europe, the United States, Canada, Israel and Japan. The bank's total cumulative lending reached $17,800 million by 1980, with energy projects absorbing about 25 percent of the total. The United States holds 34.8 percent of the voting shares of the bank. The bank provides finance on both strictly commercial terms and as soft loans for projects within the region. It also provides expert technical assistance as required. (⇛ ASIAN DEVELOPMENT BANK).

Interest, abstinence theory of. An explanation of RATES OF INTEREST in terms of a reward for choosing to abstain from consumption. (⇒⇒ INTEREST, CLASSICAL THEORY OF; SENIOR, NASSAU WILLIAM; TIME PREFERENCE).

Interest, classical theory of. In the early tradition of classical theory—e.g., ADAM SMITH, DAVID RICARDO—the RATE OF INTEREST was regarded as simply the RATE OF RETURN ON CAPITAL invested. It was considered to be an INCOME to capital rather like RENT to land. With the subsequent development of the classical system, the nature and the determinants of the rate of interest came to be regarded in terms of a more complex pattern. The rate was arrived at by the interaction of two forces operating on the SUPPLY of, and the DEMAND for, funds. On the one hand, the strength of demand was related to businessmen's expectations regarding PROFITS. This was connected with the marginal productivity of INVESTMENT. On the other hand, the supply was dependent upon the willingness to save. This willingness was in turn related to the marginal rate of TIME PREFERENCE. People judge how much a dollar is worth to them today compared with a dollar in the future. They make their decision whether to save by comparing this "rate of exchange" between now and the future with the current rate of interest. In the classical system, therefore, it was the rate of interest that brought SAVINGS into balance with investment. JOHN MAYNARD KEYNES attacked this assumption in his *General Theory of Employment, Interest and Money*. The balance was brought about, he argued, by means of changes in income and output. The rate of interest was itself more closely confined to monetary factors. (⇒⇒ LIQUIDITY PREFERENCE; LOANABLE FUNDS; HUME, DAVID).

Interest cover. The number of times the fixed-interest payments made by a company to service its LOAN CAPITAL are exceeded by EARNINGS. This ratio shows the decline in earnings that could take place before interest payments could not be met out of current income and is therefore a useful guide for the prospective fixed-interest investor.

Interest, natural rate of. One of the conditions put forward by KNUT WICKSELL for monetary EQUILIBRIUM—i.e., a situation in which there are no forces tending to make PRICES in general go on rising—was that the money RATE OF INTEREST should be equal to the "natural rate." The owner of a forest has a choice between two alternatives in any one year. He can either cut down his trees and lend out the money obtained from them, or he can let the trees grow another year. The RATE OF RETURN he gets from lending is the "money rate"; the return he gets from growing his trees heavier is the "natural rate." Wicksell thought of the natural rate, therefore, in terms of a physical investment. However, GUNNAR KARL MYRDAL in developing this theme pointed out that the natural rate should also take into account the price at which the timber was expected to sell. (⇒⇒ FISHER, IRVING; KEYNES, JOHN MAYNARD).

Interest, productivity theories of. Theories that place the emphasis of the explanation for the existence of a RATE OF INTEREST on the YIELD from INVESTMENT. EUGEN VON BOHM-BAWERK, in particular, developed this theory as one of his reasons for the existence of a positive interest rate. It was built upon his theory of "roundabout" production methods. A direct method of obtaining drinking water, for example, is to go to a stream and drink. A more roundabout method is to manufacture a bucket and use it to fetch water. An even more roundabout method is to build a water pipe, pump and tap. Each stage involves more CAPITAL and also more time, but nevertheless yields increased product. Goods available today therefore have more value than goods available tomorrow, for two reasons. First, goods today can be used in a time-consuming roundabout process to yield benefits tomorrow that are greater than could be obtained by the same goods applied to direct production tomorrow. Secondly, they also yield greater benefits over the same goods applied to roundabout production tomorrow. This is because there are diminishing returns (⇛ DIMINISHING RETURNS, LAW OF) to the extension of roundabout methods. Present goods are therefore always technically superior to future goods, and it follows that there must exist a positive rate of interest by which future goods are equated to present goods. (⇛⇛ INTEREST, CLASSICAL THEORY OF; INTEREST, NATURAL RATE OF; KEYNES, JOHN MAYNARD).

Interest rate. ⇛ RATE OF INTEREST

Interest, time preference theory of. A psychological theory of the existence of RATES OF INTEREST. An individual prefers consumption now to consumption in the future for two reasons. First, he is aware of the possibility that he may be dead before he can derive the benefits from postponing consumption. Second, and less rationally, there exists a tendency for people to undervalue future benefits—a "deficiency of the telescopic faculty." (⇛⇛ BOHM-BAWERK, EUGEN VON; FISHER, IRVING; INTEREST, CLASSICAL THEORY OF; INTEREST, NATURAL RATE OF; INTEREST, PRODUCTIVITY THEORIES OF; TIME PREFERENCE).

Interlocking directorate. The holding by an individual of directorships in two or more separate companies. Interlocking directorates between directly competing large firms are not permitted under the CLAYTON ACT.

Intermediate products. Goods that are used in the production of other goods rather than for final consumption, e.g., steel. Some goods may, of course, be both—e.g., milk, which is directly consumed but is also used to make products such as chocolate, cheese and ice cream.

Internal economies. ⇛ ECONOMIES OF SCALE

Internal rate of return. That RATE OF INTEREST which, when used to discount the CASH FLOWS associated with an INVESTMENT project, reduces its net PRESENT VALUE to zero. Hence, it gives a measure of the "break-even" RATE OF RETURN on an investment, since it shows the highest rate of interest at which the project shows neither a PROFIT nor a loss. If the internal rate of return is greater than the rate of interest that has to be paid, this would suggest that a project is profitable and should be undertaken; and conversely if it is smaller. However, as a measure of investment profitability, it suffers from two important defects: (*a*) A given project may have more than one interest rate that discounts its cash flows to zero, and so the method may not give a clear-cut answer. This can happen when cash inflows (profits) within the lifetime of the project are followed by cash outflows. And (*b*) the method may give incorrect rankings of alternative projects, in that the actual profitability of one project may be greater than that of another, even though its internal rate of return is lower. The internal rate of return is also known as the *marginal efficiency of capital,* the *investor's yield* and the *DCF yield*. (⇛ DISCOUNTED CASH FLOW).

Internal Revenue Service. The branch of the U.S. government that administers the tax laws as assembled in the Internal Revenue Code. The Bureau of Internal Revenue prepares the code and interprets the various revenue acts. The staff of the bureau numbers in excess of 60,000, operating 60 district offices in the country at a cost of over $1.5 billion, which is less than 1 percent of the tax revenue collected.

International Bank for Reconstruction and Development (IBRD). Also known as the World Bank, the establishment of the IBRD, like the INTERNATIONAL MONETARY FUND, was agreed upon by the representatives of 44 countries at the U.N. Monetary and Financial Conference at BRETTON WOODS in July 1944. It began operations in June 1946. The purpose of the bank is to encourage CAPITAL investment for the reconstruction and development of its member countries, either by channeling the necessary private funds or by making LOANS from its own resources. Two percent of each member's subscription is paid into the bank's funds in gold or dollars, 18 percent in the country's own CURRENCY, and the remainder is retained but available for call to meet any of the bank's LIABILITIES if required. The bank also raises money by selling BONDS on the world market. Generally speaking, the bank makes loans either direct to governments or with governments as the guarantor. Contributions of member countries to the capital of the bank are made in proportion to that member's share of world trade. Members' voting rights are allocated in the same way. In 1981 the capitalization of the bank was increased to $80 billion. China became a member of the bank in 1980. In 1980 the bank introduced a new policy under its structural adjustment program by which it makes loans to ease BALANCE OF PAYMENTS problems of the DEVELOPING COUNTRIES. These loans, however, are conditional on the recipient country's adopting economic policies specified by the bank. Loans to the developing countries totaled $13.1 billion in the year ending June 1981. The bank operates through its affiliates, the INTERNATIONAL FINANCE CORPORATION and the INTERNATIONAL DEVELOPMENT ASSOCIATION.

International banking. Eight of the 10 largest U.S. banks have at least 40 percent of their DEPOSITS in foreign branches. Through these overseas branches, U.S. banks have been able to deal in the rapidly growing EURODOLLAR market without the constraints of the reserve requirements of the FEDERAL RESERVE SYSTEM. Foreign banks also operate in the United States. There were some 300 of these institutions in 1980, with assets of $150 billion. (⇛⇛ BANKING; FREE-TRADE ZONE).

International Banking Act. Prior to this Act (1978), foreign banks in the United States operated under state charters, and regulations governing their operation were not strictly enforced. The Act requires foreign banks to establish a "home state" and refrain from branch banking across state lines. They are also subject to reserve requirements and examination by the Federal Reserve. (⇛ BANKING; FEDERAL RESERVE SYSTEM; INTERNATIONAL BANKING).

International Clearing Union. ⇛ KEYNES PLAN

International commodity agreements. A number of international commodity agreements have been signed in the past. They include coffee, cocoa, natural rubber, bauxite, olive oil, sultanas, sugar, wheat, tin. It has been a feature of the MARKETS in primary commodities that imbalance between SUPPLY and DEMAND gives rise to wide fluctuations in PRICES. Primary commodities often have long production cycles that are difficult to adjust to bring into EQUILIBRIUM with relatively short-run fluctuations in demand. At the same time, the development of the economies of the primary producing countries depends heavily on the export earnings of these commodities, with the result that, in response to a fall in demand, there is a tendency to increase supply to maintain total earnings in the face of intensified competition, thereby forcing prices down even further. Therefore, there are two features, of commodity agreements: They may be concluded (*a*) for the stabilization of prices or (*b*) for the raising or maintenance of prices.

The first Coffee Agreement was signed in 1962 and has since been renewed regularly. The latest agreement concluded in 1982, and will operate from 1983 to 1989. Export quotas are fixed annually and "floor" and "ceiling" prices fixed. The United States is a member. A similar arrangement is followed by the International Tin Agreement, the first of which was agreed to in 1956 and the latest, the sixth, came into force in 1982 for a five year period. An International Cocoa Agreement was concluded in 1973, and a new agreement was signed in 1980. However, the Ivory Coast, the largest exporter, did not sign the agreement nor did the United States. An agreement for natural rubber was concluded in 1980, and came into full operation in 1982. (⇛⇛ COMMON FUND; ORGANIZATION OF PETROLEUM EXPORTING COUNTRIES; UNITED NATIONS CONFERENCE ON TRADE AND DEVELOPMENT).

International company. ⇛ MULTINATIONAL CORPORATION

International Cooperation Administration. ⇛ ECONOMIC COOPERATION ADMINISTRATION

International corporation. ⇛ MULTINATIONAL CORPORATION

International Development Association (IDA). An institution affiliated with the INTERNATIONAL BANK FOR RECONSTRUCTION AND DEVELOPMENT and established in 1960. It gives long-term LOANS at little or no interest (⇛ RATE OF INTEREST) for projects in the DEVELOPING COUNTRIES. It is intended for INVESTMENTS for which finance cannot be obtained through other channels without bearing uneconomically high interest charges and is mainly for items of infrastructure, e.g., roads, power supply. The repayment period for the loan may be up to 50 years. In 1980–81 the IDA lent about $3.5 billion to developing countries. The sixth call of contributions from the member countries is $12 billion payable in the three years to 1982. The U.S. commitment is $3.24 billion, representing 27 percent of the total.

International Energy Agency (IEA). An organization established in 1974 by the member countries of the ORGANIZATION FOR ECONOMIC COOPERATION AND DEVELOPMENT, excluding Finland, France and Iceland. Its aims are to (*a*) reduce the member countries' dependence on oil supplies; (*b*) maintain an information system relating to the international oil markets; (*c*) develop a stable international energy trade; (*d*) through cooperative sharing, prepare and protect member countries against a disruption of oil supplies. Member countries agree to hold a particular level of oil stocks. At the end of 1981, these were agreed at 90 days' supply. (⇛ ORGANIZATION OF PETROLEUM EXPORTING COUNTRIES).

International Finance Corporation (IFC). An affiliate of the INTERNATIONAL BANK FOR RECONSTRUCTION AND DEVELOPMENT. In the early 1950s it was recognized that the requirement that IBRD loans should have a government guarantee was a significant handicap to the attraction of private INVESTMENT to DEVELOPING COUNTRIES. The IFC was created in 1956 so that greater advantage could be taken of private initiative in the launching of new CAPITAL projects. Until 1961, when its charter was amended, its activities were restricted because it had few resources and could not participate itself in EQUITY holdings. Since that time its activities have been able to develop rapidly. The corporation can invest directly and give LOANS and guarantees for private investors. It can hold equity interests in private companies, although its interest in any one company is generally restricted to 25 percent. The IFC is empowered to borrow from the IBRD to relend to private investors without government guarantee. It is financed by subscriptions from the 109 countries that make up its membership. At the end of 1980–81, the IFC held a portfolio of equity and loan capital amounting to $1.6 billion. About 53 percent of its investments are in Latin America and the Caribbean.

International investment. ⇛ FOREIGN INVESTMENT

International Investment Bank. ⇛ COUNCIL FOR MUTUAL ECONOMIC AID

International Labor Organization (ILO). An organization established in 1919 under the Treaty of Versailles that became affiliated with the United Nations in 1946. Its aims are the improvement of working conditions throughout the world, the spread of social security and the maintenance of standards of social justice. It has drawn up a labor code based on these aims. The ILO offers technical assistance to DEVELOPING COUNTRIES, especially in the field of training.

International liquidity. The amount of gold, RESERVE CURRENCIES and SPECIAL DRAWING RIGHTS available for the finance of INTERNATIONAL TRADE. In 1958, when sterling became convertible (⇛ CONVERTIBILITY), the leading reserve currencies were the dollar and sterling. Therefore, apart from *ad hoc* LOANS made by the INTERNATIONAL MONETARY FUND, the growth in LIQUIDITY needed to finance the expansion of world trade for the following almost 15 years had to be found in the expansion of the output of gold and the supply of dollars and sterling. The physical supply of gold is virtually limited to the output of the mines in South Africa and the USSR.

The official price of gold in terms of dollars had been fixed until the end of 1971 at its 1934 level of $35 an ounce. With the decline in the United Kingdom's position in world trade, sterling's acceptability as a reserve currency became suspect. The needed growth of liquidity was therefore met by the outflow of dollars from the United States arising from the fact that the U.S. BALANCE OF PAYMENTS for many years ran a deficit. Pressures eventually built up for the elimination of this deficit, and consequently concern developed as to whether there would be adequate liquidity in the future to finance trade. Broadly, if sufficient reserves are not available, a fall in prices and world trade could follow (⇛ QUANTITY THEORY OF MONEY). A crisis of confidence finally erupted: in November 1967 sterling was devalued (⇛ DEVALUATION), and early in 1968 control over the gold market broke down. The old fixed price survived but only for gold in international finance. A separate price appeared for FREE-MARKET gold. Again, in August 1971, the U.S. government imposed a 10 percent import surcharge, suspended the convertibility of the dollar and introduced other measures to correct the balance of payments deficit. In December 1971 the "Group of Ten" countries in the IMF (⇛ INTERNATIONAL MONETARY FUNDS), at the Smithsonian Institution, Washington, agreed to revalue their currencies to give the U.S. dollar an effective devaluation of 10 percent, and the import surcharge was lifted. Having taken measures to reverse the U.S. deficit, it was agreed to hold discussions to consider the reform of the international monetary system over the long term. There are two types of solution to the problem: (*a*) a system of flexible EXCHANGE RATES that would at the theoretical extreme make international liquidity held in the form of gold and FOREIGN EXCHANGE reserves unnecessary; and (*b*) an increase in liquidity by raising the price of gold or by inventing a new CURRENCY. The Smithsonian Agreement, in December 1971, reaffirmed that discussions take place against the need for stable exchange rates. In the event, this policy did not hold, for in June of the following year, sterling was floated, and this heralded an era in which all major currencies came off fixed parities and floated, albeit the float was "managed." In the late 1960s a new source of international liquidity began to develop, partly as a result of the U.S. deficit, in the form of the Eurocurrency, and particularly of the EURODOLLAR. JOHN MAYNARD KEYNES had already put forward a scheme for a CENTRAL BANK for central banks at the BRETTON WOODS Conference, which would issue its own currency, called BANCOR. Keynes argued, "We need a quantum of international currency, which is neither determined in an unpredictable and irrelevant manner as, for example, by the technical progress of the gold industry, nor subject to large variations depending on the gold reserve policies of individual countries, but is governed by the actual current requirements of world commerce." In 1969 the IMF's articles of agreement were revised so that it could set up and distribute to member countries special drawing rights, which have a strong affinity with Keynes' bancor. The first distribution of SDRs, valued at $3,500 million, was made at the beginning of 1970. Another important new source of liquidity emerged with the introduction of the European Currency Unit (⇛ EUROPEAN MONETARY SYSTEM), used by the members of the EUROPEAN COMMON MARKET for their internal trading. However, a dramatic change in the balance of world liquidity was caused by the increase in oil prices by OPEC (⇛ ORGANIZATION OF PETROLEUM EXPORTING COUNTRIES) in 1972–73. As a result, the foreign DEBT of less-developed countries rose from $75 billion in 1970 to $400 billion in 1980. The BALANCE OF PAYMENTS deficits of the non-oil LDCs (⇛ LEAST DEVELOPED COUNTRIES) in 1980 was about $70 billion; the developed countries together had a deficit of about $50 billion in contrast to a surplus of $115 billion earned by OPEC. The unwillingness of the OPEC countries to invest their reserves denominated in a single currency has led to a diversification of reserve currencies away from the dollar and into other currencies, such as the German deutsche mark and the Japanese yen. (⇛⇛ CREDITOR NATION; UNITED NATIONS CONFERENCE ON TRADE AND DEVELOPMENT).

International Monetary Fund (IMF). The IMF was set up by the BRETTON WOODS Agreement of 1944 and came into operation in March 1947. The fund was established to encourage international cooperation in the monetary field and the removal of FOREIGN-EXCHANGE restrictions, to stabilize exchange rates and to facilitate a multilateral (⇛ MULTILATERALISM) payments system between member countries. In 1980 the fund had 140 members. Under the IMF's articles of agreement, member countries were required to observe an EXCHANGE RATE, fluctuations in which should be confined to ±1 percent around its PAR VALUE. This par value was quoted in terms of the U.S. dollar, which was in turn linked to gold. In December 1971, the "Group of Ten" (see below), meeting at the Smithsonian Institution, Washington, agreed on new "central values" of currencies in order to achieve a dollar devaluation of 10 percent with a permissible margin of ±2.25 percent. Each member country of the IMF was required to subscribe to the fund a quota paid 25 percent in gold and 75 percent in the member's own currency. Quotas have been raised six times; the last increased the total to SDR 39,000 million (⇛ SPECIAL DRAWING RIGHTS). This fund is used to tide members over temporary BALANCE OF PAYMENTS difficulties and thus to help stabilize exchange rates. Borrowing ability and voting rights are determined by this quota. Under the present system, the United States holds about 22 percent of the voting strength and the EUROPEAN ECONOMIC COMMUNITY about 27 percent; and so, since an 85 percent majority is required to make a major change in IMF procedure, both the United States and the EEC have the power to veto. A member in temporary balance of payments deficit obtains foreign exchange from the fund in exchange for its own currency, which it is required to purchase within three to five years. Members in deficit with the fund are obliged by the terms of the agreement to consult with the IMF on the procedures being taken to improve their balance of payments.

During the early 1960s it became evident that there was a strong case for increasing the size of the fund, and in 1962 the General Agreement to

Borrow was signed by 10 countries, namely, the United States, United Kingdom, West Germany, France, Belgium, the Netherlands, Italy, Sweden, Canada and Japan—called the "Group of Ten" or the "Paris Club"—under which SDR 6,500 million credit was made available to the IMF should it be required. In addition, Switzerland, which is not a member of the IMF, made available $200 million. Countries in difficulty can also negotiate standby credit on which they can draw as necessary. The IMF cannot, however, make use of any of the currency in this scheme without prior consent of the lending country. In September 1967, at the IMF meeting in Rio de Janeiro, the creation of an international paper money was agreed in principle, and proposals for the amendment of the IMF's articles were put to members in 1968. The scheme was ratified in July 1969. The system proposed was that annual increases in international credit would be distributed to IMF members by means of special drawing rights (SDRs). These credits are distributed among member countries in proportion to their quotas and may be included in their official reserves; the first, $3,500 million, was distributed in this way on January 1, 1970. There is a limit on the acceptability for payment in SDRs, in that no country need hold more than twice its SDR quota (⇛ KEYNES PLAN). In 1976 an agreement reached in Jamaica led to a major revision of the fund's articles. First, it is no longer required for member countries to subscribe 25 percent of their quotas in gold, and gold is no longer the unit of account of the SDR. The IMF is authorized to sell its gold holding. Initially the fund sold one-sixth of its gold (25 million ounces) spaced over a period of four years. It will also return a similar amount to member countries in proportion to their quotas. The revenue from its gold sales is used to finance aid to the DEVELOPING COUNTRIES. It is the intention of the IMF to encourage the use of the SDR as the principal reserve asset (⇛ RESERVE CURRENCY) in the international monetary system. Second, the commitment to fixed par values contained in the original articles was abolished.

The increase in the price of oil in 1973 placed a severe balance of payments strain on the consuming countries, and the IMF set up an oil facility loan scheme by means of which the surpluses earned by OPEC (⇛ ORGANIZATION OF PETROLEUM EXPORTING COUNTRIES) were recycled. In 1974–75 a total of SDR 6,900 million was allocated for the facility, mostly financed by borrowings from OPEC. The scheme was wound up in 1976. (⇛ GOLD STANDARD).

International Settlements, Bank for. ⇛ BANK FOR INTERNATIONAL SETTLEMENTS

International trade. The exchange of goods and services between one country and another. This exchange takes place because of differences in costs of production between countries, and because it increases the economic welfare of each country by widening the range of goods and services available for CONSUMPTION. DAVID RICARDO showed by the law of comparative advantage that it was not necessary for one country to have an absolute cost advantage in the production of a commodity for it to find a partner willing to trade. Even if a country produced all commodities more expensively than any other, trade to the benefit of all could take place, provided only that the relative costs of production of the different commodities were favorable. Differences in costs of production exist because countries are differently endowed with the resources required. Countries differ as to the type and quantity of raw materials within their borders, their climate, the skill and size of their labor force and their stock of physical CAPITAL. Countries will tend to export (⇛ EXPORTS) those commodities whose production requires relatively more than other commodities of those resources (⇛ FACTORS OF PRODUCTION) that it has most of (⇛ HECKSCHER-OHLIN PRINCIPLE). By increasing the scope for the specialization of labor (⇛ DIVISION OF LABOR) and for achieving ECONOMIES OF SCALE by the enlargement of MARKETS, there is a presumption that international trade should be free from restrictions (⇛ FREE TRADE). The classical economists (⇛ CLASSICAL ECONOMICS) condemned MERCANTILISM for its advocacy of government control over trade in order to achieve export surpluses, and the 19th and early 20th century was a period of free trade. This philosophy gave place to the economic protectionism (⇛ PROTECTION) of the interwar years but was revived again in the GENERAL AGREEMENT ON TARIFFS AND TRADE in 1948. The latter has had some success in reducing tariffs (⇛ TARIFFS, IMPORT) on IMPORTS, culminating in the TOKYO ROUND OF TRADE NEGOTIATIONS in 1974. However, many IMPORT RESTRICTIONS still remain. At the same time, there has been an increase in the number of CUSTOMS UNIONS and FREE TRADE AREAS, such as the EUROPEAN ECONOMIC COMMUNITY, EUROPEAN FREE TRADE ASSOCIATION, LATIN AMERICAN FREE TRADE ASSOCIATION and CENTRAL AMERICAN COMMON MARKET. While these unions do establish free trade between member countries, they discriminate against outsiders. International trade since the end of the Second World War has grown rapidly, and many changes in the pattern of goods and SERVICES traded have taken and are taking place. The DEVELOPING COUNTRIES, in their attempt to achieve faster ECONOMIC GROWTH, are changing from being simply raw-material exporters to exporters of finished or semifinished goods. At the same time, the developed nations are taking advantage of technological specialization, so that trade in high-value finished manufactures is increasing between them. (⇛ WILLIAMS COMMISSION).

International Trade Commission. ⇛ IMPORT RESTRICTIONS

International Trade Organization (ITO). At the U.N. conference held at Geneva in 1947 at which the GENERAL AGREEMENT ON TARIFFS AND TRADE was signed, a charter was put forward for the setting up, within the U.N. organization, of a new agency to be called the International Trade Organization. Fifty nations signed the charter in Havana the following year, but it was never subsequently ratified by the required number of countries. The aim of the proposed organization was to work out principles for the general conduct of international trade and to draw up proposals for the implementation of policies based on these principles. Its terms of reference covered tariffs (⇛ TARIFFS, IMPORT), QUOTAS, taxes, INTERNATIONAL COM-

MODITY AGREEMENTS and whatever was considered to have a bearing on the development of international trade and was based on policies of non-discrimination and tariff reductions. In practice, the GATT has carried out most of the functions envisaged for the ITO.

Interstate Commerce Commission (ICC). A United States government regulatory body established in 1887, initially to exercise control over railroad rates. Today the ICC is responsible for considerable PUBLIC UTILITY regulation in such areas as airlines, pipelines, electricity and gas. Originally, such regulatory bodies as the ICC were concerned with NATURAL MONOPOLIES, but their power has extended somewhat further over the years. (⇛⇛ REGULATION).

Intra-European Payments Agreement. A payments system established between the member countries of the ORGANIZATION FOR EUROPEAN ECONOMIC COOPERATION in 1948 to facilitate the distribution of U.S. aid under the EUROPEAN RECOVERY PROGRAM and to encourage intra-European trade by facilitating the settlement of intra-European BALANCE OF PAYMENTS deficits. Based on a set of intra-European bilateral trade forecasts, a country for which a surplus balance of payments was expected received U.S. aid above a certain minimum only on condition that it extended drawing rights to its European partners in its own CURRENCY. A deficit country therefore received aid both from the United States and from the European countries in surplus. The surplus country, on the other hand, to obtain similar levels of U.S. aid, was required itself to extend aid to its partners. This system, based on what was known as "compensation agreements" was very ungainly, and the forecasts often proved hopelessly inaccurate. It was completely replaced by the EUROPEAN PAYMENTS UNION in 1950.

Inventories. Stocks or stores of raw materials, components, work in progress or finished goods. Inventories are held for one or more or the following reasons:

1. Deliveries of raw materials, components, etc., take place at discrete intervals, whereas production takes place continuously. Hence, inventories provide a pool from which the needed INPUTS can be continuously taken.
2. Similarly, shipments of the finished product take place at discrete intervals, whereas production yields output continuously, and so inventories permit the accumulation of output before shipment.
3. There may be economies in having production runs at a constant rate of output (say 100 units per week), while sales, and hence shipments, may fluctuate (50 units one week, 150 the next), and inventories reconcile these by taking the excess production in one time period and supplying the excess demand in another.
4. It may be impossible to forecast demand with complete certainty. Hence, inventories may be held in case demand exceeds the expected level.

Inventory analysis. A body of techniques that attempts to determine the optimum level of INVENTORIES to hold in any given situation. The problem is essentially to determine the relevant set of COSTS, to find the way in which these vary with certain key VARIABLES, to set up a MODEL of the situation using the cost relationships and then to find the values of variables that minimize the costs of holding inventories. To take a simplified example: Suppose we are considering a retailer of a single good, *X,* which he sells at a known, constant rate per week. Given this rate of sales, he has to decide how large an inventory to hold, which in effect involves two decisions: how often a delivery of *X* should be made, and how much should be delivered each time. In fact, if we assume that deliveries will be timed for when inventories should have run down to a certain minimum level, the only variable whose size has to be determined is the size of the order quantity. The relevant costs are:

1. Ordering costs: These consist of the administrative overheads of making the order (which do not depend on the quantity ordered) and the delivery costs (which may well not increase in proportion to the size of the order).

2. Inventory costs: These consist of storage and warehousing costs, INSURANCE and deterioration costs, and most important, the interest cost of money "tied up" in inventories. (⇛ RATE OF INTEREST). All these costs tend to vary directly, and possibly more than proportionately, with size of inventories.

Since the size of inventories can easily be expressed in terms of the order quantity, an equation can be written that shows how total costs (ordering *plus* inventory) depend on the order quantity. Using standard techniques, the level of the order quantity can be found that makes total costs a minimum. One of the interesting implications of this calculation is that if sales should increase, the optimal inventory level increases by the square root of the sales increase—i.e., the inventory level increases less than proportionately with the sales increase, and so there are ECONOMIES OF SCALE in inventory holding. (⇛ INVENTORY INVESTMENT).

Inventory investment. The building up or running down of INVENTORIES by permitting production to exceed or fall short of sales. The situation in which stocks are run down is known as DISINVESTMENT, or negative investment. Unanticipated inventory investment or disinvestment is often the first indication to a firm that production is not appropriately matched with sales.

Inventory investment cycle. Fluctuations in economic activity caused by changes in INVENTORY INVESTMENT. The levels of production of firms, and therefore the levels of NATIONAL INCOME and employment, are determined not only by sales but also by the extent to which firms wish to add to or run down INVENTORIES. If firms aim to maintain some fixed relationship between inventories and sales, then a change in the level of sales causes a firm to adjust its level of inventories. For instance, a firm is selling 100 units per annum and has found from experience that a ratio of 50 percent of stock to sales is the optimum. With sales constant, it will produce 100 units per annum. If sales rise by, say, 10 percent to 110 units, the firm must increase its stocks from 50 units to 55 units. In that year it must therefore increase its output by 15 percent: 10 units to meet the increase in sales and 5 units to go into stock. In the following year, if sales were constant, output would fall to 110, as no additions to stock would be necessary. It can therefore be seen that the existence of stocks "accelerates" (⇛ ACCELERATION PRINCIPLE) the growth in sales in terms of output and also generates greater fluctuations in output.

Inventory turnover. The rate at which INVENTORIES are turned into sales. It can be found by dividing the average rate of sales over a given time period by the average level of inventories in the same time period. Also known as *stock turnover*.

Investment. Strictly defined, investment is expenditure on real CAPITAL goods. However, in everyday language it is also taken to mean the purchase of any ASSET, or indeed the undertaking of any commitment, that involves an initial sacrifice followed by subsequent benefits. For example, one may speak of the purchase of an ordinary share or the decision to go to a university as an investment. However, in the theory of income determination (⇛ INCOME DETERMINATION, THEORY OF), investment means strictly expenditure on capital goods. In this sense, investment is the amount by which the stock of capital of a firm or economy changes, once we have allowed for replacement of capital that is scrapped. (⇛⇛ NET INVESTMENT).

Investment appraisal. 1. The analysis of the prospective costs and benefits of possible new INVESTMENTS and the evaluation of the desirability of committing resources to them. 2. A branch of business economics that deals mainly with the formulation of rules, techniques and criteria designed to help practical decision makers in their problem of choosing investments. (⇛⇛ DISCOUNTED CASH FLOW; INTERNAL RATE OF RETURN; PRESENT VALUE).

Investment bank. A FINANCIAL INTERMEDIARY that organizes the raising of CAPITAL by new issues of SECURITIES on behalf of clients and also buys and sells securities on its own account. The investment bank will advise the client on the timing and form of the issue, assist in preparing the registration statement and prospectus and may, for very large issues, act in syndicate with other banks. In about half of all cases, the investment bank will underwrite the issue (⇛ UNDERWRITING); in others it works on an agency basis. Issues may be made to the public via the STOCK EXCHANGE or by private placement. The bank's services are rewarded by commission or an "agency spread."

Investment companies. Savings vehicles in which shares can be purchased; these funds being invested in a range of SECURITIES and other ASSETS. (⇛ INVESTMENT TRUST; MUTUAL FUNDS).

Investment demand curve. A curve showing the total amount of money that firms wish to borrow for INVESTMENT expenditure at each possible RATE OF INTEREST. Since the rate of interest is the PRICE that has to be paid on borrowed funds, the investment demand curve is analogous to the consumer demand curve, in that it shows the quantity demanded at each price.

Investment expenditure. ⇛ INVESTMENT

Investment function. The relationship between INVESTMENT and its major determinants—namely, the rate of change of output, the CAPACITY UTILIZATION RATE and the RATE OF INTEREST. (⇛⇛ ACCELERATION PRINCIPLE).

Investment goods. ⇛ CAPITAL

Investment grant. ⇛ INVESTMENT INCENTIVE

Investment incentive. Government assistance designed to encourage firms and industries to invest in particular types of physical ASSETS or make investment expenditures in particular regions of a country. Incentives may take the form of tax allowances or cash grants. (⇛ ENTERPRISE ZONE; FREE-TRADE ZONE; INVESTMENT TAX CREDIT).

Investment, negative. ⇛ DISINVESTMENT

Investment opportunity curve. A curve showing the relationship between increasing amounts of money currently devoted to INVESTMENT expenditure and the future income that will result. The curve was extensively used in the classic work by IRVING FISHER on the theory of CAPITAL and RATE OF INTEREST.

Investment tax credit. A tax policy whereby a corporation can obtain a tax rebate equal to a specific percentage of the cost of new capital equipment rather than depreciating such an expenditure over the life of the asset. Currently, the credit takes the form of a 7 percent allowance on the cost of certain investments and, in effect, reduces the cost of an asset by 7 percent. The first use of such a credit in the United States was in 1962.

Investment trust. A company whose sole object is to invest its CAPITAL in a wide range of other companies. An investment trust issues SHARES and uses its capital to buy shares in other companies. (⇛ MUTUAL FUNDS; TRUST).

Investor's yield. ⇛ INTERNAL RATE OF RETURN

Invisible. Those "invisible" items, such as financial services, that are recorded in the BALANCE OF PAYMENTS accounts and are distinguishable from the "visible" items, such as merchandise trade, EXPORTS and IMPORTS of goods. The main categories making up the invisible account in the U. S. balance of payments are travel and transportation; interest and dividends; and miscellaneous services, which include BANKING and INSURANCE. By far the largest group is that of interest and dividends earned both by the United States from its ownership of overseas assets and by foreigners from the ownership of their assets held in the United States. The United States earned about $76 billion from overseas assets in 1980 and paid out about $43 billion to foreigners from their U.S.-owned assets. This category therefore generates a surplus of about $33 billion.

Invisible balance. ⇛ INVISIBLE

"Invisible hand". ADAM SMITH believed that society was such that, although individuals pursued their own advantage, the greatest benefit to society as a whole was achieved by their being free to do so. Each individual was "led by an invisible hand to promote an end which was no part of his intention." (⇛⇛ MANDEVILLE, BERNARD DE; PRICE SYSTEM; RESOURCES).

Irredeemable security. A SECURITY that does not bear a date at which the CAPITAL sum will be paid off or redeemed. Sometimes called undated securities.

Isoquant. A curve that shows the combinations of two INPUTS required to produce a given quantity of a particular product. For example, in the diagram, we measure units of LABOR input along the horizontal axis and units of CAPITAL along the vertical. The isoquant $Q = 100$ shows the quantities of capital and labor that can be used together to make 100 units of output—e.g., K_1 of capital, L_1 of labor; or K_2 of capital, L_2 of labor; or any other combination represented by a point on the curve. Similarly, the curve $Q = 150$ shows combinations of capital and labor required to make a given quantity—in this case 150 units—of output.

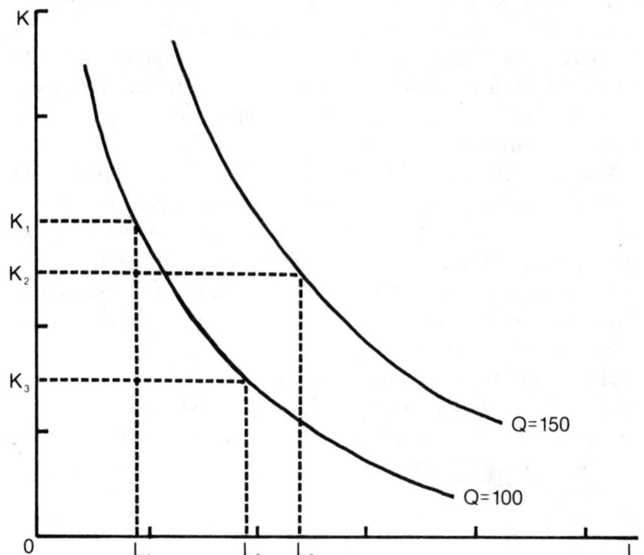

We can note several features of these isoquants and the assumptions that give rise to them:

1. The curves are smooth and continuous. This implies that both inputs are infinitely divisible—i.e., they do not come in discrete lumps, but rather we can choose any fractional value we wish (e.g., 3.7526 units of capital and 7.0004 units of labor). It also implies that they are physically substitutable—i.e., we are not forced to use labor and capital in fixed proportions, such as one man to one machine.

2. They slope downward from left to right—i.e., they have negative slopes. This implies that if we reduce the quantity of one input (say, labor), we must increase the quantity of the other in order to leave output unchanged. The amount by which we have to increase the capital input divided

by the amount by which we reduced the labor input is referred to as the RATE OF TECHNICAL SUBSTITUTION of capital for labor and is identical to the mathematical definition of the slope of the isoquant (dK/dL).

3. They are convex, that is, they are relatively flat at small amounts of capital and large amounts of labor but get steadily steeper as capital increases and labor diminishes. When there is little capital and much labor, a reduction in labor can be compensated for by a relatively small increase in capital; but at a lower level of labor input, the same size reduction in labor requires a larger increase in capital to maintain output at the same level. This is consistent with the law of diminishing marginal productivity (⇛ DIMINISHING MARGINAL PRODUCT, LAW OF): When the quantity of an input is small, the increase in output that results from increasing the quantity of the factor by one unit is larger than when a lot of the factor is being used, given a constant amount of the other input.

There is a strong similarity between isoquants and INDIFFERENCE CURVES. The crucial point of difference is, however, that output is measurable, while UTILITY is not, so that quantities can be attached to isoquants but not to indifference curves.

Isoquants are used in the theory of the firm (⇛ FIRM, THEORY OF) to derive the COST CURVES that the firm faces in making its output decision and to derive the DEMAND CURVES of the firm for the FACTORS OF PRODUCTION. The purpose of isoquants in this analysis is to summarize the technological possibilities open to the firm in combining inputs to produce outputs. That is, they are a very convenient way of illustrating aspects of the PRODUCTION FUNCTION of the firm.

Issued capital. ⇛ ISSUED STOCK

Issued stock. That part of a company's CAPITAL which has been subscribed to by stockholders. It may or may not be paid up. (⇛ PAID UP CAPITAL).

Issuing house. ⇛ INVESTMENT BANK

J

Jamaica Agreement. ⇛ INTERNATIONAL MONETARY FUND

Jawboning. The name given to economic policy that relies on voluntary cooperation from corporations and labor unions, encouraged by verbal pronouncements from government on the need for such cooperation. For example, phase two of the 1971 PRICES AND INCOMES POLICY of the Nixon administration suggested wage and price guidelines and called for voluntary adherence to these by business and unions. Economists are often skeptical of the value of this kind of "policy by exhortation," since, in the absence of effective sanctions to back up the policy, it is easily ignored.

J-curve phenomenon. This is a reference to the fact that following an EXCHANGE-RATE depreciation, the trade balance may worsen initially and then slowly improve. The cost of IMPORTS rises immediately, whereas revenue from exports does not. The latter is largely due to the fact that an improvement in exports follows an exchange-rate depreciation with a considerable lag. There are three important reasons for the lag. First, time is required to develop contracts for the export of goods. Second, potential customers for exports may have to wait for existing contracts with other suppliers to expire. Third, it takes time to increase the production of export goods and import substitutes.

Jevons, William Stanley (1835–82). He studied natural science and worked as an assayer to the Australian Mint from 1853 to 1859. He became professor of logic at Owens College, Manchester, England in 1866 and in 1876 at University College, London. His main theoretical economic work is *Theory of Political Economy* (1871). Other aspects of his work are collected in *Investigations in Currency and Finance* (1884). He was one of the three economists to put forward a MARGINAL UTILITY theory in the 1870s. He argued that one COMMODITY will exchange for another such that the ratio of the PRICES of the two commodities traded equals the ratio of their marginal utilities. FRANCIS YSIDRO EDGEWORTH criticized the way Jevons developed these ideas and in so doing invented the INDIFFERENCE CURVE. Jevons also made an important contribution to the theory of CAPITAL, many aspects of which were, in fact, taken over by the AUSTRIAN SCHOOL. He superimposed on the classical economic (⇛ CLASSICAL ECONOMICS) theory the idea that capital should be measured in terms of time as well as quantity. An increase in the amount invested is the same as an increase in the time period in which it is being employed. Output can be increased by extending the period in which the investment is available by, for instance, reinvesting the output instead of consuming it at the end of the production period. With given levels of LABOR and capital, output becomes a function of time only. He derived from this a definition of the RATE OF INTEREST as the ratio of the output gained by an increase in the time capital remains invested, divided by the amount invested (⇛ BOHM-BAWERK, EUGEN VON). Jevons was also one of the founders of ECONOMETRICS: He invented MOVING AVERAGES. He also propounded a theory of the TRADE CYCLE based on sunspots, but this is of little importance except for the stimulus it gave to the study of statistics for economic empirical work. (⇛⇛ GOSSEN, HERMANN HEINRICH; MENGER, CARL; WALRAS, MARIE ESPRIT LEON).

Job vacancy index. An index based on the number of registered job vacancies and given by the ratio of registered job vacancies to the civilian labor force. This index does not have an empirical foundation in the United States, because the data required to construct such an index are not collected. Such an index has, however, been computed for Canada since the early 1970s. (⇛ U-V CURVE).

Joint costs. COSTS that are incurred in the production of two or more products and that cannot be attributed to any one of them.

Joint demand. The demand for two goods that, for reasons of their complementarity in use, have to be bought together, e.g., left and right shoes.

Joint Economic Committee. A committee of the House of Representatives and Senate that investigates broad areas of economic policy. Among other things, it will report from time to time on the state of the U.S. economy with respect to particular economic objectives.

Joint products. Two or more products that are necessarily produced by a given process. For example, production of beef also gives leather. It is possible, however, to have alternative processes that yield differing qualities and quantities of the two products.

Joint-stock banks. ⇛ COMMERCIAL BANKS

Joint-stock company. A now virtually obsolete term for a business enterprise in which the CAPITAL is divided into small units permitting a number of investors to contribute varying amounts to the total, PROFITS being divided among stockholders in proportion to the number of SHARES they own. The joint-stock company developed from the 17th century onward because of the need for increasingly large amounts of capital by certain types of enterprise, such as overseas trading companies. By 1720 abuse of the joint-stock system (culminating in the South Sea Bubble crisis) made it necessary to control business more closely. (⇛⇛ CORPORATE LAW).

Justice Department. ⇛ ANTITRUST POLICY

K

Kennedy Round of Trade Negotiations. There has been a series of rounds of negotiations between the signatories of the GENERAL AGREEMENT ON TARIFFS AND TRADE designed to reduce TRADE BARRIERS on a multilateral basis. The first round took place in 1947, and the Kennedy Round was the sixth. It commenced in 1964 and was concluded in July 1967. This round was distinguished from its predecessors by the fact that its aim was straight percentage tariff reductions right across the board rather than item-by-item agreements. This approach was made possible by the fact that in 1962 President Kennedy obtained authority from the U.S. Congress to negotiate reductions in tariffs of up to 50 percent under the Trade Expansion Act. Forty-nine countries took part in the Kennedy Round, including all the principal industrial and trading nations of the world except the USSR and China. In the end, agreements for the reduction of industrial tariffs by up to 50 percent, with an overall average of 30 percent, were achieved. Two timetables were agreed to. The first, followed by the United States, provided for reductions in five annual stages and commenced in January 1968. The second, followed by the EUROPEAN ECONOMIC COMMUNITY, EUROPEAN FREE TRADE ASSOCIATION and Japan, laid down that two-fifths of the reduction should be made in July 1968, so coinciding with the final tariff adjustments of the EEC. Subsequent reductions took place in January 1970, 1971 and 1972. In 1973 ministers agreed in Tokyo to a seventh round of negotiations, which began in 1974. (⇛⇛ DUMPING; TOKYO ROUND OF TRADE NEGOTIATIONS).

Keynes, John Maynard (1883–1946). Educated at Eton, Keynes won prizes there in mathematics as well as in English and classics before going up to King's College, Cambridge, England. At the university he graduated with a first in mathematics. During his stay at Cambridge, he studied philosophy under Alfred Whitehead and economics under ALFRED MARSHALL and ARTHUR CECIL PIGOU. After a period in the civil service, he accepted a lectureship in economics at King's College, Cambridge. In 1911 he became editor of the *Economic Journal.* During the First World War, he held a post in the U.K. Treasury but resigned because he believed that the figure for German war reparations was set too high (*The Economic Consequences of the Peace* [1919]). He was also a severe critic of the decision of the government to return to the GOLD STANDARD and at the prewar EXCHANGE RATE (*The Economic Consequences of Mr. Churchill*). In 1930 he published *A Treatise on Money*. His major work, *The General Theory of Employment, Interest and Money,* appeared in 1936. He served a second period in the Treasury during the Second World War and was responsible for negotiating with the United States on Lend-Lease. He took a leading part in the discussions at BRETTON WOODS in 1944, which established the INTERNATIONAL MONETARY FUND.

KEYNES, JOHN MAYNARD (1883-1946)

UNEMPLOYMENT during the interwar period persisted in the United Kingdom at very high levels, never falling below 5 percent and at its worst reaching as much as 20 percent of the total LABOR force. In the United States 11.9 million were unemployed in 1933, as much as 23 percent of the labor force, and the percentage did not fall below 6 percent in the whole period from 1930 to 1941. The failure of the economy to recover from such a long Depression was unprecedented in the economic history of industrial society. Fluctuations in activity were well-known and had received much attention from theorists on the TRADE CYCLE in the past. The classical economists (⇛ CLASSICAL ECONOMICS) held that in the downturn of the trade cycle, both wage rates (⇛ EARNINGS) and the RATE OF INTEREST fell. Eventually, they reached levels low enough for businessmen to see a significant improvement in the profitability of new INVESTMENTS. The investment so induced generated employment and new INCOMES, and the economy expanded again until rising prices in the boom brought the next phase in the cycle. The classical economists therefore concluded that the failure of the economy to expand was because wages were inflexible. Their policy recommendations were that the unions should be persuaded to accept a wage cut. Keynes argued that, although this policy might make sense for a particular industry, a general cut would lower CONSUMPTION, income and AGGREGATE DEMAND, and this would offset the encouragement to employment by the lowering of the "PRICE" of labor relative to the price of CAPITAL, e.g., plant and machinery. A.C. Pigou countered Keynes' argument by pointing out that, by lowering wages, the general price level would be lowered; therefore, liquid balances that people owned would have a higher spending value. The upturn, it was agreed, was stimulated by businessmen responding to lower wages with increased investment expenditure. Why, asked Keynes, should not the government take over the businessman's function and spend money on public works? Current opinion upheld the belief that government budget deficit financing would bring more hardship than already existed. The BALANCED BUDGET was regarded as equally the correct accounting practice for the government as it was for a private household. Most economists of the period accepted that public-works expenditure would reduce unemployment, even given the need to keep the budget in balance. A.C. Pigou showed the mechanism by which this could be brought about. However, the contrary view was that public works would merely divert SAVINGS and labor from the private sector, and as the former was less productive, the net effect would be a worsening of the situation. It was not until after Keynes had written his *General Theory* and crystallized his arguments into a coherent theoretical framework that his views were accepted.

Keynes did not deny the classical theory. He agreed that a reduction in wage rates could, in theory, be beneficial, but it would operate only through the LIQUIDITY PREFERENCE schedule. A fall in prices would increase the value of the stock of money in people's hands in real terms. This would make available an increase in the amount that people were willing to lend, with a consequent drop in the rate of interest to the benefit of investment.

However, if this is so, why not operate directly on the rate of interest or the quantity of money in the economy? Moreover, Keynes argued that there exists a level of interest rate below which further increases in MONEY SUPPLY are simply added to idle balances (⇛ INACTIVE MONEY). rather than being used to finance investment. Wage cuts or not, the economy would stick at this point with chronic unemployment. In the classical system, the national product (⇛ NATIONAL INCOME) was determined by the level of employment and the latter by the level of REAL WAGES. The quantity of money determined the level of prices. Savings and investment were brought into balance by means of the rate of interest. In Keynes's system the equality of savings and investment was achieved by adjustments in the level of national income or output working through the MULTIPLIER. The rate of interest was determined by the quantity of money people desired to hold in relation to the money supply. The level of output at which savings equals investment does not necessarily correspond to full employment. The innovation in the Keynesian system was that it was the quantity of money that determined the rate of interest, and not the level of output, as in the classical system. In the Keynesian model, if you increased the propensity to invest or consume, you did not simply raise the rate of interest, you raised output and employment (⇛ CONSUMPTION FUNCTION). Keynes's study of monetary aggregates of investment, savings, etc., led to the development of national accounts. Keynes' general theory of employment is now criticized for its reliance on special cases (wage rigidity, the insensitivity of investment to the rate of interest and the idea of a minimum rate of interest at which the demand for money became infinitely elastic); its preoccupation with EQUILIBRIUM; and the fact that, despite its presentation as a radical new departure, it nevertheless embodied many of the analytical limitations of the "CLASSICAL SCHOOL" of economics. However, the transformation that Keynes brought about, in both theory and policy, was considerable. In effect, he laid the foundations for what is now MACROECONOMICS. (⇛ SUPPLY-SIDE ECONOMICS).

Keynes Plan. The U.K. Treasury submitted proposals for the establishment of an International Clearing Union for discussion at the BRETTON WOODS Conference in 1944. These proposals were primarily the work of JOHN MAYNARD KEYNES and became known as the Keynes Plan. The International Clearing Union would have basically the same functions as a domestic BANK and CLEARING HOUSE. International DEBTS would be cleared on a multilateral basis between its members. It would give OVERDRAFT facilities to a member running a temporary BALANCE OF PAYMENTS deficit and would create its own unit of CURRENCY, called BANCOR, in which the overdraft facility would be made available. Bancor would have a gold EXCHANGE RATE in the initial phases of the scheme, though it was expected that it would eventually break its gold connection and replace gold in international finance. Each member would have a quota that determined the limits of its credit facilities with the International Clearing Union. There was a set of suggested safeguards and penalties to encourage the elimination not only of deficits but also of persistent surpluses. The plan did not win approval at Bretton Woods, and the less radical INTERNATIONAL MONETARY FUND was established, which was more in line with the ideas put forward by the United States.

Klein, Lawrence Robert (1920–). When he was awarded the NOBEL PRIZE in 1980, the citation read, in part, "...the building of econometric models has attained a widespread, not to say, universal use." Klein's contribution was the application of the theory of ECONOMETRICS to the analysis of economic and social change as well as public policy.

After receiving his Ph.D. in 1944 from Massachusetts Institute of Technology he went to the Cowles Commission for three years. Following appointments at Michigan (1949–54) and at the Oxford Institute of Statistics, England (1954–58), he accepted a position at the University of Pennsylvania's Wharton School of Finance as professor of economics and finance. His work in the late 1940s and early 1950s led to the development of a large-scale econometric model of the United States—*An Econometric Model of the U.S.: 1929–52* (1955). By the early 1970s he had pioneered the development of LINK, a technique to integrate econometric models of different countries. This allows the economic analyst to study the diffusion of business fluctuations between countries, thereby forecasting international trade and capital flows. Other publications include *The Keynesian Revolution* (1960); *An Essay on the Theory of Economic Prediction* (1971).

Knight, Frank Hyneman (1885–1973). Appointed associate professor of economics at the University of Iowa in 1919 and Professor in 1922, after studying at Cornell University and the University of Chicago, Knight returned to Chicago as professor of economics in 1928. His major published works include *The Economic Organization* (1933), *The Ethics of Competition and Other Essays* (1935), *The Economic Order and Religion* (1945), *Freedom and Reform* (1947), *Essays on the History and Method of Economics* (1956) and *Intelligence and Democratic Action* (1960). His most influential work has been *Risk, Uncertainty and Profit,* published in 1921. In this work he made a clear distinction between insurable RISK and uninsurable UNCERTAINTY. It was the latter that gave rise to PROFIT. A businessman must guess future demand and selling prices and pay in advance his FACTORS OF PRODUCTION amounts based on his guesses. The accuracy of his guesses is reflected in the profit he makes. It follows that profits are related to uncertainty, the speed of economic change and business ability.

Kondratieff cycle. A TRADE CYCLE of very long duration—JOSEPH ALOIS SCHUMPETER applied the term to a cycle of 56 years in duration. Named after the Russian economist N.D. Kondratieff, who made important contributions in the 1920s to the study of long-term fluctuations. Kondratieff studied U.S., U.K. and French wholesale prices and interest rates from the 18th century through the 1920s and found peaks and troughs at regular intervals. Similar work has been carried out at Harvard, confirming a 54-year cycle in U.K. wheat prices since the 13th century.

Koopmans, Tjalling C. (1910–). Born in the Netherlands, where he initially studied mathematics and physics, Koopmans went on to earn a doctorate in economics at the University of Leiden. Following employment at the League of Nations, he went to Princeton in 1940, and during the war he worked for the Allied Combined Shipping Adjustment Board. It was here that he started on his work related to mathematical/statistical approaches to optimal resource allocation (⇛ ECONOMIC EFFICIENCY). For this work he shared the 1975 NOBEL PRIZE in Economics with Leonid Kantorovich, the Russian economist.

Following the war Koopmans went to Chicago in 1948 to do research at the Cowles Commission. When the Commission relocated at Yale (1955), he went with it and became a director of the Cowles Foundation, where he remained until 1967. Koopman's *Activity Analysis of Production and Allocation,* published in 1951, and *Studies in Econometric Methods,* published in 1953, clearly indicates the importance he played in the development of ECONOMETRICS and, in particular, LINEAR PROGRAMMING to the study of economics. His later publication in 1957, entitled *Three Essays on the State of Economic Science,* was important because of the insight it gave into the use of the scientific method in approaching economic problems.

Kuznets, Simon (1901–). Kuznets was the second American to receive the NOBEL PRIZE in Economics (1971). It was in that year that he became professor emeritus, following an 11-year career at Harvard University. Prior to his appointment at Harvard, Kuznets was at Johns Hopkins University. He was at the University of Pennsylvania earlier, from 1936 to 1954.

Much of his work has been concerned with the relationship between POPULATION and per capita income. His research led him to explain why economies with stable populations have had high rates of ECONOMIC GROWTH. By the 1960s the U.S. per capita income was considerably above that of Europe, yet there was no significant difference in population growth between Europe and the United States during the period 1840–1960. He concluded that initial endowments, especially abundant and fertile land, were important as an explanation.

Kuznets also made significant contributions to the development of NATIONAL INCOME statistics, especially the measurement of GROSS NATIONAL PRODUCT. His book *National Income and Its Composition, 1919–38* (1941) is considered a classic. Other publications include *National Product since 1869* (1941), *Income and Wealth in the U.S.: Trends and Structures* (1952), *Modern Economic growth* (1966), *Economic Growth of Nations* (1971), and *Growth, Population and Income Distribution: Selected Essays* (1979).

L

Labor One of the primary FACTORS OF PRODUCTION, "labor" is the collective name given to the productive services embodied in human physical effort, skill, intellectual powers, etc. As such, there are, of course, many types of labor INPUT, varying in effort and skill content, and in particular types of skill content. It is often a useful theoretical simplification, however, to talk of the quantity of labor as if it were homogeneous.

Labor, division of. ⇛ DIVISION OF LABOR

Labor-intensive. A process or product is called labor-intensive if it uses proportionately more LABOR in its production than the other FACTORS OF PRODUCTION. Handmade goods with a low material content are produced by a labor-intensive process. The SERVICE industries are generally labor-intensive.

Labor, marginal productivity of. ⇛ MARGINAL PRODUCT OF LABOR

Labor market. The MARKET in which wages and conditions of employment are determined.

Labor, mobility of. The mobility of labor has two aspects: (*a*) the spatial or geographical mobility of labor. This relates to the rate at which workers move between geographical areas and regions in response to differences in wages or job availability. And (*b*) the occupational mobility of labor. This relates to the extent to which workers change occupations or skills in response to differences in wages or job availability.

The importance of labor mobility is that it determines the rate at which LABOR MARKETS adjust to EQUILIBRIUM from DISEQUILIBRIUM situations. Assume the country consists of two regions, A and B, and that, initially, there is full employment (⇛ EMPLOYMENT, FULL) in each region, and wages for a given type of labor are equal. Suppose there is an increase in demand for some products in A, which causes an increase in the demand for some types of labor, and the reverse happens in B. The result would be that wages are higher in A than in B, with an excess of job vacancies over available workers in A and UNEMPLOYMENT in B. If the particular types of skills now in increased demand in A match those in reduced demand in B, then the length of time for which the "regional unemployment problem" persists depends on the geographical mobility of labor. If the skills do not match, however, then the occupational mobility of labor would also be important. One could take the persistence of a "regional unemployment problem" as evidence of a very low geographical and occupational mobility of labor. This would be an oversimplification, however, since factors such as the continued rate of decline of demand, the rate of growth of population and the extent to which CAPITAL as well as labor is geographically mobile are also important.

There are, however, many factors—economic, social and psychological—that tend to lead to low geographical and occupational mobility.

Costs of moving, reluctance to cut family and social ties, preference for a known rather than a new environment, and unemployment benefits are all well-known reasons for geographical immobility. Similarly, costs of re-training, the slow learning processes of older workers and labor union restrictions are sources of occupational and skill immobility.

Labor, specialization of. ⇛ DIVISION OF LABOR

Labor theory of value. ⇛ VALUE, THEORIES OF

Labor turnover. The rate at which workers leave a firm. Clearly, the greater this is, the higher will tend to be the labor costs of the firm, due to the administrative costs of hiring new workers, costs of training, etc. Labor turnover is normally expressed as the ratio of the number of workers who leave in a year to the firm's total work force.

Laffer curve. A graph that illustrates that if income tax rates become sufficiently high, tax revenue will decline. At a zero tax rate, no revenue is collected, and if the tax rate is 100 percent, tax revenue will also be zero because no one will bother to earn taxable income just to support the government. In between these extremes people *will* earn income and pay taxes, and at *some* rate the tax revenue will be at a maximum. This relationship was made popular by the American economist Arthur Laffer. While some economists in the United States believe that further tax rate increases will lead to lower tax revenues, others argue that the current tax rate is not so high that further increases would result in lower revenues. (⇛ DUPUIT, ARSENE JULES ETIENNE JUVENAL).

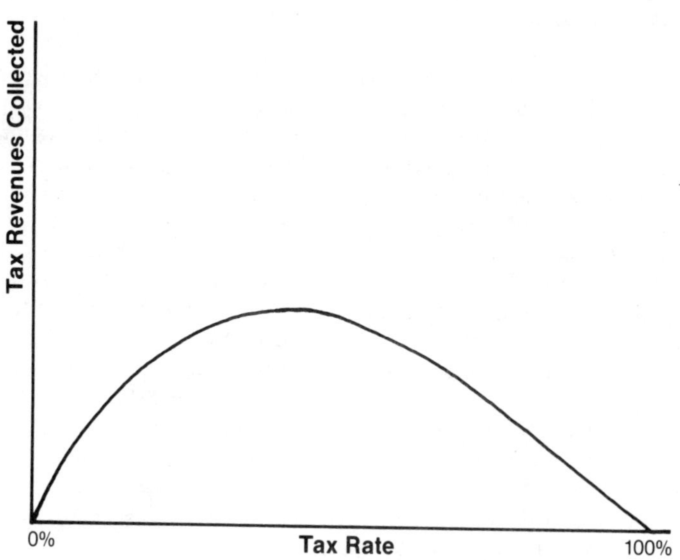

"Laissez-faire." *Laissez-faire, laissez-passer* was the term originally taken up by the PHYSIOCRATS. They believed that only agriculture yielded wealth.

Consequently, they condemned any interference with industry by government agencies as being inappropriate and harmful, except insofar as it was necessary to break up private MONOPOLY. The principle of the nonintervention of government in economic affairs was given full support by the classical economists (⇛ CLASSICAL ECONOMICS), who took up the theme from ADAM SMITH: "The Statesman, who should attempt to direct private people in what manner they ought to employ their capitals, would not only load himself with a most unnecessary attention, but assume an authority which could safely be trusted, not only to no single person, but to no council or senate whatever, and which would nowhere be so dangerous as in the hands of a man who had folly and presumption enough to fancy himself fit to exercise it"—*Wealth of Nations,* Book 4, Chapter 2. (⇛⇛ MANCHESTER SCHOOL; MANDEVILLE, BERNARD DE; SISMONDI, JEAN CHARLES LEONARD SIMONDE DE).

Land. Land in economics is taken to mean not simply that part of the Earth's surface not covered by water but also all the "free gifts of nature," such as minerals, soil fertility, etc. Land provides both space and specific resources. Much semantic argument has taken place on the extent to which land as a FACTOR OF PRODUCTION is "really distinct" from CAPITAL. Many of the services of land in fact require expenditure of RESOURCES to obtain or maintain them, and hence, they are often "produced means of production." However, although at the edges the distinction may often become blurred, it has been retained as a useful analytical convenience. Land is also meant to include the resources of the sea, so that, once again, we have a difference between the economic and everyday usage of a word.

Large numbers, law of. ⇛ LAW OF LARGE NUMBERS

Laspeyres index. An INDEX NUMBER, first published in 1864 by Etienne Laspeyres, that measures the change in some aspect of a group of items, over time, using weights based on values in some base year. For example, a Laspeyres *price index* measures the percentage change in prices of a group of commodities between now and some base year by dividing the total cost of the quantities of the commodities bought by consumers in the base year, valued at today's prices, by the total cost of those same quantities valued at the base year prices. Similarly, a Laspeyres *quantity index* finds the percentage change in quantities of commodities bought, by dividing the total cost of current quantities purchased, valued at the prices prevailing in the base year, by the total cost of the quantities purchased in the base year, again valued at base year prices. Unlike the PAASCHE INDEX, the Laspeyres index has the advantage that, since the weights are constant from year to year, a whole run of index numbers can be compared with each other. It also requires less information, since the weights have only to be calculated at intervals rather than every year. (⇛⇛ INDEX-NUMBER PROBLEM).

Last in first out (LIFO). ⇛ FIRST IN FIRST OUT

Latin American Free Trade Association (LAFTA). The treaty setting up the Latin American Free Trade Association was agreed to at Montevideo in 1960, under which the seven participating countries—namely, Argentina, Brazil, Chile, Mexico, Paraguay, Peru and Uruguay—agreed to establish a

FREE-TRADE AREA. Ecuador and Colombia joined in 1961 and Venezuela in 1966. Significant reductions in internal import tariffs (⇛ TARIFFS, IMPORT) were achieved, though little progress was made for the harmonization of a common external tariff. However, in 1969 Chile and Peru joined with Bolivia, Colombia and Ecuador to form a new economic group (⇛ ANDEAN PACT).

The members of LAFTA finally agreed to wind up the association in 1981 and to replace it by the Latin American Integration Association (ALADI). The latter will have three groups of members: (1) Argentina, Brazil, Mexico; (2) Colombia, Chile, Peru; (3) Bolivia, Ecuador, Paraguay. The intention to reduce tariffs between members has been retained but only on a pragmatic, industry-by-industry basis, compared to the across-the-board, fixed timetable approach attempted by LAFTA.

Latin American Integration Association. ⇛ LATIN AMERICAN FREE TRADE ASSOCIATION

Lausanne school. The Chair of Economics in the Faculty of Law at Lausanne was founded in 1870 with MARIE ESPRIT LEON WALRAS as the first incumbent. He retired in 1892 and was succeeded by VILFREDO FEDERICO DAMASO PARETO. The school was noted for the emphasis given to mathematics and the development of a general EQUILIBRIUM theory.

Law, John (1671–1729). A Scottish financier who put his monetary theories into practice in France through such institutions as the Banque Royale and the Compagnie des Indes. His most significant publication appeared in 1705 under the title *Money and Trade considered, with a proposal for supplying the nation with money*. He was in favor of the replacement of specie coin by paper money (⇛ BANK NOTE). Not only would this save expensive precious metals, but it would enable the state to manage the CURRENCY more effectively by making it independent of the MARKET for precious metals. Moreover, it would facilitate increasing the quantity of money in circulation and therefore the stimulation of economic activity. (⇛⇛ HUME, DAVID; QUANTITY THEORY OF MONEY).

Law of large numbers. An important proposition in statistical theory that would, in the special case of coin tossing, assert the following: As the number of times we toss a coin increases, it becomes less and less likely that the accumulated proportion of times we get heads will differ greatly from one-half. For example, for one million tosses of the coin, it is almost certain that we would have gotten heads just about half a million times. For six tosses, on the other hand, it would not be very surprising to have gotten only two heads, or four heads—in any case, proportions of heads much different than one-half. In its more general form, where it applies to any "experiment" whose outcomes are uncertain but that is capable of being repeated any number of times under identical circumstances, the proposition provides the basis for assigning as the PROBABILITY of a particular outcome the proportion of times that outcome could be expected to occur in an indefinitely large number of repetitions. For example, we would expect heads to occur half the time, and so one-half becomes the probability of getting heads in one toss of the coin.

"Leads and lags." The differences in timing in the settlement of DEBTS in INTERNATIONAL TRADE. These differences could cause a deficit or surplus for a short period in the BALANCE OF PAYMENTS, even though the underlying trade was in balance. The effect may be particularly acute when there is an expectation of a change in the EXCHANGE RATE. Importing countries will delay payment to their supplying country if it is expected that the latter's rate of exchange will fall. (⇛ DEVALUATION).

Lease. An agreement between the owner of a property (lessor) to grant use of it to another party (lessee) for a specified period at a specified RENT. The rental may be subject to review. It is possible to lease automobiles, office equipment and machinery, as well as buildings or LAND. There are many specialized forms of leasing—e.g., by equipment trusts, which lease rolling stock to railroads. The leasing of business equipment permits companies to obtain the use of capital ASSETS without borrowing; thus, it is a form of *off-balance sheet financing,* and in certain circumstances there are tax advantages.

Lease-back. An agreement in which the owner of property sells that property to a person or institution and then leases it back again for an agreed period and rental. Lease-back is often used by companies that want to free for other uses CAPITAL tied up in buildings.

Least-developed country. In 1971 the General Assembly of UNCTAD (⇛ UNITED NATIONS CONFERENCE ON TRADE AND DEVELOPMENT) approved a list of least-developed countries, made up of countries with a per capita GROSS DOMESTIC PRODUCT of $100 or less, a share of manufactures of 10 percent or less of its GDP and a literacy rate of 20 percent or less. In 1980 31 countries were classified as least-developed, of which 20 are in Africa, 9 in Asia, 1 in the Pacific (Samoa) and 1 in America (Haiti). The average per capita income of these countries is only about one-quarter of that of all DEVELOPING COUNTRIES.

Least squares regression. A method by which the relationship between two or more VARIABLES is quantified. Take, for example, the problem of quantifying the relationship between CONSUMPTION, C, on the one hand, and their DISPOSABLE INCOME, Y, on the other. Economic theory leads us to expect them to be closely related, and we may wish to test this; we may also be interested in making quantitative predictions of the consequences of certain types of change in components of AGGREGATE DEMAND (⇛ CONSUMPTION FUNCTION; INCOME DETERMINATION, THEORY OF; MULTIPLIER). We begin by measuring, at successive points in time, the observed values of C and Y. We make the linear HYPOTHESIS that $C = a + bY$; i.e., consumers' expenditure depends linearly on income (⇛ LINEAR RELATIONSHIP). This is not strictly necessary: Some other form of relationship between C and Y could be assumed, provided that, by suitable transformation of variables, we would end up with a linear relationship: $C^1 = a + bY^1$. The basic problem in regression analysis is to find, in some sense, the "best" values for a and b and then to decide whether we can really believe that this relationship in fact holds (using techniques of STATISTICAL INFERENCE). If we plot, on a "scatter diagram," the pairs of income and CONSUMPTION values we observed over the years, it may look like that shown in the first diagram.

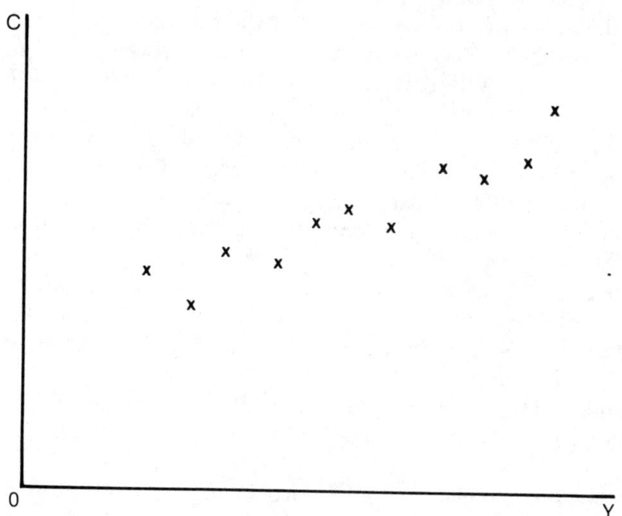

If all the data lay along a straight line, there would be no need for regression analysis. The fact that this will almost never be so in the case of economic data is rationalized by arguing that, although the true underlying relationship is as written above, there is a "random error term," which we denote by e, and which influences the actual observed value of C in an unsystematic way from year to year. *Actual C,* denoted by $\hat{C}$, is really

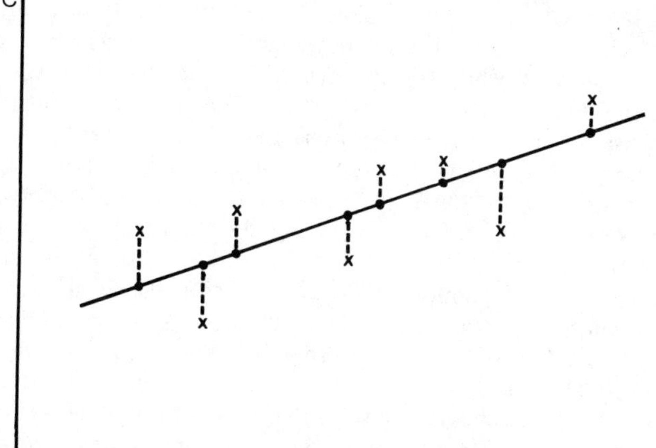

determined by the relationship $\hat{C} = a + bY + e$; and so the problem is to find a and b—i.e., to fit a line to the scatter of points in the first diagram—in the best way possible.

Least squares regression is a particular method for doing this. It proceeds as follows: Any line drawn through the scatter of points implies a particular relationship between C and Y and also implies a particular set of differences between $\hat{C}$, the actual consumption, and C, the consumption "predicted" from the fitted line. These differences, $\hat{C}$–C, are estimates of e, the error terms, as illustrated in the second diagram.

Then, the least squares method suggests that the *best* line to draw, in the sense of having certain very desirable statistical properties, is the line that makes the sum of the squares of the differences between $\hat{C}$ and C as small as possible, i.e., that involves the "least sum of squares." Out of all the possible lines that could be drawn, one and only one has this property, and there are standard procedures for finding which it is and which values of a and b it implies.

Legal tender. Money which is declared by the government to be used for the settlement of debts and the exchange of goods and services. (⇛ FIAT MONEY).

Leontief, Wassily W. (1906–). Born in Leningrad, Leontief obtained a post in the University of Kiel in Germany in 1927. In 1931 he moved to Harvard and was appointed professor of economics there in 1946. In 1973 he was awarded the Alfred Nobel Memorial Prize (⇛ NOBEL PRIZES) in Economics. Apart from the works mentioned below, his publications include *Studies in the Structure of the American Economy* (1953), *Input-Output Economics* and *Collected Essays* (1966). The interdependence of the various sectors of a country's economy has long been appreciated by economists. The theme can be traced from RICHARD CANTILLON and FRANCOIS QUESNAY and the "TABLEAU ECONOMIQUE" through KARL MARX and MARIE ESPRIT LEON WALRAS. The sheer complexity of the interactions and interrelationships between the different sectors of a modern economy was a Gordian knot, which had to be cut before the theoretical structure could be translated into a practical reflection of an actual economy and serve as the basis for policy recommendations. Leontief's achievement was to see the solution of this problem in MATRIX ALGEBRA, and modern computers have made INPUT-OUTPUT ANALYSIS a practical proposition. His book *The Structure of the American Economy, 1919–1929* was first published in 1941, and a second edition, *1919–1939,* appeared in 1951. In these studies he attempted, with the limited statistical facts available to him, to establish a "Tableau Economique" of the United States. The economy was described as an integrated system of flows or transfers from each activity of production, CONSUMPTION or distribution (⇛ DISTRIBUTION, THEORY OF) to each other activity. Each sector absorbs the outputs from other sectors and itself produces COMMODITIES or SERVICES, which are in turn used up by other sectors, either for further processing or for final consumption. All these flows or transfers were set out in a rectangular table—an input-output

MATRIX. The way in which the outputs of any industry spread out through the rest of the economy could be seen from the elements making up the rows. Similarly, the origins of its INPUTS could be seen directly from the elements of the appropriate column. Given such a structure, the implications of a specific change in one part of the economy could be traced through to all the elements in the system. (⇛⇛ SOCIAL ACCOUNTING).

Leverage. The ratio of fixed-interest DEBT to stockholders' interest plus the debt. A corporation may borrow CAPITAL at fixed interest, and if it can earn more on that capital than it has to pay for it in interest, then the additional earnings accrue to the holders of COMMON STOCKS. Leverage pushes up the RATE OF RETURN on EQUITY CAPITAL where the return on total CAPITAL EMPLOYED is higher than the rate paid for LOAN CAPITAL. However, the contrary is also true, so that the greater the leverage, the greater the risk to the holder of common stocks. Roughly speaking, if a firm's initial capital consists of $7,000 in common stock and $3,000 borrowed at fixed interest—for example, through BONDS—it would be said to have a leverage of 30 percent. Leverage is also called the *debt ratio* and *gearing* (British).

Lewis, Sir Arthur (1915–). ⇛ SCHULTZ, THEODORE

Liabilities. Sums of money for which account has to be made. The liabilities of a company include its BANK LOANS, short-term DEBTS for goods and SERVICES received (*current liabilities*), its LOAN capital and the CAPITAL subscribed by stockholders. (⇛⇛ BALANCE SHEET).

Limited liability. The restriction of an owners' loss in a business to the amount of CAPITAL that he has invested in it. If a limited company is put into LIQUIDATION because it is unable to pay its DEBTS, for example, the individual shareholders are liable only for the nominal value of the SHARES they hold. Before the principle of limited liability was recognized, investors could be made liable for the whole of their personal possessions in the event of INSOLVENCY. Limited liability is one of the advantages conferred by INCORPORATION; the owner of a PROPRIETORSHIP or most owners of PARTNERSHIPS are not protected by limited liability.

Limited partnership. ⇛ PARTNERSHIP.

Linear programming. A set of mathematical techniques for finding numerical solutions to a special class of problems. These problems involve the search for the best values of certain VARIABLES, where the "best" generally means that set of values which maximizes PROFIT or minimizes COST. An essential part of the problem will be the existence of constraints or limitations on the values of the variables that may be selected. The problem is then to choose the best possible values out of those permitted by the constraints. Examples might be:

1. The problem of deciding how much of six different products to produce and sell, when each product requires a certain amount of LABOR, machine time and warehouse space for every unit produced, and where there are fixed limits on the amounts of labor, machine time and warehouse space available. The most profitable output mix must be found within the constraint of availability of resources.

2. The problem of deciding how much of 12 different nutrients to include in an animal feed, given the cost of each nutrient and the particular combination of vitamins each contains. The object would be to minimize the cost of the feed, subject to its containing at least some minimum amount of each vitamin.

3. The problem of deciding how much crude oil to ship from each of a number of oil fields at different locations to each of a number of refineries at different locations in such a way as to minimize transport costs. The constraints here arise out of the fact that more cannot be shipped from an origin than exists there, and more cannot be shipped to a destination than is required there.

The central feature of linear programming is that, as its name suggests, all the relationships involved must be linear. (⇛ LINEAR RELATIONSHIP; KOOPMANS, TJALLING).

Linear regression model. ⇛ LEAST SQUARES REGRESSION.

Linear relationship. A mathematical relationship that, in its simplest form, gives a straight line when drawn in two dimensions. The equation $y = a + bx$ would describe a straight line once we assign particular values to a and b. The essential feature of the linear relationship is that, no matter how large x is, a change in it of one unit always leads to a change in y of b units. The linear relationship can be generalized to make y depend on two or more variables, e.g., $y = a + bx + cz + dw$.

Liquidation. The termination, dissolution or winding up of a limited company. Liquidation of a company may be initiated by the shareholders, the directors (voluntary liquidation), its creditors or by a court order if the company is insolvent (⇛ INSOLVENCY). If the company is solvent, the ordinary shareholders will receive any surplus after the company's liabilities have been met (⇛ LIMITED LIABILITY). (⇛⇛ BANKRUPTCY).

Liquidity. The ease with which an ASSET can be exchanged for MONEY. The liquidity of an asset is determined by the nature of the MARKET on which it is traded. For example, stock in a corporation is liquid because there is a well-organized market on which it can be bought and sold, and so, within quite a short time, exchanged for CASH. A house, on the other hand, tends to be illiquid, since it can take some time and effort to sell, even when DEMAND for houses may be fairly strong. The term may also be applied to an institution or individual; a firm is said to be liquid if a high proportion of its assets are held in the form of money or very liquid assets. The extent of the firm's liquidity in this sense then gives an indication of its ability to meet its expenditures quickly enough to satisfy creditors and avoid BANKRUPTCY.

Liquidity preference. The desire to hold MONEY rather than other forms of WEALTH, e.g., STOCKS and BONDS. It can be thought of as stemming from the transactions motive, SPECULATIVE MOTIVE and PRECAUTIONARY MOTIVE for holding money, and so it will be influenced by the levels of INCOME and WEALTH, RATES OF INTEREST, EXPECTATIONS and the institutional features of the economy that determine the INCOME VELOCITY OF CIRCULATION. (⇛⇛ KEYNES, JOHN MAYNARD).

Liquidity ratio. 1. The ratio of liquid ASSETS to the current LIABILITIES of a business. Also called the cash ratio or *quick ratio*, it is a very crude test of solvency. 2. The proportion of the total assets of a bank that are held in the form of CASH and liquid assets, more usually referred to as the *reserve ratio*. (⇛ BANKING).

Listed security. A security listed and tradable on a STOCK EXCHANGE. Corporations wishing to list their securities must comply with the requirements of the exchanges, and most new issues must be registered with the SECURITIES AND EXCHANGE COMMISSION. (⇛ NEW ISSUE MARKET).

LM curve. This describes the locus of points in two dimensions that illustrates the relationship between equilibrium values of the real interest rate

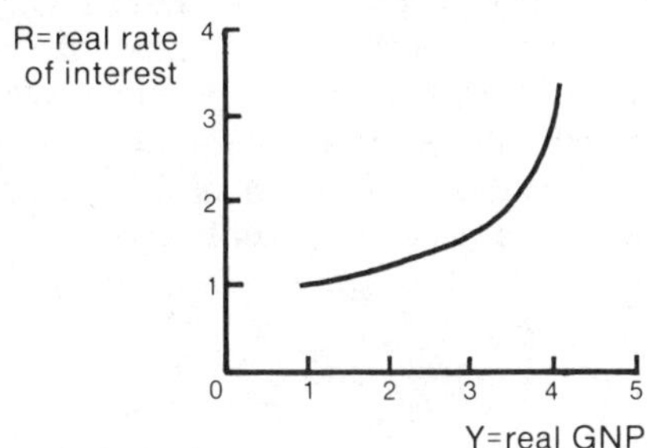

(⇛ RATE OF INTEREST) and real GNP (⇛ GROSS NATIONAL PRODUCT) for the monetary sector of the economy. The relationship is shown in the graph and assumes that the stock of money is fixed.

It shows all the points where equilibrium exists in the money market; that is, the real supply of money equals the real demand. In the lower left of the LM curve, the low income suggests a low demand for money for transaction purposes. With a fixed supply of money, this is possible only at a low rate of interest, where most assets are held as money, not, for example, as bonds. The upper right of the LM curve, with high income and high interest rates, suggests a high demand for the fixed stock of money because only a small share of assets is held as money. (⇛ KEYNES, JOHN MAYNARD).

Loan. The borrowing of a sum of MONEY by one person, company, government or other organization from another. Loans may be secured or unsecured (⇛ SECURITIES), interest-bearing or interest-free, long-term or short-term, redeemable or irredeemable. Loans may be made by individuals and companies, banks (⇛ BANK LOAN), INSURANCE and FINANCE COMPANIES, and other FINANCIAL INTERMEDIARIES, or by the issue of securities. (⇛⇛ FINANCE; TERM LOANS).

Loanable funds. MONEY that is available for lending to individuals and institutions. The main sources of these funds are: SAVINGS of individuals and firms, e.g., as RETAINED EARNINGS, DEPRECIATION allowances, etc.; DISHOARDING; and an increase in the MONEY SUPPLY made available by government and banks. Thus, loanable funds represent a flow of money onto the MARKET for LOANS of all kinds.

Loan capital. Fixed-interest borrowed funds. Alternative term for BOND and DEBENTURE.

Loaned-up bank. A bank is considered fully loaned-up when it is holding a cash reserve just about equal to its minimum required cash reserves. (⇛ REQUIRED RESERVES).

Loan stock. Synonym for LOAN CAPITAL.

Location theory. A body of theory that attempts to explain and predict the locational decisions of firms and the spatial patterns of industry and agriculture that result from aggregates of the individual decisions. The main aim of locational theorists has been to integrate the space dimension into conventional economic theory.

Location theory originated in the work of JOHANN HEINRICH VON THUNEN and Alfred Weber, who developed MODELS of location for firms in an environment of PERFECT COMPETITION. Both assumed that ENTREPRENEURS attempted to maximize PROFITS in the face of a given PRICE fixed by the MARKET and outside their control, with perfect knowledge of the COST characteristics of all locations. As a result of these assumptions, locational decisions were explained solely in terms of differences in production and transport costs between sites. The main difference between the two was that von Thunen began with an agricultural producer in a fixed location and attempted to explain his choice of product, whereas Weber took the case of a manufacturer with a given product and tried to explain his choice of location.

Until relatively recently, most work on location theory followed Weber and von Thunen in assuming perfect competition and in concentrating on cost minimization models, taking sales revenue as constant over all locations. The simplest of such models assume that producers have a market at one location and a raw-material source at another, with the problem being to predict the choice of location of the firm. If the assumption is made that production costs are constant over all locations, then the problem is simply that of finding the location that minimizes TRANSFER COSTS. Although the assumptions clearly create a highly simplified model, several definite predictions can be made that tend to be consistent with the behavior of firms for which transfer costs are a high proportion of total costs. Briefly, some of these predictions are:

1. If a production process involves loss of weight (e.g., ore refining), loss of bulk (cotton ginning) or decrease in perishability (fruit canning), the firm will locate to the raw-material source.

2. If the process involves gains in weight, bulk or perishability, the firm will locate to the market.

3. Location between the market and the raw-material source will not in general occur, for two reasons: First, freight rates per ton-mile diminish as the distance carried increases, which makes one long haul cheaper than two hauls with the same total distance; and second, a central location would mean loading and unloading charges for both raw material and finished product rather than for just one of them.

Obvious generalizations of this model have been made by introducing several markets and raw-material sources and by removing the assumption of equal production costs over all locations. However, as long as the assumptions of profit maximization and given product price were retained, the emphasis lay on determination of least-cost locations, their characteristics and the patterns of industrial location to which they give rise.

In the past 20 years or so, emphasis has shifted to the relation between location and demand, while the assumption of perfect competition has tended to be replaced by an assumption of imperfect competition (⇛ MONOPOLISTIC COMPETITION). The idea of profit maximization as the basic motivation of the firm has, however, remained.

Location theory can be viewed as an extension of the theory of the firm (⇛ FIRM, THEORY OF) to analysis of location decisions, whereas in conventional MICROECONOMICS only decisions on price, output, INVESTMENT and selling expenditures are normally considered.

Logistic curve. A curve that is often used to represent the growth process of some VARIABLE. Its shape is shown in the diagram below. Its mathematical equation is:

$$y = \frac{a}{1 + be^{-cx}}$$

where y and x are the variables; a, b and c are PARAMETERS; and e is the well-known mathematical constant, equal approximately to 2.71828, which plays an important role in growth processes of all kinds.

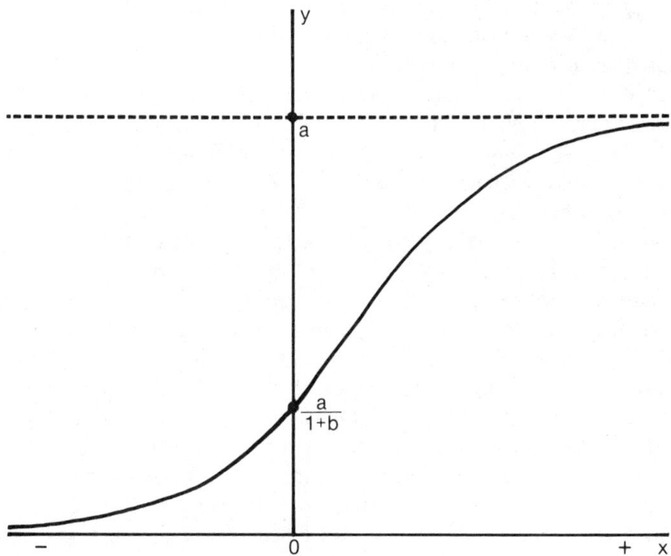

If we think of y as the total sales of a new product, for example, and x as time, the curve would imply that sales of the new product grow rather slowly at first, but then the product "takes off," and there is a period of rapid growth, followed by a leveling off as a product reaches its SATURATION POINT in the market.

Lome Convention. A convention signed in 1975 at Lome, the capital of Togo, by the members of the EUROPEAN ECONOMIC COMMUNITY and 46 DEVELOPING COUNTRIES in Africa, the Caribbean and the Pacific (ACP states). It replaced previous association agreements made by the original six members of the EEC with former colonies (Yaounde Convention) and the East African Community (Arusha Agreement). (The East African Community was a common market (⇛ CUSTOMS UNION) of Uganda, Kenya and Tanzania.) Under the Lome Convention all ACP industrial exports, and most agricultural exports, to the EEC are free of duty. Financial and technical aid—including an export income stabilization scheme, called Stabex, for agricultural exports—was also agreed upon, and the European Development Fund was set up by the EEC to administer and channel aid funds to the Lome countries.

In 1979 a second agreement was signed at Lome between the EEC and the developing countries in Africa, the Caribbean and the Pacific (ACP), of which there are now 60 members. It continues duty-free access to the EEC for most exports of ACP. The finance available for Stabex was increased to $700 million, and the conditions of the loans were eased. Lome II also introduced a scheme for supporting mineral exports. The budget for the Center for Industrial Development at Brussels, which promotes investment in ACP countries, was increased to $30 million. In general, aid through the European Development Fund and the EUROPEAN INVESTMENT BANK was increased to $7,000 million for the five-year period to 1985.

Long-dated securities. ⇛ DATED SECURITIES

Long end of the market. That part of the market for BONDS which is concerned with dealings in SECURITIES with distant MATURITY dates.

Longfield, Samuel Mountifort (1802–84). An Irish lawyer who became the first incumbent of the Chair of Political Economy at Trinity College, Dublin. His most important work in economics was *Lectures on Political Economy,* published in 1834. He argued convincingly against the LABOR THEORY of value (⇛ VALUE, THEORIES OF) and developed a marginal revenue productivity theory (⇛ MARGINAL REVENUE PRODUCT) of labor and capital. Moreover, some of his ideas on capital and the RATE OF INTEREST foreshadowed the work of the AUSTRIAN SCHOOL.

Long run. In PRICE THEORY the long run is defined as the time period long enough for the firm to be able to vary the quantities of all its FACTORS OF PRODUCTION rather than just some of them. For example, suppose that a firm uses LABOR, raw materials and machinery to make a particular product. Labor is hired on a weekly contract; raw materials take one month to arrive, from date of order; while plant and machinery take two years to design, order, construct and install. The "long run" for this firm is therefore any period longer than two years, since over this time the firm can vary all its factors of production. The implication of the definition is that the "long run" is not a fixed period of time for all firms in all industries but rather varies with the characteristics of an industry's technology. The electricity industry requires five to six years to plan, construct and install new generating capacity, and so its "long run" is five to six years. Note also that although it is normally assumed that the long run is determined by the time period required to extend plant capacity, this need not always be the case, and the definition of the long run is perfectly neutral as regards which INPUT (or inputs) actually determines the long run.

The importance of the long run in the theory of the firm (⇛ FIRM, THEORY OF) is that it is long enough to permit the firm to choose the most efficient combination of inputs to produce any given output. Suppose a firm experiences an increase in DEMAND. Initially, it can only expand output by increasing quantities of labor and raw materials, though if it expects the increase in demand to be reasonably permanent, it will set in motion the process of increasing plant capacity. In deciding on the size of this increase, it can aim at the best combination of plant, labor and raw materials to produce the planned rate of output. In the meantime, however, it must work within the limitations of its existing plant, and this will involve it in using too little plant and too much labor (and possibly other inputs) relative to that which it can achieve in the long run. Hence, it will tend to incur higher AVERAGE COSTS of production than it will in the long run, due to the fact that it is not able to use the most efficient input combination.

More generally, the long run is often loosely taken as the period long enough for underlying tendencies to change to work themselves out fully. It was in this sense that JOHN MAYNARD KEYNES was using the term in his famous dictum: "In the long-run we are all dead." (⇛⇛ MARSHALL, ALFRED).

Long-term capital. ⇛ BUSINESS FINANCE.

Lorenz curve. A curve that shows the relation between the cumulative percentage of some group of units (e.g., firms, HOUSEHOLDS) and the cumulative percentage of the total amount of some VARIABLE (e.g., employment, income) that they account for. The units are arranged in order of increasing size. For example, from information on the size distribution of corporations (⇛ SIZE DISTRUBITION OF FIRMS), we might construct the following table:

Cumulative percentage of firms	Cumulative percentage of total employment that they account for
10	2
20	6
30	11
40	18
50	26
60	38
70	51
80	65
90	80
100	100

It shows, for example, that the smallest 10 percent of firms had only 2 percent of the total employment, while the largest 10 percent of firms had 20 percent of total employment. We would then draw the Lorenz curve as shown in the diagram.

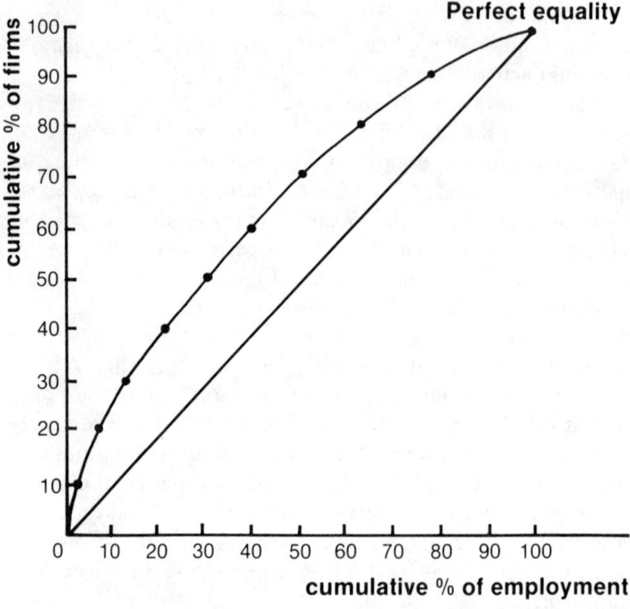

The purpose of the Lorenz curve is to show the degree of inequality in the distribution from which it is taken. If there was perfect equality, each successive equal step up in the cumulative percentage of firms, shown in the table, would be accompanied by a similar increase in the cumulative percentage of employment. Hence, the curve, when graphed, would be a straight line, as shown in the diagram. The greater the curvature of the Lorenz curve, the greater the degree of inequality, indicating the smaller the proportion of employment accounted for by the smallest firms and the greater that of the largest firms. The Lorenz curve is also often used to show the inequality in the INCOME DISTRIBUTION. (⇛ GINI COEFFICIENT).

M

McFadden Act. This legislation, enacted in 1927, embodied several recommendations of the COMPTROLLER OF THE CURRENCY of 1924. The most important aspect of the bill dealt with the matter of unit BANKING, since it allowed for the establishment of branches of national banks within the laws of individual states. There was a further restriction that called for national and state banks to relinquish their branches if they wished to be members of the FEDERAL RESERVE SYSTEM.

Macroeconomics. That part of economics which is primarily concerned with the study of relationships between broad economic aggregates, the most important of which are NATIONAL INCOME, aggregate SAVING and consumers' expenditure (or consumption), INVESTMENT, aggregate employment, the quantity of money (⇛ MONEY SUPPLY), the average price level and the BALANCE OF PAYMENTS. It is largely concerned with explaining the determinants of the magnitudes of these aggregates and of their rates of change through time. A major preoccupation is also the role of government expenditure (⇛ BUDGET; MONETARY POLICY; TAXATION) in determining the general level of economic activity. Macroeconomics proceeds by defining and analyzing, in some depth, relationships between the aggregates, finding the conditions under which the system is in static or dynamic EQUILIBRIUM and noting the characteristics of the equilibrium state. This then enables predictions to be made about the consequences of changes in certain key magnitudes, e.g., the level of investment or government expenditure. Modern macroeconomics largely dates from the publication of JOHN MAYNARD KEYNES' *The General Theory of Employment, Interest and Money* in 1936. (⇛⇛ FISCAL POLICY; INCOME DETERMINATION, THEORY OF; TRADE CYCLE).

Malthus, Thomas Robert (1766–1834). He was educated at St. John's College, Cambridge, England and became a fellow there, after studying mathematics and philosophy. He entered the Church of England and became a country parson. He was subsequently professor of history and political economy at the East India Company's Haileybury College. His *Essay on the Principle of Population as it Affects the Future Improvement of Society* was published in 1798, and a revised edition in 1803. His other works include: *An Inquiry into the Nature and Progress of Rent* (1815), *The Poor Law* (1817), *Principles of Political Economy* (1820) and *Definitions of Political Economy* (1827). Malthus is remembered for his essays on POPULATION. Population had a natural growth rate described by a GEOMETRIC PROGRESSION, whereas the natural resources necessary to support the population grew at a rate similar to an ARITHMETIC PROGRESSION. Without restraints, therefore, there would be a continued pressure on living standards, both in terms of room and of output. He advocated moral restraint on the size of families. Malthus also carried on a long argument with DAVID RICARDO against Say's Law (⇛ SAY,

JEAN-BAPTISTE). Briefly, Say's law stated that there could be no general overproduction or underproduction of COMMODITIES, on the grounds that whatever was bought by somebody must have been sold by somebody else. (JOHN MAYNARD KEYNES found some affinity between Malthus's conclusions and his own in his *General Theory.*) Malthus, however, was arguing strictly within the basic assumption of the equality of planned SAVINGS and INVESTMENT in CLASSICAL ECONOMICS and was a long way from Keynes's revolutionary assumption that they are made equal only by movements in total INCOME. Saving to Malthus was investment. His argument for underconsumption was simply that an increase in savings necessarily diminished consumption on the one hand, and on the other increased the output of consumers' goods through increased investment. At the same time, because the LABOR supply was inelastic (⇛ ELASTICITY), wages rose, and therefore so did costs. (⇛⇛ SISMONDI, JEAN CHARLES LEONARD SIMONDE DE).

Malynes, Gerald (1586–1641). An English merchant and government official and a leading exponent of MERCANTILISM. His publications include *A Treatise of the Canker of England's Commonwealth* (1601), *Saint George for England, Allegorically Described* (1601), *England's View in the Unmasking of two Paradoxes* (1603), *The Maintenance of Free Trade* (1622), and *The Center of the Circle of Commerce* (1623). He showed how an outflow of precious metals could lead to a fall in PRICES at home and a rise in prices abroad. This was an important clarification of the economic thought of the time. He suggested that higher import tariffs (⇛ TARIFFS, IMPORT) should be levied and EXPORTS of BULLION prohibited, because he believed that a country's growth was related to the accumulation of precious metals. He thought that exchange control should be used to improve the TERMS OF TRADE, supporting his policy on the belief that English exports were price inelastic (⇛ ELASTICITY). (⇛⇛ QUANTITY THEORY OF MONEY).

Managed currency. A CURRENCY is said to be managed if the EXCHANGE RATE is not fixed by FREE-MARKET forces, i.e., if the government influences the rate by buying and selling its own MONEY or by other means. Most currencies are managed in some sense today, even when they are allowed to float. (⇛⇛ EXCHANGE CONTROL; INTERNATIONAL MONETARY FUND).

Management accountancy. Business accounting practice concerned with the provision of information to management for policy-making purposes as opposed to that required for the preparation of BALANCE SHEETS and other information required by law. Insofar as the two sets of information overlap, the phrase is imprecise, but it usefully emphasizes the recent aspects of the development of accounting, notably in cost control (⇛ COST ACCOUNTING) and INVESTMENT.

Manchester school. "Manchesterism" was an epithet applied in Germany to those who subscribed to a political-economic philosophy of "LAISSEZ-FAIRE." It was applied, in particular, to the movement in England from 1820 to 1850 that was inspired by the propaganda of the Anti-Corn Law League. This was headed by Cobden and Bright, and supported by the economics of

DAVID RICARDO. The "school" believed in FREE TRADE and political and economic freedom with the minimum of government restraint.

Mandeville, Bernard de (1670–1733). Born at Dort in Holland, Mandeville obtained an M.D. at Leyden and established himself in London, England as a practicing doctor. In 1705 he published a poem called *The Grumbling Hive,* which was reissued in 1714 and 1729 under the title of *The Fable of the Bees or Private Vices, Public Benefits.* In this pamphlet he showed how, although individuals indulge in unholy vices in their private behavior, nevertheless in the aggregate they contributed to the public good and therefore could be excused. ADAM SMITH was severely critical of the satirical nature of the work. (⇛ INVISIBLE HAND).

Margin. The down payment required before money can be borrowed to purchase STOCKS. The margin is usually set as a percentage of the stock price. (⇛ REGULATIONS T, U, G).

Marginal analysis. A marginal change is a very small increase or decrease in the total quantity of some VARIABLE, and marginal analysis is the analysis of the relations between such changes in related economic variables. The importance of marginal analysis arises in two somewhat different ways, one of which is associated more with its use in MICROECONOMICS and the other with its MACROECONOMIC applications. Much of microeconomics is concerned with the analysis of optimizing behavior, i.e., the search for OPTIMUM values of particular variables. The consumer is assumed to maximize UTILITY; the firm is assumed to maximize PROFIT and, in doing so, to minimize COSTS for every level of output; the policymaker is assumed to maximize social welfare (⇛ SOCIAL WELFARE). Now the value of a variable that yields a maximum is such that a small increase and decrease from that value will cause the value of the MAXIMAND to fall. Similarly, a value of the variable that yields a minimum is such that a small increase and decrease from that value will cause the value of the MINIMAND to rise. The search for optimum values therefore involves the definition and analysis of marginal concepts, and this is how virtually all the marginal concepts in microeconomics arise. The mathematician will, of course, recognize "marginal analysis" as a straightforward application of differential calculus and the various marginal concepts as being special names given to first derivatives of particular functions; and he will also appreciate how those concepts arise in the search for maxima and minima, constrained and unconstrained, of functions such as profits as a function of output, utility as a function of quantities of goods consumed and output as a function of quantities of INPUTS used.

Marginal analysis arises in macroeconomics not so much because we are trying to find optimum solutions, but because we are directly concerned with the effects of changes in certain variables (e.g., INVESTMENT, EXPORTS and government expenditure) on certain other variables (e.g., employment and NATIONAL INCOME). (This sort of consideration also occurs in microeconomics.) The analysis of the relationship between small changes in variables is therefore of direct interest. (⇛ COMPARATIVE STATIC EQUILIB-

RIUM ANALYSIS; GOSSEN, HERMANN HEINRICH; JEVONS, WILLIAM STANLEY; MARGINAL COST; MARGINAL PRODUCT; MARGINAL PROPENSITY TO CONSUME; MARGINAL PROPENSITY TO SAVE; MARGINAL RATE OF SUBSTITUTION; MARGINAL REVENUE; MARGINAL UTILITY; MENGER, CARL; THÜNEN, JOHANN HEINRICH VON; WALRAS, MARIE ESPRIT LEON).

Marginal cost. The increase in cost resulting from a small increase in the rate of output of a good or service. For example, if a plant is producing 999 units of output per week at a total cost of $5,000, and when it steps up production to 1,000 units of output per week its total cost rises to $5,004, then $4 is its marginal cost. The concept of marginal cost plays an important role in the theory of the firm (⇛ FIRM, THEORY OF). If the firm is seeking to maximize PROFIT, it has to ask itself whether a small increase in output from its existing level would add more to sales revenue than it does to cost, because, if so, it would increase profit and should therefore be undertaken. Thus, one-half of this marginal profitability calculation is marginal cost.

It is necessary to distinguish between SHORT-RUN and LONG-RUN marginal cost. Suppose the firm is deciding upon its output levels for the coming month. Although it will be able to vary the quantities of some of the FACTORS OF PRODUCTION it uses—for example, energy, raw materials and some kinds of labor services—there will be some factors whose quantities cannot be varied (or would be prohibitively costly to vary in such a short period)—e.g., its stock of machinery and buildings, and perhaps some kinds of highly skilled labor. It must then calculate the cost of changes in output taking into account the fact that only some of its inputs are variable. The corresponding marginal cost is then a *short-run* marginal cost. Suppose, on the other hand, that the firm is planning output for a month so far into the future that, over the intervening period, it is possible to change *all* input levels. For example, it is long enough for the firm to plan, buy and install more machinery; construct new buildings; hire or train the skilled labor. Then it can calculate the cost of changes in output in that future period on the basis that all inputs are variable, and the associated marginal cost will be *long-run* marginal cost. The relevant marginal cost to use is always unambiguous: It is determined by the precise period for which output is being planned and the possibilities of varying inputs for that period.

Marginal-cost pricing. A method of setting PRICE, by which the price at which an output can be sold on the market is equated to the MARGINAL COST of producing that output. In diagrammatic terms, the required price and output are found at the point at which the DEMAND CURVE cuts the marginal cost curve. Marginal cost pricing is often recommended as an appropriate policy for PUBLIC ENTERPRISE and regulated industries (⇛ REGULATION), on the grounds that it is the pricing policy that maximizes social welfare (⇛ SOCIAL WELFARE FUNCTION). The argument goes as follows: The theory of demand (⇛ DEMAND, THEORY OF) tells us that each consumer values the marginal unit of a good he buys at exactly the price he pays for it. For example, if you buy 50 units of electricity per day at a price of 15 cents per unit, then the 50th unit is worth just 15 cents to you, no more, no less.

The marginal cost of the good shows the value of the RESOURCES absorbed in producing the marginal unit of output, and hence the value of the other goods and services that the economy could have produced with those resources. Now if a price and output were chosen such that price exceeded marginal cost, that would mean consumers place a higher value on the marginal bit of their consumption than it costs to divert resources from other uses to produce that marginal bit of consumption. Therefore, it would be possible to increase *net* consumer benefits in the economy by supplying a bit more of the output. Thus, no price greater than marginal cost can be consistent with maximizing net consumer benefit or social welfare. Likewise, if price and output were such that marginal cost exceeded price, the value of the resources absorbed in producing the marginal bit of output exceeds consumers' valuation of that output, and net benefit can be increased by reducing output. If it will not be possible to make such welfare-increasing output adjustments, it will be necessary to set price equal to marginal cost. Clearly, the whole argument rests on two underlying propositions:

1. Output price is a correct measure of the benefit consumers derive from their marginal consumption.
2. Marginal cost is a correct measure of the value of the resources absorbed in producing the marginal bit of output.

If one or both of these propositions is *not* true, the "marginal-cost pricing rule" may have to be modified (⇛ HOTELLING, HAROLD).

Marginal efficiency of capital. ⇛ INTERNAL RATE OF RETURN

Marginal efficiency of investment. ⇛ INTERNAL RATE OF RETURN

Marginal physical product. ⇛ MARGINAL PRODUCT

Marginal product. The increase in total output resulting from a small increase in one FACTOR OF PRODUCTION, all other factors held constant. In mathematical terms, it is a partial derivative of the PRODUCTION FUNCTION. We would then talk about the MARGINAL PRODUCT OF LABOR, the marginal product of capital (⇛ INTERNAL RATE OF RETURN), etc. There are as many marginal products as factors of production. (⇛⇛ DIMINISHING MARGINAL PRODUCT, LAW OF).

Marginal productivity of capital. ⇛ INTERNAL RATE OF RETURN

Marginal productivity theory of wages. A theory based on the idea that the DEMAND for LABOR is determined by its marginal productivity (⇛ DISTRIBUTION, THEORY OF), and indeed, that the wage of labor will be equal to its MARGINAL VALUE PRODUCT. This stems from the idea that it pays a firm to increase the amount of labor it employs, until the extra revenue gained by employing one more unit of labor is just equal to the wage. Just as the interaction of SUPPLY and DEMAND determines the price of a good, so the relationship between the marginal productivity and the supply of labor interacts to determine wages. (⇛⇛ BARGAINING THEORY OF WAGES).

Marginal product of labor. The increase in output resulting from increasing LABOR input by a small amount. In mathematical terms, it is the partial derivative of the PRODUCTION FUNCTION with respect to labor. In line with the law of diminishing marginal product (⇛ DIMINISHING MARGINAL PRODUCT, LAW OF), it is assumed that, after some point, increasing the input of labor results in smaller and smaller increases in output. The marginal product of labor underlies the theory of the DEMAND for labor and the determination of the wage rate, since the firm is assumed to adjust the amount of labor it seeks to hire to the point where the revenue it gets from the sale of the output of the marginal worker is just equal to the wage it has to pay him. (⇛⇛ MARGINAL PRODUCTIVITY THEORY OF WAGES).

Marginal propensity to consume (MPC). The proportion of a small increase in INCOME that will be devoted to increased CONSUMPTION expenditure. The value of the MPC is derived from the slope of the CONSUMPTION FUNCTION. Typically, it is expected to be less than one. That is, an increase in income leads to a smaller increase in consumption expenditure, the difference being saved. The MPC was first defined by JOHN MAYNARD KEYNES and forms an important part of his theory of the MULTIPLIER. Keynes in fact asserted, as a "fundamental psychological law," that as NATIONAL INCOME rose, the MPC would fall. That is, the richer people are, the greater the proportion of an increase in income that would be saved. (⇛⇛ INCOME DETERMINATION, THEORY OF; MARGINAL PROPENSITY TO SAVE).

Marginal propensity to save (MPS). The proportion of an increase in INCOME that will be saved. Since an increase in income will be partly saved and partly consumed, the MPS is equal to one minus the MARGINAL PROPENSITY TO CONSUME. The MPS plays an important part in JOHN MAYNARD KEYNES' theory of the MULTIPLIER. In fact, in its simplest form, the multiplier is calculated as 1/MPS. The corollary of Keynes' "fundamental psychological law," that the MPC falls as income rises, is that the MPS rises as income rises. (⇛⇛ CONSUMPTION FUNCTION; INCOME DETERMINATION, THEORY OF).

Marginal rate of substitution (MRS). The rate at which one good must be substituted for another as a consumer moves along his INDIFFERENCE CURVE. Let us consider the indifference curve in the diagram.

If the individual is initially at point A, representing a particular quantity of x and a particular quantity of y, we can "move him along" his indifference curve by subtracting a small amount of x and substituting for it the appropriate amount of y. What is "appropriate" depends on the shape of the indifference curve and varies along it. Thus, in moving from A to B, a relatively small increment in y is quite enough to compensate for the reduction in x. At E, however, the same reduction in x requires a much larger increment in y to compensate. Let us denote the (supposedly very small) change in x by dx and the appropriate change in y—required to "get back onto" the indifference curve—by dy. The marginal rate of substitution of y for x is then defined as dy/dx, i.e., the ratio of the required change in y to the change in x. Alternatively, if we were thinking in terms of increasing x and reducing y, we could define the MRS of x for y as dx/dy. Clearly, the two expressions are reciprocal. Mathematically, the MRS measures the slope of the indifference curve, and the type of curvature normally assumed implies a decreasing MRS, i.e., a slope that increases in absolute value but decreases in numerical value as we move from right to left.

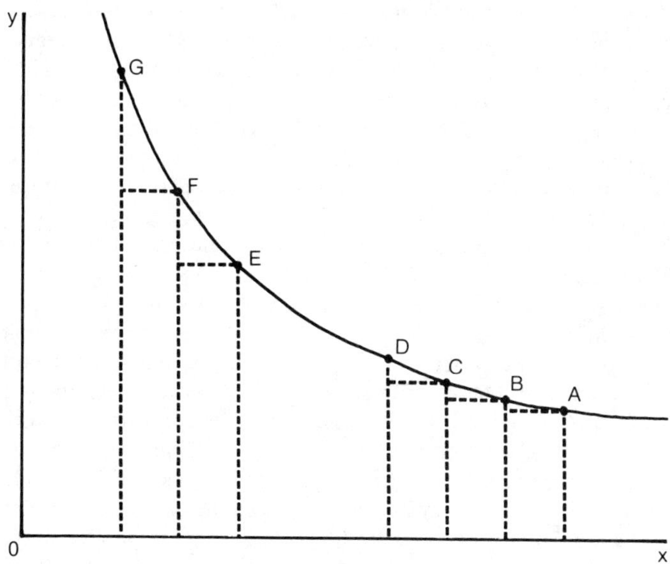

Marginal revenue. The change in a firm's total revenue that results from changing output sold by one unit. Marginal revenue to a firm will either be equal to or below PRICE. If the price of the good is the same for whatever quantity the firm sells, i.e., if the firm is in PERFECT COMPETITION, then the increase in revenue from selling one more unit is equal to price. If, however, the attempt to sell an additional unit of output forces the firm to reduce price on *all* the output it sells, then marginal revenue will equal the new price less the fall in revenue on the units that would have been sold at the higher price. The concept of marginal revenue plays an important role in theories of imperfect competition (⇛ MONOPOLISTIC COMPETITION), since equality of marginal revenue and MARGINAL COST determines the profit-maximizing EQUILIBRIUM of the firm. (⇛⇛ MARGINAL ANALYSIS).

Marginal revenue product. The marginal revenue product of an INPUT is derived by multiplying the MARGINAL PRODUCT of the input by the MARGINAL REVENUE of the good when it is sold. The marginal product of an input is defined in terms of physical units of output—hence, it is often called the *marginal physical product.* Suppose the marginal product of an input, X, is 1.2 units, while the marginal revenue of the good is \$3.00. Then the marginal revenue product of X is simply $\$3.00 \times 1.2 = \$3.60$ per unit of X. That is, we are simply finding the extra revenue that is brought in by increasing the quantity of X by one unit. (⇛⇛ MARGINAL PRODUCTIVITY THEORY OF WAGES; MARGINAL VALUE PRODUCT).

Marginal social product. The effect on social welfare (⇛ SOCIAL WELFARE FUNCTION) of a small change in the quantity of an INPUT used. The definitions of MARGINAL PRODUCT, MARGINAL REVENUE PRODUCT and MARGINAL VALUE PRODUCT are framed implicitly in terms of the private returns that can be gained through sales of the output on a MARKET and that accrue to the individual. However, there may be certain effects on social welfare resulting from an increase in quantity of an input used that differ from the direct gains to the individual, and so the marginal social product of the input may differ from its marginal "private" product. (For a further discussion of the reasons for divergence between private and social costs and returns, with examples, see EXTERNALITIES.) Where the subject of concern, in analysis or policy, is social welfare, then the appropriate concept is the marginal social product of an input rather than its private product.

Marginal utility. The increase in total UTILITY of CONSUMPTION of a good that results from increasing the quantity of the good consumed by one unit. This concept played an extremely important part in Marshallian demand theory (⇛ MARSHALL, ALFRED), but has been less important since the introduction of INDIFFERENCE ANALYSIS. It is important to appreciate the distinction between marginal and total utility. A good may have a very low marginal utility but a very high total utility, e.g., water. And since it is the *marginal utility* that (in conjunction with supply) determines PRICE, this explains the old *paradox of value* of why goods that are essential for life, i.e., have a high total utility, sell at low prices; whereas inessential goods, such as diamonds, sell at a high price. (⇛⇛ CONSUMER SURPLUS; GALIANI, FERDINANDO; VALUE, THEORIES OF; WALRAS, MARIE ESPRIT LEON).

Marginal utility, law of diminishing. A law stating that, after some point, successive equal increments in the quantity of a good yield smaller and smaller increases in UTILITY; i.e., MARGINAL UTILITY is diminishing. As a broad proposition, this hypothesis has some plausibility: Even the most ice cream-addicted child will begin to experience diminishing marginal utility after his fifth ice cream cone in a short space of time. However, economists' main objection to the "law" was directed at its implication that utility is a quantity capable of being measured in terms of fixed units, so that *n* units of a good can be said to yield "*x* units of utility." Comparison of differences in total utility requires utility to be measurable. But it has proved impossible to find an objective yardstick with which to measure utility. As a result, Marshallian demand theory (⇛ MARSHALL, ALFRED), which is based on the law of diminishing marginal utility, was superseded by INDIFFERENCE ANALYSIS. (⇛⇛ EDGEWORTH, FRANCIS YSIDRO).

Marginal utility of money. The increase in total UTILITY that results from increasing the quantity of MONEY an individual has by one unit. Since, typically, money is only valued because of the power it gives to buy goods (now or in the future), the MARGINAL UTILITY of money must ultimately derive from the marginal utilities of the goods (and SAVING) on which it is spent. Consistent with the law of diminishing marginal utility (⇛ MARGINAL UTILITY, LAW OF DIMINISHING), it is generally held that the marginal utility of money diminishes as the quantity of money possessed by an individual increases. (⇛⇛ MARSHALL, ALFRED).

Marginal value product. Analogous to the MARGINAL REVENUE PRODUCT of an INPUT, the marginal value product is a measure of the extra revenue that results from increasing the quantity of an input used by one unit, all other input quantities remaining constant. The marginal value product is found by multiplying the MARGINAL PRODUCT of the input by the PRICE of the product. Where the price at which a firm sells its output is the same whatever the quantity sold—i.e., where the market is in PERFECT COMPETITION—then MARGINAL REVENUE is equal to price, since the revenue brought in by the sale of an extra unit of output is always equal to the price. Hence, in this case, marginal revenue product and marginal value product are equal, and the latter correctly measures the extra revenue brought in by increasing the quantity of an input used by one unit. If the marginal product of an input is, say, 1.1 units, while its output price is \$2.00 per unit, then its marginal value product is \$2.00 × 1.1 = \$2.20. If, however, the firm must reduce price in order to sell a greater quantity—i.e., if it is in imperfect competition (⇛ MONOPOLISTIC COMPETITION)—then marginal revenue will generally be less than price, and so marginal value product will overstate the extra revenue actually brought in by increasing the quantity of an input used by one unit. This extra revenue will be accurately measured by the marginal revenue product. (⇛⇛ MARGINAL PRODUCTIVITY THEORY OF WAGES).

Market. A market exists when buyers wishing to exchange MONEY for a good or service are in contact with sellers wishing to exchange goods or services for money. A market is defined in terms of the fundamental forces of SUPPLY and DEMAND and is not necessarily confined to any particular geographical location. The concept of the market is basic to most of contemporary economics, since, in a FREE-MARKET ECONOMY, this is the mechanism by which RESOURCES are allocated. (⇛⇛ PRICE SYSTEM).

Market capitalization. ⇛ CAPITALIZATION

Market demand curve. ⇛ DEMAND CURVE

Market economy. ⇛ FREE-MARKET ECONOMY

Market failure. A situation in which the MARKET system produces an allocation of resources (⇛ RESOURCE ALLOCATION) that is not Pareto-efficient (⇛ ECONOMIC EFFICIENCY). It is possible to find ways of changing the resource allocation in such a way as to make some consumer(s) better off and none worse off. The prevalence of market failure would then refute ADAM SMITH's famous doctrine of the invisible hand, that individualistic self-seeking behavior by consumers and firms will be guided by the invisible hand (of market forces) to achieve the highest level of welfare for society as a whole. Market failure is predicted as likely to occur in the presence of MONOPOLY and OLIGOPOLY, EXTERNALITIES, PUBLIC GOODS and COMMON PROPERTY RESOURCES. In each case, individualistic behavior leads to a suboptimal result. A conclusion often drawn is that there is then a case for government intervention to "correct" the market failure, e.g., by regulating monopoly, taxing external diseconomies and supplying public goods

(⇛ REGULATION). It has been pointed out, however, that this is to commit the fallacy of supposing that the alternative to imperfect markets is "perfect government." In fact, government may have neither the means nor the inclination to correct adequately for market failure. The question becomes one of deciding which of two imperfect forms of organization is likely to lead to the least bad outcome, and this is a far more complex issue than the simple demonstration of market failure.

Market forces. The forces of SUPPLY and DEMAND, which together determine the PRICE at which a product is sold and the quantity that will be traded.

Market share. This can refer to (*a*) the sales of the product or products of a firm as a proportion of the sales of the product or products of the industry as a whole (e.g., sales of Ford automobiles compared with total U.S. automobile sales) or to (*b*) the sales of a particular COMMODITY compared with the total sales for the class of commodity of which it is a member (e.g., sales of automobiles with automatic transmission in a particular MARKET compared with total sales of automobiles). The presumption is that the firm's product in (*a*) and the particular commodity in (*b*) are faced with competitive SUBSTITUTES in their respective markets. Market shares may also be calculated in terms of the proportion of the product in the total existing stock of that class of products as opposed to its share of the flow of new sales (e.g., Ford automobiles as a proportion of the total number of automobiles in use). *Penetration* is an alternative term for market share. (⇛⇛ SATURATION POINT).

Market structure. The underlying characteristics of a MARKET that determine the competitive relations between sellers. The most important of these characteristics are: (*a*) the SIZE DISTRIBUTION OF FIRMS, (*b*) the size distribution of buyers, (*c*) the BARRIERS TO ENTRY of new buyers and sellers, (*d*) the degree of product differentiation (⇛ DIFFERENTIATION, PRODUCT) and (*e*) the degree of VERTICAL INTEGRATION. Other characteristics that may be important are the capital intensity (⇛ CAPITAL-INTENSIVE) of production, the elasticity of demand for the product on the market and the spatial distribution of buyers and sellers.

Market supply. The SUPPLY of a good or service forthcoming from all sellers in a MARKET. (⇛⇛ ECONOMIC GOOD).

Market supply curve. ⇛ SUPPLY CURVE

Marshall Aid. At the end of the Second World War, only the United States had the necessary productive capacity to make good the losses experienced by other countries. European countries had heavy BALANCE OF PAYMENTS deficits *vis-a-vis* the United States. In 1946, in order to alleviate the resultant shortage of dollars, the United States and Canada made substantial LOANS. It was expected that these loans would be sufficient to cover requirements over the short period, which was all that was expected to be necessary for the world economies to recover. However, in 1948 a general LIQUIDITY crisis was only avoided by further loans made under the EUROPEAN RECOVERY PROGRAM. This program was called Marshall Aid, after the then U.S. Secretary of State, General G.C. Marshall. The loans were allocated under the direction of the ORGANIZATION FOR EUROPEAN ECONOMIC COOPERATION set up for this purpose.

Marshall, Alfred (1842–1924). He was educated at Merchant Taylor's School and graduated in mathematics at St. John's College, Cambridge, England. In 1868 he was appointed to a lectureship in moral science at Cambridge, and it was during this period that he began to study economics. In 1882 he moved to the Chair of Political Economy at Bristol. In 1885 he returned to Cambridge as professor of political economy, a post he retained until his retirement in 1908. His most important works include *The Pure Theory of Foreign Trade* (1879), *The Principles of Economics* (1890), *Industry and Trade* (1919) and *Money, Credit and Commerce* (1923). Marshall was in the long tradition of the English CLASSICAL SCHOOL, which was founded by ADAM SMITH and DAVID RICARDO, and his influence on succeeding generations of economists has been very great. His achievement was to refine and develop MICROECONOMIC theory to such a degree that much of what he wrote is still familiar to readers of the elementary economic textbooks today. His theory of VALUE brought together the diverse elements of previous theories. On the one hand, he showed how the demand for a COMMODITY is dependent on a consumer's UTILITY or welfare. The more of a commodity a consumer has, the less extra utility or benefit accrues to him from an additional purchase (⇛ GOSSEN, HERMANN HEINRICH). He will not go on buying a commodity until this extra benefit falls to zero. Rather, he will stop buying more when he finds that the MONEY he has to pay for it is worth more to him than the gain from having an extra unit of the commodity. At this point of EQUILIBRIUM, a fall in the PRICE, therefore, will mean that it becomes worthwhile to him to exchange his money for more of the commodity. In general, therefore, a fall in price will increase the quantity of the commodity demanded, and in theory, a schedule could be drawn up that shows how much would be demanded at each price. The resultant graph would show a downward-sloping DEMAND CURVE. Marshall invented the expression ELASTICITY to describe his measure of the response of demand to small changes in price. Similarly, on the supply side, higher prices are necessary to bring forward increased outputs, and a supply schedule with its corresponding supply curve can be drawn up. The price of the commodity is determined at the point where the two curves intersect. These worked like a pair of scissors, neither blade of which cuts without the presence of the other.

Marshall recognized that his consumer utility theory was in some ways an oversimplification. It does not take account of complementary or competitive goods (⇛ COMPLEMENTARY DEMAND) and assumes that the MARGINAL UTILITY of money is constant. However, he argued that his analysis applied to small price changes and to goods upon which only an insignificant proportion of income was spent. It was within this framework that Marshall discussed the idea of CONSUMER SURPLUS (⇛ DUPUIT, ARSEN JULES ETIENNE JUVENAL). For a given quantity of a commodity purchased on a competitive market, the price will be the same for each unit of the commodity sold. However, for any individual purchaser the price is equal to the utility to him of the last unit of the total quantity purchased; the last but one being worth more, the last but two worth more again, and so on. These utilities can be added up, and the extra—over the price and quantity paid out—is the consumer's surplus. He was aware of the shortcomings of the "Stationary State" of the typical classical analysis and emphasized the importance of the production period. He recognized the element of time as the chief difficulty of almost every economic problem. He considered (*a*) a market period in which supplies are all fixed; (*b*) a short period in which supplies can be increased, but only to the extent possible by better use of current capacity; and (*c*) a long period in which capacity itself can be increased. The classical economists had shown how RENT is received by landowners as a surplus. As land was a FACTOR OF PRODUCTION in fixed supply, it differed from other factors of production in that its returns were not related to work done. Marshall extended the concept by pointing out that, in the short run, man-made CAPITAL was in fixed supply also, and during the period that it took to manufacture, it earned a QUASI-RENT. (⇛⇛ COURNOT, ANTOINE AUGUSTIN; MARSHALL-LERNER CRITERION; MILL, JOHN STUART).

Marshall-Lerner criterion. A rule that states the ELASTICITY conditions under which a change in a country's EXCHANGE RATE would improve its BALANCE OF TRADE. A.P. Lerner set out the appropriate formulas in his book *Economics of Control* on the basis of the elasticity concepts developed by ALFRED MARSHALL. In its simplest form, the rule states that the price elasticities of demand for IMPORTS and EXPORTS must add up to greater than unity for an improvement to be effected. The volume of exports increases and the volume of imports decreases in response to a fall in the PRICE of the former and a rise in the price of the latter when a CURRENCY is devalued (assuming, for the sake of the argument, that there are no other factors influencing the MARKET, such as SUPPLY restrictions). There would therefore be an improvement in the balance of trade in volume terms, i.e., in terms of the prices ruling prior to DEVALUATION. However, what is important for the BALANCE OF PAYMENTS is the impact of devaluation on the value of trade. If the price elasticity of exports plus the price elasticity of imports is less than unity, it means that the increased cost of imports in terms of the domestic currency outweighs the value of the growth in exports. Putting it another way, the improvement in the volume of the balance of trade is not sufficient to offset the fall in the value of the balance of trade occasioned by the devaluation. (⇛⇛ TERMS OF TRADE).

Marshall Plan. ⇛ MARSHALL AID

Marx, Karl (1818–83). Born in Trier, he studied philosophy at Bonn University and at the Hegelian Center at Berlin University, and took a doctorate at Jena. For a time he was editor of *Rheinische Zeitung*, but the paper was suppressed, and in 1843 he fled to Paris. There he began his friendship and close association with Friedrich Engels, who encouraged in him an interest in political economy. After a brief return to Germany, he was banished, and in 1849 he settled in London, where he remained until his death in 1883. The *Communist Manifesto,* written jointly by Marx and Engels, was published in 1848. In 1859 the first fruits of his long, painstaking research at the British Museum appeared: the *Critique of Political Economy*. The first volume of *Das Kapital* came out in 1867. The remaining volumes, edited by Engels, were published posthumously in 1885 and 1894.

Marx's economics was essentially that of the CLASSICAL SCHOOL, especially of DAVID RICARDO, to whom he owed a great debt. However, he lifted economics out of its preoccupation with agriculture and stationary states. For Marx, CAPITALISM was a stage in the process of evolution removed from the primitive agricultural economy and moving toward the inevitable elimination of private property and the class structure. Marx attempted a synoptic view of the development of the whole structure of human society. His economics was only a part, though a fundamental part, of his all-embracing sociological and political theories. Marx postulated that the class structures of societies, their political systems and, indeed, their culture, were determined by the way in which societies produced their goods and services. Moreover, the whole structure was evolutionary. The class structure of a capitalist state was a reflection of the split between owners and non-owners of CAPITAL, which division characterized the manner in which production was carried out, and which already had within it the necessary ingredients of change.

Marx developed from ADAM SMITH and David Ricardo their labor theory of value (⇛ VALUE, THEORIES OF), which held the central place in his economic theory. For Ricardo the amount of LABOR used in the production of COMMODITIES was a rough determinant of relative prices in the long run. For Marx, however, the quantity of labor used up in the manufacture of a product determined value, and this value was fundamental and immutable. He did not satisfactorily explain any connection with relative prices. Labor consumption determined exchange value, which differed from use value. The distinction between the two in the case of labor, regarded in itself as a commodity, was a vital one in Marx's analysis. The capitalist pays wages, which are determined by the exchange value of workers. This exchange value is, in turn, determined by the socially necessary labor time required to "produce" the worker—that is, the labor inputs required to rear, feed, clothe and educate him. However, in return the capitalist gets the laborer's use value. The value of the laborer to the capitalist who uses him is greater than the value the capitalist paid in exchange for his services. This difference Marx called "surplus value"(s). Only labor yields surplus value. Other FACTORS OF PRODUCTION, such as plant and machinery and raw materials, only reproduce themselves in the productive process. (These ideas have some affinity with the PHYSIOCRATS' *"produit net,"* although in their case it was LAND that was the only factor that produced a surplus.) The amount of capital required to pay wages Marx called variable (v) (⇛ WAGE FUND THEORY), and the remainder he called constant (c). GROSS NATIONAL PRODUCT in the Marxian system is therefore given by $c + v + s$. The ratio of constant capital in total capital $c/(c+v)$ he called the organic composition of capital. The "exploitation rate" was s/v. The rate of profit was $s/c+v$. The desire for further wealth, coupled with competition and technical change, induced capitalists to invest from the surplus (which they expropriated from the workers) and in labor-saving machinery. The organic composition of capital therefore rose over time as more was spent on plant and machinery (c) compared with wages (v), with the result that, as only variable capital produced a surplus (and assuming that the exploitation rate remained constant), the rate of profit tended downward. (⇛ PROFIT, FALLING RATE OF.) On the one hand, diminishing profits and stronger competition would lead to MONOPOLY and the concentration of WEALTH in a few hands, and on the other hand, there would be an increasing squeeze on the REAL INCOMES of workers by the capitalists in their attempt to maintain PROFITS and the emergence of a large "reserve army of unemployed" arising from mechanization. The class conflict would become increasingly acute until the environment was such that the change inherent in the economic structure would be made manifest by the overthrow of capitalism.

Matrix. An array of numbers set out in rows and columns. The following, for example, are matrices:

$$\begin{bmatrix} 1 & 2 \\ 3 & 4 \end{bmatrix} \qquad \begin{bmatrix} 5 & 2 \\ 7 & 6 \\ 0 & -3 \end{bmatrix}$$

The individual numbers are called the elements of the matrix. It is usual to denote the elements of a matrix by some letter—say, a—so we would write the matrix as:

$$A = \begin{matrix} a_{11} & a_{12} & \dots & a_{1n} \\ a_{21} & a_{22} & \dots & a_{2n} \\ \dots & \dots & \dots & \dots \\ a_{m1} & a_{m2} & \dots & a_{mn} \end{matrix}$$

where each element is now defined by two subscripts, the first of which gives the row in which the element appears, the second the column. For example, a_{21} would denote the element in the second row and first column. Since the matrix A above has m rows and n columns, it is said to be of "order $m \times n$." Matrices are of considerable importance in modern economics, since many economic MODELS have a mathematical structure that permits representation by matrices. (⇛⇛ INPUT-OUTPUT ANALYSIS; MATRIX ALGEBRA).

Matrix algebra. A branch of mathematics that defines rules by which matrices (⇛ MATRIX) may be added, subtracted, multiplied and divided. It is also concerned with analyzing the properties of particular types of matrices and of particular types of expressions involving matrices. Though initially a purely abstract branch of mathematics, it has found considerable application in economics and ECONOMETRICS, because many of the models they use have a mathematical structure that permits representation by matrices. Indeed, such is the power and relative simplicity of matrix algebra, that matrix-based models are often applied to a problem even though it is known that they are not strictly appropriate, it being argued that the degree of insight achieved more than makes up for the fact that answers will only be approximate. (⇛⇛ INPUT-OUTPUT ANALYSIS).

Maturity. The date at which documentary promises to pay are redeemable in cash, i.e., DATED SECURITIES and ASSURANCE policies.

Maximand. That which it is desired to maximize. For example, it may be desired to find the level of output that maximizes (makes as large as possible) the profits of a firm. In that case, PROFIT is the maximand.

Maximin strategy. A principle of choosing a course of action or strategy in theoretical game situations (⇛ GAMES, THEORY OF). For each strategy the "player" may choose, he should find the worst possible payoff to himself that could result from the choice of strategy by his opponent, i.e., the minimum-valued payoff for each strategy. He should then choose that strategy which yields the largest of these minimum outcomes, so that he is *maxi*mizing his *mini*mum payoff. The term *maximin* describes this. This strategy is suggested as rational strategy in ZERO-SUM GAMES, given that an opponent is rational and is seeking to make himself as well off—and, hence, you as badly off—as he can. Simultaneous use of a maximin strategy by both players may then lead to an EQUILIBRIUM outcome of the game. The strategy appears less rational in so-called games against nature, however, where the opponent is not a rational, calculating opponent but "blind chance." In this case the extreme pessimism of the strategy, which in effect assumes that nature will always do its worst, may lead to choices that a reasonable man would regard as irrational, largely because it ignores all payoffs, other than the worst, in each strategy.

Member banks. ⇛ FEDERAL RESERVE SYSTEM

Menger, Carl (1840–1921). Professor of economics in the Faculty of Law at Vienna University from 1873 to 1903. His major work, in which he developed his marginal utility theory, *Grundsatze der Volkswirtschaftslehre,* was published in 1871. He was one of the three economists in the 1870s who independently put forward the theory of VALUE based on MARGINAL UTILITY and whose work had a profound influence on the subsequent evolution of economic thought (⇛ GOSSEN, HERMANN HEINRICH; JEVONS, WILLIAM STANLEY; WALRAS, MARIE ESPRIT LEON). Exchange takes place, he argued, because individuals have different subjective valuations of the same COMMODITY. Menger saw commodities in terms of their reverse order in the productive process, i.e., bread is prior to flour and flour prior to wheat. The PRICE of the first-order commodities, which is determined by their exchange for CONSUMPTION, is imputed back through to the higher-order commodities. The theory of diminishing UTILITY was the catalyst that eventually unified the theories of production and consumption. Menger himself, however, overemphasized consumption demand in the theory of value, just as the CLASSICAL ECONOMISTS had overemphasized production supply. (⇛ MARSHALL, ALFRED).

Mercantilism. The growth in INTERNATIONAL TRADE and the establishment of the power of the merchant after the medieval era led to the emergence of a body of thought, between the mid-16th and late 17th centuries that was primarily concerned with the relationship between a nation's wealth and its balance of foreign trade. The mercantilists recognized the growing power of the national economy and were in favor of the intervention of the state in economic activity to maximize national WEALTH. Partly because the monetary system was very primitive in relation to the growing needs of economic expansion, mercantilist writing was often overburdened with the identification of national wealth with precious metals. However, its leading writers did make important progress in developing economic thought and made significant contributions to the analysis of international trade problems. (⇛⇛ MALYNES, GERALD; MISSELDEN, EDWARD; MUN, SIR THOMAS; SERRA, ANTONIO).

Merchandise trade. ⇛ VISIBLE TRADE

Merger. The fusion of two or more separate corporations into one. In current usage merger is a special case of COMBINATION, where both the merging companies wish to join together and do so on roughly equal terms, as distinct from a TAKEOVER, which occurs against the wishes of one company. However, merger, takeover, amalgamation, absorption and fusion are sometimes all used as synonyms. Where two firms in the same business—i.e., competitors—merge, this is known as horizontal, or lateral, integration. Where two firms that are suppliers or customers of one another merge, this is known as VERTICAL INTEGRATION. (⇛⇛ CONGLOMERATE; HOLDING COMPANY).

Merit goods. Those kinds of goods (⇛ ECONOMIC GOOD) that society appears to consider intrinsically good or bad and so adopts measures to stimulate or discourage their consumption. For example, it may be decided that education is desirable, not simply because it increases the PRODUCTIVITY of LABOR but because it is inherently a good thing. RESOURCES may then be devoted to making it more widely available—e.g., through the public school system—than would be the case if left to MARKET FORCES. Similarly, consumption of hard drugs may be considered intrinsically undesirable and therefore made illegal. It should be noted that there is a strong element of paternalism in policies toward merit goods. Somehow, "society" decides that the preferences of individuals cannot be left to determine the levels of consumption of such commodities.

Microeconomics. Economic theory is conventionally divided into two parts: (*a*) microeconomics and (*b*) MACROECONOMICS. As the names suggest, the difference lies in the level of aggregation at which economic phenomena are studied. Microeconomics is concerned with the study of the individual "decision units"—consumers and firms—and the way in which their decisions interrelate to determine the PRICES of goods and FACTORS OF PRODUCTION and the quantities of these that will be bought and sold. Its ultimate aim is to understand the mechanism by which the total amount of RESOURCES possessed by society is allocated among alternative uses. The central concept in microeconomics is the MARKET. (⇛⇛ FREE-MARKET ECONOMY; PRICE SYSTEM; RESOURCE ALLOCATION).

Mill, John Stuart (1806–1873). In his childhood John Stuart Mill was subjected to a regime of severe educational discipline by his father, James Mill. He was acquainted with the major works of economics of the day by the age of 12, and was correcting the proofs of his father's book, *Elements of Political Economy,* when he was 13. He learned Ricardian economics and Benthamite UTILITARIANISM from his father. In 1823 he joined the East India Company, where he remained for 35 years. For 3 years, before moving to France to spend his retirement, he was a member of Parliament. He was an extraordinarily prolific writer, especially when it is remembered that he had a full-time job to hold down. His reputation was made by his *A System of Logic, Ratiocinative and Inductive, being a connected view of the Principles of Evidence and the Methods of Scientific Investigation,* which was published in 1843. His essay *On Liberty* appeared in 1859, and *Examination of Sir William Hamilton's Philosophy* in 1865. His two most important works on economics are *Essays on Some Unsettled Questions of Political Economy* (which was published in 1844, though he actually wrote it in 1829 when he was only 23) and *Principles of Political Economy with some of their Applications to Social Philosophy* (1848). The latter was intended to be a comprehensive review of the field of economic theory at the time and was, in fact, an up-to-date version of ADAM SMITH's *Wealth of Nations.* It succeeded so well that it remained the basic textbook for students of economics until the end of the century. The work is regarded as the apogee of the CLASSICAL SCHOOL of Adam Smith, DAVID RICARDO, THOMAS ROBERT MALTHUS and JEAN-BAPTISTE SAY. Mill himself said the book had nothing in it that was original, and indeed basically it is an eclectic work, intended simply to bring together the works of others. However, it is not true that Mill lacked originality altogether. He analyzed the forces that lead to increasing RETURNS TO SCALE, arguing that as a result there will be a tendency for industries to become more and more concentrated in a few firms. The advantages this gave should be set against the disadvantages that will accrue in the form of higher prices from the loss of competition. Recognition of this tendency led him to support strike action by trade unions. Trade unions were a necessary counterweight to the powerful employer (⇛ GALBRAITH, JOHN KENNETH). In his exposition of the theory of VALUE, Mill showed how PRICE is determined by the equality of DEMAND and SUPPLY, although he did not demonstrate the relationship by means of graphs or schedules. Mill recognized as a distinct problem the case of COMMODITIES with JOINT COSTS. He showed also how reciprocal demand for each other's products affected countries' TERMS OF TRADE. Mill brought in the idea of ELASTICITY of demand (though the actual expression was invented later by ALFRED MARSHALL) to analyze various alternative trading possibilities. His father had suggested that RENT, being a surplus according to Ricardian theory, was ideally suited to TAXATION. John Stuart took this idea up, and it became quite popular with the public. Mill proposed that all future increases in unearned rents should be taxed. (⇒ GEORGE, HENRY).

Minimand. That which it is desired to minimize. For example, it may be desired to find the quantities of various INPUTS that minimize (make as small as possible) the COST of producing a particular output level. In that case, cost is the minimand.

Minorities, minority interest. Elements shown in the consolidated accounts of groups of companies where one or more of the SUBSIDIARIES is not wholly owned by the parent. Where one company acquires 95 percent of the common STOCK of a subsidiary, for example and the accounts of the subsidiary are consolidated with those of the parent, then the whole of the assets and income of the subsidiary will be included in the consolidated accounts. In showing net assets attributable to shareholders of the parent company, 5 percent in this case (the minority) belongs to the minority shareholders and must be deducted. Similarly, in calculating net income attributable to the same shareholders, earnings will be shown after minority interest. (⇒ INCOME STATEMENT).

Mises, Ludwig Edler von (1881–1973). Professor at Vienna University from 1913 until he joined the Graduate Institute of International Studies at Geneva in 1934. In 1940 he left Europe for the United States and was appointed five years later to a professorial chair at New York University, where he stayed until 1969. His published works include *The Theory of Money and Credit* (1912), *The Free and Prosperous Commonwealth* (1927), *Geldwertstabilisierung und Konjunkturpolitik* (1928), *Bureaucracy* (1944), *Omnipotent Government* (1944), *Human Action* (1949), *Theory and History: An Interpretation of Social and Economic Evaluation* (1957) and *The Ultimate Foundation of Economic Science* (1962). Von Mises argued in favor of the PRICE SYSTEM as the most efficient basis of RESOURCE ALLOCATION. A PLANNED ECONOMY must be wasteful, because it lacks a price system and cannot institute such a system without destroying its political principles. He applied the MARGINAL UTILITY theory of the AUSTRIAN SCHOOL to develop a new theory of MONEY and pointed out that UTILITY could be measured ordinally only and not cardinally (⇒ HICKS, SIR JOHN RICHARD). He also outlined a PURCHASING POWER PARITY THEORY comparable to that of Gustav Cassel (1866–1945). His TRADE CYCLE theory explained fluctuations in terms of an expansion of bank credit in the upturn that caused a fall in the RATE OF INTEREST and surplus INVESTMENT with a consequent reversal when the MONEY SUPPLY was reduced. (⇒⇒ HAWTREY, SIR RALPH GEORGE; HAYEK, FRIEDRICH AUGUST VON).

Misselden, Edward (1608–54). A leading member of the merchant adventurers and a member of the group of writers referred to as mercantilists (⇒ MERCANTILISM). He argued that international movements of specie and fluctuations in the EXCHANGE RATE depended on international trade flows and not the manipulations of bankers, which was the popular view. He suggested that trading returns should be established for purposes of statistical analysis, so that the state could regulate trade with a view to obtaining EXPORT surpluses.

Mitchell, Wesley Clair (1874–1948). ⇛ INSTITUTIONAL ECONOMICS

Mixed economy. An economy that contains elements of both private and state enterprise. The U.K. economy is an example of this, having both a large PRIVATE SECTOR and a group of large NATIONALIZED INDUSTRIES. In fact, virtually all economies are to some extent "mixed," in that no socialist economy is without some degree of PRIVATE ENTERPRISE, while even the U.S. economy has some state-regulated industries. (⇛⇛ NATURAL MONOPOLIES; REGULATION).

Mode. ⇛ AVERAGE

Model. A theoretical system of relationships that tries to capture the essential elements in a real-world situation. Any real-world problem will, in general, consist of a large number of VARIABLES and a large number of often quite complex relationships between them. If any headway is to be made in the analysis of such situations, it is necessary to try to isolate the most important elements and disregard the rest. Although this may mean that a model is "unrealistic" in the sense that it does not completely describe the real-world situation, it may still give us far more insight into a problem, and far greater predictive ability, than would a less abstract approach that tried to take everything into account. (⇛ RICARDO, DAVID).

M1, M1A, M1B, M2, M3. ⇛ MONEY SUPPLY

Monetarism. A particular approach to MACROECONOMIC theory and policy that has the following central elements:

1. In the long run, the level of REAL (⇛ REAL TERMS) NATIONAL INCOME or output is determined by the interaction of the forces of supply and demand in all markets, including those for LABOR. This full-employment level of output is therefore determined *solely* by the real underlying elements of the economy: the amounts of RESOURCES it possesses and the technology of production. PRICES and wage rates will adjust to whatever *relative* levels are necessary to establish this full-employment EQUILIBRIUM, in which by definition there is no *involuntary* UNEMPLOYMENT.

2. It follows that neither fiscal nor MONETARY POLICY can affect output and employment in the long run. The MONEY SUPPLY is, however, a key policy instrument, first, because it determines the general level of prices in the long run (⇛⇛ QUANTITY THEORY OF MONEY), and because it may have SHORT-RUN effects on output and employment. To see this, suppose there is an increase in the money supply. This will stimulate DEMAND for goods and services, first, because the RATE OF INTEREST will fall, thus increasing investment and possibly some forms of consumer expenditure; and second, because the value of money balances will have increased, thus making people feel wealthier and inducing them to spend more. The immediate effect of this increased expenditure is to increase output and employment. However, prices and wages will start to rise in response to increased demand. This then causes a rise in everyone's EXPECTATIONS of INFLATION, causing a further wage-price spiral. Therefore, though with a time lag that

may be "long and variable," the increased money supply will finally show up in more inflation.

3. FISCAL POLICY is at best irrelevant and at worst positively harmful. It can by definition have no effect on the level of full-employment output, simply changing its composition by "CROWDING OUT" private sector output. Insofar as it is financed by increasing the money supply, it will cause inflation.

4. The demand for money depends on real output and the real interest rate in a stable, predictable way. This is the modern extension of the assumption underlying the "simple" quantity theory of money that the velocity of circulation (⇛ INCOME VELOCITY OF CIRCULATION) is a constant. In effect it is saying that the latter may vary but in a way that can be explained and predicted in terms of interest rate and income changes.

5. The money supply is *controllable:* It is possible for a monetary authority such as the FED (⇛⇛ FEDERAL RESERVE SYSTEM) to determine its level and rate of growth.

6. Because, in the long run, output is independent of the money supply (as well as fiscal policy), the policy that should be adopted is to allow the money supply to grow at the same rate as the growth of output. This will ensure growth without inflation, since the quantity theory implies that, in the long run, the rate of inflation will equal the rate of growth of the money supply *minus* the rate of growth of real output. Coupled with this is a general opposition to *discretionary* policy, i.e., policy that can be varied at will by the government. This is regarded as more likely to be destabilizing and so should be replaced by non-discretionary fixed rules, such as that of allowing the money supply growth rate to grow at the same rate as output. This therefore suggests a less active economic role for government.

Within the set of economists who would accept being termed "monetarists," there are differences in emphasis and some diversity of views; for example, not all believe in RATIONAL EXPECTATIONS. The above propositions, however, are the common core. The antecedents of monetarism can be traced back at least 300 years. For example, there is a clear statement of point 2 above in the writings of DAVID HUME. However, following the work of JOHN MAYNARD KEYNES in the 1930s, almost diametrically opposed views, particularly in relation to economic policy, became dominant among economists. The revival of monetarism in its present form owes a great deal to the theoretical and empirical work of MILTON FRIEDMAN and his coworkers at the University of Chicago.

Monetary accommodation. A change in the MONEY SUPPLY, in response to a fiscal action (⇛ FISCAL POLICY), that ensures that interest rates remain unaffected by the fiscal action. For example, a tax reduction to be financed by selling bonds to the banks would be paralleled by an expansion in the money supply. Such action would prevent CROWDING OUT. (⇛⇛ MONETARISM; MONETARY POLICY).

Monetary base. ⇛ HIGH-POWERED MONEY

Monetary Control Act. ⇛ DEPOSITORY INSTITUTIONS DEREGULATION AND MONETARY CONTROL ACT

Monetary Policy. The deliberate control of the MONEY SUPPLY and/or RATES OF INTEREST by the FED (⇛ FEDERAL RESERVE SYSTEM) to try to effect a change in employment or INFLATION. By controlling interest rates, monetary policy can effect changes in the capital account of a country's BALANCE OF PAYMENTS, since relatively higher rates of interest in one country will attract funds from other countries in the short term. Monetary policy is one approach to STABILIZATION POLICY. (⇛ FISCAL POLICY; MONETARISM; QUANTITY THEORY OF MONEY).

Money. Anything that is generally accepted as a means of settling DEBTS. In present-day economies money normally consists of LIABILITIES of the government (notes and coin) and of the banks (bank accounts) (⇒ BANKING)—i.e., money consists of claims held by individuals on banks and the government, these claims being generally accepted as a means of payment. This use of claims as money is a feature of relatively sophisticated systems of finance and CREDIT. In less well developed systems, articles that possessed intrinsic VALUE (pieces of gold, cows, cigarettes) were used as a means of payment. This difference reflects the importance of economic stability and well-developed financial institutions, since the use of money that has no intrinsic value of its own depends on confidence that it will be universally accepted in exchange for goods. (⇛ GALLOPING INFLATION; INFLATION; MONEY, FUNCTIONS OF; MONEY SUPPLY).

Money, functions of. MONEY is generally regarded as fulfilling three functions:

1. As a *medium of exchange:* Since a BARTER system may be very cumbersome and inefficient, it is generally found useful to have some good or token that is widely accepted as payment in settlement of DEBTS. Goods can be exchanged for money, which can then be exchanged for other goods; and hence, money serves as the medium through which exchange is facilitated. Its ability to perform this function is, in fact, the defining characteristic of money.

2. As a *unit of account:* The units in which money is measured (dollars and cents, pounds and pence) are generally used as the units in which PRICES, ACCOUNTS, debts, financial ASSETS, etc., are measured. This is a natural consequence of the use of money as a medium of exchange, although no exchange need be involved in the use of money as a unit of account.

3. As a *store of value:* Part of an individual's INCOME may be set aside from immediate CONSUMPTION and held in some form in order to yield future consumption. Money is one form in which this may be held. Since receipts and payments are never perfectly synchronized, the medium of exchange function of money will, in any case, lead to money's being held over time as a store of VALUE or purchasing power. (⇛ TRANSACTIONS MOTIVE).

Money illusion. The propensity to respond to change in MONEY magnitudes as if they represented changes in real magnitudes. For example, suppose that your money INCOME and the prices of all goods that you could buy were simultaneously doubled. Any set of purchases you could previously afford you can still afford; any set you could not afford still cannot be bought. If the set of purchases you previously made was the one you preferred out of all those available to you, there is absolutely no reason for you to change it now. On the other hand, if, because your money income has gone up, you feel richer and now buy more of the luxury goods and less of the necessities, you would be said to be "suffering from" money illusion, since you have not realized that your REAL INCOME has remained the same.

Money, inactive. ⇛ INACTIVE MONEY

Money in circulation. MONEY that is being used to finance transactions, as opposed to idle money. (⇛ See INACTIVE MONEY).

Money market. The financial institutions that deal in short-term SECURITIES and LOANS. MONEY has a "time value," and therefore the use of it is bought and sold on the money market and long-term money on the CAPITAL MARKET. Financial instruments dealt with on the money market include TREASURY BILLS, CERTIFICATES OF DEPOSIT, *bankers' acceptances* (bills "accepted or endorsed" by a bank and used primarily to finance INTERNATIONAL TRADE) and other commercial paper. The money market is not an organized body like the STOCK EXCHANGE but consists of a large number of financial institutions that trade and keep in touch by telephone and telex, including the banks of the FEDERAL RESERVE SYSTEM, other COMMERCIAL BANKS, specialized dealers and other financial institutions. In a wider context the money market includes the FOREIGN-EXCHANGE MARKET and the BULLION or gold market. The largest money markets are in New York and London, England, and these are closely interconnected. In London specialized institutions called DISCOUNT HOUSES deal in government securities and certificates of deposit. The discount houses purchase these securities from the government and the PRIVATE SECTOR with money borrowed from the banking system and other sources. Their profit is made by borrowing at very short term (normally 24-hour call loans) and lending by DISCOUNTING securities at slightly higher RATES OF INTEREST.

Money supply. The amount of MONEY that exists in an economy at a given time. There is no single definition of exactly what constitutes the money supply. The essence of money is that it be generally accepted as a means of payment, but this characteristic does not permit a unique definition of the actual money supply. Since notes and coin (nominally, claims against the government, but, in fact, simply tokens) are an accepted means of payment, they are clearly part of the money supply. In addition, DEMAND DEPOSITS at banks are, through the use of CHECKS, also used to settle DEBTS and so are also part of the money supply. These two taken together give what can be thought of as the most narrow definition of the money supply. This "narrow" definition is often referred to as "M1." TIME DEPOSITS are, strictly speaking, not capable of being used as money—one cannot draw a check on a time deposit account and use it to settle a debt. Nevertheless, despite the formal rules, it is possible to meet a check drawn on one's demand deposit account by transferring the appropriate sum from a TIME DEPOSIT virtually at will, and hence, a broader definition of the supply of money would also include time deposit accounts. This definition is known as "M2." M3 is M2 plus CERTIFICATES OF DEPOSIT. Recently, M1 has been further separated into M1A and M1B, the former referring to what is M1 as defined above and the latter being M1A plus NOW ACCOUNTS and ATS (⇛ AUTOMATIC TRANSFER SERVICE) accounts. (⇛⇛ BANKING; DOMESTIC CREDIT EXPANSION; HIGH-POWERED MONEY; NEAR MONEY; QUANTITY THEORY OF MONEY).

Monopolistic competition. The market situation in which there is a large number of firms whose outputs are close but not perfect substitutes, either because of product differentiation (⇛ DIFFERENTIATION, PRODUCT) or geographical fragmentation of the MARKET. The fact that the products are not homogeneous means that any one firm may raise its PRICE relative to the prices of its competitors without losing all its sales, so that its DEMAND CURVE is downward-sloping rather than a horizontal straight line (as in PERFECT COMPETITION). The combination of a large number of firms, as in perfect competition, with downward-sloping demand curves, as in MONOPOLY, is responsible for the term "monopolistic competition." The theory was developed in the 1930s virtually simultaneously by EDWARD HASTINGS CHAMBERLIN in the United States and JOAN VIOLET ROBINSON in the United Kingdom. (⇛⇛ EXCESS CAPACITY).

Monopoly. A MARKET situation in which a single seller controls the entire output of a particular good or service. The seller is then able to set the price and output of the good entirely in his own interests. It is implicit in this definition that the monopolist is faced by a large number of competing buyers (⇛ BILATERAL MONOPOLY). A basic proposition in economics is that monopoly control of a good will result in too little of the good being produced at too high a price: The monopolist finds that it maximizes his PROFIT to restrict output and charge a higher price than could be obtained under PERFECT COMPETITION. In particular, he will set a price above MARGINAL COST (⇛⇛ MARGINAL-COST PRICING). Thus, economists have often advocated ANTITRUST POLICY, PUBLIC ENTERPRISE or REGULATION to control the abuse of monopoly power. Note that for monopoly to persist in the LONG RUN, it is necessary for BARRIERS TO ENTRY to exist. That is, the high profits that exploitation of monopoly power generates would attract would-be entrants into the market, and the monopolist must find some way of excluding them if he is to go on enjoying monopoly profits. Otherwise, he may be forced to deter new entry by keeping his price and profits lower than the levels implied by the standard textbook analysis, and so, in the absence of entry barriers, the undesirable effects of monopoly may not be so great.

Monopoly, discriminating. A MONOPOLY that practices PRICE DISCRIMINATION.

Monopsony. The situation in which there is only a single buyer in a MARKET. (⇛⇛ MONOPOLY).

Monte Carlo method. An approach to the problem of finding the PROBABILITIES with which the possible outcomes of a given activity, process, experiment, etc., may occur, based on experimentation and SIMULATION. This is in contrast to an "analytical" approach, which would use techniques of mathematical statistics to attempt to find a mathematical expression for these probabilities. In many real problems, the complexity of the situation may be such that an analytical solution would be difficult or impossible. The procedure of repeating a large number of times the operation of the activity in the form of a MODEL, and using the results to build up the probability values of the outcomes, may then be a cheap and accurate approach. This technique has received widespread use in OPERATIONS RESEARCH.

Mortgage. A legal agreement conveying conditional ownership of ASSETS as security for a LOAN and becoming void when the DEBT is repaid. Mortgage loans are a common form of financing for home purchase (⇛ SAVINGS AND LOAN ASSOCIATIONS) but are also used in BUSINESS FINANCE.

Mortgage bonds. ⇛ BOND

Mortgage debenture. ⇛ DEBENTURE

Most favored nation clause. The clause in an INTERNATIONAL TRADE treaty under which the signatories promise to extend to each other any favorable trading terms offered in subsequent agreements to third parties. (⇛⇛ GENERAL AGREEMENT ON TARIFFS AND TRADE).

Moving average. A series of AVERAGES that are calculated from groups of numbers that are in a series. Each group is obtained by adding the next number in the series and omitting the earliest. Consider, for example, the series

$$2 \quad 4 \quad 6 \quad 20 \quad 10$$

and $\frac{2+4}{2} = 3, \quad \frac{4+6}{2} = 5, \quad \frac{6+20}{2} = 13, \quad \frac{20+10}{2} = 15$

so that a new series is generated (3, 5, 13, 15) that is a moving average of the first series. The groups need not be of only two numbers but could be of three or more depending on the length of the original series. Note that the derived series has reduced the relative size of the jump in the fourth place of the original series. Moving averages are used to smooth out TIME SERIES so that trends can be more easily picked out. (⇛⇛ JEVONS, WILLIAM STANLEY; SLUTSKY, EUGEN).

Multi-bank deposits. ⇛ MULTI-BANK SYSTEM

Multi-bank system. A financial system where there is more than one bank, each bank having one or more branches. (⇛⇛ BANKING).

Multicollinearity. The presence of significant CORRELATION between the INDEPENDENT VARIABLES in a regression model (⇛ REGRESSION ANALYSIS). Its effect is to invalidate some of the assumptions on which LEAST SQUARES REGRESSION is based and hence to render inappropriate the use of that method, unless modified. The problem of multicollinearity occurs very frequently in econometric studies and has been extensively studied in the theory of ECONOMETRICS.

Multilateralism. INTERNATIONAL TRADE and exchange between more than two countries without discrimination between those involved. In contrast to BILATERALISM. (⇛⇛ GENERAL AGREEMENT ON TARIFFS AND TRADE; MOST FAVORED NATION CLAUSE).

Multinational corporation (MNC, MNE). A corporation—or, more correctly, an ENTERPRISE—operating in a number of countries and having production or service facilities outside the country of its origin. A commonly accepted definition of an MNE is an enterprise producing at least 25 percent of its world output outside its country of origin. There are over 10,000 corporations with direct investments outside their headquarter country with over 80,000 affiliates over which they have effective control, but less than 500 MNEs account for three-quarters of foreign affiliates, and only 200 of these MNEs derived 25 percent or more of their sales from foreign activities. The multinational corporation takes its principal decisions in a global context and thus often outside the countries in which it has particular operations. The rapid growth of these corporations since World War II and the possibility that conflicts might arise between their interests and those of the individual countries in which they operate have provoked much discussion among economists in recent years. MNEs possibly account for one-quarter of world trade, but earlier fears that they would come to dominate the world economy now seem misplaced. Also called *international companies* and *transnational corporations*. (⇛ TRANSFER PRICES).

Multiple correlation. The measurement of the degree of association between one VARIABLE on the one hand and two or more variables on the other. It is thus an extension of simple CORRELATION, which considers only the association between two variables. We may be interested in discovering how strongly expenditure on CONSUMPTION is related to INCOME, family size and WEALTH for a group of families. We would then compute the multiple correlation coefficient, a number lying between zero and one, that expresses how closely expenditure across the group of families varies with income, family size and wealth taken together. A VALUE close to one would denote a very strong association; close to zero, a very weak association. Note that the remarks made about the interpretation of the ordinary correlation coefficient apply equally here—in particular, that no causal relationship can be inferred from a high multiple correlation coefficient. (⇛⇛ PARTIAL CORRELATION; REGRESSION ANALYSIS).

Multiplier. A measure of the effect on total NATIONAL INCOME of a unit change in some component of AGGREGATE DEMAND. Suppose that an economy is initially at less than full employment (⇛ EMPLOYMENT, FULL), with given levels of aggregate INVESTMENT, CONSUMPTION and national income. Then suppose that, for some reason, firms increase the rate of investment expenditure—i.e., they increase their expenditure on plant, machinery and buildings. We then expect national income to increase by the amount of this increase in expenditure. This investment expenditure is paid out as wages, salaries and PROFITS, to suppliers of factor (⇛ FACTORS OF PRODUCTION) services to the investment goods industries. The recipients of this income will save a portion of it and will spend the rest on buying goods and services, which creates INCOME for the suppliers of those goods and services. At this stage, the total increase in national income is equal to the initial increase in investment expenditure, plus the portion of that increase that is re-spent, since this re-spending has in turn generated new income and output. The income generated by the re-spending will, again, be partly saved and partly spent, in turn generating new income, which is partly saved and partly spent, and so on, *ad infinitum*. The result of this is that the total increase in national income resulting from the initial increase in investment will, in the end, be several times larger than the increase in investment—i.e., it will be some multiple of the increase in investment. The expression that gives the value of this multiple is called the *multiplier,* and the overall effect of the investment increase is called the *multiplier effect.*

To show how the multiplier is determined, suppose that, throughout the economy a proportion (b) of any increase in income is re-spent, while the remainder ($1-b$) is saved. If investment increased by, say, 10, then the amount that is re-spent at the first "round" is given by $b \times 10$, and so the total income generated by the increase in investment is $10 + 10b$. The amount of income re-spent, $10b$, has become someone else's income, and this sum will in turn be partly re-spent. In fact, the proportion re-spent is $b \times 10b = 10b^2$. This, in turn, becomes someone's income, a proportion of which is re-spent, to give a new increase in income of $b \times 10b^2 = 10b^3$. And so on. Total new income generated is the sum of the income generated at each stage—i.e., it is $10 + 10b + 10b^2 + 10b^3 \ldots$; and it can be shown by elementary algebra that this sum is equal to $10 \frac{1}{1-b}$. That is, if we know the value of b and the amount of the increase in investment, then we can find the amount by which income will increase. Now b is, in fact, the MARGINAL PROPENSITY TO CONSUME, which is generally held to be less than one; so $\frac{1}{1-b}$ must be greater than one; e.g., if $b = 0.8$, then $\frac{1}{1-b} = 5$. Thus, the increase in income will be some multiple of the increase in investment, the value of this multiple being given by $\frac{1}{1-b}$, which is accordingly called "the multiplier."

The multiplier has played an important role in MACROECONOMIC analysis since its use by JOHN MAYNARD KEYNES as a central element in his MODEL of the economy. When the word *multiplier* is qualified by the word *investment,* the concept is used to refer only to the multiplier effects of an increase in investment. However, the multiplier concept is of general application and can be shown to apply just as well to changes in EXPORT demand, government expenditure (⇛ BUDGET) and TAXATION. Note, however, that if there is full employment in the economy, the simple multiplier described here is unlikely to provide an adequate prediction of the consequences of an increase in investment. This is because the increase in demand for investment goods will cause rising prices and RATES OF INTEREST rather than an increase in REAL INCOME. (⇛ BALANCED BUDGET).

Multi-product firm. A firm that produces more than one product. Though the standard economic analysis normally considers the single-product firm, it is not difficult to generalize it to the multi-product case. Empirically, of course, the multi-product firm is in the overwhelming majority.

Municipal bonds. Sold by local governments to raise CAPITAL for local public works. Such bonds are sold in "strips"—a 10-year issue consisting of 10 separate issues: a 1-year issue, a 2-year issue and so on. Most municipal bonds are held to maturity with only a limited amount of trading. (⇛ BOND).

Mun, Sir Thomas (1571–1641). An English mercantilist (⇛ MERCANTILISM) and a director of the East India Company. His publications include *Discourse of Trade from England unto the East Indies* (1621) and *England's Treasure by Forraign Trade* (1664). He attacked the idea that EXPORTS OF BULLION should be completely prohibited and other restrictions put on trade, pointing out that restrictions on trade invited retaliation in foreign MARKETS and raised domestic PRICES. He did emphasize, however, that an export surplus should be sought in the BALANCE OF TRADE of the country as a whole, although it was unnecessary to seek to achieve this with each trading partner.

Mutual company. A company, without issued CAPITAL STOCK, owned by those members that do business with it. The PROFITS of a mutual company, after deductions for reserves, are shared out among members. Some savings banks and INSURANCE companies are mutual companies. The term *mutual* is also used to refer to open-ended investment companies, i.e., MUTUAL FUNDS.

Mutual funds. A company or a branch of a financial organization that invests its funds subscribed by the public in SECURITIES and in return issues units that it will repurchase at a price reflecting the value of the fund's investment portfolio. This is referred to as an "open-end" fund. A "closed-end" fund sells SHARES to raise CAPITAL, and once it is closed, the sale and purchase of shares is done through the STOCK EXCHANGE or OVER-THE-COUNTER MARKET. Within the classification of closed- and open-ended funds, there are a wide variety of classes of funds. A balanced fund is likely to hold a significant portion of its portfolio in BONDS, DEBENTURES and PREFERRED STOCK to offset COMMON STOCK price fluctuations. A fully managed fund has virtually no ground rules—managers take advantage of investment opportunities as they arise. A fixed trust fund may contain 20 to 30 stocks, the composition being left unchanged in the short run, thereby minimizing management costs. Some funds have become sufficiently specialized that one can invest in mortgages, real estate or energy through a particular type of fund. (⇛ INVESTMENT TRUST; MUTUAL COMPANY).

Mutual savings banks. Organized in the early 19th century, these institutions were founded by wealthy businessmen whose aim in part was to encourage savings and property ownership for the "working classes." They are controlled by a self-perpetuating board of trustees and make MORTGAGE loans, installment loans and invest in corporate BONDS. The bulk of mutual savings banks are in New England and New York. (⇛ BANKING; COMMERCIAL BANKS; THRIFTS).

Mutual Security Agency. ⇛ ECONOMIC COOPERATION ADMINISTRATION

Myrdal, Gunnar Karl (1898–). Born in Sweden, Professor Myrdal graduated in law at Stockholm University in 1923. After a period in private practice, he obtained a degree in economics in 1927 and took up a post as lecturer in political economy at Stockholm University, eventually succeeding Gustav Cassel to the Chair of Political Economy and Financial Science in 1933. From 1936 to 1938 he was a member of Parliament as a Social Democrat. After a period as economic adviser to the Swedish legation in the United States, he was appointed minister of commerce in the Swedish government, a post he held from 1945 to 1947. He resigned from this post to become Secretary General of the U.N. Economic Commission for Europe at Geneva, where he stayed until 1957. In 1957 he was appointed professor at the Institute for International Economic Studies of Stockholm University, and in 1974 he was awarded the Alfred Nobel Memorial Prize (⇛ NOBEL PRIZES) in Economics jointly with FRIEDRICH AUGUST VON HAYEK. His published work includes *Price Formation under Changeability* (1927), *Vetenskap och Politik i Nationalekonomin* (1929), *Om Penningteoretisk Jamvikt* (1931), *An American Dilemma* (1944), *Economic Theory and Underdeveloped Regions* (1957), *Value in Social Theory* (1958), *Beyond the Welfare State* (1960), *Challenge to Affluence* (1963), *Asian Drama: An Inquiry into the Poverty of Nations* (1968), *Objectivity in Social Research* (1969), *The Challenge of World Poverty* (1970), *Against the Stream—Critical Essays in Economics* (1973).

Professor Myrdal invented the terms and formulated the distinction between EX ANTE and EX POST, in particular in relation to the equality of aggregate SAVINGS and INVESTMENT in EQUILIBRIUM. He emphasized the need to study the dynamics of macroeconomic (⇛ MACROECONOMICS) processes. His book *Monetary Equilibrium,* published in 1931, which developed the economics of KNUT WICKSELL, foreshadowed many aspects of JOHN MAYNARD KEYNES's *General Theory*. In recent years he has argued that economists should accept the need to make explicit VALUE JUDGMENTS, without which their theoretical structures are unrealistic. He has become an advocate of INSTITUTIONAL ECONOMICS. Professor Myrdal believes that such a framework is necessary in any economic studies of the DEVELOPING COUNTRIES.

N

National Commission for Manpower Policy. This 17-member commission was established under the COMPREHENSIVE EMPLOYMENT AND TRAINING ACT to study and evaluate manpower programs, especially as they relate to the Act. The commission included the secretaries of labor; health, education and welfare; defense; commerce; and agriculture; plus other members appointed by the President.

National Debt. The national, or public, debt represents the federal government's borrowing of money by selling BONDS to households, firms, banks and other financial institutions (⇛ BANKING). By the end of 1980 the amount was close to $900 billion, or roughly $4,000 per capita. The FEDERAL RESERVE SYSTEM holds roughly 40 percent of the total debt. The national debt rose dramatically during World War II, reaching over 100 percent of GROSS NATIONAL PRODUCT (GNP) and has, as a share of GNP, declined since then to just under 40 percent of GNP. Interest on the debt was a constant share of GNP from the early 1950s to 1974 but has been rising since then. The size of the national debt has been the subject of intense debate in recent years. One viewpoint is that the optimal size of the debt is something that must be judged by viewing the willingness of borrowers to hold public bonds at various RATES OF INTEREST. Furthermore, the debt should be allowed to fluctuate according to the needs of full employment policy. An alternative view, sometimes attributed to fiscal conservatives, is that there is among public officials bias toward public expenditure financed by borrowing, not taxation, which has fueled INFLATION in the economy, causing more debt to be issued to pay for the interest on existing debt. Intervention, to control inflation or unemployment, by way of the budget balance, is more than likely to be unsuccessful and destabilizing. (⇛ MONETARY POLICY).

National Income. A measure of the MONEY value of the total flow of goods and services produced in an economy over a specified period of time. It can be calculated in three ways:

1. As the value of the outputs of all goods and SERVICES in the economy, net of indirect taxes (⇛ DIRECT TAXATION) and SUBSIDIES, and corrected for inter-industry sales so as to avoid double counting (⇛ VALUE ADDED).

2. As the total flow of INCOMES paid out to HOUSEHOLDS in return for the supply of FACTORS OF PRODUCTION, plus PROFITS retained by firms as reserves.

3. As the sum of expenditure on consumers' goods and INVESTMENT goods, government expenditure (⇛ BUDGET) and expenditure by foreigners on EXPORTS, less domestic expenditure on IMPORTS.

In principle, each of these methods of measurement should give the same result, since the flow of expenditure on goods and services must equal the sales value of those goods and services, which in turn must equal the incomes paid out by firms as wages, salaries, interest (⇛ RATE OF INTEREST), DIVIDENDS and RENT, plus undistributed profits. However, in practice, because of measurement problems, the three separate estimates of national income usually diverge, and the value finally adopted is a "compromise estimate" of the three. Since national income measures the flow of goods and services produced, its level can be taken as an indicator of the well-being of the economy, though, clearly, it can never be a perfect indicator of this. The latter depends not only on the size of the flow of goods and services but also on the way in which this is distributed among households (⇛ INCOME DISTRIBUTION), the quality of the goods themselves, the state of the environment, etc., which need by no means improve with a rising national income.

National income is defined to include not only the incomes that arise from production within the economy but also income that accrues to domestic residents from activities carried on abroad. If these overseas earnings are excluded, we would have GROSS DOMESTIC PRODUCT. (⇛ GROSS NATIONAL PRODUCT).

Nationalized industries. Industries owned and controlled by the government, rather than by private individual stockholders. In many countries outside the Soviet bloc, governments have taken industries into public ownership because it is believed that certain objectives of economic policy can be better achieved in this way. For example it is thought that a MONOPOLY can be prevented from abusing its power if it is state-owned. In many developing countries, state ownership and control is thought to facilitate more rapid development of industry. The quantitative significance of nationalization does, however, vary greatly across economies. In countries such as the United Kingdom, Italy and Sweden, basic industries such as electricity, coal, rail transport and iron and steel are state-owned, and nationalized industries as a whole account for roughly 10% of total national output. In less developed countries such as Turkey and Brazil this proportion is much greater, reaching almost 80%. In the United States the climate of opinion is generally unfavorable toward government ownership. Concern with monopoly power is met by REGULATION, which leaves ownership of corporations in the hands of private stockholders.

Natural monopolies. Monopolies with ECONOMIES OF SCALE over a large range of outputs, so that one firm can produce at lower AVERAGE COSTS than could more than one. Examples of natural monopolies are electricity and natural gas utilities. Having several companies supplying the same area would result in multiplication of cables, transformers, pipelines, etc., and a granting of MONOPOLY rights would seem the most efficient thing to do. The recognition of the inevitable trend toward monopolization in such industries has meant that, from their early history, and in most countries, including the United States, there has been REGULATION of these monopolies.

Natural resources. Those COMMODITIES which are found in nature, as opposed to commodities that are entirely fabricated in production processes. It is usual to distinguish between *renewable* and *nonrenewable* natural resources.

Examples of the former are forests, fish stocks and wild game animals. The essential characteristic of these natural resources is that by appropriate choice of the level of current consumption, the total amounts in existence need not diminish and could in fact increase. It is also possible to increase their amounts by activities such as planting forests or breeding fish. In the case of nonrenewable resources, such as crude oil, coal and mineral deposits, it is not possible to replace the amounts consumed. Since the amounts of them in existence must be finite, continued consumption must ultimately result in their exhaustion. This difference has to be reflected in the economic MODELS by which analysis of the optimal time path of consumption of the resources is carried out. Note that all natural resources require application of other FACTORS OF PRODUCTION to make them available for their end uses in consumption or production, and so in this respect they are similar to other commodities. The essential difference is that it is impossible to ignore the time-related or "dynamic" aspects of production in the case of natural resources. In the case of nonrenewable resources, we have to take account of the cumulative total of consumption over time as well as the rate of consumption at one period of time. In the case of renewable resources, we have to take account of how consumption at one time period affects the dynamic process of growth and reproduction of the resource. Thus, natural resource problems were among the first areas of MICROECONOMICS to be examined using methods of OPTIMAL CONTROL THEORY.

Near money. An asset that serves as a store of value and can be readily converted into a medium of exchange (⇛ MONEY). A deposit at a SAVINGS AND LOAN ASSOCIATION qualifies as near MONEY, since it can be converted into cash or transferred to a CHECKING ACCOUNT. STOCKS and BONDS are not generally considered near money because, while they may be converted to cash, their value can fluctuate considerably. CERTIFICATES OF DEPOSIT (CD), on the other hand, would qualify.

Negotiable certificate of deposit (NCD). ⇛ CERTIFICATE OF DEPOSIT

Negotiable orders of withdrawal (NOW). ⇛ DEPOSIT

Neoclassical economics. A school of economic thought in the tradition of CLASSICAL ECONOMICS, which has developed since 1945 and which contrasts with that of the CAMBRIDGE SCHOOL. Neoclassical economics is characterized by microeconomic (⇛ MICROECONOMICS) theoretical systems constructed to explore conditions of STATIC EQUILIBRIUM (⇛ COMPARATIVE STATIC EQUILIBRIUM ANALYSIS). The analysis often takes the form of the comparative study of equilibrium states that are timeless, in the sense that they do not explore the dynamics of the economic system. Statements about macro events are often derived from the aggregation of micro relationships, and this has led to criticism, particularly from the Cambridge school. Equilibrium is achieved at full employment by changes in factor prices. Essentially, the neoclassical school has been concerned with the problems of equilibrium and growth at full employment, in contrast to J.M. Keynes, who was primarily concerned with the underemployment of resources.

Neo-Keynesianism. An approach to macroeconomic (⇛ MACROECONOMICS) theory and policy that has developed from the work of JOHN MAYNARD KEYNES. The qualification "neo-" appears because, although firmly rooted in the approach and assumptions of Keynes' MODEL of income determination (⇛ INCOME DETERMINATION, THEORY OF), the neo-Keynesian analysis incorporates subsequent extensions such as the reformulation of the CONSUMPTION FUNCTION and may take a less extreme view on some issues, for example, the significance of the MONEY SUPPLY. Within the group of economists who would accept being labeled neo-Keynesians, there may, of course, still be differences of emphasis and some diversity of views, but they would hold the following common beliefs:

1. FISCAL POLICY has an important effect on NATIONAL INCOME and employment through the MULTIPLIER process. Changes in the MONEY SUPPLY, on the other hand, have a very small effect on output and the general level of prices, and so, for all practical purposes, MONETARY POLICY is irrelevant.

2. There is no necessary or strong LONG-RUN tendency for the economy to reach EQUILIBRIUM at full employment (⇛ EMPLOYMENT, FULL; ⇛⇛ UNEMPLOYMENT, NATURAL RATE OF), and so government intervention will be required to stabilize the economy at full employment.

3. This STABILIZATION POLICY can and should be "discretionary," i.e., *not* fixed in accordance with some simple rule but capable of being varied at will in response to circumstances.

4. The EXCHANGE RATE should be used as a policy instrument in achieving a desired outcome on the BALANCE OF PAYMENTS rather than being left to be determined by MARKET FORCES.

5. INCOMES POLICY may very well be required to moderate inflationary wage claims and ensure price stability at full employment (⇛ PRICES AND INCOMES POLICY).

These tenets of neo-Keynesianism are in direct contrast to those of MONETARISM.

Net assets. The CAPITAL employed in a business. It is calculated from the BALANCE SHEET by taking fixed ASSETS plus current assets less current LIABILITIES. Often used as a basis for calculating RATE OF RETURN on capital.

Net capital employed. ⇛ CAPITAL EMPLOYED

Net capital formation. ⇛ CAPITAL FORMATION

Net cash flow. ⇛ CASH FLOW

Net income. Net PROFIT on earnings after tax and, where appropriate, after minority interest. (⇛ MINORITIES, MINORITY INTEREST).

Net investment. Gross expenditure on capital formation, minus the amount required to replace worn-out and obsolete plant and equipment. This therefore gives a measure of the change in CAPITAL STOCK. It may in fact be negative, if not enough expenditure is made to replace DEPRECIATION fully.

Net profit. ⇛ PROFIT

Net worth. ⇛ BALANCE SHEET

New Deal. The U.S. federal government, under President Roosevelt, began, in 1933, a number of projects designed to give financial assistance and work to the large number of people thrown out of employment by the great DEPRESSION, which followed the stock market collapse on Wall Street in 1929. This change of policy was called the New Deal. It met with a certain amount of opposition, because it led to budget deficits (⇛ BALANCED BUDGET). (⇛⇛ KEYNES, JOHN MAYNARD).

New issue market. That part of the CAPITAL MARKET serving as the market for new long-term CAPITAL. Those institutions needing capital (industrial, commercial and financial companies and public authorities) offer SHARES and other SECURITIES, usually through FINANCIAL INTERMEDIARIES, which are then purchased by each other and the general public. Internally generated funds provide the bulk of the capital required by business, and the new issue market is not large, although it is important. The new issue market does not include certain other sources of new long-term external finance, such as MORTGAGES and other LOANS from financial institutions. The new issue market consists primarily of the STOCK EXCHANGES, but some issues are privately placed (⇛ PLACING), and the INVESTMENT BANKS play an important role. Well-established companies can greatly reduce the cost of raising new capital by offering shares to their existing shareholders by what are known as "rights issues." The new issue market, like the rest of the capital market, is increasingly becoming an international one, and both large companies and public sector bodies raise money in overseas capital markets.

New York Cotton Exchange. Established in 1870, the exchange initially dealt in the trading of FUTURES for cotton. Futures trading of other commodities was added, and today the exchange deals in cotton, wool, frozen orange juice, propane and petroleum.

New York Stock Exchange. ⇛ AMERICAN STOCK EXCHANGE

Nixon's control program. ⇛ PRICES AND INCOMES POLICY

Nobel Prizes. The sixth Nobel Prize, for Economics, in memory of Alfred Nobel (1833–96), the Swedish chemist, was introduced in 1969 and is financed by the Swedish National Bank. The following economists have been awarded this prize in each year: 1969—J. Tinbergen and R. Frisch; 1970—PAUL ANTHONY SAMUELSON; 1971—SIMON KUZNETS; 1972—SIR JOHN RICHARD HICKS and KENNETH J. ARROW; 1973—WASSILY W. LEONTIEF; 1974—FRIEDRICH AUGUST VON HAYEK and GUNNAR KARL MYRDAL; 1975—L.V. Kantorovich and TJALLING C. KOOPMANS; 1976—MILTON FRIEDMAN; 1977—J.E. Meade and BERTIL OHLIN; 1978—HERBERT A. SIMON; 1979—THEODORE W. SHULTZ and Sir A. Lewis; 1980—LAWRENCE ROBERT KLEIN; 1981—JAMES TOBIN.

Nominal value. The FACE VALUE of a STOCK or BOND, which may be more or less than its market price. (⇛ PAR VALUE).

Nominal yield. The return or YIELD on a SECURITY in which DIVIDEND or interest (⇛ RATE OF INTEREST) is expressed as a percentage of the NOMINAL VALUE of the security as opposed to its market price.

Nonlinear programming. A mathematical technique for solving certain classes of problems. Just like LINEAR PROGRAMMING, the problem is to find the best values of some set of VARIABLES, given the existence of constraints. The main difference, as the name suggests, is that at least one of the relationships in the problem will not be linear. It is true to say that nonlinear problems occur in practice more often than linear problems. However, because of its special nature, the linear version is much easier to solve, and so a linear form will always be substituted for a nonlinear form whenever it is thought to be a close enough approximation.

Non-price competition. Policies that a seller may use to attract customers away from rival sellers but that do not involve PRICE reduction. The most common of such policies are ADVERTISING; use of "free-gift" schemes; exclusive contracts with distributors; and style, quality and design changes.

Normal competitive return. ⇛ PROFIT

Normal profit. ⇛ PROFIT

Normative. Concerned with values, ethics, opinions of what *ought* to be rather than what is. Normative propositions would be: sin is bad; UNEMPLOYMENT is too high; the faster the rate of growth of NATIONAL INCOME, the better for the country; INFLATION ought to be stopped.

North-South. ⇛ BRANDT REPORT

Note. A written promise to pay a specified amount, usually at a specified date. When notes are issued to a bank in return for a short-term LOAN, the interest is usually deducted at the time the loan is made. This is known as DISCOUNTING. Notes are rarely issued for less than 30 days.

NOW (Negotiable Order of Withdrawal) Account. An arrangement that enables funds to be transferred from a TIME DEPOSIT to a DEMAND DEPOSIT. Presentation to a financial institution of a check drawn on a NOW account causes funds to be moved from a time deposit to the NOW account to cover the payment. (⇛ AUTOMATIC TRANSFER SERVICE).

O

OASDI. ⇛ OASI (OLD AGE AND SURVIVOR'S INSURANCE)

OASI (Old Age and Survivor's Insurance). Instituted in 1934, this is the core of the U.S. social INSURANCE system. It was revised to include disability insurance/benefits in 1956 (OASDI), and in 1966 a health plan known as "Medicare" was added, giving medical benefits to those over 65 years of age. OASDI is financed by a PAYROLL TAX, with employer and employee each contributing one-half to the premium. Over 25 million people receive benefits under OASDI. OASDI and "Medicare" are financed by a 1 percent payroll tax, up to a maximum wage.

Obsolescence. A reduction in the useful life of CAPITAL good or consumer DURABLE GOOD through economic or technological change or any other external changes, as distinct from physical deterioration in use (⇛ DEPRECIATION). For example, a new process or machine may be developed which renders existing equipment uneconomic, because a firm could significantly reduce its costs by scrapping its existing machinery, even though it might still have many years of physical life. Then the old equipment has become obsolescent. "Planned obsolescence" is a term used to describe the way certain consumer durables, e.g. automobiles, are altered in appearance or performance so that users will wish to buy new models earlier than they would otherwise have done. In this instance a consumer's UTILITY or satisfaction is said to be reduced subjectively by the knowledge that his automobile is not the latest model, even though its performance has not deteriorated in any way and may be indistinguishable from that of a new one.

Occupational Safety and Health Administration (OSHA). ⇛ ENVIRONMENTAL PROTECTION AGENCY

Off balance sheet financing. ⇛ LEASE

Office of Price Administration. ⇛ PRICES AND INCOMES POLICY

Ohlin, Bertil (1899–1979). After studying at Harvard, Ohlin returned to Stockholm to complete his Ph.D. in 1924. The following year he became professor of economics at Copenhagen. He became active in politics and from 1944 to 1967 was chairman of the Swedish Liberal Party, serving as minister of commerce in 1944–45.

Ohlin's major contribution was his extension of the theory of INTERNATIONAL TRADE originally developed by E. Heckscher, resulting in what is commonly known now as the HECKSHER-OHLIN PRINCIPLE. Ohlin emphasized the fact that, as trade expands, the special advantage in a country that enables it to export becomes increasingly important. Increased demand for these specialized factors eventually makes them more expensive, and thus international trade equalizes the initial relative advantage one nation has over its trading partners (⇛ RICARDO, DAVID). Ohlin's contributions were first published in his *Interregional and International Trade* (1933). In 1977 Ohlin was awarded the NOBEL PRIZE in Economics.

Okun, Arthur M. (1928–80). In 1962 Okun's work on the full employment level of GROSS NATIONAL PRODUCT was published in the *American Statistical Association Proceedings*—"Potential GNP: Its Measurement and Significance." This work led to what is now referred to as OKUN'S LAW, conceiving the relationship between GNP and employment (⇛ EMPLOYMENT, FULL). His graduate studies, completed in 1956, were undertaken at Columbia University. After a period at Yale University, Okun went to the COUNCIL OF ECONOMIC ADVISORS (1964–69) and was its chairman in 1968–69. From 1970 until May of 1980, he was a senior fellow at the Brookings Institution. His other publications include *The Political Economy of Prosperity* (1970); *Upward Mobility in a High Pressure Economy,* (1973); and *Prices and Quantities: A Macroeconomic Analysis,* published posthumously in 1981. This last work reflects Okun's interest in implicit contract theory and the way multiple contracts in product and FACTOR MARKETS render wages and prices less sensitive to changes in AGGREGATE DEMAND.

Okun's Law. The close negative relationship between the rate of unemployment and the ratio of actual GROSS NATIONAL PRODUCT to full employment GNP. It was first pointed out by ARTHUR OKUN in 1962. In the United States the relationship in the 1960s and 1970s was such that a one percentage point change in the rate of unemployment was matched by a one-third percentage point change in the opposite direction in the ratio of actual to full employment GNP.

Oligopoly. A type of MARKET in which there is a relatively high degree of CONCENTRATION; that is, a small number of firms account for a large proportion of output and employment. The essential feature of this market form is the high degree of interdependence among the decisions of the firms, which will generally be recognized by them. The result of this is that each seller must predict the reactions of his competitors before he can determine the consequences of any decision he might make. This obviously creates considerable UNCERTAINTY in the industry, and partly because of this, and partly because their PROFITS will be higher, it is generally argued that oligopolists will adopt some kind of policy of COLLUSION. The most usual form will be an agreement to avoid price competition, although the firms may well compete through product differentiation (⇛ DIFFERENTIATION, PRODUCT), particularly in consumer good industries. Because of the tendency for prices to be well above costs and for expenditures on product differentiation to be excessive, collusive oligopolies have received a good deal of criticism from economists (⇛ ANTITRUST POLICY; FEDERAL TRADE COMMISSION). It appears that oligopolies are becoming an increasingly important feature of the modern economy. (⇛ GAMES, THEORY OF; MONOPOLY).

Open-ended investment company. ⇛ MUTUAL FUNDS

Open-end investment company. ⇛ MUTUAL FUNDS

Open Market Committee. ⇛ FEDERAL OPEN MARKET COMMITTEE

Open-market operations. The purchase or sale of SECURITIES by the Federal Reserve banks (⇛ FEDERAL RESERVE SYSTEM) to influence the supply of funds in the CAPITAL MARKET and so interest rates and the volume of credit.

Purchase of securities by the Federal Reserve System increases the reserves of member banks, while sales reduce them. Since the banks aim to keep reserves near to the minimum so as to maximize the return on their funds, whenever reserves are increased by open-market operations, the banks tend to acquire additional assets such as loans; expanding credit and depressing interest rates. Reductions in reserves by open-market operations have the opposite effect. Policy on open-market operations by the Federal Reserve System is established by the Federal Open Market Committee. (⇛⇛ MONEY SUPPLY; MONETARY POLICY).

Open shop. An arrangement whereby a union is recognized as representing a group of workers but does not have *exclusive* jurisdiction over all employees. An employee is not compelled to join the union to work in such a firm. (⇛ CLOSED SHOP; UNION SHOP).

Operating cost. A term for prime or VARIABLE COSTS.

Operating expenses. Outflows of cash or other resources incurred in the normal running of a business. They include operating COSTS such as wages and supplies, plus all other expenses, including DEPRECIATION. (⇛ INCOME STATEMENT; VARIABLE COSTS).

Operating profit. 1. Profit on current activities. 2. The difference between total revenue and total operating costs (or VARIABLE COSTS) and before deduction of fixed costs. (⇛⇛ PROFIT; INFLATION ACCOUNTING).

Operating ratios. Various measures of the efficiency of a business—e.g., the operating rate or CAPACITY UTILIZATION RATE, the stock-sales ratio, the RATE OF RETURN, the LABOR turnover ratio, the creditor-debtor ratio and other FINANCIAL RATIOS.

Operations research. An interdisciplinary field of activity that attempts to develop procedures for finding OPTIMUM solutions to management problems. To do this, it has to identify the problems, construct MODELS of them and then use suitable techniques to obtain from the models solutions that can be applied to the real problems. It draws heavily on mathematics, engineering and economics for both its personnel and its methods. At the same time, its concern with practical problems has provided considerable stimulus to these disciplines to extend the analysis of problems of optimization in general. Among the most useful techniques in operations research are CRITICAL-PATH ANALYSIS, DISCOUNTED CASH FLOW, INVENTORY ANALYSIS and LINEAR PROGRAMMING.

Opportunity cost. ⇛ COST

Optimal control theory. A set of mathematical techniques and theorems concerned with finding optimal time paths of particular systems. The state of the system at any point in time is completely described by the numerical values of a set of VARIABLES called *state variables*. The values of these variables, and so the state of the system, change over time according to some dynamic relationships, which must be specified mathematically. There is a second set of variables, called the *control variables,* whose values at each point in time are to be chosen by the decision maker, which values then determine the time paths of the state variables. The decision maker will have a preference ordering (⇛ INDIFFERENCE ANALYSIS) over alternative time paths of the system, and this must also be specified mathematically. Optimal control theory then studies the problem of choosing those time paths of the control variables out of the set of paths that are feasible, which leads to the most preferred time path of the entire system.

The main application of optimal control theory in economics has been in the theory of optimal ECONOMIC GROWTH. The system concerned is an aggregate macroeconomic (⇛ MACROECONOMICS) model of the economy. The problem is to find the time path of INVESTMENT that meets some objective, such as maximizing CONSUMPTION per capita of the population. However, many other applications of the theory exist, and it has been a vital tool in the development of dynamic analysis (⇛ ECONOMIC DYNAMICS) in all areas of economics.

Optimal growth theory. That area of ECONOMICS which is concerned with finding OPTIMAL time paths in two main types of economic MODEL. The first type is a macroeconomic (⇛ MACROECONOMICS) model in which the main VARIABLES of interest are CONSUMPTION, SAVING, INVESTMENT, CAPITAL employment and NATIONAL INCOME. Using methods of OPTIMAL CONTROL THEORY, the problem is usually formulated as that of finding the time paths of saving and investment that will give the preferred time path of consumption, given the PRODUCTION FUNCTION for the economy, the rate of growth of the LABOR force and the initial values of all the relevant variables. The second type of model was originated by the physicist John von Neumann (1903–1957), (⇛ GAMES, THEORY OF), and studies a model in which there are many COMMODITIES or sectors. The production of each commodity at one point in time requires INPUTS of other commodities produced at the preceding point in time. The question then arises of whether it is possible to find a time path of outputs of commodities such that they are all growing at the same rate and, if so, to investigate the properties of such a BALANCED GROWTH path. The question of *optimality* is concerned with finding the *maximal* such growth path, i.e., that along which the common growth rate is the largest possible. (⇛⇛ TURNPIKE THEOREMS).

Optimal resource allocation. ⇛ ECONOMIC EFFICIENCY

Optimum. A word that occurs frequently in economics and that means simply the best value that some VARIABLE can take, with reference to some particular objective. For instance, if a firm's objective is to maximize PROFITS, its optimum, or best, output is that at which profits are a maximum; alternatively, this output might simply be referred to as the optimum. (⇛ SATISFICING).

Option. An agreement with a seller or buyer permitting the holder to buy or sell if he chooses to do so at a given price within a given period. Options may be purchased for cash or may be granted along with a transaction. In the STOCK EXCHANGE an option may be purchased from a broker, giving the right to purchase a certain number of SHARES at a certain price within a certain time, e.g., a three-month option. If, in the meantime, the price falls by more than the cost of the option, then the broker will lose, and the purchaser will gain, and vice versa. An option to buy is a *call option;* an option to sell is a *put option;* and one to buy or sell is a *double option.* The purchase of options allows the speculator to limit the amount of money at risk on a share price movement.

Ordinal utility. A concept of UTILITY that is based on the idea of a preference ordering, or ranking, rather than on the Marshallian (⇛ MARSHALL, ALFRED) concept of measurable utility. It is assumed that a consumer is capable of comparing any two alternative "baskets" of goods and deciding whether he prefers one to the other or is indifferent between them. Several assumptions are made about the nature of this preference ordering (⇛ INDIFFERENCE CURVE), which lead to the conclusion that all possible "baskets" of goods can be grouped into sets in such a way that the consumer is indifferent between all the "baskets" in one set and is not indifferent between sets. These "indifference sets" can be arranged in increasing order of preference. It is often convenient, though not necessary, to assign numbers to these sets, adopting the convention that the higher a set is in the order of preference, the higher its number should be. Any increasing sequence of numbers could perform this function. For example, we could indicate successive indifference sets by the sequence 1, 2, 3, 4 . . . or by the sequence 1, 10, 2,000, 2,001 . . . or by any other rising sequence. It has become the practice to call such numbers "utility numbers," and since they simply describe the ordering of indifference sets, they are said to represent "ordinal utility." This usage is rather unfortunate, since the word *utility* bears no relation to the Marshallian notion of the intrinsic satisfactions induced by the consumption of a good. Indeed, the theory of ordinal utility has tried to purge itself entirely of this notion. (⇛ INDIFFERENCE ANALYSIS; SOCIAL WELFARE FUNCTION).

Organization for Economic Cooperation and Development (OECD). The OECD came into being in September 1961, renaming and extending the ORGANIZATION FOR EUROPEAN ECONOMIC COOPERATION. It was based on the convention signed in Paris in December 1960 by the original member countries of the OEEC, plus Spain, the United States and Canada. Later Japan, New Zealand, Australia and Finland also became members (with Yugoslavia as an observer). The aims of the OECD are (*a*) to encourage economic growth and high employment with financial stability among member countries and (*b*) to contribute to the economic development of the less advanced member and nonmember countries and the expansion of world multilateral trade (⇛ MULTILATERALISM). The organization carries out its functions through a number of committees—namely, the Economic Policy Committee, the Committee for Scientific Research, the Trade Committee, the Development Assistance Committee—serviced by a large secretariat. It publishes regular statistical bulletins covering the main economic statistics of member countries and regular reviews of the economic prospects of individual members. It also publishes *ad hoc* reports of special studies covering a wide range of subjects, e.g., world POPULATION growth, agricultural surpluses. The OECD has been particularly important as a forum for the industrial countries to discuss international monetary problems and in promoting aid and technical assistance for DEVELOPING COUNTRIES. (⇛⇛ INTERNATIONAL MONETARY FUND).

Organization for European Economic Cooperation (OEEC). After a speech by the U.S. secretary of state, General Marshall, offering U.S. aid to postwar Europe, a conference was held in Paris in July 1947 that established a Committee of European Economic Cooperation for the coordination of the economic recovery program of Western Europe. In April 1948 a convention was signed in Paris by the ministers of 16 European countries and allied representatives for Germany. The 16 countries were Austria, Belgium, Denmark, France, Greece, Iceland, the Republic of Ireland, Italy, Luxembourg, the Netherlands, Norway, Portugal, Sweden, Switzerland, Turkey and the United Kingdom. Under the agreement, multilateral trading (⇛ MULTILATERALISM) was to be reestablished with a multilateral payments system, and trade adjustments or restrictions were to be reduced. Its immediate function was to propose a recovery program and carry it out. This meant the efficient distribution of American aid under the EUROPEAN RECOVERY PROGRAM between 1948 and 1952. At the same time, quantitative IMPORT restrictions were steadily reduced by the OEEC. The EUROPEAN PAYMENTS UNION, which was established in July 1950, was the agency through which the OEEC fulfilled its obligation to institute a multilateral payments system. In subsequent years considerable progress was made in freeing LABOR and CAPITAL movements and payments among member countries. The OEEC opened negotiations for the setting up of a EUROPEAN FREE TRADE AREA linking the EUROPEAN ECONOMIC COMMUNITY with the other member countries, but they proved abortive in the face of opposition from the EEC. In September 1961, to mark its widening and changing functions, the OEEC was replaced by the ORGANIZATION FOR ECONOMIC COOPERATION AND DEVELOPMENT, which included Canada and the United States as full members.

Organization of Petroleum Exporting Countries (OPEC). A group of 13 countries that are major producers and exporters of crude petroleum. The organization, set up in 1960, acts as a forum for discussion of and agreement on the level at which the member countries should fix the price of their crude petroleum EXPORTS. The organization also acts as a coordinator for determining the level of aid to DEVELOPING COUNTRIES granted by the members. The 13 member countries are: Algeria, Ecuador, Gabon, Indonesia, Iran, Iraq, Kuwait, Libya, Nigeria, Qatar, Saudi Arabia, the United Arab Emirates and Venezuela. These countries account for about 60 percent of total world crude oil production and about 90 percent of total world exports. In 1976 a split in the organization led to the introduction of a dual price system because of the decision by Saudi Arabia and the U.A.E. that oil price rises should be kept to a minimum. In 1976 the organization voted $800 million for aid to developing countries, of which $400 million was offered to the International Agricultural Development Fund, a fund set up by the World Food Council in Rome in 1974. (⇛ INTERNATIONAL ENERGY AGENCY).

Origin. ⇛ CERTIFICATE OF ORIGIN; EUROPEAN FREE TRADE ASSOCIATION

Overdraft. A LOAN facility on a customer's checking account at a bank permitting him to overdraw up to a certain agreed limit for an agreed period. Overdrafts are often unsecured. U.S. banks do not normally permit overdrafts but make personal loans against credit cards without requiring COLLATERAL SECURITY; they will also make installment loans. (⇛ TERM LOANS; PERSONAL LOANS).

Over-full employment. Empirical studies, especially those made in connection with the Phillips curve (⇛ PHILLIPS, ALBAN WILLIAM HOUSEGO), have suggested that there is some minimum level of UNEMPLOYMENT consistent with maintenance of wage and PRICE stability. If unemployment should fall below this level, there will tend to be wage and price INFLATION, and, correspondingly, such a level of employment of the LABOR force is referred to as "over-full employment." Essentially, it refers to a condition where DEMAND for goods and services is high relative to the maximum productive capacity of the economy, thus creating inflationary pressures in markets for goods and labor. (⇛ UNEMPLOYMENT, NATURAL RATE OF).

Overheads. ⇛ FIXED COSTS

Overseas banks. ⇛ INTERNATIONAL BANKING

Over-the-counter market. A secondary MARKET in which unlisted shares are bought and sold outside the organized STOCK EXCHANGE. Prices are set, not by auction but by negotiation between firms of dealers and between them and investors. Bid and offer prices tend to be much wider apart than for listed SECURITIES, especially for the majority of securities in which the market is relatively narrow. The market is important for the stocks of smaller industrial companies, although listed securities, including government BONDS, are also traded on the OTC. Companies whose securities are listed and traded on a national securities exchange are required to register their securities with the SECURITIES AND EXCHANGE COMMISSION, but this is not necessary for OTC securities. However, OTC dealers and brokers are required to register with the Securities and Exchange Commission.

Overtime. The hours worked in excess of the standard number of hours of work laid down in the conditions of employment. Hourly paid employees are normally paid at a higher rate per hour for overtime than for standard hours, and it is therefore in their interests to get the number of standard hours reduced. The amount of overtime worked fluctuates in response to movements in AGGREGATE DEMAND.

Overvalued currency. ⇛ UNDERVALUED CURRENCY

Own rate of interest. The RATE OF INTEREST that is implied by the change in price of a particular COMMODITY. If p_t is the commodity's price at time *t*, and p_{t+1} that at one period later, then the own rate of interest can be calculated simply as $(p_{t+1} - p_t)/p_t$, which is the proportionate rate of change of the price. The idea here is that if you buy one unit of the commodity at time *t* and hold it for one period, then the own interest rate gives the RATE OF RETURN you will have earned. This can be compared to the rate of interest earned on buying ASSETS such as BONDS, in order to determine the most profitable opportunity for INVESTMENT.

P

Paasche index. An INDEX NUMBER, named after a nineteenth century German economist, that measures the change in some aspect of a group of items over time, using weights based on current rather than past values. For example, the Paasche PRICE index finds the percentage increase of current prices over prices at some base period by dividing the total cost of the current purchases made by consumers, at today's prices, by the total cost of those same purchases at the prices prevailing at the base date. Similarly, a Paasche quantity index finds the percentage increase of current quantities purchased over quantities purchased at some base date by dividing the total cost of the quantities currently purchased, valued at today's prices, by the total cost of the quantities purchased at the base data, again valued at current prices. In the first of these examples, the weights (⇛ WEIGHTED AVERAGE) used are current quantities purchased. In the second, the weights are current prices. A disadvantage of the Paasche index is that, because the weights are changing from year to year, comparison can only be made between any given year and the base year. (⇛⇛ INDEX-NUMBER PROBLEM; LASPEYRES INDEX).

Paradox of voting. This refers to a problem of inconsistency that may arise in majority voting systems and is also known as "Condorcet's paradox," after the French philosopher who first formulated it in the 18th century. It shows that majority voting over pairs of alternatives may lead to inconsistent or internally contradictory rankings of the alternatives.

The paradox can be illustrated as follows: Three individuals—Tom, Dick and Harry—must vote on three policy alternatives, A, B and C. Suppose their preferences are as follows:

Ranking	*Tom*	*Dick*	*Harry*
Most preferred	A	B	C
Next preferred	B	C	A
Least preferred	C	A	B

In voting on A over B, A collects Tom and Harry's votes and so by a majority vote is ranked ahead of B. In voting on B over C, B collects Tom and Dick's vote and so by a majority vote is ranked ahead of C. But in voting on C over A, C collects Dick and Harry's vote, and so C is ranked ahead of A. But then we have that "the group prefers" A to B, and B to C, but C to A, thus displaying the kind of inconsistency known as intransitivity. This paradox therefore shows that if we allow any pattern of preferences to be held by each individual, pairwise majority voting does not guarantee a consistent ranking of alternatives by the group. It also shows that choice of the order in which pairwise votes are taken can determine which alternative finally gets selected. For example, Tom could ensure that his preferred alternative A is selected by insisting that the vote first be taken on B over C, and then on A over B, and then claiming that A is best because C has already been "eliminated."

The main achievement of KENNETH J. ARROW's famous IMPOSSIBILITY THEOREM is to show that this paradox can be extended to *all* voting schemes, or "constitutions," that possess certain minimal desirable properties. (⇛ SOCIAL WELFARE FUNCTION).

Parameter. A specified term in an algebraic equation. For example, in the relationship $y = 3x + 2$, the numbers 3 and 2 are parameters.

Pareto-optimal. ⇛ ECONOMIC EFFICIENCY

Pareto's law. ⇛ PARETO, VILFREDO FEDERICO DAMASO

Pareto, Vilfredo Federico Damaso (1848–1923). An Italian, born in Paris, Pareto was trained as, and practiced as, an engineer. He succeeded his father to a post in the Italian railways, and in 1874 was appointed superintendent of mines for the Banca Nazionale, Florence. He succeeded MARIE ESPRIT LEON WALRAS to the Chair of Economics in the Faculty of Law at Lausanne University in 1892. His publications include *Cours d'économie politique* (1896–97) and *Manuale di Econimica Politica* (1906). He retired in 1907. He developed analytical economics from the foundation laid by Walras. He pointed out the shortcomings of any theory of VALUE insofar as it rested upon assumptions of measurable or "cardinal" rather than ORDINAL UTILITY. He demonstrated that an effective theory of consumer behavior and exchange could be constructed on assumptions of ordinal utility alone. Exchange would take place in a competitive MARKET between individuals such that the ratios of the MARGINAL UTILITIES of the goods traded equaled the ratio of their prices. An optimum point of exchange could be defined without the need to compare one individual's total UTILITY with another's. He defined an increase in total welfare as occurring under those conditions in which some people are better off as a result of the change, without at the same time anybody's being worse off (⇛ COMPENSATION PRINCIPLE). Pareto's work in this field, coupled with the development of INDIFFERENCE CURVE analysis, invented by FRANCIS YSIDRO EDGEWORTH, was the foundation upon which modern WELFARE ECONOMICS is based. A study of the distribution of personal incomes in an economy led him to postulate what became known as *Pareto's law,* that whatever the political or TAXATION conditions, INCOME will be distributed in the same way in all countries. He noted that the distribution of the number of incomes is heavily concentrated among the lower income groups and asserted that the number of incomes fell proportionately with the size of income. Pareto's law has not, in fact, proved valid in its strict sense. (⇛⇛ ECONOMIC EFFICIENCY; INCOME DISTRIBUTION; SLUTSKY, EUGEN).

Paris Club. ⇛ INTERNATIONAL MONETARY FUND

Par rate of exchange. ⇛ EXCHANGE RATE

Partial correlation. Analysis of the CORRELATION between two VARIABLES that takes into account the fact that one or both of those variables is also correlated with some other variable or variables. Procedures are then used to eliminate the influence of the other(s) from the measure of the correlation between the two in question. The resulting correlation coefficient is known as the *partial correlation coefficient.*

Partial equilibrium analysis. The analysis of the determination of EQUILIBRIUM positions for a small part of the economy. That is, we take a single MARKET and examine the determination of its equilibrium position and the change in this position that follows from a shift in its underlying determinants (⇛ COMPARATIVE STATIC EQUILIBRIUM ANALYSIS). The assumption underlying partial equilibrium analysis is that the interaction between the market under study and the rest of the economy can be ignored, as having little effect on the final result. In effect, we make the "other things being equal" assumption that the rest of the economy remains the same throughout the analysis of one market, and so there are no "feedback effects" on the single market under study. Many economists would regard partial equilibrium analysis as being valid only for expositional purposes or for studying very SHORT-RUN effects. In general, interdependence among markets in the economy is strong enough to warrant a GENERAL EQUILIBRIUM ANALYSIS. The method of partial equilibrium analysis was characteristic of ALFRED MARSHALL's approach to economic theory, in contrast to the explicitly general equilibrium approach of MARIE ESPRIT LEON WALRAS. (⇛ INPUT-OUTPUT ANALYSIS).

Participation rate. The proportion of the population who are of working age and who are part of the labor force of the economy, i.e., the "economically active" part of the population. The size of the labor force will be altered if the participation rate should increase. For example, the increase in the participation rate of women in the 1970s caused the labor force to grow faster than the population of working age. Other empirical evidence shows that the higher the education level, the higher the participation rate for women. This latter rate falls, however, in periods of general high unemployment.

Partnership. An unincorporated business formed by the association of two or more persons who share RISKS and PROFITS. There are two main types of partnerships: (1) *general partnership,* in which each partner is liable for the DEBTS and the business actions of the others, to the full extent of his own RESOURCES (including his personal property); and (2) *limited partnership,* in which the liability of certain partners is limited, by agreement with the others, to the amount of their SHARE in the capital of the partnership. The distribution of the partnership income and the other rights and duties of its members are governed by the partnership agreement. Partnerships are a common form of organization in the legal, medical and accounting professions and in businesses where CAPITAL requirements are relatively small, e.g., retail distribution and other services. Partnerships, with sole PROPRIETORSHIPS, account for the vast majority of the total number of businesses and are subject to little government regulation of a specific nature. Each state in the United States has a separate general partnership statute (most of them similar in form), but neither registration nor statutory audit is required, although limited partnerships need to file a certificate with the state listing the names of general and limited partners and their shares in capital and profits. Except in certain cases where a corporation is a member of a partnership, the partners are assessed for tax on their share of partnership income as individuals. The partnership itself is not subject to tax and is therefore "fiscally transparent." This is an advantage compared with a corporation, whose stockholders are taxed on the income they receive as dividends in addition to the taxation that the corporation pays on its profits. Among the disadvantages of partnerships are legal complications involved in changes in ownership and—for some partners, at least—lack of protection from unlimited liability. (⇛ CORPORATION INCOME TAX).

Par value. The PRICE at which a SHARE or other SECURITY is issued, i.e., FACE VALUE or NOMINAL VALUE of STOCK. A security is said to be standing above par if its quoted price on the STOCK EXCHANGE is greater than that at which the security was issued.

Pay-back. The period over which the cumulative net revenue from an INVESTMENT project equals the original investment. It is a commonly used but crude method for analyzing CAPITAL projects. Its main defects are that it takes no account of the PROFITS over the whole life of the investment, nor of the time profile of the CASH FLOW. (⇛ INVESTMENT APPRAISAL).

Pay board. Established in 1971, and appointed by the COST OF LIVING COUNCIL, the Pay Board was responsible for setting maximum nominal pay increases of 5.3 percent per annum in the second phase of the incomes policy from November 1971 to January 1973. Exceptions were allowed, especially in those instances where a union contract had been signed prior to November 1971. Wage increases for "the working poor" were not restricted to this 5.3 percent limit. (⇛⇛ PRICE COMMISSION; PRICES AND INCOMES POLICY).

Payment-in-kind. A phrase to describe compensation of a nonmonetary nature for services rendered. If a doctor accepted a painting from a patient instead of the usual fee, he would receive payment-in-kind. (⇛ BARTER; HIDDEN ECONOMY).

Payments, balance of. ⇛ BALANCE OF PAYMENTS

Payout ratio. ⇛ COVER

Payroll tax. A tax levied on employers' wage bills. It is favored by many economists in developed economies as a means of encouraging both capital intensiveness (⇛ CAPITAL-INTENSIVE) and the more efficient use of LABOR, and of discouraging labor hoarding. A payroll tax has operated in the United States since 1935, when it was introduced to finance the Old Age and Survivor's Insurance (⇛ OASI). Today it is a tax on employers and employees, and the proceeds are used to help finance several social security programs.

Peg. ⇛ EXCHANGE RATE

Penetration. Synonym for MARKET SHARE.

Pension funds. Sums of money laid aside and normally invested to provide a regular INCOME on retirement, or in compensation for disablement, for the remainder of a person's life. Nearly all developed countries have state pension plans—e.g., the OASI plan—but unlike these plans, private pension plans for which contributions receive favorable tax treatment are usually funded, i.e., placed in managed invested funds. Many private pension plans are based upon ASSURANCE. Occupational pension plans may be contributory or noncontributory by the employee; the benefits of private plans are normally related to the length of service of the employee and the level of his salary or contributions. Pension funds have considerable economic significance and provide an important flow of funds to the CAPITAL MARKET. The pension funds of the largest corporations are often significant shareholders in other companies. Higher rates of inflation since 1973 have raised acute problems for pension funds, since it has not proved possible to invest these funds at rates that would maintain their value in REAL TERMS. Under the OASI employee contributions or premiums are not tax deductible, while employer contributions are. Benefits and interest are not taxed. For private retirement plans, contributions are treated the same way, but employer benefits and interest are taxed. Self-employed plans are limited to 10 percent of adjusted gross income with an annual ceiling. For tax purposes they are treated like employer contributions and benefits. The OASI was instituted in 1934 as an insurance program equal to a combined employer-employee rate of 2 percent on the first $3,000 of wages. The combined rate and the ceiling to which the rate applies have been adjusted upward frequently since that time. (⇛ INSTITUTIONAL INVESTOR).

Percentile. The *n*th percentile of a set of numbers, arranged in ascending order of magnitude, is that number below which *n* percent of the numbers fall. For example, suppose that we have the numbers 1, 2, 3, 4, 5, 6, 7, 8, 9, 10, then the 80th percentile will equal 9 (since 80 percent of the numbers lie below it), the 40th percentile will be 5 and so on.

Perfect competition. A MARKET in which the following assumptions hold:

1. There is a large number of buyers.
2. There is a large number of sellers.
3. The quantity of the good bought by any buyer or sold by any seller is so small relative to the total quantity traded that changes in these quantities leave market PRICE unaffected. The individual seller can therefore take the DEMAND CURVE he faces as a horizontal straight line at the going price. Similarly, the individual buyer can take the SUPPLY CURVE he faces as a horizontal straight line at the going price.
4. Units of the good sold by different sellers are identical—i.e., the product is homogeneous.

Perfect competition is sometimes distinguished from *pure competition* by two further assumptions, although pure and perfect competition are normally used as synonyms.

5. There is perfect information, in the sense that all buyers and all sellers have complete information on the prices being asked and offered in all other parts of the market.
6. There is perfect freedom of entry—i.e., new sellers are able to enter the market and sell the good on the same terms as existing sellers.

The consequences of these assumptions are:

A. The market adjusts rapidly to discrepancies between SUPPLY and demand, since such discrepancies will cause price changes that are transmitted throughout the market by the process of ARBITRAGE, which relies on an unimpeded flow of information.

B. When an EQUILIBRIUM is achieved, it can only be at a single price.

C. In the LONG RUN, there can be no PROFITS, other than a normal competitive return to the ENTREPRENEUR, because, if there are, entry (⇛ BARRIERS TO ENTRY; FREEDOM OF ENTRY) takes place, and they are competed away.

The assumptions underlying perfect competition are obviously "unrealistic," in that they are not an accurate description of many real-world markets. Some markets conform to some assumptions, but few, if any, conform to them all. The STOCK EXCHANGE, for example, in general conforms to the assumptions of perfect information (or nearly so) and large number of buyers. On the other hand, stringent restrictions on entry exist, and there is considerable specialization by dealers in particular shares, and so the stock exchange is better described as a closely-knit group of OLIGOPOLIES.

Given this "unrealism" of the assumptions, there has been considerable debate among economists over the usefulness of the theory. One result of this was the development of theories of MONOPOLISTIC COMPETITION and oligopoly in the 1930s and later. At the present time, there is still conflict of opinion on the degree of applicability of the MODEL of perfect competition. Partly this is a result of the difficulties surrounding EMPIRICAL TESTING in economics, since it is not easy to establish just how useful the perfectly competitive model is as compared to alternative theories. Partly, also, it is a result of conflict of political views, since one's belief in the efficiency of the FREE-MARKET ECONOMY tends to depend on how closely one believes the markets conform, or can be made to conform, to the competitive ideal. There does seem to be a fairly general consensus of opinion, however, that first, as a limiting case (the other being absolute monopoly), the theory can give useful insights into the workings of the economy, just as a physicist might begin his study of gravity by considering an object falling in a vacuum. Extreme simplification, and then the gradual introduction of complications, may be a far more fruitful methodology than the attempt to take all the complications of the real world into account at once. Second, the model may give reasonably accurate predictions of the consequences of certain types of change, even if its assumptions are descriptively unrealistic. If we are interested only in predicting results and not in explaining the details of the process by which they come about, then, on the grounds of expediency, we may be prepared to use the theory. The cost of making a theory more realistic is generally an increased complexity, with the result that it becomes more difficult to use, and even possibly less accurate, in its predictions. Third, the perfectly competitive model fulfills certain conditions of optimal resource allocation (⇛ ECONOMIC EFFICIENCY) and gives important insights into the extent to which decentralized decision making can be expected to lead to an economic optimum. In this respect, it acts as a standard against which to assess the efficiency of real-world economic systems.

Peril point. A term used by the U.S. Tariff Commission to describe the point beyond which tariff (⇛ TARIFFS, IMPORT) reductions would threaten the existence of domestic industry. (⇛ TRIGGER PRICE).

Permanent income hypothesis. A theory of the CONSUMPTION FUNCTION, proposed by MILTON FRIEDMAN, that was designed to explain certain results that had been obtained from attempts to make empirical estimates of JOHN MAYNARD KEYNES' consumption function. Friedman argued that people relate their consumption in a given period not to their level of DISPOSABLE INCOME *in that period* but rather to an estimate of what their long-run or permanent income is. For example, a worker in the automobile industry may figure that over the years his income will average out at about $20,000 per year. In some periods he may make more because of overtime and bonus payments, at other times less because of short-time working and layoffs. The hypothesis is that he regards these changes in income as *transitory* and does not fully adjust his consumption pattern to them—he continues to consume to some extent as if his income had been $20,000. It therefore follows that the relationship between consumption and short-run income will be relatively flat—a large change in current income causes relatively little change in consumption—even if the relation between consumption and permanent income is a close proportional one. To make this appealing idea operational, it is then necessary to measure "permanent income." Friedman's suggestion was to express consumption as depending on current and recent past (lagged) values of disposable income, where these latter could be taken as the basis for the individual's estimate of permanent income. In this form the hypothesis has become an important element in modern work on the consumption function.

Personal disposable income. That portion of NATIONAL INCOME which flows to HOUSEHOLDS, *minus* personal direct tax (⇛ DIRECT TAXATION), *plus* TRANSFER PAYMENTS. Personal disposable income per person in the United States in 1980 was equal to $4,879. (⇛⇛ CONSUMPTION FUNCTION).

Personal loan. A loan from a bank, trust company or financial institution to an individual without COLLATERAL SECURITY. Personal loans are granted for a fixed period, from one month to normally not more than five years, and are usually repayable in monthly installments. The most popular use of personal loans is for the acquisition of consumer goods. (⇛ INSTALLMENT CREDIT).

Petrodollars. The excess purchasing power in the hands of producers of oil. This has been generated by the large increases in the price of oil since 1973. The stock of petrodollars may well exceed $500 billion. Petrodollars find their way back to oil-consuming countries through the BALANCE OF PAYMENTS capital account, creating problems in the FOREIGN-EXCHANGE MARKET. It has also been speculated that the rise in the price of gold in 1979–80 was induced by the expenditure of petrodollars on gold. Petrodollars may also cause domestic problems for oil-consuming countries if those dollars are used to purchase specific assets such as land and buildings in oil-consuming countries. The result is INFLATION and eventually a fall in the real price (⇛ REAL TERMS) of oil. (⇛⇛ ORGANIZATION OF PETROLEUM EXPORTING COUNTRIES).

Petty, Sir William (1623–87). The pioneer of numerical economics. His main interest lay in public finance, and he made important contributions to monetary theory (⇛ MONETARISM) and FISCAL POLICY. His approach to these subjects contributed to the development of CLASSICAL ECONOMICS, and his work in the field of comparative statistics is in direct line of descent to the work of modern economists in the field of comparative economic statistics. His best-known work is *Political Arithmetic,* published in 1691. The so-called *Petty's law* was a remarkably farsighted statement of the tendency for the proportion of the working population engaged in SERVICES to increase as an economy develops.

Petty's law. ⇛ PETTY, SIR WILLIAM

Phillips, Alban William Housego (1914–75). After a number of jobs in electrical engineering, and after serving in the British Royal Air Force during the Second World War, Phillips began lecturing in economics at the London School of Economics, England, in 1950. From 1958 until 1967 he was Tooke Professor of Economics, Science and Statistics in the University of London. In 1968 he accepted the Chair of Economics at the Australian National University. Professor Phillips published many articles exploring the relationships between the MULTIPLIER and accelerator in mathematical MODELS (⇛⇛ ACCELERATOR-MULTIPLIER MODEL) with various time lags and applied the engineering technique of closed-loop control systems to the analysis of macroeconomic (⇛ MACROECONOMICS) relationships.

In an article in *Economica* in 1958, Professor Phillips set out empirical evidence to support the view that there was a significant relation between the percentage change of money wages and the level of UNEMPLOYMENT —the lower the unemployment, the higher the rate of change of wages. This relationship, which became known as the *Phillips curve,* has attracted considerable theoretical and empirical analysis. Its main implication is that, since a particular level of unemployment in the economy will imply a particular rate of wage increase, the aims of low unemployment and a low rate of INFLATION may be inconsistent. The government must then choose between the feasible combinations of unemployment and inflation, as shown by the estimated Phillips curve—e.g., 3 percent unemployment and no inflation, or 1½ percent unemployment and 8 percent inflation, etc. Alternatively, it may attempt to bring about basic changes in the workings of the economy—e.g., a PRICES AND INCOMES POLICY—in order to reduce the rate of inflation consistent with low unemployment. However, the relation between unemployment and inflation has not been sufficiently stable in practice to permit exact judgments to be made.

Phillips curve. ⇛ PHILLIPS, ALBAN WILLIAM HOUSEGO

Physiocrats. A group of 18th-century French economists, led by FRANCOIS QUESNAY, who later became known as the Physiocrats or *"Les Economistes."* They believed in the existence of a natural order and regarded the state's role as simply that of preserving property and upholding the natural order. They held that agriculture was the only source of WEALTH, and therefore this sector should be taxed by *l'impot unique.* In this, and in their advocacy of free trade, their views were directly opposed to those of the mercantilists (⇛ MERCANTILISM). In their belief in LAISSEZ-FAIRE, they had much in common with, and certainly influenced, British CLASSICAL ECONOMICS, and especially ADAM SMITH. Quesnay's *Tableau Economique,* published in 1758, has in it the origins of modern ideas on the circulation of wealth and the nature of interrelationships in the economy. (⇛⇛ CANTILLON, RICHARD; GEORGE, HENRY; MILL, JOHN STUART).

Pigou, Arthur Cecil (1877–1959). A pupil of ALFRED MARSHALL, whom he succeeded to the Chair in Political Economy at Cambridge, England, in 1908; Pigou continued in this chair until he retired in 1944. His major publications include *Principles and Methods of Industrial Peace* (1905), *Wealth and Welfare* (1912), *Unemployment* (1914), *Economics of Welfare* (1919), *Essays in Applied Economics* (1923), *Industrial Fluctuations* (1927), *The Theory of Unemployment* (1933) and *Employment and Equilibrium* (1941). His work on monetary theory (⇛ MONETARISM), employment and the NATIONAL INCOME, which was in the tradition of the CLASSICAL SCHOOL, led him into controversy with JOHN MAYNARD KEYNES. He was the first to enunciate clearly the concept of the real balance effect, which, as a consequence, became known as the *Pigou effect.* The Pigou effect is a stimulation of employment brought about by the rise in the real value of liquid (⇛ LIQUIDITY) balances as a consequence of a decline in prices—as the real value of WEALTH increases, so CONSUMPTION will increase, thus increasing income and employment. This was one of the processes by which the classical MODEL envisaged that full-employment EQUILIBRIUM could be obtained as a result of a reduction in real wages. Although his work on MACROECONOMICS was partly superseded by Keynes, he made a lasting contribution with his original work in WELFARE ECONOMICS. He strongly resisted the belief that practical policies based on propositions from welfare economics were impossible because interpersonal comparisons of UTILITY cannot be made. He argued that, though this may be true for individuals, it was possible to make meaningful comparisons between groups. His distinction between private and social product now plays an important role in the formation of government economic policy in the field of PUBLIC EXPENDITURE.

Pigou effect. ⇛ PIGOU, ARTHUR CECIL

Placing. The sale of a new issue of SHARES (⇛ NEW ISSUE MARKET) directly to investors instead of by means of a public issue. Placings are made by a financial intermediary, such as an INVESTMENT BANK acting on behalf of the company issuing the shares, usually with INSTITUTIONAL INVESTORS. This method of *private* placing of shares minimizes the cost of a new issue for small firms. If the shares are quoted on the STOCK EXCHANGE, a proportion of the issue must be made to the general public.

Planned economy. An economy in which the basic functions of RESOURCE ALLOCATION are carried out by a centralized administrative process as opposed to a price mechanism (⇛⇛ PRICE SYSTEM). Decisions on the total outputs of all goods in the economy are taken by an administrative body, and these decisions may reflect to varying degrees the wishes of consumers and the perceived need to expand particular sectors of the economy more rapidly than others, e.g., heavy industry, armaments industries, export industries. At this stage, of course, consistency must be achieved between outputs of FINAL PRODUCTS and outputs of the INTERMEDIATE PRODUCTS required to produce them. Similarly, the total requirements for LAND, LABOR and CAPITAL must not exceed the total amount available. The "plans" or output programs are then communicated to the individual production units—factories, plants and farms—and these units are expected to fulfill their plans with the resources that have been allocated to them; indeed, incentives often exist for output plans to be over-fulfilled, since this represents greater PRODUCTIVITY of resources than was envisaged in the plan. INCOME DISTRIBUTION is determined centrally, since wages and salaries are set by the administrative machinery (there are, of course, no RENT, PROFIT or INTEREST (⇛ RATE OF INTEREST) earners, apart from the state). This extreme form of centralized economic organization is most closely approached in the USSR and China, but even these economies do not correspond perfectly to the description given above, since there are certain important sectors, notably agriculture, in which PRIVATE ENTERPRISE and some elements of a MARKET mechanism still operate. A planned system was the most obvious form of economic organization for any economy that wanted to eliminate the characteristics of the capitalist economy. In addition, it permits the economy to be run in a way that corresponds to particular objectives, e.g., the rapid expansion of heavy industrial sectors at the expense of consumer goods. Such political imposition of priorities is rather more difficult in a capitalist system. Finally, an administrative process of allocation may be the only way to secure ECONOMIC DEVELOPMENT in an economy that does not possess the necessary institutions, skills and mores for a capitalist system to work. On the other hand, the major defects of a centralized system (assuming one does not regard the absence of private enterprise as in itself a defect) lie in its possible inefficiency as a means of allocating RESOURCES. In any industrialized economy, the scale of the problem is very large. Inevitably, the planning process requires a large BUREAUCRACY, with the resulting problems of securing administrative efficiency faced by any large organization. Costly mistakes may occur, and the rigidities in the system may mean that they remain long uncorrected. Because the system is not sensitive to the detailed wishes of consumers, a planned economy is probably better suited to an economy attempting to industrialize rapidly than to a high mass-consumption economy. This, among other things, may account for the fact that the wealthier socialist economies in Eastern Europe are beginning to develop methods of giving greater discretion to managers of production units and even to experiment with price mechanisms that would enable CONSUMERS' PREFERENCES to be more accurately measured.

Plowback. ⇛ SELF-FINANCING

Poll tax. A tax levied equally on each person in the community. Also called a *head tax*. (⇛ TAXATION).

Population. 1. The number of people living in any defined area, such as New York, California or the entire United States. 2. In statistics, a term applied to any class of data of which counts are made or samples taken, e.g., the population of business corporations.

The statistical study of the characteristics of human populations is called *demography*. While total population statistics derived from the registration of births and deaths and from CENSUSES of population are reasonably accurate in advanced countries, the population of many DEVELOPING COUNTRIES can only be estimated within wide margins of error because the necessary administrative machinery is not available. Population growth is a central problem of economic development. In many instances developing countries have seen their real economic growth more than consumed by rapidly growing populations. This has led economists to study what is referred to as the critical minimum effort; the amount of population growth needed to increase CAPITAL fast enough so that it exceeds population growth. Projections of population depend on several factors, the most important for the United States being net immigration and the fertility (⇛ BIRTHRATE) rate. In 1910 the fertility rate was 126. This fell to about 80 in the DEPRESSION of the 1930s and rose to 120 by the mid- to late 1950s. It has fallen now to well below 100. The population of the United States is currently about 200 million people and is forecast to rise to between 245 million and 280 million by the year 2000. (⇛⇛ MALTHUS, THOMAS ROBERT).

Population, census of. In the United States, a count, or census, of the number of inhabitants is taken every 10 years. Enumerators visit every house in areas assigned to them, leave census forms, which they later collect, and check on the accuracy of the answers. Information is collected on place of residence, age, sex, marital condition, occupation and certain supplementary information on living conditions, education and occasionally other matters. All advanced countries have regular censuses, but many DEVELOPING COUNTRIES are now in the process of organizing them for the first time. It is not possible to obtain information accurately by other means. Calculations based on births, deaths and migration have not proved in the past to be very precise means of estimating population growth, except as a means of interpolation between censuses. Annual estimates of the present and future population are prepared and published by the government. The latest census in the United States was in 1980.

Portfolio. The collection of SECURITIES held by an investor.

Potential competition. The doctrine, enshrined in the CELLER-KEFAUVER ACT, that MERGERS should not be allowed between two firms that do not at present compete in a particular geographical territory or product market should not be allowed if they were likely to compete in the event of the merger's not taking place.

Precautionary motive. A motive for holding MONEY that arises out of the possibility of unforeseen or imperfectly anticipated needs for expenditure. A need for money that can only be met by selling some nonmoney form of holding WEALTH—e.g., a SHARE, a BOND—may involve the holder in a loss, perhaps because of unfavorable MARKET conditions, cost penalties or transactions costs. Alternatively, it may involve borrowing and thus incurring interest (⇛ RATE OF INTEREST) costs. Hence, given that future needs for money cannot be predicted with complete certainty, some margin over the most likely required money sum will have to be held. This part of the individual's money holding then arises out of a precautionary motive.

Predatory pricing. A policy of setting PRICES, the purpose of which is to weaken or eliminate competitors or to discourage and prevent entry of new sellers into a MARKET. It is therefore a means by which MONOPOLY power may be built up or preserved and for this reason has often been criticized by economists. (⇛⇛ BARRIERS TO ENTRY; DUMPING).

Preemptive right. A legal right to purchase SHARES from any new issue so as to preserve a stockholder's ownership proportion. (⇛ STOCK RIGHT).

Preferential duty. ⇛ TARIFFS, IMPORT

Preferred stock. Holders of preferred stocks take precedence over the holders of COMMON STOCKS, but after BOND holders, in the payment of DIVIDENDS and in the return of CAPITAL in the event of LIQUIDATION of the corporation. Preferred stock normally entitles the holder to a fixed rate of dividend and carries limited voting rights. Preferred stock may be cumulative or non-cumulative. Cumulative preferred stocks carry forward the right to preferential dividends, if unpaid, from one year to the next. From the investors' point of view, preferred stocks lie between bonds and common stocks in terms of RISK and INCOME, while to the issuing corporation they permit some flexibility in distribution policy at a lower cost than bonds. Preferred stock issues are now unusual, mainly because their dividend payments are not treated as an expense to the issuing corporation, unlike bond interest, and are subject to CORPORATION INCOME TAX.

Premium. 1. The difference, where positive, between the current PRICE or VALUE of a SECURITY or CURRENCY and its issue price or PAR VALUE. 2. A regular payment made in return for an INSURANCE policy.

Prepayments. Payments for services such as rent, insurance and interest made in one accounting period for consumption wholly or partly in a following period. Prepaid items are written into the BALANCE SHEET as a current ASSET.

Present value. The VALUE now of a sum of MONEY arising in the future. Money now is worth more than money in the future, because it could be invested now to produce a greater sum in the future. The present value of money in the future is calculated by DISCOUNTING it at a RATE OF INTEREST equivalent to the rate at which it could be invested. Thus, \$105 in a year's time has a present value of \$100 if the interest rate is 5 percent per annum. The net present value of an investment is the difference between the CAPITAL cost of an investment and the present value of the future CASH FLOWS to which the investment will give rise. It is defined as:

Net present value $= \frac{R_1}{(1+r)} + \frac{R_2}{(1+r)^2} \ldots + \frac{R_n}{(1+r)^n} - C_o$ where R_1, R_2, ...

R_n are gross PROFITS arising in years 1, 2, . . . n, C_o is the present value of capital expenditure, and r is the annual interest rate (assumed constant throughout the period). The calculation of net present values is an important part of INVESTMENT APPRAISAL. (⇛ DISCOUNTED CASH FLOW; INTERNAL RATE OF RETURN).

Presidential committee on income maintenance programs. Appointed in January 1968 to review existing programs and make recommendations on income maintenance, this committee reported in November 1969. The committee concluded that existing programs were inadequate to deal effectively with poverty and recommended a federal universal income supplement program.

Price. The quantity of MONEY that must be exchanged for one unit of a good or service. In addition, economists often use price in a broader sense to refer to anything, whether money or some COMMODITY, that has to be paid—e.g., in a BARTER economy the price of a bride may be 25 cows. (⇛ PRICE SYSTEM; PRICE THEORY; SHADOW PRICE).

Price Commission. Like the PAY BOARD, this commission was established in 1971 to administer the second phase (November 1971 to January 1973) of the U.S. PRICES AND INCOMES POLICY. The commission was an agency of the COST OF LIVING COUNCIL, and its responsibilities were to carry out the policies of the council with respect to price increases. Firms were prohibited from raising prices, as of August 1971, by more than increases in costs. Even when prices were raised, a firm's ratio of profit to sales could not exceed the best ratio in two of the three years prior to August 1971. Farm products, timber and some fishing products were exempt from this requirement on price increases.

Price discrimination. The practice of charging different prices to different consumers for the same good, where the price differences do not reflect differences in cost of supply. In order to practice any form of price discrimination, it must be possible to prevent ARBITRAGE, since otherwise buyers at a lower price could resell to buyers at a higher price, and both parties would gain, which would undermine the price discrimination. "Perfect" price discrimination exists when each buyer is taken separately and is charged the maximum he is prepared to pay for each unit of good. In this way, the seller appropriates all the CONSUMER'S SURPLUS. In practice, perfect price discrimination is rarely feasible, and instead buyers are divided into broad groups, on the basis perhaps of income, location or type of economic activity (e.g., "domestic" versus "industrial" consumers). Provided the ELASTICITIES of DEMANDS of the groups differ (and a major purpose of the division into groups will be to isolate such elasticity differences), a profit-maximizing seller will charge different prices to the groups, setting a higher price to a group with a lower elasticity of demand. A firm practicing price discrimination will earn a relatively greater PROFIT margin in more or less captive markets and a lower margin in more competitive markets. (⇛ ROBINSON-PATMAN ACT).

Price-earnings (P/E) ratio. The quoted price of a company's STOCK divided by the most recent year's EARNINGS per share. The P/E ratio is thus the reciprocal of the earnings YIELD and a measure of the price that has to be paid for a given income from a stock. A company whose stock was quoted at $10 on the STOCK EXCHANGE and that, in the previous year, had earnings of $1 per share would have a P/E ratio of 10 to 1—i.e., the earnings yield would be 10 percent, and it would cost $10 to buy every dollar's worth of earnings. The price of earnings will vary with the stock market's assessment of the risks involved: A high P/E ratio could mean that a company's earnings are expected to grow rapidly; a low ratio could indicate a poor earnings record or a high risk, so that the share with the higher P/E could be the better buy.

Price rigging. ⇛ PRICE SIGNALING

Prices and incomes policy. A policy to control the rate of increase of wages and prices in an attempt to reduce the rate of INFLATION. In the United States the first major prices and incomes policy was introduced during World War II, when prices were tightly controlled by the Office of Price Administration. In August of 1971 the president announced a 90-day freeze on wages and prices. This was followed by a second phase, lasting from November 1971 to January 1973, during which a set of wage and price guidelines were laid down, or suggested. The third phase, which relied on "self-enforcement," terminated in June of 1973, with a 60-day freeze on prices, following a dramatic rise in food prices. The last phase, that of decontrol, lasted until April 1974. (⇛ JAWBONING; PAY BOARD; PRICE COMMISSION; TAX-BASED INCOMES POLICY).

Price signaling. A commercial practice by which firms achieve agreed prices. The market leader publishes a price change sufficiently in advance for other suppliers in the MARKET to bring their prices into line. This method means that overt agreement across the table is avoided and, thus, accusations of conspiracy. (⇛⇛ ANTITRUST POLICY; SMITH, ADAM).

Price support. A situation whereby the government or its agency sets a price for a commodity above market price (⇛ PRICE SYSTEM) and purchases unsold production. The first intervention of this kind in the United States took place in 1929, when the Federal Farm Board was established. It ceased to operate effectively when its funds were exhausted through the accumulation of stocks. Price supports were introduced again in the 1930s and persisted, with minor modifications, until the mid-1970s, when major changes were made to U.S. price support programs. Most important, schemes whereby the government bought and stored crops were canceled and replaced by (1) cash payments to farmers when market prices fall below a government-designated target price; (2) low-interest loans to farmers to assist them in purchasing their own storage facilities. (⇛⇛ INTERNATIONAL COMMODITY AGREEMENTS; COMMON AGRICULTURAL POLICY).

Price system. The system of RESOURCE ALLOCATION based on the free movements of PRICES. In an economy in which MARKETS are permitted to work without outside intervention, the decisions made by individual buyers and sellers are coordinated and made consistent with each other by movements in prices. If buyers wish to purchase more than sellers wish to supply, price will rise. As price rises, this causes buyers to reduce the quantities they wish to buy and sellers to increase the quantities they wish to sell, until, at some particular price, these quantities are equal, and the separate decisions of buyers and sellers are made consistent. Similarly, if sellers wish to sell more than buyers are prepared to take, price falls, causing sellers to reduce the quantities they wish to sell and buyers to increase the quantities they wish to buy, until the quantities are again equal, and decisions are consistent. If every good, service and FACTOR OF PRODUCTION in the economy is sold on such a market, then we can see how the movements in prices bring about consistency of decisions or plans of all buyers and sellers. This mechanism by which movements in prices coordinate individual decisions is known as the price system.

Several things should be noted. First, the process of coordination is quite decentralized. No single central authority collects information on buyers' and sellers' decisions, finds the level at which they are consistent and then transmits information on the necessary sales and purchases to individual buyers and sellers. Whatever one's view of the ethics of centralization, a decentralized system is, other things being equal, likely to be more efficient as a coordinating device; simply because it saves the costs of a two-way transmission of information, it may operate more quickly and with fewer mistakes (⇛ ADAM SMITH). Second, however, we must take care not to identify the workings of the idealized price system too readily with the workings of any actual FREE-MARKET ECONOMY. Many frictions and imperfections may exist in the real world that reduce the efficiency of the decentralized price system. Finally, even if markets in the real world worked smoothly, without frictions and imperfections, the price system does not solve all the problems of resource allocation. Some goods, often called PUBLIC GOODS, cannot be bought and sold on markets. The price system does not take into account EXTERNALITIES and so does not ensure that the socially optimal level of an activity is in fact achieved. The ability to buy goods and services through the price system depends on one's INCOME, and this may create social problems. The conditions under which the price system will bring about an optimal allocation of resources (⇛ ECONOMIC EFFICIENCY) form a major area of study of WELFARE ECONOMICS. (⇛ MARKET FAILURE).

Price theory. That part of economics concerned with analyzing the ways in which prices are determined in a FREE-MARKET ECONOMY and the role they play in solving the problems of RESOURCE ALLOCATION (⇛ ECONOMIC EFFICIENCY). Another name for MICROECONOMICS. The central concept of price theory is the MARKET. Since the essential elements in a market are the behavior of buyers, the behavior of sellers and the ways in which these interact, the study of markets is normally organized into "sub-theories": (*a*) a theory of the behavior of buyers, or the theory of DEMAND; (*b*) a theory of the behavior of sellers, or the theory of SUPPLY, in which the theory of the firm (⇛ FIRM, THEORY OF) plays a central role; and (*c*) a theory of market behavior, which examines how prices are determined by the interaction of buyers and sellers in various states of the environment. (⇛ MONOPOLISTIC COMPETITION; MONOPOLY; OLIGOPOLY; PERFECT COMPETITION; ⇛⇛ INDIFFERENCE ANALYSIS; MARSHALL, ALFRED).

Pricing policy. The rules adopted by a firm or public enterprise that determine the PRICES it sets. For example, it is often argued that PUBLIC ENTERPRISES should adopt MARGINAL-COST PRICING policies. In analyzing the pricing policies of PRIVATE SECTOR firms, economists predict that, if a firm's objective is to maximize PROFITS, its pricing policy will consist of setting prices in such a way that MARGINAL COST equals MARGINAL REVENUE. In PERFECT COMPETITION, where price and marginal revenue coincide, the firm will adopt a marginal-cost pricing policy. In imperfect competition, however, price exceeds marginal revenue, and hence it will exceed marginal cost. In practice, a firm might simply adopt the pricing policy of setting price equal to VARIABLE COSTS plus a markup; though if the markup is responsive to MARKET conditions, this may well give much the same result as that predicted by the economist.

Primary reserves. In some banking systems these are part of a bank's REQUIRED RESERVES and consist of cash held by the CENTRAL BANK against the DEPOSITS of a bank. In such circumstances there may also be SECONDARY RESERVES, such as short-term government SECURITIES, which banks are required to hold as ASSETS. Primary and secondary reserves would constitute a bank's required reserves. (⇛ BANKING).

Prime costs. Strictly, VARIABLE COSTS plus administrative and other FIXED COSTS that can be avoided in the short or long term if there is no output, even while the firm remains in business. Often used loosely as a synonym for variable costs. (⇛ SUPPLEMENTARY COSTS).

Prime rate. The RATE OF INTEREST on LOANS charged by banks to their most credit-worthy customers.

Private enterprise. Private economic activity, as opposed to government economic activity, or PUBLIC ENTERPRISE. More generally, private enterprise means an economic system in which CAPITAL resources and other property are owned by individuals and in which production is undertaken for private PROFIT. All modern economies are, to varying degrees, mixed systems of public and private economic activity. (⇛ MIXED ECONOMY; ⇛⇛ MARX, KARL; WELFARE ECONOMICS).

Private net product. A term first used by ARTHUR CECIL PIGOU for the net NATIONAL INCOME or product, to distinguish it from the SOCIAL NET PRODUCT.

Private placing. ⇛ PLACING

Private sector. That part of the economy not under direct government control. Beyond the productive activities of PRIVATE ENTERPRISES, the private sector also includes the economic activities of non-profit-making organizations and private individuals, these sometimes being referred to as the *personal sector.*

Probabilistic sample. ⇛ RANDOM SAMPLE

Probability. The likelihood of occurrence of some event. More formally, the probability of the occurrence of some event may be represented by a number lying between zero and one, and this number is called the probability of the event. A probability of zero would imply that the event stands no chance whatsoever of happening. A probability of one implies that the event is certain to happen. Although, once probabilities have been assigned to events, there is a very well worked-out body of mathematical theory concerning manipulations with probabilities and their applications to real problems, there is still considerable debate about the philosophical basis of probabilities.

Producer goods. Those goods which are bought and used by firms in producing other goods and services, as opposed to goods which are bought and used by final consumers. For example, coal used for making steel is a producer good, while coal used to fuel a furnace in a private home is a CONSUMPTION GOOD. Note therefore that the distinction refers to the *use* of the good, rather than its physical or technological characteristics. Producer goods are often also known as intermediate goods. (⇛ CAPITAL).

Producer's surplus. The excess of the total earnings of a supplier of a good or service, over the payment he would require just to induce him to continue to supply the amount he currently does. This payment is equal to the total avoidable COST of supplying the output, and so producer's surplus can also be expressed as the excess of revenue over total avoidable costs of supply. The surplus arises in the following way: As output expands, the cost of the marginal unit of output (⇛ MARGINAL COST) rises, due to diminishing returns (⇛ DIMINISHING RETURNS, LAW OF). Since price must equal marginal cost, total revenue will be marginal cost *times* output. Total avoidable costs, however, are the sum of the incremental costs of each successive unit of output, and, since the intra-marginal units of output had a lower marginal cost than that of the marginal unit, the total costs must be less than revenue. (⇛⇛ CONSUMER SURPLUS; DUPUIT, ARSENE JULES ETIENNE JUVENAL; QUASI-RENT).

Product differentiation. ⇛ DIFFERENTIATION, PRODUCT

Production, factors of. ⇛ FACTORS OF PRODUCTION

Production function. A mathematical relationship between the quantity of output of a good and the quantities of INPUTS required to make it. It is written as: $q = f(x_1 x_2 \dots x_n)$, where q is output; $x_1 x_2 \dots x_n$ are inputs (say, labor, machinery, raw materials, etc.); and $f(\ \ )$ is the mathematical notation for "is a function of," i.e., "is related to" or "depends on." The equation would read: The quantity of output of the good depends on the quantities of the inputs x_1 (say, labor), x_2 (machinery), x_3 (raw materials) and so on. This is, of course, a very general statement. The next step is to specify a precise mathematical form for the equation. For example, we might consider that the relation between output and inputs is best described by a *linear* equation (⇛ LINEAR RELATIONSHIP), such as: $q = a_1 x_1 + a_2 x_2 \ \dots + a_n x_n$, where $a_1, a_2, \dots a_n$ are numbers that tell us by how much output increases if the input to which they are attached increases by one unit, all other inputs remaining the same. Alternatively, we might consider the relation best described by a multiplicative function of the form:

$$q = a_o x_1^{b_1} x_2^{b_2} \dots x_n^{b_n}$$

the numbers tell us the percentage increase in output when input x_1 increases by 1% and similarly for b_2, which is often called the COBB-DOUGLAS

PRODUCTION FUNCTION. Many other functional forms exist. Choice of a particular functional form is important, since different functions have different mathematical properties and involve different assumptions about the technological characteristics of the production process being described. In choosing a particular form, the aim is to achieve a good compromise between simplicity and ease of manipulation on the one hand and accuracy in describing the technological relationships on the other. Production functions may be specified for individual firms, in which case they are useful for deriving the COST CURVES of firms and their DEMAND CURVES for FACTORS OF PRODUCTION; and they may relate to the economy as a whole, in which case they are useful in GROWTH THEORY, the theory of INCOME DISTRIBUTION and the theory of INTERNATIONAL TRADE. (⇛ ISOQUANT).

Production possibility curve. ⇛ TRANSFORMATION CURVE

Production, theory of. The branch of economics concerned with analyzing the determinants of the firm's choice of quantities of INPUTS, given its PRODUCTION FUNCTION, the PRICES of the inputs and the level of output it wishes to produce. The theory is based on the hypothesis that the firm will wish to use that set of quantities of the inputs which minimizes the overall COST of producing a given output. Then, by varying output, it is possible to construct the output-cost relationships that are the basis for much of the theory of the firm (⇛ FIRM, THEORY OF). In addition, the analysis in production theory forms the basis for the theory of marginal productivity (⇛ INTERNAL RATE OF RETURN) and the determination of factor prices. (⇛⇛ DIMINISHING MARGINAL PRODUCT, LAW OF; ECONOMIES OF SCALE; FACTORS OF PRODUCTION; ISOQUANT—all of which are important concepts in production theory).

Productive efficiency. ⇛ ECONOMIC EFFICIENCY

Productivity. A measure of the rate at which output flows from the use of given amounts of FACTORS OF PRODUCTION. If factors are being used inefficiently, there will be scope for productivity improvements, since by definition more output can be produced from the given amounts of inputs. In practice, productivity is usually measured by expressing output as a ratio to a selected input. The input selected will give its name to the productivity measure—e.g., labor productivity is the ratio of output to labor input (and is therefore the same thing as the average product of labor). Some care must be taken in making efficiency comparisons across firms, industries or countries on the basis of just one productivity measure, since differing technological conditions or relative input PRICES may mean that different productivities of specific inputs are quite consistent with efficiency. For example, a country in which labor is abundant and cheap, such as India, will have lower labor productivity in its agriculture than a country such as the United States, where labor is relatively scarce, because it is economically efficient to use more LABOR-INTENSIVE production methods in India. Similarly, when comparing industries, the electricity industry will have higher labor productivity and lower capital productivity than the automobile industry because electricity-generation technology is inherently more CAPITAL-INTENSIVE.

Serious attempts to assess the efficiency of firms, industries or entire economies require a more fundamental procedure than the mere comparison of specific productivity measures.

Product, marginal. ⇛ MARGINAL PRODUCT

Product-moment correlation coefficient. ⇛ CORRELATION

Products, final. ⇛ FINAL PRODUCTS

Products, joint. ⇛ JOINT PRODUCTS

Professional corporation (PC). ⇛ INCORPORATION

Profit. It is important to distinguish clearly between the definition of profit used in *accounting* calculations in firms and the definition of profit used in economic theory. In many ways, the distinction reflects that made between accounting and economic definitions of COSTS. In accounting terms, we can define:

1. *Gross profit:* total sales revenue, less payments of wages, salaries, rents, fuel, raw materials, etc. This therefore represents the difference between receipts and money outlays incurred directly in carrying on the operations of the firm.

2. *Net profit:* gross profit, less INTEREST (⇛ RATE OF INTEREST) on LOANS and DEPRECIATION. Thus, net profit is the residual value arrived at after deducting all MONEY costs. After deduction of tax, it represents the surplus available for distribution to the firm's owners as INCOME and as a source of reserves and funds for new INVESTMENT.

The economic concept of profit need not quite correspond to that of the accountant, because the economist would deduct IMPUTED COSTS as well as money outlays. If the firm owned its own LAND and buildings, the RENTS that the firm would have had to pay if it had to lease them will be part of the accountant's profit figure and would not be separately identifiable, whereas the economist would deduct a sum equal to the rent that could be obtained if the land and buildings were let out to the highest bidder—i.e., he would deduct the "imputed" rent. Some firms might be making an accounting profit but a loss in the economic sense. This might arise, for example, where a firm is operating in premises that were purchased a long time ago but have risen substantially in value through, say, urban development, and that if newly leased or rented would command a very high rental.

Assessable profit on which tax has to be paid differs from both accounting profit and the economic concept.

Economics distinguishes between two types of profit:

1. *Normal profit:* Profit is regarded as the income that accrues to the ENTREPRENEUR, i.e., the residual left after payment of all *opportunity costs* to the INPUTS he employs. The entrepreneur need not devote his energies to the particular line of business he is in: He could just as well devote them to some other activity, and the best return he could obtain in some alternative line of business is the opportunity cost to him of remaining in the activity he is in. Then normal profit is defined as that profit which is just sufficient to induce the entrepreneur to remain in his present activity; it is the oppor-

tunity cost of remaining in that activity. It follows that if actual profits are less than normal profits, the entrepreneur will switch to a more profitable activity; on the other hand, if profits exceed normal profits, we would expect entrepreneurs in other activities to move into the one in question. The essential point about normal profit is that it is not a surplus over all costs but is rather the cost of the services that the entrepreneur provides.

2. *Supernormal profit:* Profit over and above normal profit, also referred to as *excess profit.* If entry into an activity is perfectly free, then, in the long run, supernormal profits would be zero, due to the competition of entrepreneurs attracted to the activity by the prospect of higher incomes than they were currently earning. Thus, supernormal profits are either a SHORT-RUN, DISEQUILIBRIUM phenomenon or the result of BARRIERS TO ENTRY. This suggests the role of supernormal profits in the processes of adjustment of a FREE-MARKET ECONOMY as being an indicator of "resource deficiency"—they indicate that RESOURCES are relatively more scarce than in other areas in the economy that are just earning normal profits and at the same time provide the attraction that, in the absence of entry barriers, leads to the appropriate expansion in scale of resources devoted to that particular activity. (⇛ KNIGHT, FRANK HYNEMAN).

Profit-and-loss account. ⇛ INCOME STATEMENT

Profit center. A division or department of a business or other organization for which costs and revenues are separated out for MANAGEMENT ACCOUNTANCY purposes so that the profitability of the unit can be calculated.

Profit, falling rate of. The early classical economists (⇛ CLASSICAL ECONOMICS) believed that it was a feature of the economic system for the general rate of PROFIT to decline. ADAM SMITH argued that CAPITAL accumulation took place at a faster rate than the growth of total output. Although the absolute level of profits rose, competition lowered the RATE OF RETURN on capital. For DAVID RICARDO the decline of the general rate of profit was induced by the decline in the marginal productivity of LAND, to which all profits were linked. KARL MARX took up ideas similar to Smith's and predicted a fall in the rate of profit because of an intensification of competition between capitalists (⇛ CAPITALISM). There would follow, he concluded, a strong pressure to reduce REAL WAGES.

Program planning, budgeting system (PPBS). An approach to the activities of government and other non-profit-making organizations that attempts to take into account the objectives it is desired to achieve, the RESOURCES available and how these all interrelate in such a way as to use limited resources in the most effective manner. It proceeds by (*a*) breaking down broad programs (health, defense, education, etc.) into detailed subprograms; (*b*) devising methods of measuring the level of output of the subprograms and of evaluating the resources required to provide this output; (*c*) clarifying the objectives laid down by the policymakers with respect to the broad programs and possibly subprograms; (*d*) finding the least-COST ways of meeting these objectives; (*e*) clarifying the "opportunity costs" of these objectives—e.g., 1 extra university implies 50 fewer high schools—and thus in turn helping to formulate future policy objectives. It is an attempt to introduce rational methods of management into an area where considerable difficulties of measurement and evaluation exist.

Progressive tax. A TAX which takes an increasing proportion of INCOME as income rises. (⇛ TAXATION).

Promissory note. A legal document between a lender and borrower whereby the latter agrees to certain conditions for the repayment of the sum of money borrowed. When one borrows from a COMMERCIAL BANK, one signs a promissory note. Particular forms of promissory notes, known as commercial paper, can be bought and sold. They are usually issued by large corporations, especially when MONETARY POLICY is so restrictive as to make it difficult to get CREDIT. (⇛ MONEY SUPPLY).

Propensity to consume. ⇛ AVERAGE PROPENSITY TO CONSUME; MARGINAL PROPENSITY TO CONSUME

Propensity to import. A relationship between INCOME and IMPORT levels. We would expect the DEMAND of a HOUSEHOLD for foreign goods to depend on its income, just as does its demand for domestically produced goods. Similarly, we would expect firms' demands for foreign goods—raw materials, machine tools, components, etc.—to depend on their output. The whole economy's demand for imports thus depends on NATIONAL INCOME.

1. *The average propensity to import:* the ratio of the total value of imports to national income. It is the proportion of national income spent on imports.

2. *The marginal propensity to import:* the proportion of an increase in national income that is spent on imports. For instance, if national income increased by \$100, and imports increased by \$20, then the marginal propensity to import would be $\frac{\$20}{\$100} = \frac{1}{5}$.

The marginal propensity to import is a useful concept in two ways. First, if it can be accurately measured, and if it is relatively constant over time, then it can be used to predict the increase in imports that will result from an increase in income. To continue the above example, if the marginal propensity to import is estimated as $\frac{1}{5}$, and national income is expected to increase by \$10 billion, then we can predict that imports will increase by \$2 billion, and this may be very useful from the point of view of control of the economy and the BALANCE OF PAYMENTS. Second, the marginal propensity to import determines, among other things, the value of the MULTIPLIER, and so an estimate of it will be required if we are going to be able to predict the effects on national income of a change in INVESTMENT, government expenditure (⇛ BUDGET), exports or TAXATION.

Though, in the short run, the average and marginal propensities to import may be taken as relatively constant, it must be remembered that they reflect demands for foreign goods by firms and households and therefore are influenced by (*a*) relative prices of foreign and domestic goods and the exchange rate, (*b*) tastes, and (*c*) technology and other factors, any or all of which may change over time.

Propensity to save. ⇛ AVERAGE PROPENSITY TO SAVE; MARGINAL PROPENSITY TO SAVE

Property rights. Legally defined and enforceable rights that relate to the ownership and use of RESOURCES and COMMODITIES. The particular structure of property rights in an economy will have an important effect on the way in which that economy works. For example, in the U.S. economy individuals are able to own the ASSETS of business corporations and to buy and sell their ownership shares on the stock market. In centrally planned economies (⇛ PLANNED ECONOMY), on the other hand, this is not possible; all productive assets can only be owned by the state. Likewise, in market economies (⇛ FREE-MARKET ECONOMY) individuals are able to sell goods and services directly to each other, and when such a transaction takes place, there is *not only* an exchange of some physical quantity of the good but also an exchange of the rights to use that good in certain ways that are sanctioned by the legal system. Explicit awareness of and interest in property rights has developed only relatively recently in ECONOMICS, but the "property-rights approach" has led to important new insights into the way economic systems work.

Proprietorship. In such an organization, a single owner makes all decisions and is responsible for all debts (⇛ LIMITED LIABILITY). While full control is in the hands of one person, such an organization is somewhat limited in the amount of CAPITAL it can raise. Excluding farms, there are approximately 7 million single proprietorships in the United States. (⇛ CORPORATION; PARTNERSHIP; SMALL BUSINESS).

Protection. The imposition of tariffs (⇛ TARIFFS, IMPORT) or QUOTAS to restrict the inflow of IMPORTS. Arguments in favor of protectionism and against FREE TRADE have their origin in the earliest periods of economic discussion but became paramount during the Mercantilist era (⇛ MERCANTILISM). The arguments take many forms. Domestic industries, especially agriculture, must be maintained at a high level in case foreign sources are cut off during a war. Similarly, key industries that have a significant defense role should be protected to avoid reliance on a foreign supplier. In conditions of EXCESS CAPACITY, protection increases employment by switching demand away from foreign to domestic production and, through an increase in the surplus on the BALANCE OF PAYMENTS, enables aggregate INCOME to be raised through the MULTIPLIER effect. Protection also enables new industries to develop to an optimum size (⇛ INFANT INDUSTRY ARGUMENT). Protection can be used as a counter to DUMPING and as a retaliatory measure against other countries' restrictions. (⇛⇛ CUSTOMS UNION; GENERAL AGREEMENT ON TARIFFS AND TRADE; IMPORT RESTRICTIONS).

Public debt. ⇛ NATIONAL DEBT

Public enterprise. An ENTERPRISE engaged in producing and selling goods and services that is entirely owned and controlled by the state. This is a fairly common form of business organization in Europe and Canada, but in the United States REGULATION is preferred to state ownership as a means of achieving control over MONOPOLY. (⇛⇛ NATIONALIZED INDUSTRIES).

Public expenditure. Spending by federal, state and local government and PUBLIC ENTERPRISES on goods and services (including capital formation), SUBSIDIES, grants and DEBT servicing. Defined in this way, public expenditure in the United States rose from 6.5 percent of GROSS NATIONAL PRODUCT (GNP) in 1890 to 32.5 percent in 1978. The increase in public expenditure has taken place in all developed countries. The largest components of public expenditure in the United States are social welfare, followed by defense and education; though other items include civil safety, transportation and foreign aid. Much of public expenditure consists of TRANSFER PAYMENTS; if these are excluded, the share of government expenditure in GNP falls to 20.6 percent. Transfers are made both from the various levels of government to individuals and between the levels of government. Federal grants to state and local government now account for about 20 percent of the total revenue of the two lower tiers of government. If these grants are included at the level of origin, then the federal government accounts for over half of public expenditure. (⇛⇛ BUDGET; FISCAL FEDERALISM).

Public finance. A branch of economics concerned with the identification and appraisal of the effects of government financial policies. It attempts to analyze the effects of government TAXATION and expenditure on the economic situations of individuals and institutions and to examine their impact on the economy as a whole. It is also concerned with examining the effectiveness of policy measures directed at certain objectives and with developing techniques and procedures by which that effectiveness can be increased. (⇛ BUDGET; COST-BENEFIT ANALYSIS; FISCAL POLICY; PROGRAM, PLANNING, BUDGETING SYSTEM; STABILIZATION POLICY).

Public goods. Goods that, because they cannot be withheld from one individual without withholding them from all, must be supplied communally. For example, it would not be possible to exclude any one individual from "consuming" national defense or street lighting or general police protection. Unless this exclusion could be made, a private ENTREPRENEUR would not undertake to supply these services, because he would not have the power to force the community as a whole to pay him, and he could not exclude anyone who did not pay him from consuming the good. Since the state can raise revenues by TAXATION, it alone can finance the provision of public goods. A further important property of a public good is that consumption of it by one individual does not reduce the amount available for consumption by others. Note that this definition does not apply to *all* goods publicly supplied. Many of the goods supplied by the state could be supplied privately, and some indeed are, the best examples being housing, education and specific police protection. The non-pure, or "quasi"-public, goods are supplied by the state and financed out of taxation because it is considered that their quality and/or quantity of supply would be inadequate under private provision. (⇛ PRICE SYSTEM; MERIT GOODS).

Public utility. An enterprise producing and supplying one of a particular set of outputs—namely, electricity, transport, gas, telephones and water supply. The nature of the technology of these goods is such that the enterprises supplying them tend to have considerable MONOPOLY power. This may be due to ECONOMIES OF SCALE and to the prohibitive cost of replication of distribution networks—e.g., if each household on a street received its electricity supply from a different company, then there would be as many different power lines in the neighborhood as there were households. Because of this tendency to monopoly, and also because of the importance of these goods to modern life, some form of REGULATION of public utilities is almost universal.

Pump priming. The policy of increasing government spending in order to expand NATIONAL INCOME and employment. It is based on the view that even if only a portion of the deflationary gap is filled by an increase in government spending, there will be an improvement in EXPECTATIONS leading to increases in INVESTMENT expenditure and thus a return to full employment. (⇛⇛ KEYNES, JOHN MAYNARD).

Purchasing power parity theory. A theory that states that the EXCHANGE RATE between one CURRENCY and another is in EQUILIBRIUM when their domestic purchasing powers at that rate of exchange are equivalent. For example, the current rate of exchange of £1 = $1.70 would be in equilibrium if £1 will buy the same goods in the United Kingdom as $1.70 will buy in the United States. If this holds true, purchasing power parity exists. The theory has its source in the mercantilist (⇛ MERCANTILISM) writings of the 17th century, but it came into prominence in 1916 through the writings of the Swedish economist Gustav Cassel (1866–1945). The basic mechanism implied by the theory is that, given complete freedom of action, if $1.70 buys more in the United States than £1 does in the United Kingdom, it would pay to convert pounds into dollars and buy from the United States rather than in the United Kingdom. The switch in demand would raise prices in the United States and lower them in the United Kingdom and at the same time lower the U.K. exchange rate until equilibrium and parity are reestablished. Cassel interpreted the theory in terms of changes in, rather than absolute levels of, prices and exchange rates. He argued that the falls in the FOREIGN-EXCHANGE MARKETS in the postwar period were a result of INFLATION due to unbalanced BUDGETS' increasing the quantity of MONEY. In practice, the theory has little validity, because exchange rates, which are determined by the DEMAND and SUPPLY of currency in the foreign-exchange markets, are related to such forces as BALANCE OF PAYMENTS disequilibriums, CAPITAL transactions, SPECULATION and government policy. Many goods and services do not enter into INTERNATIONAL TRADE, and so their relative prices are not taken into account in the determination of the exchange rate. Moreover, it is impossible to measure satisfactorily what purchasing power a currency in one country has relative to that in another because of the difficulty of determining the appropriate mix of commodities and also of measuring their average price level. This means that international comparisons of standards of living based on current exchange rates have to be interpreted with great care. (⇛⇛ INDEX-NUMBER PROBLEM; MISES, LUDWIG ELDER VON).

Pure competition. ⇛ PERFECT COMPETITION

Put option. ⇛ OPTION

Q

Quantitative restrictions. ⇛ QUOTAS

Quantity equation. ⇛ QUANTITY THEORY OF MONEY

Quantity of money. ⇛ MONEY SUPPLY

Quantity theory of money. A theory of the relationship between the quantity of MONEY in an economy and the PRICE level. This long-established theory begins with the identity (known as the "Fisher equation," after the economist IRVING FISHER): $MV = Py$, where M is the stock of money, V is the INCOME VELOCITY OF CIRCULATION of money, P is the average price level, and y is a measure of the flow of real goods and SERVICES, i.e., the flow of REAL INCOME. This is an identity, because the left-hand side measures the total money value of transactions over a given period—i.e., the stock of money multiplied by the number of times it has circulated through the economy financing transactions—while the right-hand side measures the total money value of goods sold. Since the total money value of transactions is necessarily the same as the money value of goods sold, the two sides of the equation are equal by definition. However, it is hypothesized (1) that y is a constant, because the economy is at full employment (⇛ EMPLOYMENT, FULL) and will remain there; and (2) that V is a constant, being determined by certain institutional features of the economy, e.g., time intervals between wage and salary payments, which determine the extent to which the buyers' spending pattern coincides with the sellers' requirements for money. (These features change only very slowly over time and so can be taken as constant in the SHORT RUN.) Then we could rewrite the above identity as the equation $M = \frac{y}{V} \cdot P$, which since y/V is a constant, implies that changes in the stock of money are proportional to changes in the price level. This relationship is the core of the quantity theory of money.

Several important policy recommendations flow from this simple theory. It suggests that INFLATION can be controlled by the monetary authorities (⇛ MONETARY POLICY) through control of the quantity of money in existence. Alternatively, if a certain rate of growth in real income is anticipated, then this can be achieved without inflation by allowing the quantity of money in the economy to increase at the same rate, but no faster.

Although the macroeconomic theory of JOHN MAYNARD KEYNES (⇛ MACROECONOMICS) was concerned very much with showing that the level of real income, y, could not be assumed to remain constant at the full-employment level, it nevertheless retained the quantity theory of money in the form of the TRANSACTIONS DEMAND FOR MONEY, which is a component of the overall demand for money. The quantity theory was heavily criticized in the 1950s and early 1960s, however. Criticism centered on the alleged constancy of V. Because of the existence of quasi-money (⇛ NEAR MONEY), and because of the ingenuity of nonbank FINANCIAL

INTERMEDIARIES in developing and extending forms of CREDIT, it was argued that variations in the money value of total expenditure and income need not bear any stable relationship to variations in the quantity of money—i.e., V is unstable in the short run. It was argued that what matters are the determinants of desired expenditure and the total LIQUIDITY in the economy. This leads logically to a *"Keynesian"* view of economic policy, which concentrates on the determinants of AGGREGATE DEMAND and stresses FISCAL POLICY rather than monetary policy as a method of controlling the economy.

The quantity theory has regained support recently, largely as a result of the work of MILTON FRIEDMAN at the University of Chicago. Friedman showed that, on the basis of an analysis of the demand for money by an individual consumer, the overall velocity of circulation, V, would be determined as an ENDOGENOUS VARIABLE, by, among other things, the level of interest rates (⇛ RATE OF INTEREST) and the value of WEALTH in REAL TERMS. Although the value of V might vary, this variation is not capricious or random but can be accounted for and predicted within an economic model. Moreover, in the longer term, the value of V, at least in the United States, could be shown to be fairly stable. He concluded that monetary policy can have an effective role. As a result of these refinements, it can be said that the theories of the DEMAND for money based on a quantity theory of money approach do not differ a great deal from the theories based on the Keynesian framework. The relative emphasis on the practical importance of the MONEY SUPPLY and the nature of policy recommendations still differ significantly between the two approaches, however. The controversy has considerable practical importance, and the greater emphasis placed on monetary policy by policymakers over the past decade has probably been the result of the influence of the money supply school.

Quasi-money. ⇛ NEAR MONEY

Quasi-rent. An excess of total revenues over total avoidable COSTS that accrues to a seller of a good or service as a PROFIT in the SHORT RUN but is transformed into a cost, or otherwise eliminated, in the LONG RUN. Quasi-rents generally arise either because it takes time for new firms to enter and compete within a market where profits are being earned or because certain PRICES of FACTORS OF PRODUCTION may be fixed over the short run but can be renegotiated in the long run. As an example of the latter, suppose that a store is located on a particular site, and its rental is fixed on the basis of a 10-year lease. Halfway through the duration of the lease, a new housing development is built nearby, and the amount of business done, and the profits the shopkeeper makes, treble. When the time comes for renegotiation of the lease, the owner of the site will raise the rental to equal the PRESENT VALUE of the future stream of profits from the shop, since this is the maximum amount the shopkeeper would pay before he would move elsewhere (note that the "salary" or opportunity cost of a shopkeeper is included in costs and so is not a part of profit). Either the shopkeeper can pay this new rental or leave, and so the excess profits have now been turned into a genuine opportunity cost. What were profits in the short run have become costs in the long run, and such temporary profits, arising essentially because the system is not in long-run EQUILIBRIUM, are known as quasi-rents.

Quesnay, Francois (1694–1774). A surgeon by profession, he held the post of secretary of the French Academy of Surgery and edited its official journal. He became physician to Madame de Pompadour. His major economic works appeared in various articles in the *Encyclopedie* in 1756 and 1757 and in the *Journal de l'agriculture du commerce et des finances* in 1765 and 1767. The *Tableau Economique* and *Maximes,* a commentary on the *Tableau,* were both published in 1758. The *Tableau* set out three classes of society and showed how transactions flowed between them. The three classes were (*a*) landowners, (*b*) the farmers and farm laborers and (*c*) others, called the "sterile class." Only the agricultural sector produced any surplus value, the rest only reproducing what it consumed (⇛ MARX, KARL). He anticipated THOMAS ROBERT MALTHUS's fear of underconsumption arising from excessive SAVINGS. Net INCOME would be reduced if the flows in the *Tableau* were interrupted by delays in spending. This was the first attempt to construct a macroeconomic (⇛ MACROECONOMICS) input-output MODEL of the economy (⇛ INPUT-OUTPUT ANALYSIS). In fact, progress in this field had to await the application of MATRIX ALGEBRA and computerization (⇛ LEONTIEF, WASSILY W.) Quesnay suggested a single tax, *"l'impot unique,"* on the net income from land, arguing that by so doing the nation would save tax-collecting costs. Only agriculture yielded a surplus, and therefore it ultimately bears all taxes anyway (⇛ GEORGE, HENRY; MILL, JOHN STUART). He was the central figure in the group of economists called the PHYSIOCRATS, who flourished in France between 1760 and 1770.

"Quick" ratio. Cash, marketable SECURITIES and net accounts receivable as a proportion of current LIABILITIES. A measure of the ability of a company to meet short-term debt or sudden demands upon current ASSETS without being forced to dispose of INVENTORIES. A more immediate test of credit-worthiness than the CURRENT RATIO and for this reason also referred to as the *acid test ratio.*

Quotas. 1. The quantitative limits placed on the importation of specified COMMODITIES. The PROTECTION afforded by quotas is more certain than can be obtained by raising IMPORT tariffs (⇛ TARIFFS, IMPORT), as the effect of the latter will depend on the price ELASTICITIES of the imported commodities. Quotas, like tariffs, can also be used to favor preferred sources of supply. Quotas have virtually disappeared among industrial trading countries, except for primary products. 2. Quantitative restrictions set by CARTELS, colluding OLIGOPOLY or governments to restrict supply (⇛ COLLUSION). (⇛⇛ GENERAL AGREEMENT ON TARIFFS AND TRADE).

Quota sample. A SAMPLE that is carried out on the basis of a "stratification" of the population (⇛ STRATIFIED SAMPLE), but, unlike a stratified sample, the entities within each stratum are not then selected by a SIMPLE RANDOM SAMPLE procedure but rather by the interviewers themselves as they conduct the survey. Each interviewer would have a specified number of entities of each kind—e.g., HOUSEHOLDS and individuals by income level, shops by type of trade, firms by size—that he or she would have to interview, but the actual choice of the entities is left for the interviewer to decide. In the stratified sample, on the other hand, an objective procedure is used to select the entities that the interviewer must then visit. The advantage of a quota sample is that it is generally cheaper: It avoids the costly process of drawing a simple random sample within each stratum of entities; on the other hand, it may be biased and unreliable, since the interviewers will still have considerable discretion in choosing entities even within the limits set by the quotas for the strata, and so conscious or unconscious biases may exist (⇛ RANDOM SAMPLE). In actual practice, because of their lower costs and greater speed, quota samples are by far the most prevalent form of sample.

R

Random sample. Any method of taking a SAMPLE by which each member of the POPULATION of items has a *known chance* of being included in the sample. A special case of a random sample is a simple random sample, whereby each item in the population has an equal chance of being included in the sample, and therefore all possible samples of a given size (number of items) have an equal chance of being selected. It is important to distinguish between the meaning of *random* here and its meaning in everyday usage. An intuitive interpretation of the phrase "a random sample of voters" would be that one goes out on to the street and questions the first, say, 20 people one meets or picks out 20 people "at random." This is not, however, a random sample, since we do not know what chance each member of the population (the people of voting age in a particular electoral zone) had of being chosen, and it is quite possible that many of them had no chance at all. A random sample, properly defined, may well be the result of a careful calculation, and there may be a very precise specification of how many of which types of item are to be included in the sample. The word *random* is not being used in the sense of "haphazard" or "fortuitous" but rather in the more specialized sense of "probabilistic" (in fact *probabilistic sample* is the term also used often in the United States for *random sample*). The importance of devising a random sample is that only if a definite PROBABILITY of being included in the sample is assigned to each item in the population can the probable error in using the information derived from the sample to make statements about the population be estimated. An incidental, but important, advantage of random sampling is that by specifying beforehand which types of item, or even exactly which items, are to be included in the sample, on the basis of an objective procedure, the inevitable biases that arise from an on-the-spot choice of the sample are avoided. An interviewer may unconsciously select better-dressed people, or apartments on lower floors, in a sample that is supposedly to be chosen without bias, and such unconscious biases may influence the results in ways that cannot be estimated. For particular types of sampling procedure based on the idea of random sample, see STRATIFIED SAMPLE and SIMPLE RANDOM SAMPLE.

Rate of interest. The PRICE of borrowed MONEY. If a sum of money is lent for a specified period of time, the amount that is repaid by the borrower to the lender will be greater than the amount that was initially lent. It is convenient to have a standardized way of expressing this PREMIUM, and so we define the rate of interest to be the difference between what is lent and what must be repaid after a specified period, expressed as a proportion of the amount lent. If \$100 is lent and \$105 is repaid after one year, then the yearly interest rate is $\frac{\$105 - \$100}{\$100} = 0.05$, or, in percentage terms, 5 percent. If \$105 were to be repaid after six months, then 0.05, or 5 percent, would be the six-month interest rate. The time period should always be carefully specified—e.g., a six-month interest rate of 5 percent is not equivalent to a yearly interest rate of 10 percent (⇛ COMPOUND INTEREST). Normally, interest rates are calculated for a year, and when a time period is not specified, a yearly period is generally implied.

It is an oversimplification to talk about "the" rate of interest. At any one time, there will be a whole set of different interest rates, each associated with a particular form of lending: bank loans, savings and loan (⇛ SAVINGS AND LOAN ASSOCIATIONS) accounts, short-term government debt (⇛ TREASURY BILLS), long-term government debt, industrial bonds, etc. The reason for differences in these interest rates can be understood by considering the reasons for the existence of interest rates.

1. *Time preference:* Money that is lent generally represents saving, i.e., a sacrifice of CONSUMPTION at the present time. The lender is, in effect, postponing consumption from the present to some time in the future. It is argued that, as a fact of human psychology, people in general prefer to consume now rather than later and hence must be paid something to induce them to postpone consumption. The stronger their preference for present as opposed to future consumption, the more they must be paid to induce them to postpone consumption—i.e., the higher must be the rate of interest (⇛⇛ TIME PREFERENCE).

2. *The possibility of illiquidity:* Lending money generally implies exchange of money for some ASSET that is not money—in the sense that it is not universally acceptable as a payment for goods and services, e.g., a treasury bill or a BOND. If, within the duration of the loan, the lender should require money in excess of the amount he has available, he must either convert his asset into money or borrow. The ease with which he can do the former depends on the asset in question. For example, he may have to wait for one month before he can receive some of his money from a savings and loan account. On the other hand, there may not be a time delay if a well-organized MARKET exists for the asset—e.g., the stock market—but, at the same time, he may be forced to sell the asset for less than he paid for it and so sustains a capital loss. Alternatively, he might borrow, in which case he must himself pay a rate of interest. The fact that the lender is exchanging a liquid asset, money, for a less liquid asset involves him in the risk of loss should the need for liquidity subsequently arise. In making the loan, the lender must therefore be compensated for this risk, and this makes for the existence of an interest rate.

3. *The possibility of default:* The lender may not be absolutely sure that the borrower will repay the loan—he may default. Hence, this risk will also make for a positive interest rate. Again, the extent of the risk depends on the type of loan being made.

4. *Inflation:* The three factors just mentioned would make for a positive rate of interest, even if the general level of prices were expected to remain constant over the duration of the loan. We would call a rate of interest determined on such a basis the "real rate of interest." However, if

the price level were expected to rise by, say, 3 percent over the duration of the loan, then, in real terms, the sum lent is worth 3 percent less when it is repaid. If inflation is anticipated, the lender will therefore wish to take this fall in the value of money into account by raising the rate of interest by enough to offset it—in this case by three percentage points.

The above factors suggest why positive rates of interest exist. Further, since different types of loans have different characteristics with respect to at least some of those factors, we have a partial explanation for differences in interest rates. The rate of interest paid on any type of loan is essentially a price—the price that is paid for the use of that money. Hence, economists have discussed the determinants of the levels of interest rates in terms of DEMAND and SUPPLY: The demand for loans by consumers wishing to buy on credit and by firms wishing to invest and the supply of SAVINGS available for lending. The demand for loans for investment is determined by the marginal productivity of capital (⇛ INTERNAL RATE OF RETURN). JOHN MAYNARD KEYNES, however, stressed also the role that the demand for money to hold as an asset, in expectation of changes in prices of paper assets (bonds), plays in determining the rate of interest. (⇛⇛ INTEREST, ABSTINENCE THEORY OF; INTEREST, CLASSICAL THEORY OF; INTEREST, NATURAL RATE OF; INTEREST, PRODUCTIVITY THEORIES OF; INTEREST, TIME PREFERENCE THEORY OF; LIQUIDITY PREFERENCE).

Rate of return, return on investment (ROI). Usually net income (⇛ PROFIT) after DEPRECIATION as a percentage of average CAPITAL EMPLOYED. Profit is usually defined as net of tax but before interest. Interest is added back to net income from operations because it is the cost of obtaining borrowed capital and is thus part of the return on capital employed. Alternatively, the rate of return on owners' EQUITY may be calculated as INCOME FROM OPERATIONS, in this case net income after interest, as a percentage of NET ASSETS. The use of simple rates of return in the analysis of alternative investment projects is open to the serious criticism that it does not take account of the timing of capital outlays and earnings and hence does not allow for the time value of money (⇛ INVESTMENT APPRAISAL). Strictly speaking, the rate of return on capital employed in a business does not measure the return to capital alone or the efficiency of the use of RESOURCES by that business, since the returns to each of the FACTORS OF PRODUCTION cannot be separated out. However, in normal circumstances a firm that is earning a long-term rate of return lower than its cost of capital (⇛ CAPITAL, COST OF) could be said to be using resources inefficiently.

Rate of technical substitution. The rate at which one INPUT can be substituted for another along an ISOQUANT. Just as an isoquant is closely analogous to an INDIFFERENCE CURVE, so the rate of technical substitution is exactly the same kind of concept as the MARGINAL RATE OF SUBSTITUTION.

Rate of time preference. ⇛ TIME PREFERENCE

Rational expectations. A decision maker is said to hold EXPECTATIONS that are rational when he uses available knowledge and information to form those expectations in such a way that he does not make systematic errors. As an example of expectations that are not rational, take the case of the market involved in the COBWEB THEOREM. Here, suppliers expect that this period's price will continue to prevail next period, despite the fact that in every period they are proved wrong. An economist who knew the cobweb theorem could make a killing as a speculator in such a market. Can such expectations therefore persist? If there is a profit to be made out of forming expectations in a superior way, surely this will occur. The usual postulates of rationality in economics therefore suggest that expectations that are systematically wrong will be revised, so that in the end expectations will be formed that are correct *on the average*. That is, although they may turn out to be wrong at any one time, these errors will be randomly distributed about the correct value.

Real balance effect. An increase in the real money supply, caused by a fall in prices, increases household wealth, and this in turn induces consumers to purchase more goods. (⇛⇛ PIGOU, ARTHUR CECIL).

Real capital. ⇛ CAPITAL

Real economy. A term used to distinguish the flow of actual goods and services between firms and households from the flow of money payments. The flow of labor services to businesses and the flow of commodities from firms to households are real flows and part of the real economy. Wages paid to labor and household payments for goods are money flows. (⇛⇛ REAL TERMS).

Real income. INCOME measured in terms of the real goods and services it can buy. It can be calculated by dividing MONEY income by a suitable index of prices. (⇛ INDEXATION; REAL TERMS).

Real terms. A variable is "in real terms" when its value has been adjusted for changes in the purchasing power of MONEY. For example, in order to calculate NATIONAL INCOME, goods and services are valued at their money prices, and these values aggregated. In order to find how real income has changed over time—i.e., how the physical flow of goods and services has changed—it is necessary to allow for the changes in prices. This is done by deflating by an appropriate INDEX NUMBER of prices, and the resulting value is real national income or the national income at *constant prices.* (⇛⇛ REAL WAGES).

Real wages. A wage rate will normally be expressed in money units per unit of time, e.g., $500 per week, $26,000 per year, etc. However, we may be interested in knowing the increase in purchasing power that a given increase in money wage implies, and hence, we define the real wage as the money wage divided by an INDEX NUMBER of the overall price level. If money wages rose by 5 percent while the price level also rose by 5 percent, the real wage would remain unchanged, implying that the volume of goods and services that can be bought with the new money wage is equal to that which could be bought with the old. Note that *real* is used as the opposite of *monetary,* not the opposite of *imaginary*. (⇛ MONEY ILLUSION).

Recession. A downturn in the business cycle characterized by two successive quarters of negative growth in the real GROSS NATIONAL PRODUCT. (⇛⇛ DEPRESSION; UNEMPLOYMENT).

Reciprocal demand. ⇛ EQUATION OF INTERNATIONAL DEMAND

Reciprocity. The practice, sometimes called "fair trade" or "beggar-my-neighbor policy," by which governments extend to each other similar concessions or restrictions in trade. It is reflected in U.S. trade policy in the Reciprocal Trade Agreements Acts of 1934; the Trade Expansion Act of 1962, which made the KENNEDY ROUND OF TRADE NEGOTIATIONS under the GENERAL AGREEMENT ON TARIFFS AND TRADE possible; and, more recently, in the TRADE ACT OF 1974.

Recycling. The process by which funds are transferred through the international financial institutions from countries with current account BALANCE OF PAYMENTS surpluses to countries running deficits. The large increase in the price of oil made by the ORGANIZATION OF PETROLEUM EXPORTING COUNTRIES in 1973 and 1974 generated an unprecedented recycling problem. In 1974 the OPEC countries had a current account surplus of $59.5 billion, in contrast to the corresponding deficit of $27 billion for the member countries of the ORGANIZATION FOR ECONOMIC COOPERATION AND DEVELOPMENT (OECD) and a similar deficit among the DEVELOPING COUNTRIES. The transfer of funds from the countries with surpluses for lending for investment or for economic aid in the countries with deficits was achieved mainly through the banks (⇛ BANKING) in the advanced countries.

Redeemable securities. STOCKS or BONDS that are repayable at their PAR VALUE at a certain date, dates or specified eventuality. Most fixed-interest SECURITIES are redeemable, though COMMON STOCKS and some PREFERRED STOCKS are not. (⇛⇛ REDEMPTION DATE).

Redemption date. The date at which a LOAN will be repaid or release given from other obligations. (⇛⇛ REDEEMABLE SECURITIES).

Redemption yield. ⇛ YIELD

Reducing balance. A means of recording DEPRECIATION expenses in which the original COST of an ASSET is "written down" by a fixed fraction each year. In this way, the amount of depreciation allowed falls each year—e.g., a machine costing $10,000 could be written down by 20 percent per annum, i.e., $2,000 in the first year and then 20 percent of its written-down value of $8,000 (i.e., $1,600) in the following year, and so on.

Reflation. Macroeconomic (⇛ MACROECONOMICS) policy designed to expand AGGREGATE DEMAND in order to restore full-employment levels of NATIONAL INCOME. Typical reflationary measures include expansion of the MONEY SUPPLY, with consequent reductions in interest rates (⇛ RATE OF INTEREST), increases in government expenditure and reduction in taxation. (⇛ KEYNES, JOHN MAYNARD).

Registered bond. ⇛ BOND

Regression analysis. A set of statistical techniques, the purpose of which is to quantify the relationship between two or more VARIABLES. The object of this may be to permit quantitative prediction or forecasting, or simply to apply the techniques of STATISTICAL INFERENCE to find out whether or not the variables can be expected to be closely related in the population of items under study. It also permits the testing of different hypotheses about the forms of the relationship and the variables that should be included in it. In these respects, it is clearly of considerable importance in economics and, in fact, is the major tool of ECONOMETRICS. Much of econometric theory has been concerned with the theoretical problems arising out of the application of classical regression MODELS, based on certain quite stringent assumptions, to economic data for which those assumptions do not necessarily hold. Most of "applied" econometrics is concerned with the measurement and testing of economic relationships using regression techniques. Precisely as in CORRELATION, to which it bears a very close relation, regression analysis is concerned with measuring statistical association only and does not in itself imply causation. (⇛ AUTO-CORRELATION; LEAST SQUARES REGRESSION; MULTICOLLINEARITY).

Regression model. ⇛ REGRESSION ANALYSIS

Regressive tax. A tax that takes a decreasing proportion of INCOME as income rises. (⇛ TAXATION).

Regulation. Government policy to monitor and control the economic activities of certain types of PRIVATE ENTERPRISE. Such policy arises because of the need to prevent the abuses of unrestrained MONOPOLY power or because certain outputs are characterized as PUBLIC GOODS or generate EXTERNALITIES. In the United States PUBLIC UTILITIES are governed by regulation because they are permitted to operate as monopolies in a geographic area. Railroads have been regulated since 1887, and since then airlines, pipelines and trucking have also come under various government regulations (⇛ INTERSTATE COMMERCE COMMISSION).

In recent years regulations and regulatory commissions have emerged to provide consumer protection. The Food and Drug Administration maintains a surveillance network in an attempt to ensure that harmful products do not enter the market. The ENVIRONMENTAL PROTECTION AGENCY attempts to control the negative externalities associated with the production and distribution of goods and services. The Federal Maritime Commission, the Federal Aviation Commission and the Federal Communications Commission are federal agencies that have been assigned the task of (among other things) enforcing regulations governing shipping, the use of the skyways and media broadcasting, respectively. In recent years there has been increasing pressure on Congress to remove or limit regulation in the belief that existing legislation is impeding ECONOMIC GROWTH. (⇛ LAISSEZ-FAIRE).

Regulation Q. A FED (⇛⇛ FEDERAL RESERVE SYSTEM) regulation established in 1933 that placed interest rate ceilings on commercial bank deposits prior to the DEPOSITORY INSTITUTIONS DEREGULATION AND MONETARY CONTROL ACT (1980). Under this Act, deregulation will be phased out by 1986. The ceiling was regulated by the FED in conjunction with MONETARY POLICY, but even with this flexibility, it initially enabled the THRIFT institutions to expand rapidly in the late 1940s and throughout the 1950s in the absence of rate competition. When the ceilings were allowed to rise on several occasions between 1957 and 1965, the growth in thrifts slowed considerably. By the late 1960s the FED had approved a regulation whereby thrift institution could set a ceiling rate for deposits .5 percent above the maximum rates for banks. Pressure from the commercial banks and the general feeling that such control was inhibiting efficient capital market operation led to the change in legislation noted above.

Regulations T, U, G. The FEDERAL RESERVE SYSTEM controls the use of CREDIT to purchase STOCKS by setting the MARGIN for such purchases. The three regulations—T, U and G—control the margins for dealers, banks and others, respectively, who may extend credit for stock purchases. The Federal Reserve is free to vary the margin.

Regulation W. ⇛ CREDIT CONTROL ACT

Rent. The PRICE paid per unit of time for the services of a DURABLE GOOD and, in particular, LAND and buildings. One may rent a computer rather than buy it outright, or rent a television set, and the payments for this will be referred to as rents or rentals. In economics the term *rent* is also given a more specific meaning. (⇛ ECONOMIC RENT; QUASI-RENT; RICARDO, DAVID).

Rental. ⇛ RENT

Rentier. A supplier of CAPITAL who is paid in the form of interest (⇛ RATE OF INTEREST) and DIVIDENDS. He does not, however, supply entrepreneurial services—he does not participate in managing the firm (⇛ ENTREPRENEUR). The word is of French origin and is derived from *rente,* meaning interest (not the English RENT, meaning, *inter alia,* the payment for LAND).

Repressed inflation. INFLATION that exists when the state of the economy is essentially inflationary—AGGREGATE DEMAND for goods and services exceeding the AGGREGATE SUPPLY, and so, other things being equal, PRICES would tend to rise—but the rise in prices is not allowed to happen. An example would be a perfectly effective PRICES AND INCOMES POLICY, which prevented prices of goods, services and FACTORS OF PRODUCTION from rising. Most economists would argue that if the underlying DISEQUILIBRIUM of aggregate supply and demand is allowed to remain uncorrected, inflation will not be repressed for long, since no administrative mechanism will be sufficiently comprehensive to control the tendency for prices (including wages) to rise in one way or another. (⇛ WAGE DRIFT).

Required reserve ratio. ⇛ REQUIRED RESERVES

Required reserves. The amount of cash reserves that member banks of the FEDERAL RESERVE SYSTEM (the FED) must hold. These reserves may be held as cash in the vault or in the form of reserve accounts held with the FED. The amount required depends upon the size of the member bank and type of DEPOSITS it holds as LIABILITIES. The power to change reserve requirements was established in 1933. A banking system based on reserve requirements is known as *fractional reserve banking.* During the 1970s required reserves as a percentage of deposits varied between 14.4 percent and 17.2 percent with a slight downward trend over the decade. By controlling the reserves that must be held by member banks, the FED can control the availability and cost of CREDIT. A higher required reserve places restrictions on the ability of banks to make LOANS, giving rise to *tight money* and a higher interest rate (⇛ RATE OF INTEREST). Lower required reserves allow banks to increase loans and reduce interest. (⇛⇛ MONETARY POLICY).

Resale price maintenance. An attempt by producers to force all retailers to sell their product at a fixed, given price. This would, in effect, eliminate price competition among retailers. Without legal sanction, it is extremely difficult to enforce if there is any degree of competition, and hence there has, over the years, been pressure to have legislation passed that would enforce resale price maintenance. By 1936 all but three states had enacted laws permitting resale price maintenance for intrastate trade. In 1937 Congress passed an act exempting from antitrust laws resale price maintenance for certain classes of goods in interstate commerce. The exemption was upheld in 1951 as a fair-trade law but was struck down in 1975 by another act of Congress that forbade resale price maintenance on any interstate commerce. Resale price maintenance is easier to enforce if the producer/supplier maintains a MONOPOLY position, and because of this possibility, some countries, notably Canada, have prosecuted firms for this practice.

Research and development (R&D). Basic research, i.e., research without a specific commercial objective; applied research, i.e., research with a commercial objective or the pursuit of an invention; and development work, i.e., the perfection of an invention, the work of turning research into products or processes, including the improvement of existing products. R&D expenditure is a matter of great relevance to economic policy because of its contribution to innovation and, through innovation, growth. (⇛ ECONOMIC GROWTH).

Reserve. 1. In business accounting an amount appropriated or put aside for a future eventuality, a contingency reserve, for example. 2. Reserve requirements in the FEDERAL RESERVE SYSTEM determine the percentage of cash that member banks must hold in relation to deposits. 3. CENTRAL BANKS hold GOLD AND FOREIGN-EXCHANGE RESERVES, and members of the IMF (⇛ INTERNATIONAL MONETARY FUND) have reserve positions in the fund.

Reserve currency. A CURRENCY that governments and international institutions are willing to hold in their GOLD AND FOREIGN EXCHANGE RESERVES and that finances a significant proportion of INTERNATIONAL TRADE. The prerequisites for these two conditions are normally that: (*a*) the value of the currency must be stable in relation to other currencies; (*b*) the currency is that of a country that holds an important share of world trade; (*c*) there exists an efficient FOREIGN-EXCHANGE MARKET in which the currency may be exchanged for other currencies; and (*d*) the currency is convertible (⇛ CONVERTIBILITY). The U.S. dollar had been the dominant reserve currency in the period since 1945 until the early 1970s. Since the upheaval in international finance in 1973–74 caused by the increase in oil prices, governments have diversified their foreign-exchange holdings away from the U.S. dollar. For instance, in 1973 the U.S. dollar holdings in these reserves were 12 times those held in German deutsche marks, but by 1980 this ratio had fallen to 6 times. (⇛ INTERNATIONAL LIQUIDITY).

Reserve holding ratio. The ratio of cash reserves to deposits of BANKS.

Reserve ratio. ⇛ BANKING

Resource allocation. 1. The process by which scarce RESOURCES in the economy are distributed among their alternative uses. A basic assumption underlying the whole of ECONOMICS is that resources are "relatively scarce." That is, if all PRICES were zero, the combined demands of all consumers in the economy for all goods and services would greatly exceed the capacity available to produce them. This capacity is determined by the resources the economy possesses, on the one hand, and the technological possibilities of production, on the other. This is held to be true, however abundant, in some absolute sense, resources may appear to be. Given relative scarcity, it is necessary to know how much of each resource will be allocated to production of each good and how much of each good will be allocated to each consumer. Economics as an academic discipline is concerned with the study of how this allocation problem is solved, especially (though not exclusively) in economies where the mechanism by which resources are allocated is based upon MARKET FORCES.

2. A resource allocation can be thought of as a specific list of quantities: A level of output for every good and service in the economy—steel, milk, haircuts, college tuition, corn flakes and so on; a level of consumption of each good and service by each consumer in the economy; an amount of each FACTOR OF PRODUCTION used by each production unit in the economy; and an amount of each factor of production supplied by each owner of resources in the economy—labor services of carpenters, plumbers, stevedores, mailmen; supply of capital by savers and ENTREPRENEURS; and so on. Thus, a specific resource allocation is a very long and detailed list, indeed. Nevertheless, each day, the economic system arrives at such an allocation. The main purpose of economics, then, is to understand how this comes about, what the determinants of the achieved allocation are and whether the specific allocation actually achieved is in some sense the best possible.

Resources. These are the "agents" or FACTORS OF PRODUCTION used in an economy or firm to produce and distribute goods and services. They are conventionally classified into LAND, LABOR and CAPITAL, where each of these is a generic name for a possibly large set of productive services. The category *land* includes natural resources, properties of soil and waterways, or simply its ability to be built upon. *Labor* is a term that summarizes the services of both manual and non-manual labor, the services yielded by a broker in bringing two parties together, as well as those yielded by a machine operator or auto mechanic. Finally, the category *capital* refers to the services provided by machinery, buildings, tools and other productive instruments that are goods made to produce other goods, which considerably increase the PRODUCTIVITY of land and labor, and which are only obtained by sacrificing current consumption possibilities. In certain problems the distinctions between categories may not be rigidly applied—e.g., a highly skilled worker may be better regarded as a capital good than as a unit of labor.

The most important characteristic of resources is that they are relatively scarce—scarce, that is, relative to the total flow of goods and services that society would like to produce with them. This relative scarcity correspondingly creates a need for allocation, and the study of the way in which capitalist (⇛ CAPITALISM) economies carry out this process of resource allocation has long been the main preoccupation of MICROECONOMICS.

Retail Price Index. ⇛ CONSUMER PRICE INDEX

Retail trade. The final link in the chain of distribution from the manufacturer to the consumer. A retail outlet may maintain stocks at the point of sale or, as in the case of mail-order businesses, centralize stocks in one location. Retail outlets have gone from being small and highly specialized to very large and all-encompassing in terms of what they sell. A shopping mall is an attempt to combine specialized retailing in one central location.

Retained earnings. Undistributed PROFITS. (⇛⇛ SELF-FINANCING).

Retentions. Undistributed PROFITS. (⇛ SELF-FINANCING).

Return on capital employed. ⇛ RATE OF RETURN, RETURN ON INVESTMENT

Return on investment (ROI). ⇛ RATE OF RETURN

Returns to scale. The increases in output that result from increasing the scale of some production activity. Suppose that the quantities of all the INPUTS used in producing a given output of a good are increased by the same proportion, e.g., 50 percent. Then, if output increases by a greater proportion—e.g., 55 percent—returns to scale are said to be increasing; if output increases in the same proportion (50 percent), then returns to scale are said to be constant; and if output increases by a smaller proportion—e.g., 45 percent—returns to scale are said to be decreasing. Thus, returns to scale refer to the way in which output changes when the whole scale of input changes. The nature of returns to scale will clearly influence the way in which costs of production vary with scale of output. If returns to scale are increasing, then a given proportionate change in output requires a smaller proportionate change in quantities of inputs, and we would therefore expect COSTS to rise less than proportionately with output, implying a fall in cost per unit of output, i.e., a fall in AVERAGE COST. Similarly, decreasing returns to scale imply increasing average costs. Since they relate to changes in all inputs, returns to scale are necessarily a LONG-RUN concept.

The usefulness of the concept of returns to scale lies in its role as a classifying device. It provides a convenient way of classifying particular types of technological condition. For a discussion of the reasons for increasing and decreasing returns to scale, see ECONOMIES OF SCALE and DISECONOMY. Note that returns to scale refer to the relationship between input and output, while economies of scale refer to the relationship between cost and output, so that only those sources of economies and diseconomies of scale that are based on the input-output relationship are also sources of increasing and decreasing returns to scale, respectively.

Revealed preference. An analysis of consumer behavior based only on the information on choices actually made by the consumer in various price-income situations. A given INCOME level and set of PRICES will determine for the consumer a particular set of "baskets" of goods he could purchase. If, in that situation, we observe that he chooses one particular basket, that basket is then "revealed preferred" to all the other baskets that were attainable. Another price-income situation will lead to (in general) another basket's being revealed as preferred. By making certain quite plausible assumptions about the consistency of the choices of the consumer in the various price-income situations, it is possible to prove some of the important propositions in consumer demand theory (⇛ DEMAND, THEORY OF), without having to assume measurability of UTILITY or even that INDIFFERENCE CURVES can be constructed. The revealed preference approach was first formulated by PAUL ANTHONY SAMUELSON.

Revenue expenditures. The cost of repairs and maintenance on existing ASSETS to maintain capacity, and charged to the current year's revenues. Counted as a CAPITAL EXPENDITURE.

Revenue sharing. In a federal state, one level of government may collect tax revenue and—by virtue of an agreed-upon formula with a subordinate, or lower, level of government—share the tax collections with that level of government. For example, in Canada the federal government collects the personal income tax on behalf of nine of the provinces, returning to each province a share of the revenue collected in that province. While this is the historical use of the term, it has a slightly different, and more widespread, interpretation in the United States. Originally proposed by Walter Heller in 1966 (and known as the Heller-Pechman plan), general revenue sharing was enacted in 1972. Under the State and Local Fiscal Assistance Act, *unconditional grants* are made from the federal treasury to the states, the sizes of which are based on a state's population, the effort it makes in raising its own revenue, its per capita income and urban population. One-third of the total remains with the state government, while the rest is passed to local government.

Ricardo, David (1772–1823). The son of Jewish parents who were connected with the MONEY MARKET, first in the Netherlands, and later in London, Ricardo had little formal education. At the early age of 14, however, he was already working in the money market himself. It was James Mill (the father of JOHN STUART MILL) who persuaded Ricardo, himself diffident about his own abilities, to write. Nevertheless, Ricardo succeeded in making a fortune on the STOCK EXCHANGE, sufficient for him to be able to retire at 42. Not surprisingly, many of his earlier publications were concerned with money and banking. In 1810 he published a pamphlet on *The High Price of Bullion, a Proof of the Depreciation of Bank Notes;* in 1811 appeared the *Reply to Mr. Bosanquet's Practical Observations on the Report of the Bullion Committee;* and in 1816 *Proposals for an Economical and Secure Currency.* However, his work on monetary economics did not have the originality or exert the influence comparable to his studies in other branches of economics. In 1815 he published his *Essay on the Influence of the Low Price of Corn on the Profits of Stock,* which was the prototype for his most important work. This first appeared in 1817 under the title *The Principles of Political Economy and Taxation,* a work that was to dominate English CLASSICAL

ECONOMICS for the following half-century. In his *Principles* Ricardo was basically concerned "to determine the laws which regulate the distribution (between the different classes of landowners, capitalists and labor) of the produce of industry." His approach was to construct a theoretical MODEL that abstracted from the complexities of an actual economy so as to attempt to reveal the major important influences at work within it. His economy was predominantly agricultural. With DEMAND rising as a result of increasing POPULATION, and a level of subsistence that tended, by custom, to rise also over time, more and more less-fertile LAND had to be brought into cultivation. The return (in terms of the output of corn) of each further addition of CAPITAL and LABOR to more land fell. This process continued until it was no longer considered sufficiently profitable to bring any additional plots of land under cultivation. However, COSTS and PROFITS must be the same on all land, whether or not it was marginal. Laobr cost the same wherever it was applied. If profits were higher at one place than at another, it would encourage capital to be invested at the place of high return, until by the process of diminishing returns, profit fell into line with profits elsewhere. Therefore, as costs and profits were the same throughout, a surplus was earned on the non-marginal land, and this was RENT (shaded in diagram).

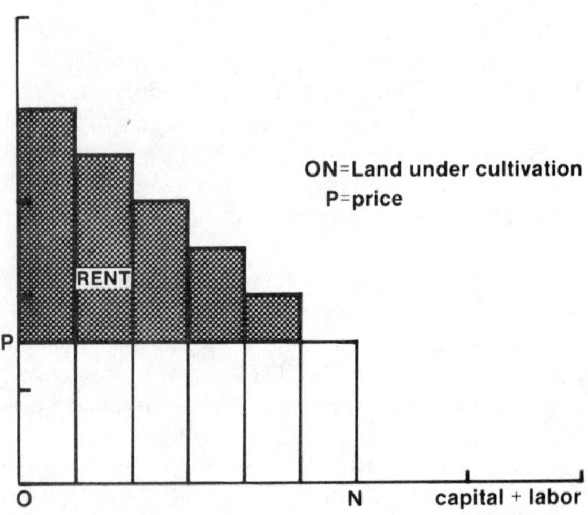

The consequence of this was that, as the population expanded and more less-fertile land was brought into cultivation, profits became squeezed between the increasing proportion of total output that went in rent and the basic minimum level of subsistence allocated to the wages of labor. Ricardo assumed that prices were determined principally by the quantity of labor used during production (⇛ VALUE, THEORIES OF). However, he recognized that capital costs did nevertheless also have an influence on prices and that the effect of a rise in wages on relative prices depended on the proportion of these two FACTORS OF PRODUCTION in the various COMMODITIES.

With a rise in wages, CAPITAL-INTENSIVE goods became cheaper relative to LABOR-INTENSIVE goods, with a consequent shift in the demand and output in favor of the former (⇛ RICARDO EFFECT). In the theory of INTERNATIONAL TRADE, Ricardo stated explicitly for the first time the law of comparative costs. This law can best be illustrated by means of the example of two countries (A and B) producing two commodities (say cloth and wine). If the relative cost of cloth to wine is the same in both countries, then no trade will take place because there is no gain to be had by exchanging wine (or cloth) for cloth (or wine) produced abroad for that produced at home. Trade will take place where cost differences exist. These can be of two kinds. First, if wine is cheap in A and cloth in B, A will specialize in wine and B in cloth, and exchange will take place to their mutual advantage. Second, the law of comparative costs states the condition under which trade will take place, even though both commodities may be produced more cheaply in one country than in another.

Man-hours per unit of output

Country	Wine	Cloth
A	120	100
B	80	90

Country B exports one unit of wine to A and imports in exchange $\frac{120}{100}$ units of cloth. If Country B had devoted the 80 man-hours employed in making wine for exports to making cloth instead, it would have produced only $\frac{80}{90}$ units of cloth. Country B therefore gains from trade by the difference $(\frac{120}{100} - \frac{80}{90})$ units of cloth. As long as B can exchange wine for cloth at a rate higher than $\frac{80}{90}$, it will therefore gain from the trade. If Country A exports a unit of cloth to Country B, it will obtain in exchange $\frac{90}{80}$ units of wine. If the 100 man-hours required by A to produce a unit of cloth had been devoted to the home production of wine, only $\frac{100}{120}$ units of wine would be obtained. The gain from trade therefore is $(\frac{90}{80} - \frac{100}{120})$ units of wine. Provided, therefore, that A can exchange cloth for wine at a rate higher than $\frac{100}{120}$, it will gain from the trade. Within the range of exchange of wine for cloth of $\frac{120}{100}$ and $\frac{80}{90}$, both countries therefore benefit.

The law of comparative costs survives as an important part of the theory of international trade today. Otherwise, Ricardo's main contribution is the analytical approach of theoretical model building, which has contributed substantially to economists' methodological tool kits. (⇛⇛ EQUATION OF INTERNATIONAL DEMAND; HECKSCHER-OHLIN PRINCIPLE).

Ricardo effect. FRIEDRICH AUGUST VON HAYEK argued that, if the PRICES that firms received for their outputs increased more than the COSTS of their raw materials and wages, the average rate of PROFIT on CAPITAL employed per year increased more for those firms with a short than for those with a long turnover period. This can best be illustrated by a simple arithmetical example. If the rate of profit per year is 5 percent, $100 of capital will yield $105 in one year and $110 in two years (approximately, ignoring COMPOUND

INTEREST). If output prices rise by, say, 1 percent, the YIELD rises to $6 for one year and to $11 in two years. The rate of profit therefore rises to 6 percent per annum for the capital that can be turned over in one year but only to $5\frac{1}{2}$ percent per annum for capital with a two-year turnover period. Consequently, in a boom, when COMMODITY prices rise faster than wages, firms are discouraged from investing in capital-goods industries because of the long production time required. This reaction is called the Ricardo effect because of its affinity to Ricardo's argument that, if REAL WAGES fall, firms tend to substitute LABOR for machinery. This conclusion contrasted sharply with JOHN MAYNARD KEYNES's views based on the principle of the accelerator. (⇛ ACCELERATION PRINCIPLE).

Rights issue. ⇛ STOCK RIGHT

Right-to-work laws. These laws permit the OPEN SHOP or the right to work without belonging to a union. The option to pass such laws rests with individual states, and the right to pass such laws is guaranteed through the TAFT-HARTLEY ACT of 1948.

Risk. A decision is said to be subject to risk when there is a range of possible outcomes that could flow from it and when objectively known PROBABILITIES can be attached to these outcomes. Risk is therefore distinguished from UNCERTAINTY, where there is a plurality of outcomes to which objective probabilities cannot be assigned. The decision to accept a gamble involving the toss of a coin is a decision subject to risk, since there is more than one possible outcome (heads, tails) and the odds can be calculated. The term *risk* is being defined at once more broadly and more narrowly than in its everyday usage. A "risky situation" in everyday terms is generally one in which one of the outcomes involves the decision maker in losses—a businessman would not feel he was "taking a risk" if an investment had two outcomes, one of which resulted in a PROFIT of $10,000, the other of which resulted in a profit of $5,000. Yet, according to the strict definition, this is a situation involving risk. On the other hand, the fact that objective probabilities often cannot be assigned means that many situations that, in practice, are called "risky" are, according to the strict definition, really subject to uncertainty, not risk. (⇛ BERNOULLI'S HYPOTHESIS).

Risk capital. Long-term funds invested in enterprises particularly subject to RISK, as in new ventures. Sometimes used as a synonym for EQUITY capital, it is also used instead of the term *venture capital*, a somewhat more precise term meaning CAPITAL provided for a new business undertaking by persons other than the proprietors. Neither term is unambiguous, since all capital except that secured by fixed assets is at risk, and even extensions to an existing business may be described accurately as a new venture. Venture capital is provided by private investors and by institutions such as the INVESTMENT BANKS. There are also a number of specialized venture capital institutions and the SMALL BUSINESS INVESTMENT COMPANIES.

Robinson, Joan Violet (1903–). Educated at Girton College, Professor Robinson took up a post as assistant lecturer at Cambridge University, England, in 1931, becoming reader in 1949. She was elected to the Chair of

Economics in 1965 on the retirement of her husband, Professor Sir E.A.G. Robinson, and remained in this post until 1971. Economic theorists in the 1920s were much concerned with the problem of the meaning of a theory of VALUE based on PERFECT COMPETITION. In particular, it was felt of doubtful validity to assume a situation in which there were so many firms supplying a COMMODITY that none of them individually could affect the PRICE—in the face of the existence of the economies of large-scale output. Professor Robinson broke out of the analytical framework of perfect competition and built up her analysis on the basis of firms in "imperfect competition" (⇛ MONOPOLISTIC COMPETITION). Each firm had a MONOPOLY in its products that was based on the preferences of consumers (⇛ CONSUMERS' PREFERENCE), in spite of the existence of very close substitutes produced by other firms. (EDWARD HASTINGS CHAMBERLIN developed similar ideas simultaneously and independently.) These ideas were set out in her book *Economics of Imperfect Competition,* published in 1933. Her other published works include *An Essay on Marxian Economics* (1942); *Accumulation of Capital* (1956); *Essays on the Theory of Economic Growth* (1963); *Collected Economic Papers* (5 volumes—1951, 1960, 1965, 1973 and 1979); *Economics: An Awkward Corner* (1966), the "awkward corner" being the present-day confusion of "partial LAISSEZ-FAIRE"; *Freedom and Necessity* (1970); *Economic Heresies* (1971); *Contributions to Modern Economics* (1978); and *Aspects of Development and Underdevelopment* (1979). Government economic controls are confined to the regulation of aggregate effective demand (⇛ AGGREGATE DEMAND), and the allocation of the country's economic RESOURCES is left to FREE-MARKET competition. There is, however, no more reason to suppose that competition efficiently allocates available resources, given the political and social aims of society, better than it can regulate AGGREGATE DEMAND. Professor Robinson has played a dominant role in the CAMBRIDGE SCHOOL of economic thought, with the development of post-Keynesian MACROECONOMICS linked to the early classical period of DAVID RICARDO and KARL MARX. (⇛ CAPITAL RESWITCHING).

Robinson-Patman Act. An amendment in 1948 to the Clayton Merger and Acquisitions Act of 1914 (⇛ CLAYTON ACT), making it unlawful to engage in PRICE DISCRIMINATION. (⇛⇛ ANTITRUST POLICY).

Rostow, Walt Whitman (1916–). Educated at Yale and at Oxford, as a Rhodes Scholar, Rostow served during the Second World War in the Office of Strategic Services and was the assistant chief of the Division of German-Austrian Economic Affairs of the U.S. Department of State from 1945 to 1946. He was Pitt Professor of American History at Cambridge University, England, for 1949–50 and professor of economic history at Massachusetts Institute of Technology from 1950 to 1965. Since 1969 he has been professor of economics and history at the University of Texas. He was appointed special assistant to the president in 1966. His major publications include *The Process of Economic Growth* (1952), *Stages of Economic Growth* (1960), *Politics and the Stages of Growth* (1971), *How it all Began—Origins of the Modern Economy* (1975), *The World Economy: History and Prospect*

(1978), and *Why the Poor Get Richer and the Rich Slow Down* (1980). He postulated that societies passed through five stages of economic development: (*a*) the traditional society; (*b*) the preconditions for takeoff; (*c*) the takeoff, when growth becomes a normal feature of the economy; (*d*) the drive to maturity; and, some 60 years after takeoff begins, (*e*) maturity, reached in the age of high mass CONSUMPTION. (⇛ ECONOMIC GROWTH, STAGES OF; GROWTH THEORY).

S

Sales tax. 1. A tax levied as a proportion of the retail PRICE of a COMMODITY at the point of sale. *Retail sales taxes* are an important source of state and local government revenues and are imposed by all but four states at rates that vary from 2 percent to 5 percent or more. These are general taxes, but federal and state sales taxes are also levied on a selective basis, i.e., on specific products such as gasoline. Federal or excise taxes are mostly levied on manufacturers and are on a unit rather than an ad valorem basis (⇛ UNIT TAX). 2. More generally, sales taxes are levied on business firms. The base may be selective—i.e., it may include all or only some consumer goods and CAPITAL goods; sales taxes may be imposed at retail, wholesale or manufacturer level and may be single-stage, as with retail sales taxes, or multiple-stage, as with VALUE-ADDED TAX or TURNOVER TAX. A sales tax is a REGRESSIVE TAX, since it is the same for all consumers irrespective of income or personal circumstances. Because INCOME TAX discriminates against SAVING, economists have long been attracted to a personalized expenditure tax. Such a tax would be levied at progessive rates upon total consumption expenditure calculated on an annual basis. The taxpayer would have to make an annual return of his expenditure (whether financed by borrowing, capital gains or other sources of income). Not the least of the practical difficulties of introducing an expenditure tax would be the need for a complete recording of cash balances at the outset and the scope for *tax evasion* (⇛ TAX AVOIDANCE) through BARTER.

Sample. In everyday terms, a sample is a quantity of something that has been selected as representative. A wine taster takes a sample of a particular type of wine and tastes it in order to evaluate the whole vintage. In economic and social research, however, a sample is given a somewhat more restricted meaning; rather than being just any "part" of the "population," it must be selected by certain statistical methods designed to ensure that it is really representative of the POPULATION as a whole. Thus, the term *sample* should strictly be applied only to a properly chosen set of items. (For discussion of what constitutes "proper" choice, see QUOTA SAMPLE; RANDOM SAMPLE; SIMPLE RANDOM SAMPLE; STRATIFIED SAMPLE.) The purpose of a sample is to provide information about the population from which it is selected. Since the sample is only a part of the population, it follows that we would expect some inaccuracy. For example, by questioning a sample of voters, it might be found that 30 percent of the sample intended to vote for presidential candidate A, 50 percent intended voting for presidential candidate B and 20 percent for other candidates. On the other hand, if an election were held, we might well get shares of 33 percent, 49 percent and 18 percent, respectively, simply because a sample is unlikely to give a perfect representation of the population. However, if the sample is properly designed, the size of the likely error is kept to a minimum, and it is possible to calculate and specify its size. Furthermore, it is possible to find how varying the number of items included in the sample affects the size of the likely error.

The advantages of taking a sample, even if the information gained is not likely to be perfectly accurate for the whole population, are often substantial. In the extreme case, where evaluating the sample destroys the items (tasting wine, testing a machine or component to destruction), it is quite clear that the relevant information can only be gained from a sample. In economic and social research, the relevant consideration is the relation between the size of the sample and the cost and quality of the information-gathering procedure. The larger the sample, the greater the number of questionnaires, interviewers, etc., and the greater the cost of analyzing the data.

Samuelson, Paul Anthony (1915–). Professor Samuelson was appointed to the Chair of Economics at Massachusetts Institute of Technology in 1940. He served in the U.S. Treasury for seven years after the end of the Second World War. In 1970 Professor Samuelson received the Alfred Nobel Memorial Prize in Economics. His publications include *Foundations of Economic Analysis* (1947) and *Linear Programming and Economic Analysis* (1958). Samuelson developed the HECKSCHER-OHLIN PRINCIPLE by showing how an increase in the PRICE of a COMMODITY can raise the INCOME of the FACTORS OF PRODUCTION that is used most intensively in producing it (⇛ CAPITAL-INTENSIVE). This led to his formulating the *factor price equalization theorem,* which states the conditions under which, as FREE TRADE in commodities narrows differences in commodity prices between countries, the prices (incomes) of factors of production are also brought into line. In other words, free trade is a substitute for the free mobility of factors of production. Professor Samuelson has made important contributions to the development of mathematical economics, general EQUILIBRIUM theory and the theory of consumer behavior. To free the latter from what he considered to be the constraint of the traditional concept of UTILITY, he invented REVEALED PREFERENCE. In macroeconomic theory (⇛ MACROECONOMICS), he was, in an article in 1939, the first to formulate the interaction between the accelerator and the multiplier. (⇛ ACCELERATOR-MULTIPLIER MODEL; SOCIAL WELFARE FUNCTION).

Satisficing. Decision-making behavior directed at finding a *satisfactory* rather than an OPTIMUM choice in any given situation. Virtually all of conventional MICROECONOMICS is based on the assumption that an individual always seeks the *best* alternative out of those available. Thus, firms are assumed to *maximize* profit and consumers to *maximize* UTILITY. HERBERT A. SIMON has, however, consistently pointed out that to do so may require far better information and greater computational ability than individuals in fact possess. Given the existing real limitations on these, individuals are more likely to select an alternative that meets some criterion of acceptability rather than to go on looking for the best alternative ("the best is the enemy of the good"). This hypothesis underlies the development of the BEHAVIORAL THEORY OF THE FIRM. Despite its intuitive appeal, it must be said that the principle of satisficing has not replaced that of optimization in mainstream economics.

Saturation point. A level beyond which the *relative* absorption of a product or service is not expected to increase. It is defined in terms of a ratio, e.g. ownership of refrigerators per household or per hundred persons. Once the saturation point is reached, the growth of demand slows down to levels determined by population growth and replacement, although in some cases predictions of saturation points have been falsified by the emergence of multiple ownership, e.g. of autos and television sets. (⇛⇛ MARKET SHARE).

Saving. Not spending INCOME on CONSUMPTION. Income that is not spent on consumption is by definition saved. An important thing to note about this definition is that it is rather wider than the conventional usage of the word: It is not necessary for an income earner to place money in a savings account or buy some kind of ASSETS to be saving in the sense used here. Simply leaving money in a jar on the shelf, as long as it represents non-spending of current income, is saving. Economists choose this definition because the important feature of saving is that it represents money that, having been paid out as income to HOUSEHOLDS, does not flow back to firms in the form of expenditure on goods and services. If there were not some other source of expenditure on goods and services to "make up for" the amount saved, firms would find that they were producing too much and would therefore reduce production, implying in turn a fall in income and employment. In fact, another source of expenditure does exist, and this is INVESTMENT. If the amount invested just equals the amount saved, income and employment will show no tendency to change—i.e., they will be in EQUILIBRIUM. If investment is less than saving, total expenditure will be inadequate to maintain the previous level of output, income and employment, which will all tend to fall. If, however, investment is greater than saving, expenditure must be more than enough to maintain the previous levels of income, which will tend to rise. Thus, we can say that for income and employment to be in equilibrium, expenditure on investment must be just equal to saving or nonexpenditure on consumption. This is the basis of the theory of income determination. (⇛ INCOME DETERMINATION, THEORY OF).

Savings and loan associations. These financial institutions originated on the basis of self-help. A group of individuals would pool their savings and issue shares in proportion to their contribution to the total. A MORTGAGE loan was then made to a member— randomly selected (⇛ RANDOM SAMPLE) —to build a house, and when funds were again sufficient, another loan would be made. Repayments plus more savings allowed all members to eventually secure a home. As new members entered the association, its continuation was assured. Most savings and loan associations are now organized as CORPORATIONS and may be either state or federally chartered. (⇛ FEDERAL HOME LOAN BANK BOARD; THRIFTS).

Savings banks. ⇛ MUTUAL SAVINGS BANKS

Savings ratio. The percentage of PERSONAL DISPOSABLE INCOME that is saved by households. The average in the United States during the 1960s and 1970s was 6.3 percent, with a high of 7.8 percent in 1973 and a low of 4.7 percent in 1963. The savings ratio began to decline steadily starting in 1976, and by 1980 it was below 5 percent. Preliminary figures suggest that the ratio was close to 4 percent in 1981. The decline is generally thought to be the consequence of INFLATION. Consumers, expecting a rise in prices, spend a greater share of their increase in disposable income on goods and services. On the other hand, consumers also attempt to restore the real value of the savings, which inflation otherwise diminishes. (⇛ REAL TERMS).

Say, Jean-Baptiste (1767–1832). A practical businessman, Say developed an interest in economics and began lecturing in the subject in 1816. In 1819 he was appointed to the Chair of Industrial Economy at the Conservatoire National des Arts et Métiers. In 1831 he was appointed professor of political economy at the College de France. His most important published works are *Traite d'economie politique,* which appeared in 1803, and *Cours complet d'economie politique pratique,* which was published in 1829. Although he can claim some credit for the introduction of the concept of an ENTREPRENEUR into economic theory, and also the division of the fundamental FACTORS OF PRODUCTION into three—LAND, LABOR and CAPITAL—his fame and notoriety spring from his *"lois des debouches,"* or "law of markets." It is probable that his "law" would not figure so prominently in economics today had not JOHN MAYNARD KEYNES accused the CLASSICAL SCHOOL of being gravely misled by accepting it as the pivot of their macroeconomic theory (⇛ MACROECONOMICS). According to Keynes, the law said that the sum of the values of all COMMODITIES produced was equivalent (always) to the sum of the values of all commodities bought. By definition, therefore, there could be no underutilization of RESOURCES; "supply created its own demand." However, there is some considerable doubt about what Say actually meant. Several versions have been put forward; some are incontrovertible platitudes, such as in barter a seller must also be a buyer, and if a good is sold somebody must have bought it. Probably the most meaningful interpretation is that of Keynes, but only as a condition that must be satisfied for EQUILIBRIUM to exist. (⇛⇛ WALRAS, MARIE ESPRIT LEON).

Say's law of markets. ⇛ SAY, JEAN-BAPTISTE

Scarce currency. Synonym for HARD CURRENCY.

Scarcity. A condition where there is less of something than people would like to have if it cost nothing to buy. This word is used in economics in a relative sense. Most people would say that there were many automobiles about, and that they were hardly scarce in the usual sense of the word; but since there are certainly not enough to give everyone as many automobiles as he would like to have, we can say that they are, relatively speaking, scarce. Similarly, since the total quantity of goods and services that people would like to have far exceeds the amount that the economy's resources are capable of producing, we can say that there is a scarcity of RESOURCES (even though the economy might have a very large LABOR force, many factories, etc.). The importance of the existence of scarcity is that it gives rise to a need to allocate the available RESOURCES among alternative uses. If this allocation is done through a FREE-MARKET capitalist system (⇛ CAPITALISM) rather than through a centralized command economy (⇛ PLANNED ECONOMY), then scarcity will necessarily imply positive PRICES for goods. Air does not have a price because it is not relatively scarce: Everyone has as much as he wants; food has a price because it requires resources—LAND, labor, machinery, seed, fertilizer, etc.—that are relatively scarce and could be used to produce other things.

Schultz, Theodore W. (1902–). Following an undergraduate degree at South Dakota University, Schultz received his Ph.D. at Wisconsin in 1930, and from that year to 1943, he taught agricultural economics at Iowa State University. He went next to Chicago and was chairman of the Economics Department from 1946 to 1972.

His early work was related to the role that education played in leading to productivity gains—*Agriculture in an Unstable Economy* (1945)—but his work later branched out, encompassing a broader outlook on the role of education in all sectors of the economy—*The Economic Value of Education* (1963) and *Transforming Traditional Agriculture* (1964). He was awarded the NOBEL PRIZE in Economics in 1979 jointly with Sir Arthur Lewis of Princeton University. The citation stated: "Both are deeply concerned about need and poverty in the world, and engaged in finding ways out of underdevelopment."

Schumpeter, Joseph Alois (1883–1950). In 1919 he was appointed professor of economics at Czernowitz, subsequently moving to Graz. He was appointed minister of finance in the Austrian Republic for a short period after the First World War. From 1925 until 1932 he held the Chair of Public Finance at Bonn. From 1932 until his death, he was at Harvard University. His major publications include *Theory of Economic Development* (1912), *Business Cycles* (1939), *Capitalism, Socialism and Democracy* (1942) and *History of Economic Analysis,* which appeared posthumously and unfinished in 1954. He built up a theory of the TRADE CYCLE that was based on three time periods: (*a*) short, (*b*) medium and (*c*) long, to each of which he attributed different causes. He tested his theory against actual fluctuations from the 18th to the 20th centuries. Although it was reasonably successful, he was doubtful of the predictive efficiency of his theory for future periods. He attempted to work out a theory of economic growth and fluctuation around an explicit recognition of the contribution of technical INNOVATION. He tried to argue that, without the latter, an economy would reach a static EQUILIBRIUM position of a "circular flow" of goods with no net growth. He emphasized the evolutionary nature of the capitalist system. He argued that under MONOPOLY capitalism, firms would place less emphasis on PRICE competition but would increasingly compete in technical and organizational innovation, thus sending "gales of creative destruction" through the economic system. He predicted that capitalism would evolve gradually into socialism. (⇛ KONDRATIEFF CYCLE).

Scitovsky paradox. ⇛ COMPENSATION PRINCIPLE

Scrip issue. The issue of new SHARES to shareholders in proportion to their existing holdings, made—as distinct from a rights issue (⇛ STOCK RIGHT) —without charge. Like a STOCK SPLIT, a scrip issue does not raise new CAPITAL. It is merely an adjustment to the capital structure that capitalizes reserves, usually consisting of past PROFITS, and in this sense is distinguished from a stock split, which consists simply of dividing up existing shares into smaller units. Commonly referred to also as a *stock dividend.* The word *scrip* is an abbreviation of *subscription certificate.* (⇛⇛ CAPITALIZATION).

Seasonal adjustment. An adjustment made to the values in a statistical TIME SERIES that is intended to correct for changes that are due entirely to the point in time at which the data were recorded rather than to the underlying forces we may really be interested in. For example, the number of workers unemployed will be recorded in each quarter of the year; it will usually rise sharply in winter and drop in spring. If we want to evaluate the impact that macroeconomic (⇛ MACROECONOMICS) policies are having on the economy, we will want to remove the influence of these purely seasonal factors—layoffs of outdoor workers because of winter weather, and so on—from the data. Therefore, we can try to measure the amount of unemployment that is due to the seasonal factors and eliminate the influence of these from the data. However, it is rarely possible to estimate with perfect accuracy the influence of purely seasonal factors, and so we run the risk that seasonal adjustment will distort the data by removing variation in which we are interested as well as that in which we are not. Hence, "smoothing" time series to eliminate seasonal variation is not an uncontroversial activity.

Seasonal unemployment. UNEMPLOYMENT due to the seasonal nature of activity in some industries—e.g., unemployment in the construction industry increases in winter.

Secondary market. A MARKET for the resale and purchase of SECURITIES or other titles to property or COMMODITIES. The term is potentially a confusing one, since primary and secondary markets may be one and the same. For example, organized STOCK EXCHANGES are involved in primary distributions (⇛ NEW ISSUE MARKET) as well as in trading in SHARES and BONDS once they have been issued. In some cases, shares are issued by INVESTMENT BANKS by private placing and are traded on the secondary market (the stock exchange) later. The secondary MORTGAGE market, in which holders of mortgages who need funds can dispose of their holdings before maturity, is, however, uniquely a secondary market. (⇛⇛ OVER-THE-COUNTER MARKET).

Secondary reserves. ASSETS of COMMERCIAL BANKS that are not quite as *liquid* as PRIMARY RESERVES but provide considerable protection against an unexpected withdrawal of DEPOSITS. (⇛⇛ REQUIRED RESERVES).

Second best, theory of. An area of economics concerned with the analysis of situations in which PERFECT COMPETITION does not prevail throughout the economy, or, for some reason, the state of the economy that would result from a perfectly competitive EQUILIBRIUM cannot be achieved by the market system. The most important proposition of the theory is that, if some part of the economy does not attain the perfectly competitive equilibrium position—e.g., because of MONOPOLY—it need not be optimal for any other sector of the economy to attain that position. Rather, optimality may require that the other sectors of the economy adopt positions that diverge from the perfectly competitive one. This apparently rather abstract proposition, first advanced by R.G. Lipsey and K. Lancaster, has, in fact, very important implications for such subjects as the pricing of NATIONALIZED INDUSTRY outputs and OPTIMUM tariff (⇛ TARIFFS, IMPORT) policies in INTERNATIONAL TRADE. For example, it may imply that nationalized industries should not adopt MARGINAL-COST PRICING, or that FREE TRADE is not an optimum policy.

Secured bonds. ⇛ BOND

Securities. 1. In the widest sense, documents giving title to property or claims on INCOME that may be lodged, e.g., as security for a BANK LOAN. 2. Income-yielding paper traded on the STOCK EXCHANGE or in SECONDARY MARKETS. A synonym for STOCKS and BONDS. An essential characteristic of a security is that it is saleable. The main types of security are (*a*) *fixed-interest:* BONDS of various kinds, PREFERRED STOCK; (*b*) *variable-interest;* ordinary SHARES; (*c*) other: NOTES, INSURANCE policies. Securities may be redeemable (⇛ REDEEMABLE SECURITIES) or irredeemable. (⇛ IRREDEEMABLE SECURITY; SECURITIES AND EXCHANGE COMMISSION).

Securities and Exchange Commission (SEC). A regulatory agency of the U.S. government charged with the supervision of the federal securities laws. The SEC was created in 1934. The Securities Act of 1933 requires registration with the SEC of most securities offered for sale to the public. PLACINGS and issues that are offered and purchased within only one state are exempt. The Securities Exchange Act of 1934 regulates exchanges and dealers and, among other provisions, requires companies whose securities are listed and traded on a national securities exchange to file regular registration statements with detailed information about their financial position and operations (the 10-K Report). The 1934 Act also requires the registration of BROKERS and dealers who trade in the OVER-THE-COUNTER MARKET. The Public Utility Holding Company Act of 1935 is another Act administered by the SEC.

Self-financing. CAPITAL generated from INCOME. A firm that is self-financing is generating its INVESTMENT funds from internal sources, i.e., the plowing back of retained PROFITS and DEPRECIATION, as opposed to external borrowing. (⇛⇛ BUSINESS FINANCE).

Self-financing ratio. INVESTMENT funds derived from undistributed INCOME as a proportion of total investment funds in any accounting period. (⇛⇛ SELF-FINANCING).

Self-liquidating. A low-risk financial transaction or LOAN that incorporates a procedure for the simultaneous termination and clearing of indebtedness. An INSTALLMENT CREDIT transaction is self-liquidating, in that regular payments culminate in a final installment that clears the DEBT. More generally, the term is applied to any form of financing to fill a temporary shortfall of funds, such as bank credit lines provided to customers in the process of selling one home and buying another or to commercial customers on an acceptance basis.

Senior, Nassau William (1790–1864). Educated at Oxford University, England, Senior was called to the bar in 1819 and became a master in chancery in 1836. In 1825 he was appointed the first Drummond Professor of Political Economy at Oxford. He held this position twice, the first time until 1830 and the second from 1847 to 1852. He served on many royal commissions. His major work on economics was an *Outline of the Science of Political Economy,* which appeared in 1836. He is remembered mainly for his abstinence theory of interest. Interest was a reward for abstaining from the unproductive use of SAVINGS. The creation of new capital involved a sacrifice. A positive return must therefore be expected to make the sacrifice worthwhile. Senior can be regarded as one of the first pure theorists in economics. He attempted to elaborate economic theory on the basis of deductions from elementary propositions. (⇛ INTEREST, ABSTINENCE THEORY OF).

Separation of ownership from control. The situation where the owners of a corporation do not actively participate in its management. In its earliest form, business was owned and managed by the same people. Economic and technological development led to the advent of the JOINT-STOCK COMPANY in the 17th century to meet the need for larger amounts of CAPITAL. This began the process of the separation of ownership from control that continued with the introduction of LIMITED LIABILITY for both public companies and private companies, and the gradual emergence of the modern giant corporation, in which none of the directors or managers have more than a minority financial interest. This process has given rise to the possibility that the interests of those who control the business and those who own it may conflict, a subject of continuing controversy among economists since the publication of *The Modern Corporation and Private Property* by A. A. Berle and G. C. Means in 1932. (⇛⇛ FIRM, THEORY OF; GALBRAITH, JOHN KENNETH).

Serial correlation. ⇛ AUTO-CORRELATION

Serra, Antonio (15? –16?). A Neapolitan writer in the mercantilist tradition (⇛ MERCANTILISM), who was the first to analyze and fully use the concept of the BALANCE OF TRADE, both visible and INVISIBLE. He explained how the shortage of precious metals in the Neapolitan kingdom was a result of a deficit in the BALANCE OF PAYMENTS. In so doing, he rejected the idea, current at the time, that the SCARCITY of money was due to the unfavorable EXCHANGE RATE. The solution was to be found in the encouragement of EXPORTS.

Services. Those types of COMMODITIES that are intangible and do not take concrete physical form. For example, an accountant who prepares your tax return, a barber who cuts your hair, or a bank clerk who cashes your check is "producing" a service rather than a tangible physical commodity like automobiles or bread. In economic analysis, however, no significance is attached to the distinction between goods and services: the same approach is adopted to each.

Shadow price. 1. In general terms, a PRICE that is imputed as the true marginal value of a good or opportunity COST of a resource and that may differ from the MARKET price. For example, it is often argued that if a certain type of labor being used to produce a particular good would, if not producing that good, be otherwise unemployed, then society foregoes no alternative output by keeping it employed; its opportunity cost is zero (ignoring the value of the workers' leisure time foregone), and so a shadow price of zero should be imputed to it. Its actual market price, on the other hand, may be whatever wage rate the relevant labor union can secure for it by using its bargaining power. Hence, the market price exceeds the shadow price. To take a converse example: A number of firms located around a lake may dispose of their effluent by discharging it into the lake, using the "services" of the lake as a waste-disposal unit. The lake is being used as a free good, since the firms do not have to pay for its services, and the market price is therefore zero. However, suppose that it is desired, on grounds of SOCIAL COST, to restrict the extent of lake pollution. Corresponding to a specified degree of pollution will be a price that, if charged to the firms, would lead them to choose a rate of effluent discharge that pollutes the lake to that degree and no more. This price is then the shadow price of the lake's service as an industrial waste-disposal unit. If controls are imposed on the physical quantity of pollution, the market price continues to be zero. The idea of the shadow price, however, suggests an alternative solution: If the firms were actually charged the shadow price, then they would adjust to this, and the desired standards would again be met. There are often arguments made for using a pricing mechanism, rather than quantitative controls, in cases of this sort, on grounds of simplicity, flexibility and lower costs of administration and enforcement. These two examples suggest the importance of the shadow price concept in COST-BENEFIT ANALYSIS and applications of WELFARE ECONOMICS generally.

2. Specifically, in mathematical programming problems—e.g., LINEAR PROGRAMMING—a solution, if it exists, will always have associated with it a set of so-called dual variables, which are often called "shadow prices." For example, suppose the problem is to choose outputs of three goods, given the per-unit PROFIT on each good, in such a way that total profit is maximized. Each good requires specified amounts of labor time, machine time and raw material per unit produced. There are fixed total amounts of labor time and machine time available, and so no set of outputs can be produced with total labor and machine time requirements in excess of these. By methods of mathematical programming, three output levels can be found that can be produced and that yield at least as much profit as any other output levels that could be produced. The solution will also produce money values, one for labor time and one for machine time, that measure the gain in total profit that would result if the fixed quantity of the corresponding resource were increased very slightly. These money values are the *shadow prices* of the

resources. They can play an important role in planning. For example, if additional machine time can be leased at a price below the shadow price of machine time, then the firm will increase its profit by doing so. Similarly, if another branch of the firm wished to divert a small amount of labor away from production of these three products, it could be "charged" a price equal to the shadow price of labor time, since this is the loss of profit caused by such a diversion.

The concept of a shadow price originated in the development of mathematical programming methods, and its extension to more general usage is closely associated with the recognition that all problems of RESOURCE ALLOCATION are essentially mathematical programming problems.

Share. One of a number of equal portions in the CAPITAL of a business entitling the owner to a proportion of distributed PROFITS and of residual VALUE if the company goes into LIQUIDATION. A synonym for STOCK.

Shareholder. The owner of SHARES. A synonym for STOCKHOLDER.

Shareholders' interest. ⇛ BALANCE SHEET

Sherman Antitrust Act. The Sherman Price Fixing and Monopolies Act of 1890 was the first legislation designed to control the market power of large firms. The Act made it illegal to set up a MONOPOLY or to carry out any activities in restraint of trade. The Act is enforced through the Justice Department. (⇛⇛ ANTITRUST POLICY; BANK HOLDING COMPANY ACT; CLAYTON ACT; TRUST).

Short run. A time period within which a firm is not able to vary all its FACTORS OF PRODUCTION. There will, in fact, be several "short runs," of varying lengths, corresponding to the particular possibilities that the firm has of varying particular INPUTS. For example, in the very short run—say, one week—the firm may not be able to change the amounts of any of the inputs it uses. Over a month, however, it may be able to expand its LABOR force and increase the flow of raw materials. Over a year, it may be able to increase all its inputs, except perhaps certain types of machinery, which may take two years to obtain and install. However, the firm may itself have it within its power to shorten the short run by incurring higher costs. For example, the firm could rent the machinery, at a premium, and so obtain it in less than two years; or the firm may pay more to shorten the delivery time. This means that what is the short run to a firm is as much an economic as a technological question. More generally, the term *short run* may be applied to any time period not long enough to allow the full effects of some changes to have operated. (⇛⇛ HUME, DAVID; LONG RUN; MARSHALL, ALFRED).

Short-run cost curves. Curves showing the relationship between SHORT RUN total, AVERAGE and MARGINAL COSTS, on the one hand, and output on the other. They are a useful analytical tool in the theory of the firm. (⇛ FIRM, THEORY OF).

Simon, Herbert A. (1916–). In 1978 Simon was awarded the Nobel Prize in Economics for his contributions to mathematics, organization behavior, computer science and economics. Following a doctorate in political science at the University of Chicago, he went to the Bureau of Public Information at the University of California. He then moved, in 1949, to Carnegie Mellon as professor of computer science and psychology.

Early in his career, Simon challenged the view that the corporation was a profit-maximizing, rational entity. He argued that decision making was based on limited information, making it necessary to plan for the short term and/or to restrict analysis to one activity. In his book *Administrative Behavior* (1947), Simon argued that the corporation is an adaptive system, seeking satisfactory alternatives to a series of problems. Corporations were therefore directed to "SATISFICING" behavior, not strict profit maximization. His other publications include *The New Science of Management Decision* (1960) and *Models of Thought* (1977). (⇛ FIRM, THEORY OF).

Simple random sample. A RANDOM SAMPLE in which each item in the POPULATION has an equal chance of being included in the sample. Suppose the population to be sampled consists of 12 students, and we wish to find, by taking a sample of 3 students, the average annual expenditure on books. If we want to take a simple random sample, we could number the students from 1 to 12, write each number on a separate piece of paper, put them into a bag and draw out three pieces. The numbers on them would then identify the 3 students for our sample. Each piece of paper has the same chance of being selected; any other procedure that has the property of giving the items in the population an equal chance of being included would be suitable, and choice of a procedure depends on its cost and convenience. A simple random sample shares the general properties of random samples in being independent of human judgment, and therefore of the biases this might impart, and in permitting the size of the likely error in generalizing from sample to population to be estimated. However, there may well be situations in which, although we wish to retain the properties of the random sample, we do not want each item in the population to have the same chance of being selected—we may wish to have consistently more of one type of item than another in our sample. This then requires a STRATIFIED SAMPLE.

Simulation. The use of a MODEL of some activity or process to examine the way it works and to solve problems associated with it. The model may be a physical construction; e.g., the stresses to which an airplane design may be subject can be examined by simulating its flight by means of a scale model in a wind tunnel. More generally, however, a mathematical model of the system concerned will be constructed and a computer used to reproduce the essential workings of the system. In this latter sense, simulation has come to play a very important role in OPERATIONS RESEARCH. The reason for its use is, of course, that it is generally much cheaper to construct a model, physical or mathematical, than to operate the process itself. (⇛⇛ MONTE CARLO METHOD).

Sinking fund. ⇛ AMORTIZATION

Sismondi, Jean Charles Leonard Simonde de (1773–1842). A Swiss historian and economist, who after a period in exile in England, began lecturing at Geneva Academy in 1809 on history and economics. His economic works include *Richesse commerciale* (1803), *Nouveaux principes d'economie poli-*

tique (1819) and *Etudes sur l'economie politique* (1837). Sismondi argued against the doctrine of LAISSEZ-FAIRE in favor of state intervention. He recommended UNEMPLOYMENT and sickness benefits, and pension plans for workers. Along with THOMAS ROBERT MALTHUS, he attacked DAVID RICARDO for not recognizing the possibility of economic crisis developing from underconsumption. He tried to emphasize the dynamic nature of the economic process, compared with the comparative statics of Ricardo (⇛ COMPARATIVE STATIC EQUILIBRIUM ANALYSIS), and was the first to use sequence analysis as an analytical device. Increased output in one period, he argued, is faced with a level of INCOME generated by a lower level of output in the previous period. Total demand falls short of the available supply. Lags in the economic system, therefore, could give rise to underconsumption.

Size distribution of firms. A description of the size pattern of firms in an industry or economy. It is constructed, first, by choosing some suitable measurement of size (total sales, number employed, NET ASSETS, etc.) and then by establishing size classes, e.g.:

Number employed: less than 10
11– 20
21– 50
51–100
and so on

Then, the number of firms falling within each size class is calculated, and these numbers are tabulated against the size classes. This then gives the size distribution of firms. (⇛⇛ CONCENTRATION RATIO; FREQUENCY DISTRIBUTION).

Slump. ⇛ DEPRESSION

Slutsky, Eugen (1880–1948). In 1918 he was appointed a professor at Kiev University, where he remained until 1926. In 1934 he accepted a post at the Mathematics Institute of the Academy of Sciences of the USSR, where he remained until his death. He published an article in the Italian journal *Giornale degle Economiste* in 1915 on consumer behavior. In this article he showed how the concept of ORDINAL UTILITY could be used to build a theory of consumer behavior of the same scope as that of ALFRED MARSHALL but without the underlying assumption of the measurability of UTILITY. However, the article lay unnoticed until SIR JOHN RICHARD HICKS and SIR ROY GEORGE DOUGLAS ALLEN rediscovered it in 1934. In his book *Value and Capital,* Hicks applied Slutsky's name to the mathematical formulas that illustrate how a consumer would react to PRICE and INCOME changes (⇛ PARETO, VILFREDO FEDERICO DAMASO). Slutsky did little further work in economic theory but made important contributions to statistics and PROBABILITY theory that are of relevance to economics. He emphasized the danger of assuming causes for observed fluctuations in TIME SERIES by showing how regular cycles could be generated in the derivation of MOVING AVERAGES from a series, even though the latter was made up of random (⇛ RANDOM SAMPLE) numbers. He also made important advances in the study of serial CORRELATION.

Small business. A firm that is managed in a personalized way by its owners or part owners, has only a small share of its market and is not sufficiently large to have access to the STOCK EXCHANGE in raising CAPITAL. The Small Business Act (1953) defines a small business as one that is independently owned and operated and that is not dominant in its field of operation. For administrative purposes (such as determining eligibility for SMALL BUSINESS ADMINISTRATION loans), the SBA sets industry-specific limits in terms of employment and dollar sales volume. These limits are higher in industries with a relatively high CONCENTRATION RATIO and lower in fragmented industries where the promotion of freedom of entry is unnecessary (⇛ BARRIERS TO ENTRY). In the automobile industry, for example, the SBA defines a small firm as one with less than 2,500 employees, while in refrigerated warehousing the limit is set at 25 employees. There are well over 10 million small businesses in the United States, but statistics on small firms are very unreliable, partly because of the high mortality rate of new businesses. Most small businesses (about 90 percent) are single PROPRIETORSHIPS and PARTNERSHIPS, but the vast majority of the 1 million business corporations are also small. In U.S. manufacturing, establishments employing less than 250 people accounted for 43 percent of total manufacturing employment in 1972. (⇛ ESTABLISHMENT; EXPORT TRADING COMPANY).

Small Business Administration (SBA). An independent agency of the U.S. government that advises and assists SMALL BUSINESS. Its origins can be traced to the Reconstruction and Finance Corporation, founded in 1932 and ended in 1953 when the SBA was created, and the Smaller War Plants Corporation. The authorizing legislation for the SBA, the Small Business Act (1953), states that "The preservation and expansion of . . . competition is basic not only to the economic well-being but to the security of this Nation. Such security and well-being cannot be realized unless the actual and potential capacity of small business is encouraged and developed." The activities of the SBA include: (1) vetting proposed legislation and exerting pressure for change if small business interests are threatened; (2) taking measures to increase the share of small business in public procurement; (3) making loans directly and in participation with the COMMERCIAL BANKS; (4) guaranteeing loans made by banks and other financial institutions. (⇛ CREDIT GUARANTEES). Of the $3.2-billion total of SBA regular business loans made in 1979, 86 percent were commercial bank loans guaranteed by the agency; (5) licensing, regulating and helping to finance the SMALL BUSINESS INVESTMENT COMPANIES; (6) providing information and consultancy services, partly through the use of the Service Corps of Retired Business Executives (SCORE) working out of local SBA offices; (7) providing aid to victims of floods and other disasters. The management of the SBA is vested in the administrator, who is appointed from civilian life by the President with the advice and consent of the Senate. In 1976 an Office of Advocacy was established in the SBA. The chief counsel for advocacy (also appointed by the President with the approval of the Senate) serves as a focal point for the receipt of complaints and suggestions about government policies as they affect small business and advises small firms on their relations with the federal government. The United States is the only country with an independent agency to look after the interests of small business. In Canada similar functions are carried out by the Small Business Secretariat in the Department of Industry and Commerce.

Small Business Development Corporations (SBDCs). ⇛ SMALL BUSINESS INVESTMENT COMPANIES

Small Business Investment Companies (SBICs). Privately owned companies licensed by the SMALL BUSINESS ADMINISTRATION to provide equity and long-term loans to SMALL BUSINESS. The SBICs enjoy favorable tax treatment, and stockholders are allowed to deduct losses on the sale of SBIC stock from taxable income. The SBICs are eligible for long-term loans from the Federal Financing Bank at rates of only ⅛ percent to 1 percent above the cost of the funds to the TREASURY. These loans are guaranteed by the SBA. SBICs in the United States were established by the Small Business Investment Act of 1958 with the object of increasing investment, particularly EQUITY investment, in small business by both individuals and financial institutions. There are now some 250 active SBICs in the United States, a major proportion of them subsidiaries of large corporations and financial institutions. They made 2,257 financings for $280.1 million in 1979. Similar institutions have been authorized by three provincial governments in Canada, where they are called *Small Business Development Corporations.* SBDCs do not receive favorable tax treatment (although they are exempt from capital tax), but individuals purchasing stock in an SBDC get an immediate cash grant of 30 percent of the amount invested; corporations receive a credit against provincial corporation tax.

Smith, Adam (1723–90). A Scotsman, brought up by his mother at Kirkcaldy, he became a student under Francis Hutcheson at Glasgow University at the age of 14 and won a scholarship to Oxford, England, where he spent six years until 1746. He lectured at Edinburgh University from 1748 to 1751. From 1751 until 1763 he was at Glasgow, first in the Chair of Logic and a year later the Chair of Moral Philosophy, which he took over from Hutcheson. From 1764 to 1766 he toured France as the tutor to the Duke of Buccleugh. His major work on economics, *An Inquiry into the Nature and Causes of the Wealth of Nations,* appeared in 1776. This work of Adam Smith's became the foundation upon which was constructed the whole subsequent tradition of English CLASSICAL ECONOMICS, which can be traced from DAVID RICARDO through ALFRED MARSHALL to ARTHUR CECIL PIGOU. Smith was primarily concerned with the factors that led to increased WEALTH in a community, and he rejected the PHYSIOCRATS' view of the preeminent position of agriculture, recognizing the parallel contribution of the manufacturing industry. He began his analysis by means of a sketch of a primitive society of hunters. If it cost twice the labor to kill a beaver as it does a deer, one beaver would exchange for two deer. Labor was the fundamental measure of VALUE, though actual PRICES of COMMODITIES were determined by SUPPLY and DEMAND on the MARKET (⇛ MARX,

KARL). There were two elements in the problem of increasing WEALTH: (*a*) the skill of the labor force and (*b*) the proportion of productive to unproductive labor. (According to Smith, the SERVICE industries did not contribute to real wealth.) The key to (*a*) was the DIVISION OF LABOR. To illustrate his point, he quoted the example of the manufacture of pins. If one man were set the task of carrying out all the operations of pin manufacture—drawing the wire, cutting, head fitting and sharpening—his output would be minimal. If, however, each man specialized in a single operation only, output would be increased a hundredfold. The size of the output need only be limited by the size of its market. The key to (*b*) was the accumulation of CAPITAL. Not only did this enable plant and machinery to be created to assist labor, but it also enabled labor to be employed. Capital for the latter was the wages fund (⇛ WAGE FUND THEORY). The workers must be fed and clothed during the period of production in advance of the INCOME earned from their own efforts. Smith believed that the economic system was harmonious and required the minimum of government interference (⇛ LAISSEZ-FAIRE). Although each individual was motivated by self-interest, they each acted for the good of the whole, guided by a "hidden hand" (⇛ INVISIBLE HAND) made possible by the free play of competition (⇛ MANDEVILLE, BERNARD DE). Free competition was the essential ingredient of the efficient economy. However, from his *Wealth of Nations,* it is clear that not only did his scholarship range widely over the fields of history and contemporary business, but that, at the same time, he was a very practical man. He was quite aware, for instance, of the forces that were at work to limit competition: "People of the same trade seldom meet together even for merriment and diversion, but the conversation ends in a conspiracy against the public, or on some contrivance to raise prices" (Book 1, Chapter 10, Part 2). In his discussions of PUBLIC FINANCE, he laid down four principles of TAXATION, namely (*a*) equality (taxes proportionate to ability to pay), (*b*) certainty, (*c*) convenience and (*d*) economy. (⇛⇛ HUME, DAVID).

Smithsonian Agreement. An agreement concluded in December 1971 between the "Group of Ten" of the INTERNATIONAL MONETARY FUND at the Smithsonian Institution, Washington. Under the agreement, the major currencies were restored to fixed parities but with a wider margin, ± 2.25 percent of permitted fluctuation around their par values. The dollar was effectively devalued by about 8 percent and the dollar price of gold increased to $38 per ounce. (⇛⇛ EXCHANGE RATE; WILLIAMS COMMISSION).

Smithsonian parities. ⇛ SMITHSONIAN AGREEMENT

Social accounting. The presentation of the NATIONAL INCOME and expenditure accounts in a form showing the transactions during a given period between the different sectors of the economy. The tabulations are set out in the form of a MATRIX showing the source of INPUTS of each sector or part of a sector and the distribution of their outputs. The production sector, for instance, shows for an industry how much of its inputs were bought from other home industries; how much it imported; and how much it spent on wages, salaries and DIVIDENDS. At the same time, it shows how much of its output it sold to other industries, how much it exported and how much was consumed by private individuals or the government sector. These transactions of the producers' sector are counterbalanced by corresponding transactions of the other sectors. For instance, the personal sector shows the value and sources of INCOMES earned from the producers' sector and others, and the way these incomes are spent on the outputs of the various industries or on IMPORTS or are saved. (⇛⇛ INPUT-OUTPUT ANALYSIS; LEONTIEF, WASSILY W).

Social benefits. A term sometimes used in two senses: (1) all the gains in welfare that flow from a particular economic decision, whether or not they accrue to the individual or institution making the decision—i.e., the total improvement in welfare of the society as a whole, *including* the decision maker. (2) Those gains that accrue not to the individual or agency making the decision but to the rest of society. In this sense, social benefits are equivalent to beneficial EXTERNALITIES or "spillover" effects. The first sense is the more widely used.

Social capital. The total stock of CAPITAL possessed by the economy as a whole. This includes not only the buildings, machinery, etc., that are used in producing marketable outputs but also those that are engaged in producing goods and services that are not marketed, e.g., schools, roads, defense equipment, etc.

Social cost. COSTS of some activity or output that are borne by society as a whole, not restricted to the costs borne by the individual or firm carrying out that activity or producing that output. Social costs therefore consist of the opportunity costs of RESOURCES used, together with the value of any loss in welfare or increase in costs that the activity causes to any other individual or firm. The social cost of an automobile trip exceeds the private cost by the amount of the increase in costs to other drivers caused by an increase in congestion and the cost of maintaining the road facilities (which are not reflected in the cost of an additional journey to any one road user). The social cost of building a factory in an area of high UNEMPLOYMENT is less than the private cost to the extent that workers are employed who would otherwise be unemployed and therefore have zero opportunity costs. The idea of social cost is closely related to the idea of EXTERNALITIES: If the social opportunity costs of resources are correctly reflected in their MARKET prices, then they will be reflected in private costs, and individual decisions will be socially optimal. (⇛⇛ PIGOU, ARTHUR CECIL; SHADOW PRICE).

Social net product. The difference between the SOCIAL BENEFIT and the SOCIAL COST arising from the use of some FACTOR OF PRODUCTION or from some form of economic activity.

Social welfare function. This term has been used in economics in two senses:

1. As defined by A. Bergson and PAUL ANTHONY SAMUELSON, it is a mathematical relationship that associates a number with any allocation of COMMODITIES among consumers. The relationship will reflect some particular set of VALUE JUDGMENTS concerning the well-being of different consumers, and underlying it is a preference ordering (⇛ INDIFFERENCE

ANALYSIS) over alternative allocations. The higher a particular allocation is in the ordering, the higher the number it will be assigned by the social welfare function. Different sets of value judgments will, of course, imply different social welfare functions in this sense. The concept of the social welfare function was proposed to enable economists to conduct analysis of the desirability of particular RESOURCE ALLOCATIONS in as objective a way as possible. Before "desirability" can be discussed, it is necessary to have a set of value judgments to define what should be regarded as good or bad. By expressing these in terms of a social welfare function, the economist can examine the consequences of different kinds of value judgments without himself being committed to any of them. This is then likely to be a more open and healthy analytical procedure than one by which an economist begins with a commitment to one specific set of value judgments and makes policy prescriptions accordingly. Economists should then stand ready to analyze the implications of *anybody's* value judgments, by representing them as a social welfare function.

2. In a fundamental analysis of the *possibility of the existence* of a social welfare function of the Bergson-Samuelson type just described, or rather, more generally of the preference ordering over resource allocations that underlies it, KENNETH J. ARROW in fact introduced a *second* meaning of the term. Arrow defined a social welfare function as a *set of procedures* for devising a social preference ordering, given the preference orderings possessed by the individuals in society. Arrow's concept of a social welfare function is therefore akin to a "constitution," i.e., a set of rules for transforming the opinions and desires of the members of a social group into concrete choices made from the alternatives that confront that group. The degree of abstraction with which Arrow pursued his analysis was such that his conclusions are applicable to all social groups, from the executive board of a large corporation to the U.S. government or the Security Council of the United Nations, and to all types of constitution, from simple majority voting to complex voting schemes. Arrow posed the following question: Suppose we require of our constitution that it possess certain general properties—e.g., that it should be responsive to the wishes of every member of the group, but no member of the group should play the role of dictator; that if everyone in the group prefers alternative A to B, then A should exceed B in the social ranking; and a number of other technical properties. Then, is it possible to design a constitution with these properties that will produce a complete, consistent ranking of the alternative social states? Arrow's famous IMPOSSIBILITY THEOREM shows that no such constitution is possible. It is in this sense that Arrow proved the impossibility of a social welfare function. An entire area of research has developed from this fundamental contribution, and most attention has been directed at the reasonableness of the properties that must be possessed by the constitution. On further analysis, some are less reasonable than might at first be supposed, and a weakening of the requirements can reverse the impossibility result. The area has become a fruitful field for mathematical logicians.

Bergson's and Arrow's concepts of the social welfare function are related, in that Arrow's social welfare function is the process by which Bergson's social welfare function would be generated. Thus, Arrow's analysis could be viewed as more fundamental than, and logically prior to, that of Bergson. However, it has been argued that Arrow's work is of more significance for political theory than for economics, since in the economic analysis of public policy, economists are concerned with the nature of the given social welfare function in Bergson's sense rather than with the properties of the political process that brings it about. (⇛⇛ PARADOX OF VOTING).

Soft currency. A CURRENCY whose EXCHANGE RATE is tending to fall because of persistent BALANCE OF PAYMENTS deficits or because of the building up of speculative selling of the currency in expectation of a change in its exchange rate. Governments are unwilling to hold a soft currency in their foreign-exchange reserves. (⇛ GOLD AND FOREIGN EXCHANGE RESERVES).

Soft loan. A LOAN bearing either no RATE OF INTEREST or an interest rate that is below the cost of the CAPITAL lent. It is the policy of the INTERNATIONAL BANK FOR RECONSTRUCTION AND DEVELOPMENT, working through its affiliate, the INTERNATIONAL DEVELOPMENT ASSOCIATION, to give "soft" loans to DEVELOPING COUNTRIES for long-term capital projects.

Special drawing rights (SDRs). The instruments for financing international trade in the postwar period were predominantly the RESERVE CURRENCIES and gold. Dependence on the latter, as JOHN MAYNARD KEYNES pointed out, is an anachronism that had been successfully terminated as far as domestic economies were concerned. The problem of depending on the former was that the supply of these currencies was regulated by their countries' BALANCE OF PAYMENTS deficits or surpluses. The deficit on the U.S. balance of payments had been an important source of the flow of LIQUIDITY into CENTRAL BANK reserves. The difficulty was that persistent deficits led to doubts about the maintenance of the currency's EXCHANGE RATE and made central banks less willing to hold dollars. In the mid-1960s, indeed, it was the declared policy of France to sell dollars for gold. This problem came to a head in August 1971, when the U.S. government imposed various measures to correct its balance of payments deficit. In December 1971 the dollar was devalued by about 10 percent. The "Group of Ten" (⇛ INTERNATIONAL MONETARY FUND) countries agreed that discussions should be held to review the whole problem of international liquidity. J.M. Keynes had put forward the idea of an international currency, to be called BANCOR, regulated by a central institution (⇛ KEYNES PLAN). This idea was turned down then for fear that the creation of liquidity would generate INFLATION. The "Group of Ten" agreed to establish SDRs, which are similar in principle to Keynes' original idea, and their agreement was ratified by the IMF. The SDR was linked to gold and equivalent to $1 (U.S.) at the gold rate of exchange of $35 per ounce. Until December 1971 an SDR was equivalent to $1, but with the effective devaluation of the dollar following the SMITHSONIAN AGREEMENT, the rate became 1 SDR = $1.08571. With the subsequent breakdown of the fixed parity system, the IMF valued the SDR in terms of a "basket" of 16 currencies, so that, from July 1974, the rate in relation to the dollar "floated." At the beginning of 1976, the rate was 1 SDR = $1.17183. At the beginning of 1970, a total of SDR 3.414 billion were distributed. The allocation agreed upon for the period 1979 through 1981 amounted to SDR 12 billion. These sums are distributed to each member country in proportion to its IMF quota. The total holding of SDRs in 1980 was SDR 16.25 billion, of which the United States held SDR 2.946 billion. In 1981 the SDR was simplified to a weighted AVERAGE of U.S. dollars (42 percent), German deutsche marks (19 percent), French francs, Japanese yen and U.K. sterling (13 percent each). The SDR has slowly become more acceptable, and now commercial BANKS accept SDR-denominated deposits.

Specialization. ⇛ DIVISION OF LABOR

Specie points. The limits between which the EXCHANGE RATE between two CURRENCIES on the GOLD STANDARD fluctuated. For instance, before 1916–1918 the same amount of gold could be bought in London, England, for £1 and in New York for $4.87, and therefore the par rate of exchange was £1 for $4.87. If the pound fetched less than $4.87 in London, it would pay a merchant to ship gold to the United States to settle his DEBTS, provided the cost of freight and INSURANCE were less than the difference between the par rate and the London rate. Therefore, in practice the rate never fell by an amount more than the cost of shipment. Similar forces applied in reverse to prevent the rate from rising by an amount in excess of the cost of shipment.

Speculation. Buying and selling with a view to buying and selling at a PROFIT later when PRICES have changed. (⇛⇛ ARBITRAGE; BEAR; BULL).

Speculative motive. A motive for holding MONEY that arises from the possibility that the money value of other forms of WEALTH may change. Suppose an individual can hold his wealth either in BONDS or in money. If he expects the PRICE of bonds to fall in the future, he will wish to switch from bonds to money—i.e., he will sell his bonds. This is because a fall in the price of bonds involves him in a loss of wealth. On the other hand, if he expects the price of bonds to rise, he will reduce his holdings of money and buy bonds. Since his desire to hold money is therefore related to his EXPECTATIONS of the variations in value of other ASSETS and the way in which he can take advantage of them, this part of the individual's money holdings is said to be determined by the speculative motive. (⇛⇛ KEYNES, JOHN MAYNARD; LIQUIDITY PREFERENCE; PRECAUTIONARY MOTIVE).

Spot market. A MARKET in which goods or SECURITIES are traded for immediate delivery, as distinct from a FORWARD MARKET. "Spot" in this context means "immediately effective," so that *spot price* is the price for immediate delivery.

Spot price. ⇛ SPOT MARKET

Stability analysis. An analysis of the behavior of the VARIABLES of an economic system when it is out of EQUILIBRIUM, concerned specifically with the question of whether they will tend to converge toward, or diverge from, their equilibrium values over time. For example, the COBWEB THEOREM analyzes the time path of price and output in an agricultural market and establishes conditions under which price oscillations will diminish through time as price converges to its equilibrium. Clearly, since time must enter explicitly, stability analysis forms an important part of ECONOMIC DYNAMICS.

Stabilization policy. The name given to the measures that governments take to reduce the amplitude of cyclical fluctuations. Left to themselves, FREE-MARKET capitalist economies tend to exhibit over time cyclical fluctuations in NATIONAL INCOME and employment. The determinants of the timing and amplitude of these fluctuations are analyzed in that part of economics known as the theory of the TRADE CYCLE. Thus, as the economy approaches the "peak" of a cycle, there is rapid wage and price INFLATION, IMPORTS rise relative to EXPORTS, and BALANCE OF PAYMENTS deficits occur. On the other hand, in the "trough" of a cycle, UNEMPLOYMENT is undesirably high, particularly in certain regions that typically have unemployment rates much higher than the national average. Hence, the aim of stabilization policy is to restrain the economy when it is nearing the peak of the cycle and to stimulate the economy when it approaches the trough.

The principal instruments of stabilization policy are MONETARY POLICY and FISCAL POLICY, and the policy is facilitated by the existence of BUILT-IN STABILIZERS. Stabilization policy is not so straightforward and simple as its description might suggest. Not only are there limitations arising out of the bluntness of the instruments available, but the imperfections in the information available to the managers of the economy also create serious difficulties. These imperfections may interact with certain time lags that exist within the system, so that stabilization policy may actually be destabilizing. Thus, we could divide the overall time period that elapses between the time an event requiring correction occurs and the time a corrective measure takes effect into three phases: (*a*) the time between occurrence of the event and recognition that corrective action is required (this depends, among other things, on the time lags in information flow); (*b*) the time between recognition of the need for action and actually taking action (which depends on the speed with which the policy-making processes work, the administrative arrangements for putting policy into effect, etc.); and (*c*) the time between the action and the impact of that action on the VARIABLES under consideration (which depends on the time lags in the institutional and behavioral relationships in the economy). Given the existence of these time lags, it is generally pointless to take action to correct something that is currently happening. Rather, current events must be used to predict future events, and then the policy measures must be designed to influence these. But this, of course, involves the difficulty that the future can never be predicted completely accurately. But, even worse than this, the knowledge of the present is based on estimates of national income magnitudes—CONSUMPTION, INVESTMENT exports, imports, etc.—and since these estimates are known to contain (sometimes considerable) errors, knowledge of the present is also extremely imperfect. Thus, predictions about an uncertain future have to be made on the basis of an incompletely known present. The costs of inappropriate policies may be high. Suppose, for example, that measures designed to restrain "overheating" in the economy come into effect just as the economy is past the peak and beginning to turn down. The measures will then accelerate the downturn and cause INCOME and employment to fall farther and faster than they might otherwise have done. It is considerations such as this that make stabilization policy more of an art than a science at the present time.

In the United States, considerable faith was placed in short-run stabilization following the Kennedy-Johnson tax cuts of the early 1960s. By the mid- to late 1970s, however, such an approach was not as enthusiastically received, as both inflation and unemployment persisted in the face of an increasing federal deficit. (⇛ ECONOMIC STABILIZATION ACT).

Stagflation. A situation in which rapid inflation is accompanied by stagnating or declining output and employment. It is a characteristic of COST-PUSH INFLATION rather than DEMAND-PULL INFLATION. Companies experience increased costs of raw materials and/or of labor, which reduce their profitability and force them to raise their own prices and cut investment. The government is then faced with the dilemma that measures to reduce the rate of inflation generated in this way may exacerbate unemployment. (⇛ PRICES AND INCOMES POLICY).

Standard and Poor's Index. A daily index of the STOCK price of 500 U.S. corporations. The prices used are based on the closing value of transactions in stocks that traded that particular day. (⇛⇛ DOW-JONES).

Standard deviation. A statistical measure of the extent to which a set of numbers are dispersed about their arithmetic mean (⇛ AVERAGE). It is the square root of the VARIANCE. An advantage of the standard deviation is that, whereas the variance will be measured in terms of the square of the units of measurement of the original set of numbers, the standard deviation is measured in terms of the original units. The variance of a baseball batter's scores over a season would be in units of "runs squared," while the standard deviation will be in runs. Clearly, the latter is easier to interpret in everyday terms. The formula for the standard deviation is:

$$\text{Standard deviation} = \sigma = \sqrt{\frac{1}{n}\sum_{i=1}^{n}(x_i - \bar{x})^2}$$

where x_i is the ith number, and $\bar{x}$ is the arithmetic mean. Everything said regarding the relation between the variance and the degree of dispersion of numbers about their mean also applies to the standard deviation.

Standard rate. ⇛ INCOME TAX

Statement of operations. ⇛ INCOME STATEMENT

Static equilibrium. An EQUILIBRIUM that, once achieved, does not change over time. The values of the VARIABLES at that equilibrium position continue to hold for all time. This is in contrast to a *dynamic* equilibrium such as BALANCED GROWTH, in which the values of the variables are changing systematically over time.

Statistical inference. That branch of statistics which is concerned with making general statements about a group, or "POPULATION," of items, on the basis of imperfect information about that group. For example, we may be interested in trying to know in advance who will win the next presidential election. By taking a RANDOM SAMPLE of voters, we may obtain information on voting intentions, but this information is imperfect, since it does not describe with certainty what all the voters will in fact do. Nevertheless, it is possible to generalize about the population on the basis of the sample. The techniques of statistical inference are primarily concerned with the question of the degree of confidence that can be placed on the generalizations and the margins of error that may be involved. In this, they rely heavily on methods of PROBABILITY theory It is rarely possible, especially in economics, to obtain perfect information about the group of things under study, yet it is desired to examine relationships, test hypotheses and make measurements for the group as a whole, and so techniques of statistical inference have become extremely important.

Steady-state growth. A state in which the rates of growth of the VARIABLES in an economic system remain constant over time. Take, for example, an economy consisting simply of firms and HOUSEHOLDS (no government, no foreign trade), where firms receive consumers' expenditure in return for goods and pay this back to households in return for productive SERVICES; households spend part of what firms pay them on CONSUMPTION expenditure and save the rest; and firms spend on new INVESTMENT exactly the same amount as households save. If, now, NATIONAL INCOME, consumption expenditures, SAVING and investment expenditures were all growing at, say, 5 percent per annum, every year without change, then we would say that the economy was in steady-state growth. It need not be the case that the growth rates of the variables are all equal (although theory tells us that in this simple example they would be), but the growth rate of each variable must be constant through time for steady-state growth to exist. The steady-state solution is generally the starting point in the analysis of most models of economic growth. It therefore fulfills much the same role as the concept of EQUILIBRIUM in static theory; as a useful theoretical abstraction that may hardly ever be realized in practice.

Sticky prices. Refers to situations where, in the presence of a reduction in demand, prices do not, at least in the short run, decline. Price rigidity can occur if firms find it more profitable to reduce their work force in the face of lower demand than to cut prices to stimulate demand.

Stochastic. Probabilistic or random. Thus, a VARIABLE is called a "stochastic variable" if it is capable of taking one of a number of alternative values, each with a stated probability. For example, if you bet \$10 that a coin will land heads, then your income from the gamble is a stochastic variable: +\$10 or −\$10, each with a probability of one-half. Likewise, a "stochastic process" is a time path of some variable, each step in which depends upon chance. For example, if you stand at a telephone pole, toss a coin to decide whether to take two steps forward or one step back, move, toss the coin again, and repeat after each move, then your progress (or lack of it) from the pole is determined by a stochastic process.

Stock. 1. A SHARE in the ownership of a corporation. 2. The amount of a COMMODITY, MONEY or CAPITAL in existence at any point in time, at a defined location. 3. Synonym for inventory.

Stockbroker. A member of the STOCK EXCHANGE who buys and sells STOCKS on his own account or for nonmembers in return for a COMMISSION on the PRICE of the SHARES. (⇛⇛ BROKER).

Stock dividend. ⇛ SCRIP ISSUE

Stock exchange. A MARKET in which SECURITIES are bought and sold. The economic importance of stock exchanges is that they facilitate SAVING and INVESTMENT, first by making it possible for investors to dispose of securities quickly if they wish to do so and, second, by channeling savings into productive investment. However, they are declining in importance as a source of new capital for industrial and commercial corporations. Ready marketability requires that new issues (⇛ NEW ISSUE MARKET) be made or backed by reputable borrowers or institutions, that information be available on existing securities, and that there should be both a legal framework and market rules to prevent fraud and sharp practice. Stock exchanges have their own rules and conventions, in addition to the normal laws of the land, but their functioning depends also on the existence of company and other legal and FINANCIAL INTERMEDIARIES. The largest of several stock exchanges in the United States is the New York Stock Exchange, often referred to as Wall Street. The New York and other stock exchanges are supervised by the SECURITIES AND EXCHANGE COMMISSION. The Federal Reserve System regulates stock MARGINS. There are two major stock exchanges in Canada: the Montreal and the Toronto exchanges.

Stockholder. ⇛ SHAREHOLDER

Stockholders' equity. The claims of the owners to the assets of a corporation. (⇛⇛ BALANCE SHEET; EQUITY).

Stock options. ⇛ OPTION

Stock right. An offer of new SHARES to existing shareholders. A company will offer the "rights" in a certain proportion to existing holdings, depending upon the amount of new EQUITY capital it wishes to raise. Thus, stockholders may be offered "one for one," i.e., the right to purchase one new share for every one held. To ensure that the issue is taken up, the new shares are offered at well below the market price of the existing shares. The choice of the DISCOUNT below the ruling price is not as critical in normal circumstances as is often supposed, because when the rights issue is announced, the market price of the shares will adjust to the market's view of the value of the rights price. If the price of existing shares falls, because, for example, it is thought that the new money will be used on projects that are less profitable than existing ones, then there will be a dilution of market values. The stock right will have a value where it remains below the price of existing shares and can be sold in the STOCK EXCHANGE. A date is typically designated after which the stock is traded free of rights, or *ex-rights.* Where it is traded with rights before that date, it is referred to as *cum-rights,* or with rights. Rights issues are a relatively cheap way of raising CAPITAL for a listed company, since most of the costs of a new issue, including UNDERWRITING commission and press advertising, are avoided. (⇛ NEW ISSUE MARKET).

Stock split. An issue of new SHARES to stockholders without increasing total CAPITAL. The object of a stock split is to reduce the average quoted price of shares to promote their marketability.

Stop-go. Refers to rapid changes in the direction of STABILIZATION POLICY. Advocates of MONETARISM charge that such approaches to short-run economic policy do more harm than good because, in part, of the lengthy lags required for the economy to adjust to new directions of policy.

Strategic stockpiling. An arrangement whereby a government makes large purchases of certain raw materials, such as copper or tin, that it does not produce itself. This is done to ensure that in the event of a war a nonproducer will have sufficient supplies of the raw material for military purposes at least.

Strategy. 1. In general terms, a general set of principles that will determine specific actions and decisions and that are designed to achieve certain long-run goals. Thus, a business strategy might be to build up—through specific advertising campaigns, product design and pricing policy—a reputation for good quality at a low price in order to achieve a dominant MARKET position.

2. More specifically, the term is used in the theory of games (⇛ GAMES, THEORY OF) to denote an entire sequence of specific actions or decisions that completely determine the way an individual will play the game. The player could give his chosen strategy to an independent umpire—or to a computer—and leave the actual playing of the game to him—or to it. To take chess as an example: A strategy would select an opening move (if the player has white) and then would specify a move in response to each possible first move of his opponent, then a move for each possible second move of the opponent, and so on for the entire game. A strategy could then be an extremely complex thing—in fact, no one has yet succeeded in writing out one strategy for chess, let alone defining *all possible* strategies. It must be assumed that in the kinds of games with which game theory is most concerned—in economics, politics, diplomacy, etc.—the possible strategies are far less complex. A strategy is the basic object of choice in game theory: A decision maker is assumed to choose a strategy in the light of its consequences, which will also depend on the strategy choices made by the other players(s).

Stratified sample. A type of RANDOM SAMPLE that is designed by first classifying the overall population into subgroups or strata according to some principle and then taking a SIMPLE RANDOM SAMPLE within each stratum. Its purpose is to ensure that the sample is, in fact, representative of the various groups that make up the POPULATION, a property that a simple random sample need by no means possess. For example, in order to design a sample to estimate the expenditure by families on house RENTS, we might divide the total population into broad income groups, decide on the sample size appropriate for each group and then choose the families in each group according to the same procedure as would be used for a simple random sample. If this stratification were not done, the sample chosen might, by chance, contain an overrepresentative figure for one income group and an underrepresentative figure for another, and thus the estimate of AVERAGE expenditure on rent per HOUSEHOLD would be biased upward or downward, as the case may be. In designing a stratified sample, we need some information about the population before the sample is carried out. This information is then used to increase the representativeness of the sample. The stratified sample is still a random sample, since each item in the population has a known chance of being selected. The basis of the stratification, or the "stratification factor," is chosen so as to be relevant to the problem at hand. As well as increasing the representativeness, and therefore the accuracy, of the sample, stratification may also be used because it is of interest to see how the results differ between the strata—e.g., how rent expenditures vary between income groups.

Structural inflation. A theory of inflation based on the notion of resource immobility or limited mobility. A decline in economic activity in some sectors does not lead to lower prices, and resources do not move quickly enough to expanding sectors; thus, prices in the latter rise rapidly. Consequently, there is a general rise in the price level.

Structural unemployment. UNEMPLOYMENT that is due to basic changes in the structure of the economy, that is to say, changes in technology or tastes that cause major changes in the pattern of demand for goods and services. Given such a change in the pattern of DEMAND, it will take time for labor to retrain and relocate so as to shift from industries and occupations in which labor demand has fallen to those in which it has risen. As a result, while the process of reallocation is taking place, there will be unemployment. (⇛⇛ U-V CURVE).

Subsidiaries. Companies legally controlled by other companies. The controlling, or parent, company may have acquired the subsidiary in a MERGER or may have set it up for a specific purpose. Risky ventures distinct from the mainstream business can be conveniently administered in a separate limited company (⇛ LIMITED LIABILITY). Although a share holding of less than 50 percent may be sufficient to control a company effectively, it is not correctly described as a subsidiary unless between 50 percent and 100 percent of the SHARES are owned by another. Companies may choose to retain subsidiaries rather than integrate them fully into their own organizations not only because of risk but for other reasons—e.g., the desire to allow local participation, a wish to conceal the business connection or to avoid the cost and complication of integrating an acquired company. (⇛⇛ CONGLOMERATE).

Subsidy. A payment by a government agency to producers of goods, intended to make PRICES lower than they otherwise would be. The payment will also in general have the effect of raising the INCOME of the recipients above the level it would otherwise have reached and of increasing the REAL INCOMES of the buyers of the subsidized products. The main purpose of a subsidy may be the achievement of any one or more of these effects.

Substitutes. Two goods are substitutes if a rise in the price of one causes an increase in DEMAND for the other. This substitute relationship arises because the goods perform a similar function or serve a similar taste. However, we can generally think of a whole spectrum of substitution possibilities for a particular good, and so we often refer to "close" substitutes or "weak" substitutes. For example, a Pepsi would be a close substitute for a Coke, but a Martini would not. The closer are the available substitutes for a product, the greater, other things being equal, will be its price ELASTICITY of demand.

Substitution effect. The change in the quantity of a good a consumer demands as a result *only* of a change in its PRICE relative to prices of other goods, the consumer's REAL INCOME OR UTILITY level being held constant. Suppose the price of coffee falls. We then expect two kinds of effect on the consumer's DEMAND for coffee. First, coffee is now cheaper relative to its substitutes—tea, orange juice, milk, etc.—and so we would expect the consumer to drink a little more coffee and a little less of its substitutes. Second, the consumer's real income has gone up—his fixed money income can buy more because coffee is cheaper, and so he is better off as a result. This increased real income will result in increased demands for at least some goods, and coffee (as well, possibly, as some of its substitutes) may be one of these. The price fall has therefore affected the demand for coffee in two ways, and it is of interest to separate out these two effects. We could imagine that, when the coffee price falls, we could make an equivalent reduction in the consumer's *money* income so as to cancel out completely the effect of the price fall on his *real* income (⇛ REAL TERMS)—he is left just as well off as he was before. We could then observe the change in his demand that results solely from the change in coffee's relative price, and this change is called the substitution effect of the price fall. Economic theory predicts that this substitution effect is always unambiguous—more will be demanded following a relative price fall, less following a price rise. On the other hand, the *overall* change in demand resulting from both the substitution effect and the effect of increased real income (the INCOME EFFECT) *is* ambiguous: In general, a consumer's demand for coffee is predicted to increase, decrease or stay the same following a price fall! The reason is that the increase in real income could work *with* the substitution effect, therefore causing an overall increase in demand; or it could work *against* the substitution effect, possibly causing an overall decrease in demand. The latter case can only happen if the good is an INFERIOR GOOD, and if it should indeed occur, the good concerned is called a GIFFEN GOOD. The purpose of the analysis of income and substitution effects is to allow economists to say more than the rather empty statement that after a price change anything can happen. In fact, for all except strongly inferior goods, we can be confident that a price fall will cause an increase in the quantity demanded of a good, and so DEMAND CURVES can safely be drawn sloping downward from left to right.

"Sunspot" theory. ⇛ JEVONS, WILLIAM STANLEY

Supplementary costs. A now little-used synonym for FIXED COSTS.

Supply. The flow onto a MARKET of a good or service (⇛ ECONOMIC GOOD) that is available to meet DEMAND. For example, the supply of gasoline is the amount of gasoline that sellers are prepared or wish to sell over some specified time period, e.g., a week. It should be emphasized that "supply" refers to the quantity of a good sellers wish, plan or seek to sell rather than the amount *actually* sold, which may well be different if the market is not in EQUILIBRIUM. An important determinant of the supply of any good is its PRICE. In general, we would expect that the higher the price, the greater the supply. Other important determinants would be costs of production, taxes or subsidies. The general importance of the *concept* of supply is that it refers to one set of forces that jointly determine the market price and quantity traded, the other, of course, being those forces grouped under the heading "demand." (⇛⇛ MARSHALL, ALFRED).

Supply curve. A curve showing the relationship between the PRICE of a good and its SUPPLY. It is usually drawn as in the diagram, embodying the HYPOTHESIS that the higher the price, the greater the supply.

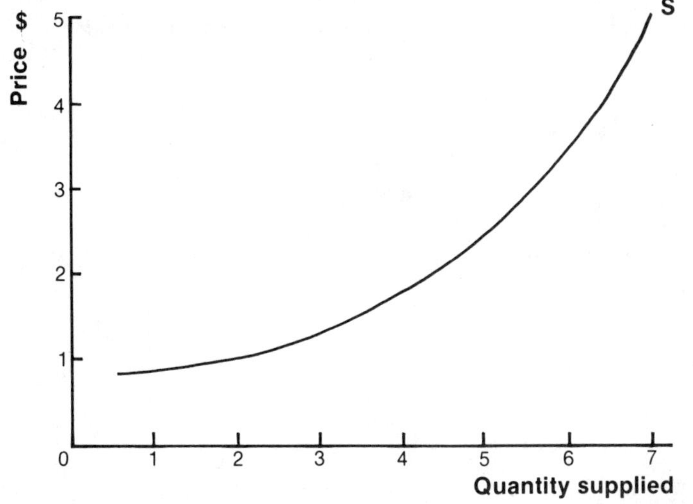

The *steepness* of the curve reflects the extent to which producers of the good respond to an increase in price by increasing supply. It will depend on the expansion of output that it is *profitable* to make given a price increase, and thus it depends on the underlying costs of production. The *position* of the curve will change if there is a change in the underlying costs of production; for example, if prices of FACTORS OF PRODUCTION change, the technology of production changes, or if factors of production that previously were available to the firm in a fixed quantity become capable of being varied in quantity. The analysis of the underlying determinants of the supply curve is the major purpose of the theory of the firm. (⇛ FIRM, THEORY OF).

Supply-side economics. A term popularized in the late 1970s that emphasizes the importance of the AGGREGATE SUPPLY in determining prices and employment. Supply-side price shocks refer to events and/or circumstances that cause the price level to rise in the absence of increases in AGGREGATE DEMAND. A series of supply-side shocks, such as OPEC (⇛ ORGANIZATION OF PETROLEUM EXPORTING COUNTRIES), food shortages, reduced PRODUCTIVITY and lower INVESTMENT, are blamed for much of the STAGFLATION in the 1970s. The emphasis on supply-side economics has led to a set of policy proposals quite different from the Keynesian (⇛ KEYNES, JOHN MAYNARD) prescriptions. SAVING is to be encouraged to permit investment to take place at a higher rate; taxes should be lowered to encourage work effort and risk taking; and welfare should be adjusted to encourage labor mobility.

Surplus value. ⇛ MARX, KARL

T

"Tableau Economique." The table by which FRANCOIS QUESNAY analyzed the circulation of WEALTH in the economy by setting out the different classes of society. The table showed how the *"produit net"* produced by the agricultural sector circulated between the owners of the LAND, the tenant farmers and other classes, such as artisans and merchants. Only agriculture produced any net additions to wealth; all other activities were "sterile." The table showed, too, how output is annually reproduced. The sterile classes were essential in that they created the necessary demand for the agricultural sector. (⇛⇛ CANTILLON, RICHARD; LEONTIEF, WASSILY W.; PHYSIOCRATS).

Taft-Hartley Act. An Act of the U.S. Congress in 1948 that defined unfair labor practices, severely limited the CLOSED SHOP and subjected pending strikes in certain areas of the economy to an 80-day cooling-off period. It encouraged states to pass right-to-work laws. The Act was precipitated by the wave of strikes in 1946–47 and widespread jurisdictional disputes between the AFL and CIO.

Takeover. The acquisition of one company by another. Takeovers are sometimes financed by paying CASH at an offer PRICE in excess of the MARKET price of the SHARES, but more frequently for large acquisitions, they are financed by the exchange of STOCK, possibly with some cash adjustment, issued by the acquiring company for the shares of the acquired company. The term *takeover* is often used to imply that the acquisition is made on the initiative of the acquirer and without the full agreement of the acquired company, as distinct from a MERGER.

Tariffs, import. Taxes imposed on commodity IMPORTS. They may be levied on an *ad valorem* basis, i.e., as a certain percentage of VALUE; or on a specific basis, i.e., as an amount per unit. Their purpose may be solely for raising revenue, in which case the home-produced product corresponding to the import would bear an equivalent compensatory tax. However, import duties are generally applied for the purpose of carrying out a particular economic policy and in this context may be used to serve many functions:

1. To reduce the overall level of imports by making them more expensive relative to their home-produced SUBSTITUTES, with the aim of eliminating a BALANCE OF PAYMENTS deficit (⇛⇛ DEVALUATION).

2. To counter the practice of DUMPING by raising the import price of the dumped commodity to its economic level.

3. To retaliate against restrictive measures imposed by other countries (⇛ RECIPROCITY).

4. To protect a new industry until it is sufficiently well established to compete with the more developed industries of other countries (⇛ INFANT INDUSTRY ARGUMENT).

5. To protect "key" industries, such as agriculture, without which the economy would be vulnerable in time of war.

Tariffs may be either preferential or nondiscriminatory. For instance, with respect to members compared with nonmembers of the EUROPEAN FREE TRADE ASSOCIATION and the EUROPEAN ECONOMIC COMMUNITY, tariffs are preferential. However, it was an accepted principle, under the MOST FAVORED NATION CLAUSE of the GENERAL AGREEMENT ON TARIFFS AND TRADE, that tariffs should be nondiscriminating, and any concessions agreed upon between two or more countries should automatically be extended to all. It has, however, been accepted that this principle may be waived in the interests of the DEVELOPING COUNTRIES. Through the GATT significant progress has been made in the reduction of tariff levels by means of a series of negotiations, of which the TOKYO ROUND OF TRADE NEGOTIATIONS was the latest.

Tatonnement process. The process by which PRICES are adjusted in the Walrasian model of GENERAL EQUILIBRIUM (⇛ WALRAS, MARIE ESPRIT LEON). It underlies the analysis of the stability of EQUILIBRIUM in this model. Thus, suppose initially the prices prevailing on the MARKETS in the model are not equilibrium prices, so that demand exceeds SUPPLY in at least one market, and supply exceeds demand in at least one other market. Then prices will tend to change in response to this DISEQUILIBRIUM, and we are interested in whether these changes will lead the system back to equilibrium or not. This will depend in part on the precise process by which the price adjustments are made, and the tatonnement process is one possible specification of this. It is assumed there is a single market coordinator who announces a set of prices and then collects from each buyer or seller information on the amount demanded or supplied at those prices. He is then able to determine the overall balance of supply and demand in each market. If demand does not equal supply in every market, he then changes the price in each market according to the following rules:

1. Raise price in a market where demand exceeds supply.
2. Lower price in a market where supply exceeds demand.
3. Leave price unchanged in a market where demand and supply are equal.

Where price *is* changed, the size of the increase or decrease in price is proportional to the gap between demand and supply, so that the greater the disequilibrium in a market, the bigger the price change. Having changed prices in this way, the coordinator again collects information on demands and supplies at these prices, computes the balance of supply and demand in each market and proceeds as before. Only when demand equals supply in each market does he call a halt to the process. The corresponding prices are the equilibrium prices, and so he allows trade to take place at those prices. Note that no actual buying or selling takes place until the equilibrium is reached; throughout the adjustment process buyers and sellers simply communicate their desired transactions to the coordinator. In this economy actual trade only takes place at equilibrium prices.

This process is clearly a very idealized picture of how market adjustments work. Nevertheless, it is not in itself sufficient to guarantee stability:

It is possible to construct examples in which the adjustment process never actually reaches an equilibrium. Further assumptions have to be made about the economic system, concerning in particular the nature of the CROSS-ELASTICITIES OF DEMAND among goods, in order to guarantee that the system will be stable.

Two of the least desirable aspects of the tatonnement process (the idea of a "market coordinator" is simply a convenient fiction) are, first, that no trading takes place out of equilibrium and, second, that buyers and sellers are always fully informed about the (single) market price. Recent research in economics has taken important steps in relaxing these assumptions. Models have been analyzed in which trading takes place at disequilibrium prices and in which buyers have to search to find information on prices, and in equilibrium different sellers may sell at different prices. These models have particular relevance to LABOR economics, and the microeconomic (⇛ MICROECONOMICS) foundations of MACROECONOMICS.

Taussig, Frank William (1859–1940). Apart from a period from 1917 to 1919 when he was chairman of the U.S. Tariffs Commission, Taussig spent his whole career at Harvard University. His works on economics include *Tariff History of the United States* (1888); *Wages and Capital* (1896); a textbook, *Principles of Economics* (1911); and *International Trade* (1927). An economist in the tradition of DAVID RICARDO and ALFRED MARSHALL, Taussig attempted to relate his theory to established statistical data.

Tax. ⇛ TAXATION

Taxable income. The PROFIT of a corporation or the income of an individual upon which government taxes are levied. Taxable income may not be the same as income reported in the annual financial statement. (⇛ INCOME STATEMENT).

Tax, ad valorem. An indirect tax (⇛ TAXATION) that is expressed as a proportion of the PRICE of a good—hence, it is "by value."

Taxation. A compulsory transfer of MONEY (or occasionally of goods and SERVICES) from private individuals, institutions or groups to the government. It may be levied upon WEALTH, INCOME or CAPITAL GAINS, or in the form of a surcharge on PRICES or the quantity of a good sold. In the first case, it would then be called a direct tax (⇛ DIRECT TAXATION); in the latter, an indirect tax. Taxation is one of the principal means by which a government finances its expenditure. The total tax bill in the United States amounted to 30.7 percent of the NATIONAL INCOME in 1980. This compares with an AVERAGE of 36.4 percent for all the members of the ORGANIZATION FOR ECONOMIC COOPERATION AND DEVELOPMENT. (⇛⇛ CORPORATION INCOME TAX; INCOME TAX; PUBLIC GOODS; SALES TAX; SMITH, ADAM; UNIT TAX).

Tax avoidance. Arranging one's financial affairs within the law so as to minimize taxation LIABILITIES, as opposed to *tax evasion,* which is failing to meet actual tax liabilities through, for example, not declaring INCOME or PROFIT.

Tax base. The object to which the tax (⇛ TAXATION) rate is to be applied, e.g., INCOME, WEALTH, the PRICE of a good.

Tax-based incomes policy (TIP). The idea of a TIP was made popular by Henry Wallich and Sidney Weintraub in 1972. A TIP imposes a tax at very high rates on wage and/or profit increases beyond government-announced guidelines. It is believed by the advocates of a TIP that such taxation would encourage firms and unions not to go beyond the guidelines. In contrast to a PRICES AND INCOMES POLICY, the TIP relies on incentives to secure certain wage and price objectives. Critics have argued that unless the tax penalties are 100 percent, there is always a net gain to be reaped for going beyond the guidelines. That, combined with the myriad administrative problems involved, has to date deterred the use of a TIP. A TIP would also frustrate the working of the PRICE SYSTEM in allocating resources.

Tax burden. The amount of MONEY that an individual, institution or group must pay in tax (⇛ TAXATION). It should include all costs to the taxpayer that he incurs in paying the tax, e.g., the net of tax cost of employing an accountant to complete a tax form.

Tax evasion. ⇛ TAX AVOIDANCE

Tax expenditures. Provisions in the tax laws that give preferential treatment to certain individuals or businesses by way of tax exemptions, deductions, lower rates of tax or tax credits. The idea behind tax expenditures is to provide an incentive to certain behavior, such as saving for retirement, investment in specific industries or the encouragement of work effort. A tax expenditure reduces government revenue as opposed to direct spending in the same area. The United States has published a tax expenditure summary since 1969, and it became law to do so in 1974. (⇛ TAXATION).

Tax-push inflation. Indirect tax increases may be inflationary, to the extent that they are shifted forward onto prices, which in turn raise wages. Similarly, if workers are largely concerned about after-tax wage rates, higher personal income taxes may contribute to wage INFLATION by stimulating demands for higher gross wage rates. (⇛ COST-PUSH INFLATION).

Tax, Single. ⇛ GEORGE, HENRY

Tax, turnover. ⇛ TURNOVER TAX

10-K Report. ⇛ SECURITIES AND EXCHANGE COMMISSION

Term loan. A bank advance for a specific period repaid, with interest (⇛ RATE OF INTEREST), usually by regular periodical payments. Term loans are common practice in the commercial banking system for business finance, and for larger borrowings the LOAN may be syndicated—i.e., the provision of funds and the interest earned are shared between several banks. In principle, term loans are intended to finance investment projects that generate CASH FLOWS to pay interest and amortize the loan and used to be secured on the assets purchased with the loan. Increasingly, term loans are made on an unsecured basis to large corporations. Loan agreements are complicated documents giving the lender powers to monitor the loan and providing for interest-free periods that may be for 2 to 10, or even up to 15, years. Since the early 1970s, interest rates (⇛ RATE OF INTEREST) have been variable, though originally they were fixed for the period of the loan.

Terms of trade. The ratio of the index (⇛ INDEXATION) of EXPORT prices to the index of IMPORT prices. An improvement in the terms of trade follows if export prices rise more quickly than import prices (or fall more slowly than import prices). However, the United States suffered a sharp fall in its terms of trade following the increase in oil prices in 1973. In 1974 export prices were about 30 percent above the 1973 level, but import prices rose by 50 percent. By the end of the decade, export prices had risen by over 90 percent, but this rise fell considerably short of the 160 percent rise in import prices.

Third-party effects. ⇛ EXTERNALITIES

Third World. ⇛ DEVELOPING COUNTRIES

Thornton, William Thomas (1813–80). ⇛ WAGE FUND THEORY

Thrifts. A general term covering nonbank institutions such as SAVINGS AND LOAN ASSOCIATIONS, CREDIT UNIONS and MUTUAL SAVINGS BANKS. Like banks, they receive DEPOSITS and make LOANS. They originated in the 19th century to serve the needs of households and small savers and borrowers. (⇛ BANKING).

Thunen, Johann Heinrich von (1783–1850). A member of the land-owning Prussian class of *junkers,* after completing his education at agricultural college, he attended the University of Gottingen. For the remainder of his life, he farmed his estate at Mecklenburg. The first volume of his work *Der isolierte Staat in Beziehung auf Landwirtschaft und Nationalökonomie* was published in 1826, and part 1 of volume 2 in 1850. The rest of volume 2 and volume 3 appeared in 1863. He used his farm as a source of facts for his theoretical work in agricultural economics. He built a theoretical MODEL that he used to find the important factors that determined the most profitable location of various branches of agriculture in relation to their sources of DEMAND. In so doing, he devised a theory of RENT similar to that of DAVID RICARDO. He set out a theory of distribution (⇛ DISTRIBUTION, THEORY OF) based on marginal productivity, using calculus, which was considerably ahead of his own time, and he could be considered one of the founders of MARGINAL ANALYSIS. (⇛⇛ LOCATION THEORY).

Tight money. MONEY is said to be "tight" when SUPPLY is low relative to DEMAND, so that INTEREST RATES tend to be high and rising. A policy of tight money may be deliberately pursued by the monetary authorities (⇛ FEDERAL RESERVE SYSTEM) in order to reduce the rate of INFLATION.

Time deposit. A time deposit account earns a higher interest (⇛ RATE OF INTEREST) than a demand DEPOSIT, but checks cannot be drawn on such an account. In some instances, the holder of the account must give the bank prior notice of his intention to withdraw money from a time deposit account. (⇛ NOW ACCOUNTS).

Time preference. A person's preference for current as opposed to future CONSUMPTION. Suppose we asked an individual the following question: "If you were to give me $1.00 today, in exchange for a promise to pay you a sum of money in one year's time, what would that sum of money have to be to compensate you for the loss of the current consumption?" We stipulate that the sum of money is certain to be paid and that there is no INFLATION. We mean by the word *compensate* that we wish to leave the individual feeling just as well off as if he hadn't given up the \$1.00—no more and no less. Then his answer will tell us the degree of his time preference. If, for example, our individual replied "\$1.25," then he is showing a preference for current as opposed to future consumption: \$1.00 now is worth more than \$1.00 in the future, and in fact it is worth 25 percent more, since he requires \$0.25 more than the amount he is giving up to leave him feeling just as well off. On the other hand, if he had answered "\$1.00," then he clearly is indifferent between consuming now or in the future, since he feels equally well off by consuming \$1.00 in the future as \$1.00 now. Finally, if he had said "\$0.75," then he is showing a preference for future as opposed to current consumption, since \$0.75 worth of consumption in one year's time is worth as much to him as \$1.00 of consumption now. We can make this idea more precise by defining the "rate of time preference," which is a kind of subjective RATE OF INTEREST. Let us take the two numbers in our time preference experiment, namely the \$1.00 given up now and the sum required to be paid in compensation. Taking the ratio of the latter to the former in each example given above, we can write:

A. $\frac{\$1.25}{\$1.00} = (1 + 0.25)$

B. $\frac{\$1.00}{\$1.00} = 1$

C. $\frac{\$0.75}{\$1.00} = (1 - 0.25)$

We now define in these three examples the consumer's rate of time preference as the number, in the form of an interest rate, that expresses the individual's relative evaluation of future and current consumption. In the first case, the individual required to be paid 25 percent more than he gave up to compensate him for postponing consumption. In the second case, nothing extra had to be paid. In the third case, 25 percent less had to be paid. So 25 percent, 0 and −25 percent, respectively, are the rates of time preference in the three cases. Clearly, the larger the value of this subjective interest rate, the more highly is current consumption valued relative to future consumption.

An individual's rate of time preference will depend to a large extent on his tastes and personality, which in turn could depend, *inter alia,* on his age and social situation. In addition, it will depend on the total amount of INCOME he currently has and the amount he expects in the future. One might expect, for example, that an individual who anticipated that his income would double in the near future would have a high rate of time preference—a dollar's worth of consumption now is more valuable to him than it will be later; conversely, if he anticipates a falling income, then he will tend to have a low or even a negative rate of time preference—consumption later will have a high value relative to consumption now. Generally, we can say that the higher is current relative to future income, the lower will be the rate of time preference, while the lower is current relative to future income, the higher will be the rate of time preference. Note also that although, in the example used above, a time period of one year was chosen, a rate of time preference can be defined for any time period.

The concept of time preference plays an important part in the theories of CAPITAL, of SAVING and hence of the RATE OF INTEREST. The nature of its role can be suggested by the following propositions: An individual will postpone consumption and lend on the CAPITAL MARKET as long as the rate of interest exceeds his rate of time preference. If his rate of time preference increases as the quantity lent increases, then his total saving is determined by equality between the rate of interest and his rate of time preference. If firms invest up to the point at which the RATE OF RETURN on INVESTMENT is equal to the rate of interest, then, in EQUILIBRIUM, the rate of time preference will equal the rate of return on investment. (⇛ FISHER, IRVING).

Time series. The values taken by some VARIABLE over several consecutive periods of time. (⇛ CROSS-SECTION ANALYSIS).

Tobin, James (1918–). The winner of the 1981 Nobel Prize in Economics, Tobin was educated at Harvard, receiving his Ph.D. in 1947. He taught at Yale from 1950 to 1961, including six years with the Cowles Commission. In 1961 he became a member of the Council of Economic Advisors. He returned in 1962 to Yale, where he is currently Sterling Professor of Economics.

One of Tobin's major contributions was his rigorous formulation of just what constitutes an asset and of the role that money plays within a range of household assets. The publication of "Liquidity Preference as Behavior Towards Risk" (*Review of Economic Studies,* 1958) by Tobin set the stage for a new approach to the analysis of portfolio choice. The paper postulates that there exists a spectrum of assets with YIELD and RISK moving together. Households, desiring both high yield and low risk, must make a trade-off in deciding upon their portfolio of assets. In recent years Tobin has been regarded as a leading exponent of the Keynesian school (⇛ KEYNES, JOHN MAYNARD) of macroeconomists in the United States and a critic of MONETARISM (⇛ FRIEDMAN, MILTON).

Other publications include *Financial Markets and Economic Activity* (1967), *Essays in Economics* (1971) and *Asset Accumulation and Economic Activity* (1980).

Tokyo Round of Trade Negotiations. Agreement was reached in Tokyo in 1973 to initiate a seventh round of trade negotiations under the auspices of the GENERAL AGREEMENT ON TARIFFS AND TRADE. These negotiations began in 1974, after the passing in the United States of the TRADE ACT, which gave the President powers to negotiate. The negotiations were concluded at the end of 1979. Agreement was reached on the following:

1. The major developed countries agreed to reduce their tariffs (⇛ TARIFFS, IMPORT) by, on the average, one-third over a period ending on January 1, 1987.

2. A new code of conduct has been drawn up covering customs valuation procedures, barriers caused by technical specifications, import licenses and government procurement policies. For instance, the American Selling Price system has been abolished. Under this system the United States revalued imports of chemicals to the higher level of that charged by U.S. domestic producers and then calculated the import duty on this higher figure.

3. A new code has also been agreed upon on the application of COUNTERVAILING DUTIES. These duties may only be applied when it can be demonstrated that material injury is being caused to the domestic producers of a commodity because of the importation of that commodity from a subsidized overseas source.

Trade accounts payable. TRADE CREDIT

Trade Act (1974). This Act gave the president of the United States wide powers enabling him to negotiate effectively in the multilateral discussions of the seventh round of negotiations for the liberalization of INTERNATIONAL TRADE under the GENERAL AGREEMENT ON TARIFFS AND TRADE known as the TOKYO ROUND OF TRADE NEGOTIATIONS. These powers were limited to a five-year period ending in January 1980. The Act also enabled workers, under certain conditions, to be given financial assistance and job retraining, if they had been made redundant and their jobs displaced by IMPORTS. (⇛ DEVELOPING COUNTRY).

Trade barrier. A general term covering any government limitation on the free international exchange of merchandise. These barriers may take the form of tariffs (⇛ TARIFFS, IMPORT), QUOTAS, IMPORT DEPOSITS, restrictions on the issue of IMPORT LICENSES or stringent regulations relating to health or safety standards. (⇛⇛ PROTECTION).

Trade credit. Mainly short-term CREDIT extended by one business to another in the course of normal business operations—for example, in accepting a delay in payment for goods or services rendered. Trade credit is an important source of finance, comparable with bank credit, and at the same time, it does not come under the direct control of the authorities as does the latter. In accounting, short-term credit obligations are known as "*trade accounts payable*" or "*accounts payable*" and are reported on the BALANCE SHEET under current LIABILITIES. (⇛⇛ FACTORING).

Trade cycle. Regular oscillations in the level of business activity over a period of years. In the postwar years the trade cycle has been controlled to the point where absolute downward movements in the level of output have been infrequent in the Western industrial economies. The trade cycle has, in consequence, been replaced by the recession (⇛ DEPRESSION), in which temporary pauses in the advance of total output occur and are followed by a resumption of growth.

Considerable attention has been given to the trade cycle phenomenon by economists, culminating in the work of PAUL ANTHONY SAMUELSON, SIR JOHN RICHARD HICKS, R. M. Goodwin, ALBAN WILLIAM HOUSEGO PHILLIPS and M. Kalecki in the late 1940s and the 1950s. Most explanations of the existence and nature of the cycle are based on the determinants of business investment and its effects, through the MULTIPLIER process, on the level of NATIONAL INCOME. The accelerator theory of investment (⇛ ACCELERATION PRINCIPLE), in conjunction with the multiplier, can be used to show that the adjustment of the level of investment to the rate of change of sales gives rise to cyclical fluctuations in national income. (⇛⇛ ACCELERATOR-MULTIPLIER MODEL; INCOME DETERMINATION, THEORY OF; STABILIZATION POLICY).

Trade discount. The percentage below the published retail PRICE at which a manufacturer sells to his distributors (wholesale or retail) or at which a wholesaler sells his goods to a retailer. In addition, further discounts are sometimes given on a scale related to the quantities of goods taken. (⇛⇛ ROBINSON-PATMAN ACT).

Trade Expansion Act (1962). ⇛ KENNEDY ROUND OF TRADE NEGOTIATIONS

Trade restrictions. ⇛ IMPORT RESTRICTIONS; TRADE BARRIER

Trading stamps. Coupons given by a retailer to a customer according to the VALUE of goods purchased. The trading-stamp firm sells the stamps to the retailer and redeems them by exchanging them for goods or CASH when presented by the retailer's customer. The trading-stamp firm makes a PROFIT from selling the stamps to the retailer at a price greater than their value and from the fact that not all of its stamps are redeemed. The retailer benefits insofar as he would lose business if his rival gives stamps. The customer benefits only insofar as he likes collecting stamps, the financial benefit being generally small, and being in any case a cumbersome method of getting a TRADE DISCOUNT.

Transactions demand for money. That component of the overall DEMAND for MONEY which is due to the need to finance the buying of goods and services. According to the original form of the QUANTITY THEORY OF MONEY, the demand for money was essentially for transactions purposes and was, in the aggregate, simply proportional to the level of real national income (⇛ NATIONAL INCOME; REAL INCOME). The factor of proportionality depended on certain institutional and structural features of the economy that determine the rate at which money circulates through the economy to finance transactions. For example, suppose you receive a salary of $1,000 on the last day of each month and choose to spend this in equal daily amounts to finance your transactions over the following month. Then, *on the average,* over the month your desired money holding for transactions purposes is $500. If now your salary increased to $2,000, and you continued to spend it all in the same way, then your transactions demand for money—the average money holding over the month—would also double to $1,000, increasing proportionately with your desired expenditure. To see how all this depends on the precise way in which payments are made, suppose your $2,000 salary is now paid in weekly installments of $500, all of which is spent in equal daily amounts over the following week. Then your average money holding over the week is $250, and since this is the same from week to week, this is also the average money holding per month. Thus, increasing the frequency of salary payments, everything else remaining the same, reduces the transactions demand for money. Finally, suppose that it becomes possible to pay for *all* your transactions at precisely the same time as you receive your salary. Then, in either of the above examples, your transactions demand for money falls to zero! You simply do not need to carry a money balance. This suggests why the advent of credit cards tends, other things being equal, to reduce the demand for money.

In the foregoing discussion, the relation between the transactions demand for money and income was taken to be determined by "institutional" factors. However, as JAMES TOBIN and William J. Baumol showed, we would in general expect this demand also to be sensitive to the RATE OF INTEREST, which is the COST of holding money. Suppose again that you are paid monthly. It would surely seem a good idea to put your salary into interest-bearing ASSETS as soon as you get it and then gradually resell those assets as you require the money to make transactions. The problem here is that this will involve costs—brokerage fees, time costs, etc.— and so will only be worthwhile if the rate of interest is high enough to compensate. In their development of this idea, Tobin and Baumol show that the transactions demand for money will then vary inversely with the rate of interest on nonmonetary assets (or with the excess of this rate of interest over the rate of interest on money holdings, if positive). (⇛ PRECAUTIONARY MOTIVE; SPECULATIVE MOTIVE).

Transfer costs. The COSTS incurred in transporting raw materials and finished products between raw-material sources and factory on the one hand, and factory and MARKET on the other. They should include all costs of achieving these physical transfers, including loading and unloading costs, administrative costs, etc., and not simply freight charges.

Transfer earnings. The earnings of a FACTOR OF PRODUCTION that are just sufficient to keep it in its present employment. Any excess of actual earnings over transfer earnings is known as ECONOMIC RENT. Not to be confused with TRANSFER PAYMENTS.

Transfer payments. Payments to individuals from government that are not in exchange for any productive or employment activity. Examples are OASI and welfare payments, unemployment insurance and Medicare. In 1980 U.S. federal government transfer payments amounted to almost $200 billion, the bulk going to below-average-income individuals. They are financed by TAXATION and, in some instances, by premiums paid by employees and employers.

Transfer prices. PRICES that are set in transactions between different branches or divisions of a business corporation. Use of transfer pricing represents an attempt to replace administrative coordination by a market mechanism in allocating resources within a large corporation. For example, suppose division A of a corporation mines a raw material and then passes it on to division B for processing. Under a centralized system, information on the costs of mining in division A and the costs of processing and revenue from output in division B would be collected by "the center," and the appropriate amount of the raw material to be transferred from A to B determined centrally. Under a transfer-pricing system, each division would be made a PROFIT CENTER, and a price for division A's output would be set. Each division would then be expected to maximize its PROFIT at this transfer price. The advantage of this system is held to be the savings in information and coordination costs, and improvements in management efficiency and morale because of greater autonomy.

Transfer pricing is also the practice by which MULTINATIONAL CORPORATIONS sell their products to their own overseas subsidiaries at artificially low prices. This enables the company to reduce its overall tax bill by transferring income from a high-tax to a low-tax country.

Transformation curve. A curve that shows for an economy as a whole how one good—say, X—can be "transformed" into another good—say, Y—by reducing output of X and transferring the RESOURCES thus saved into production of Y. It is drawn on the assumption that resources in the economy are fixed in total and so shows the alternative combinations of X and Y that are technically feasible. An example of a transformation curve is shown in the diagram.

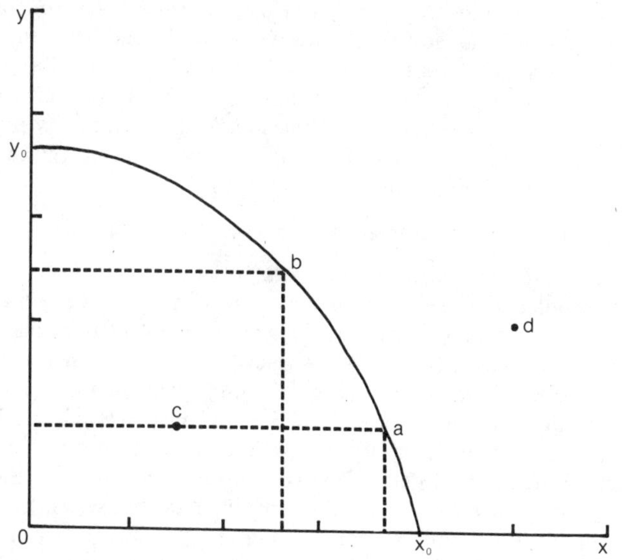

The curve shows that, if all resources are devoted to Y, a total of Y_o can be produced; if all resources are devoted to X, a total of X_o can be produced; or some intermediate combination of X and Y can be produced, e.g., such as that at *a* or *b*. It is also possible to produce at a point within the transformation curve—e.g., at *c*—that implies that resources are not being used fully, or with full efficiency, since it is possible to have more of both goods by being on the transformation curve, e.g., at *b*. On the other hand, it is not possible to be at a point such as *d*, since this is outside the transformation curve—it requires more resources or greater efficiency than are in fact possessed by the economy. The shape of the curve is due to the operation of the law of diminishing returns (⇛ DIMINISHING RETURNS, LAW OF). It represents the fact that as X is reduced from X_o by small, equal amounts, the increases in Y get smaller and smaller, because the resources being released from X are encountering diminishing returns when they are moved into Y, and similarly if we reduce Y from Y_o.

The transformation curve is an important analytical device in several areas of economics, particularly in GENERAL EQUILIBRIUM theory, WELFARE ECONOMICS and INTERNATIONAL TRADE theory. It is also useful in pointing up some basic economic lessons—e.g., in an economy with a fixed quantity of resources and a given technology it is not possible to have more of one thing without having less of another. The curve is also often referred to as the *production possibility curve.*

Transitivity. A particular type of consistency property that is assumed to be possessed by the preference ordering of a consumer. Suppose we take three specific baskets of goods, A, B and C. The consumer tells us he prefers A to B and B to C. We would then predict that he will prefer A to C. His preferences are transitive if this is in fact the case. Likewise, transitivity requires that if he is indifferent between A and B, and between B and C, then he is also indifferent between A and C. We would tend to think that if the consumer's preferences were not transitive, he was being in a way inconsistent in his choices. The implication of this transitivity property is that the consumer's INDIFFERENCE CURVES cannot intersect (given also that he always prefers more of a good to less of it).

Transnational corporation. ⇛ MULTINATIONAL CORPORATION

Treasury, The. This department acts as financial agent for the U.S. government, manufactures coins and currency, is responsible for certain aspects of law enforcement, and develops and makes recommendations on economic policy and changes in TAXATION and FISCAL POLICY. The Treasury is one of 13 departments of the executive branch of government and in terms of its budget is the third largest after Health and Human Services and Defense. The functions of the Treasury are illustrated by the titles of its various services; Bureau of Alcohol, Tobacco and Firearms; Office of the Comptroller of the Currency (which supervises the BANKING system); U.S. Customs Service; Bureau of Engraving and Printing; Federal Law Enforcement Training Center; Bureau of Government Financial Operations (which provides a central accounting system and cash management); Internal Revenue Service; Bureau of the Mint; Bureau of the Public Debt; United States Savings Bonds Division and the Secret Service. The Secretary of the Treasury is the chief financial officer of government; he serves as chairman of the President's Economic Policy Group and also as the U.S. Governor on such institutions as the INTERNATIONAL MONETARY FUND and the INTERNATIONAL BANK FOR RECONSTRUCTION AND DEVELOPMENT.

Treasury bills. Short-term securities (usually 30, 60 or 90 days) issued by the federal TREASURY (⇛⇛ FEDERAL RESERVE SYSTEM). The minimum holding is $10,000. Such securities are purchased both by the private sector and by COMMERCIAL BANKS. The banks are permitted to use these securities as collateral (⇛ COLLATERAL SECURITY) if they wish to borrow from the FED. This permits the FED to exercise some degree of MONETARY POLICY, because (1) it can agree or refuse to discount the bills; (2) it can set the rate of discount; and (3) it can determine the amount of collateral (Treasury bills) necessary for a LOAN.

Treaty of Rome. ⇛ EUROPEAN ECONOMIC COMMUNITY

Treaty of Stockholm. ⇛ EUROPEAN FREE TRADE ASSOCIATION

Trigger price. A minimum price level applied to IMPORTS of steel into the United States. If import prices were below this minimum, there was a presumption of DUMPING, and a countervailing duty (⇛ TARIFFS, IMPORT) could be imposed or a QUOTA set. This price was based on Japanese delivered prices to certain areas of the United States. The system was suspended in 1982, when the steel producers issued antidumping lawsuits against the importers.

Trust. 1. MONEY or property vested wtih an individual or group of individuals to administer in the interests of others. Trusts of this kind are usually set up to continue interests in accordance with the general instructions of the initiator and to protect them from outside interference. Thus, people set up trusts or appoint trustees to administer their estates after their death. Certain newspapers are administered by trusts and so are many charitable organizations. The term is a legal one, and state law governs the powers of trustees in investing and disposing of assets where these are not specified in the trust deed. 2. Financial trusts are also established for commercial purposes where particular protection is required against fraud, e.g., INVESTMENT TRUSTS. 3. At the end of the 19th century, trusts were used to form monopolistic groups of companies—for example, the Standard Oil Trust, which was established in 1882. The SHERMAN ACT made such trusts illegal, and the term is still used to refer to large MONOPOLY groups. (⇛ ANTITRUST POLICY).

Turgot, Anne Robert Jacques, Baron de l'Aulne (1727–81). Educated for the Church, he became an abbe at the Sorbonne in Paris but then took up a career in the civil service, where he remained for the rest of his life. He was the administrator of the District of Limoges from 1761 to 1774, when he became secretary of state for the navy. For a short time he held the post of controller of finance. His economic work appeared in *Reflections sur la formation et la distribution des richesses,* published in 1766. In this work he gave a clear analysis of the law of diminishing returns (⇛ DIMINISHING RETURNS, LAW OF). He demonstrated how more and more applications of a FACTOR OF PRODUCTION (CAPITAL) to a constant factor (LAND) will first increase, then decrease, the return at the margin. He was the first to equate capital accumulation with SAVING, a view that became a central feature of CLASSICAL ECONOMICS.

Turnover. The total sales revenue of a business.

Turnover tax. A tax (⇛ TAXATION) levied as a proportion of the PRICE of a COMMODITY on each sale in the distribution chain; also called a *cascade tax*. (⇛⇛ VALUE-ADDED TAX).

Turnpike theorems. Propositions about the nature of OPTIMAL paths of ECONOMIC GROWTH for an economy. Suppose one wants to get from location A to a reasonably distant location B, neither of which may be at a turnpike access point and which may be connected by an ordinary highway network. Given the speed differential between travel on a turnpike and on an ordinary highway, and given the distance between A and B, the quickest way of making the trip may be to drive from A to the turnpike, travel along it, and then leave it and drive to B. This is a very simple example of the kind of proposition presented by the turnpike theorems.

The analogue to the turnpike is the maximal balanced-growth path of the economy—i.e., a time path of outputs of each industrial sector of the economy that has the two properties that (*a*) at each point in time, supply of each output is equal to its demand, so that the economy is continuously in equilibrium; and (*b*) the growth rate of the economy (which, in the kind of MODEL analyzed, is the common growth rate of each industrial sector) is greater than that along any other balanced-growth path. The counterpart to location A is the current set of outputs in the economy; and the counterpart to location B is a future desired set of outputs. Turnpike theorems analyze the conditions under which the fastest growth path from one set of outputs to the other will involve moving along—or, more accurately, moving close to—the maximal balanced-growth path. The significance of the analysis lies in the point that if, under a wide range of circumstances, the maximal balanced-growth path does have this "turnpike" property, then it must play a central role in models that plan for optimal growth.

In fact, the theorems do not establish the *extreme* turnpike property of our motoring example, in that it is not in general best to move as quickly as possible to the maximal balanced growth path, move along it, then come off as close as possible to the final destination. Rather, the theorems prove weaker propositions of the following type: Provided that the terminal date is "sufficiently" far away, the optimal-growth path will require that "much" of the time be spent traveling "close" to the maximal balanced-growth path (where, of course, the terms *sufficiently, much* and *close* are given precise mathematical expression). Given the two end points, the optimal path between them will curve away from the straight line joining them, in the direction of the maximal balanced-growth path. (Note that in the economic model, there is no disadvantage in traveling across country!) The significance of the maximal balanced-growth path to planning economic growth is established, but in a more limited sense than would be so if the full turnpike property were to hold.

Tying contract. An agreement whereby a purchaser of one article agrees to buy the seller's supplies of some other commodity as a condition of the initial purchase (⇛ EXCLUSIVE DEALING). Given MONOPOLY power over one product, a producer could exploit this further by a tying contract or use the tying contract as a means of PRICE DISCRIMINATION. ANTITRUST POLICY has dealt severely with such arrangements. In 1936 the Supreme Court rejected IBM's claim that purchasers of its card-sorting machines had to use IBM cards to prevent damage to the machines.

U

Uncertainty. One of a number of terms defined much more narrowly in economics than in everyday usage (others are INVESTMENT, COST and PROFIT). The classical definition of uncertainty, first given by FRANK HYNEMAN KNIGHT, is that uncertainty exists when there is more than one possible outcome to a course of action, the form of each possible outcome is known, but the PROBABILITY of getting any one outcome is not known. If the probabilities of obtaining the outcomes are known, then this situation is one of RISK. For example, suppose I make a bet with you that if I toss a coin and it falls heads, I pay you $1, while if it falls tails, you pay me $1. To you, there are two possible outcomes of the decision to play this game: Receiving $1, paying $1. If the coin has not been tampered with in any way, we can say that the chances of its falling heads are 50-50—i.e., there is a probability of 0.5 that it will be heads or tails. Since the probabilities of the outcomes are known, this is a situation of risk. Suppose, however, instead of tossing a coin, I had made the bet contingent on whether or not the next automobile that passes us has an *A* or an *E* in its license number. Since you are not likely to know the probabilities of these two events, the problem facing you is one of uncertainty. (⇛ BERNOULLI'S HYPOTHESIS).

Unconditional grants. ⇛ FISCAL FEDERALISM

Undated securities. SECURITIES not bearing a REDEMPTION DATE or OPTION; hence, IRREDEEMABLE SECURITIES.

Underdeveloped country. ⇛ DEVELOPING COUNTRY

Undervalued currency. A CURRENCY whose EXCHANGE RATE is below either its FREE-MARKET level or the EQUILIBRIUM level that it is expected to reach in the LONG RUN. Conversely, an *overvalued currency* may develop as a consequence of balance of payments deficits. This was the experience of the United States when the dollar became overvalued in terms of gold. The dollar was devalued in 1971 (⇛ DEVALUATION). (⇛⇛ INTERNATIONAL MONETARY FUND; SMITHSONIAN AGREEMENT).

Underwriting. The business of insuring against RISK. An underwriter, in return for a COMMISSION or PREMIUM, agrees to bear a risk or a proportion of a risk. (⇛⇛ INSURANCE).

Unemployment. A situation that exists when members of the LABOR force wish to work but cannot get a job. It is therefore used in the sense of "involuntary" unemployment rather than the voluntary decision on the part of someone to choose leisure rather than work. Most postwar governments up until the mid 1970s took it as a prime object of policy to keep aggregate national unemployment at a minimum that was consistent with little or no inflation. This minimum was, from the 1950s to the early 1970s, believed to be in the neighborhood of 3 percent to 4 percent of the labor force. The rapid acceleration in the rate of inflation through the 1970s led, however, to increased emphasis on control of inflation, and rates of unemployment throughout the OECD (⇛ ORGANIZATION FOR ECONOMIC COOPERATION AND DEVELOPMENT) economies have risen sharply. In the U.S., unemployment reached at least 10.1 percent of the labor force in 1982 (⇛ KEYNES, JOHN MAYNARD). In a general sense, unemployment represents a waste of resources: The economy is producing below its potential capacity, and so the total output of goods and services is less than it could be—*everyone* is worse off than they need be. The burden of unemployment also tends not to be equally shared: It bears particularly heavily on youth and ethnic minorities and on particular localities and regions. It is arguable that high rates of unemployment create greater social tensions and stresses than high rates of inflation. Several types of unemployment have been distinguished: DISGUISED UNEMPLOYMENT; FRICTIONAL UNEMPLOYMENT; SEASONAL UNEMPLOYMENT; STRUCTURAL UNEMPLOYMENT. (⇛ STAGFLATION; UNEMPLOYMENT, NATURAL RATE OF).

Unemployment, cyclical. UNEMPLOYMENT that is due to a downturn in the business cycle and that can therefore be expected to occur and disappear with a fairly regular periodicity.

Unemployment, natural rate of. The rate of UNEMPLOYMENT corresponding to a GENERAL EQUILIBRIUM, i.e., equilibrium on all MARKETS in the economy, including those for labor. Though this might appear paradoxical, it is therefore the rate of unemployment that would be observed when the economy is at a "full-employment equilibrium." All PRICES and wage rates have adjusted to the levels at which all markets "clear"—SUPPLY equals DEMAND in each market in the economy—and so any observed unemployment is actually *voluntary,* as opposed to the "involuntary unemployment" that JOHN MAYNARD KEYNES was so concerned to explain. It arises because, at the prevailing equilibrium wage rates, some workers prefer to quit, possibly to search for another job that they think will pay a higher wage. (⇛⇛ FRICTIONAL UNEMPLOYMENT). The natural rate of unemployment is a LONG-RUN concept: At any particular period of time, actual unemployment may differ from it, but it is the rate around which the actual rate moves and to which it would tend in the long run. It is determined by *real* (⇛ REAL TERMS) elements in the economy—consumers' and workers' tastes and the efficiency with which search takes place, for example—and in particular is independent of purely *monetary* factors such as the MONEY SUPPLY. It follows that in the long run monetary factors influence only nominal values such as the price level and not real values such as output, employment and relative prices. The natural rate of unemployment is therefore a central concept in MONETARISM.

Unemployment rate. The rate of UNEMPLOYMENT is given by the number of adult persons (15 years and over) actively seeking employment as a proportion of the civilian labor force (adult persons seeking work or having a civilian job). In the United States the unemployment rate was close to 6 percent in the early 1970s and fell to 4.8 percent in mid-1973. It rose to almost 9 percent in early 1975, falling to 5.6 percent by mid-1979. By the end of 1981, it had risen once again to 8.9 percent, the highest level since the 1930s. (⇛⇛ UNEMPLOYMENT, NATURAL RATE OF).

Union shop. A very common arrangement in the United States whereby an employer can hire anyone he wants at the union wage, as opposed to the case where the union controls employment. Within some reasonable specified period of time, the employee must then join the union. (⇛ CLOSED SHOP; OPEN SHOP).

Unit-branch state. A state that prohibits a bank from having branches of that bank in the state. (⇛ BANKING).

Unit of account. ⇛ EUROPEAN UNITS OF ACCOUNT

Unit tax. A SALES TAX assessed as a given number of dollars and cents per unit of the product produced or sold. For example, a tax of $5 per bottle of wine, regardless of its selling price, would be a unit tax. Most federal sales taxes in the United States (imposed on alcohol, tobacco, gasoline and tires) are unit taxes. (⇛ TAX, AD VALOREM; TAXATION).

United Nations Conference on Trade and Development (UNCTAD). A conference convened in 1964 in response to growing anxiety among the DEVELOPING COUNTRIES over the difficulties they were facing in their attempts to bridge the standard of living gap between them and the developed nations. A further full meeting was held in 1968, a third meeting in 1972 and a fourth in 1976. The then director-general of UNCTAD, Professor R.D. Prebisch, summed the problem up in his report *Towards a New Trade Policy for Development.* The growth rate of 5 percent per annum, which was required for the developing countries to make progress in terms of REAL INCOME per capita, implied a required IMPORT growth of 6 percent. However, the trend rate of growth of their EXPORTS had been only about 4 percent in value, and this had been reduced to the low figure of 2 percent because of the deterioration in their TERMS OF TRADE. If this relationship continued, they would suffer chronic BALANCE OF PAYMENTS deficits, which would lead to a worsening in their economic welfare. The problem could be tackled on two fronts: (*a*) through measures to offset the deterioration in the terms of trade, and (*b*) through measures to promote their exports. The terms-of-trade approach could be through INTERNATIONAL COMMODITY AGREEMENTS, which would be designed to prevent primary prices from falling, and through compensatory finance arrangements. Many compensatory financing schemes had been put forward before the convening of UNCTAD but had not generally got beyond the proposal stage. An exception is the compensatory facility of the INTERNATIONAL MONETARY FUND, which came into operation in 1963. It is, however, available in principle to all members of the fund. It extends LOANS to finance short-term balance of payments deficits caused by a fall in exports below trend. The loan is limited to a proportion of the member's IMF quota. The UNCTAD recommended that the IMF should study the possibilities of extending this facility. Professor Prebisch suggested that the developed countries that benefited from the terms-of-trade shift should contribute to a fund that would be used to reimburse the losers. Professor J.E. Meade (1907–) (⇛ NOBEL PRIZES), has suggested that the transfer should be between the importers and exporters of primary COMMODITIES and based on the movement of price levels above or below agreed limits. A report by the Group of Experts of UNCTAD, *International*

Monetary Issues and the Developing Countries (1965), linked the problem with INTERNATIONAL LIQUIDITY. They proposed that the IMF should be authorized to increase LIQUIDITY by the issue of certificates, distributed in proportion to agreed quotas, to the developed countries in exchange for their CURRENCY. This currency would then be lent through the INTERNATIONAL BANK FOR RECONSTRUCTION AND DEVELOPMENT to the developing countries. Many of the proposals aired in UNCTAD are still under discussion. Professor Prebisch had suggested that the developing countries should be free to combine to discriminate against imports of manufactures from the developed countries, and at the same time the latter should give preferences (⇛ INFANT INDUSTRY ARGUMENT). The distaste felt by the developing countries for the MOST FAVORED NATION CLAUSE of the GENERAL AGREEMENT ON TARIFFS AND TRADE was recognized by that institution. A new chapter to the GATT was added in 1965 on trade and development, which called for the reduction of tariffs (⇛ TARIFFS, IMPORT) and QUOTAS on developing countries' exports. It became possible for preferential duties to be given to imports from developing countries without having to extend these preferences to all the contracting parties of GATT. In 1970 agreement was reached by which the developed nations in the EUROPEAN FREE TRADE ASSOCIATION and the EUROPEAN ECONOMIC COMMUNITY, as well as the United States, gave preferences in specified manufactured goods to the developing countries. This agreement came into force in 1971 for a period of 10 years, subject to annual review. However, a report prepared by UNCTAD in 1981 accused the United States, the EEC and Japan of abandoning this commitment. The fourth conference in 1976 agreed that discussions should be pursued with a view to the negotiating of a COMMON FUND to finance an integrated commodity price-support scheme. (⇛⇛ BRANDT REPORT).

United Nations Relief and Rehabilitation Administration (UNRRA). An emergency organization established toward the end of the Second World War to supply the basic food and clothing, raw materials and machinery requirements of the countries of Western Europe that had suffered extensive war damage. The organization was particularly active in Greece, Italy, Yugoslavia, Austria, Czechoslovakia, Poland and the Ukraine. It was financed by the British Commonwealth and the United States and extended its aid to the Pacific upon the conclusion of the war there. It was wound up officially in August 1946, and the major task of rehabilitation was taken over by the EUROPEAN RECOVERY PROGRAM.

Unrequited exports. EXPORTS for which there is no reverse flow of goods or finance in payment. They generally take place in settlement of past debts or for aid.

Unsecured bond. ⇛ BOND

Utilitarianism. The philosophy by which the purpose of government was the maximization of the sum of UTILITY, defined in terms of pleasure and pain, in the community as a whole. It was not hedonistic insofar as pleasure could include, for instance, the satisfaction of helping others. The purpose of government was to ensure the "greatest happiness of the greatest number."

It implied that utility could be measured and interpersonal comparisons made. Its chief advocate was JEREMY BENTHAM.

Utility. The satisfaction, pleasure or need-fulfillment derived from consuming some quantity of a good. It is essentially a psychological concept that is incapable of direct measurement in absolute units. The concept of utility lay at the heart of the classical theory of DEMAND, in the form of the law of diminishing MARGINAL UTILITY, until the 1930s, when SIR JOHN RICHARD HICKS and R. G. D. Allen rediscovered and extended the work of EUGEN SLUTSKY and VILPREDO FEDERICO DAMASO PARETO on INDIFFERENCE ANALYSIS. The objection was that if utility is essentially unmeasurable, it is invalid to construct a theory that proceeds as if it *could* be measured. Demand theory was therefore recast in terms of ORDINAL UTILITY—i.e., the consumer was assumed simply to be able to rank quantities of goods on the basis of preference (⇛ CONSUMERS' PREFERENCE) or indifference. Then, to say that some combination of goods has a "greater utility" than some other combination simply means that the consumer prefers the first combination to the second. Though most of the results of demand theory are unchanged, this interpretation of utility as preference, rather than as some "crude hedonistic calculus," is held to have put the theory on a much sounder footing. (⇛⇛ REVEALED PREFERENCE).

U-V curve. A curve that plots observations of the UNEMPLOYMENT RATE against the vacancy rate. It has a negative slope, indicating that high unemployment rates are associated with low vacancy rates. Shifts in the relationship over time can be used to explain STAGFLATION. A vacancy rate of 4 percent may have been compatible both with an unemployment rate of 5 percent in 1970 and with a rate of 8 percent in 1978 if there had been a rapid increase in young, unskilled entrants into the labor market who had difficulty in obtaining immediate employment.

V

Value. 1. The total UTILITY that is yielded by an object in question. This is often referred to as its "value in use." 2. The quantity of some other COMMODITY for which the object in question can be exchanged. This is then referred to as its "value in exchange." Thus, if the other commodity is MONEY, the value of the object is its PRICE. If the other commodity is fur coats, the value of the object is the number of fur coats for which it can be exchanged.

In most economic contexts the term *value* is used in the second sense. Thus, "value theory" could just as well be termed PRICE THEORY and consists of the analysis of what determines the EQUILIBRIUM rates of exchange between commodities directly, or between commodities and money. (⇛ VALUE, THEORIES OF).

Value added, or net output. The difference between total revenue of a firm and the cost of bought-in raw materials, SERVICES and components. It thus measures the VALUE which the firm has "added" to these brought-in materials and components by its processes of production, Since the total revenue of the firm will be divided among CAPITAL CHARGES (including DEPRECIATION), RENT, DIVIDEND payments, wages and the costs of materials, services and components, value added can also be calculated by summing the relevant types of cost. (⇛ VALUE ADDED TAX).

Value-added tax (VAT). A general tax (⇛ TAXATION) applied at each point of exchange of goods or services from primary production to final consumption. It is levied on the difference between the sale price of the goods or services (outputs) to which the tax is applied and the cost of goods and services (⇛ INPUTS) brought in for use in its production. The cost of these inputs is taken to include all charges, including all taxes except VAT itself. The method of payment and collection is as follows: Each trader sells his output at a price increased by the appropriate percentage of VAT. He is then liable for the payment to the government of the tax that he has obtained from his customers but can claim a refund of any VAT included in the invoices for the inputs that he himself purchased from his suppliers. His customers do likewise, and so on down to the final consumer. At each point of exchange, the tax is passed on in the form of higher prices. Being at the last point in the chain of exchange, the final consumer bears the whole tax. The traders within the chain do not bear any tax but act as collecting agencies. Value-added tax has the same base as a SALES TAX if the coverage is the same, but sales taxes normally have less coverage. There are fewer collection points for a sales tax, but value-added tax has a self-policing feature in that each buyer (other than the final consumer) will demand a tax invoice so that he can claim his tax credit. Value-added taxes are levied in the EUROPEAN ECONOMIC COMMUNITY and are the basis for contribution to the community budget. (⇛ TURNOVER TAX).

Value judgment. A statement of opinion or belief that is not capable of being falsified by comparison with fact. It is therefore essentially a NORMATIVE rather than a *positive* statement. Thus, the statement "UNEMPLOYMENT should not exist" is a value judgment, while the statement "Unemployment does not exist" is not. In economics, the desirability of making a clear distinction between value judgments and positive analysis is always stressed. Where the object is to understand and make predictions about actual economic phenomena, opinions and beliefs may only obscure the issues—e.g., if one is trying to analyze the role of excess PROFITS in the mechanism of RESOURCE allocation (⇛ ECONOMIC EFFICIENCY) in a FREE-MARKET ECONOMY, or to predict the consequences of a 45 percent corporation tax (⇛ CORPORATION INCOME TAX) on this process, it helps to put to one side one's belief that profits are iniquitous/virtuous. This is not to say, however, that economists should not make value judgments or make prescriptions about the objectives of economic policy. Indeed, some of the most successful "positive" economists have been the most vocal advocates of particular policy objectives, e.g., JOHN MAYNARD KEYNES, MILTON FRIEDMAN. Rather, it is simply to argue that value judgments must not be allowed to obscure analysis of what is, as opposed to what ought to be. This is, in essence, simply part of scientific method, but it is something that is especially difficult to achieve in economics.

Value, theories of. There have been three broad approaches to the analysis of VALUE in use or exchange in economic theory. (*a*) *General use theories:* Theories that were based on the assumption that the value of a COMMODITY was related to the use to which it could be put. (⇛⇛ GALIANI, FERDINANDO.) (*b*) *Labor theory:* Value is interpreted as reflecting the cost of production measured in terms of LABOR time absorbed. (⇛⇛ MARX, KARL; RICARDO, DAVID; SMITH, ADAM). (*c*) *Marginal utility theory:* The UTILITY of the final small increment in DEMAND and SUPPLY determines the value of commodities in exchange. (⇛⇛ GOSSEN, HERMANN HEINRICH; JEVONS, WILLIAM STANLEY; MARGINAL UTILITY; MARSHALL, ALFRED; WALRAS, MARIE ESPRIT LEON).

Variable. A number capable of taking different values. In mathematics, a variable is regarded simply as a general abstract concept, with no necessary real-world counterpart (so one solves an equation for the variables x or y, which are not any particular things). In any applied science such as economics, however, variables are usually identified with real-world magnitudes of interest—e.g., CONSUMPTION and INVESTMENT will be regarded as variables in a MODEL of income determination. (⇛ INCOME DETERMINATION, THEORY OF).

Variable costs. Costs that vary directly with the rate of output, e.g., LABOR costs, raw-material costs, fuel and power. Also known as *operating costs, prime costs, on costs* or *direct costs.*

Variance. A number that measures the extent to which a set of numbers are dispersed about their arithmetic mean. (⇛⇛ AVERAGE). It is defined as: The average of the sum of the squares of deviations from their mean, of a given set of numbers. The bigger the variance, the greater the dispersion of the numbers. Given a set of numbers—x_1, x_2 . . . x_n—we calculate their mean as an average or representative value, a measure of the "central tendency" of the numbers. It is then useful to consider the extent to which the numbers are dispersed about the mean. For example, suppose we have the three numbers 100, 101, 102. Then their mean is:

$$\bar{x} = \frac{100 + 101 + 102}{3} = \frac{303}{3} = 101.$$

On the other hand, suppose we have the three numbers 31, 71, 201. Then their mean is also

$$\bar{x} = \frac{31 + 71 + 201}{3} = \frac{303}{3} = 101.$$

Clearly, in the first case the numbers are far more closely grouped around their mean than in the second case, and so we would tend to say that the mean is a far better representation of the whole set of numbers than in the second case. Therefore, given that we might often wish to use the mean to tell us something about a set of numbers, it would appear to be useful to have another number that would tell us how widely or narrowly the numbers are clustered around the mean.

A seemingly obvious way to get such a measure might be to subtract the mean from each number and add up the differences. The larger this sum, the more widely must the numbers be dispersed about their mean. The trouble with this measure is that the sum of the differences will always be zero. For example:

$$\begin{array}{rr} 100 - 101 = & -1 \\ 101 - 101 = & 0 \\ 102 - 101 = & \underline{1} \\ \text{Total} = & 0 \end{array} \qquad\qquad \begin{array}{rr} 31 - 101 = & -70 \\ 71 - 101 = & -30 \\ 201 - 101 = & \underline{100} \\ \text{Total} = & 0 \end{array}$$

This is not an accident of the numbers chosen—it is a property of the mean that this is always so. The solution proposed by statisticians is to take the square of the difference between the mean and each number, and then to sum these squared differences. This trick of squaring the difference solves the problem, because the square of a negative number is always a positive number, and the square of a positive number is also always a positive number; and hence, the sum of these squared differences must be a positive number. To the above calculations, we can add:

$$\begin{array}{rr} (-1)^2 = & 1 \\ (0)^2 = & 0 \\ (1)^2 = & \underline{1} \\ \text{Total} = & 2 \end{array} \qquad\qquad \begin{array}{rr} (-70)^2 = & 4{,}900 \\ (-30)^2 = & 900 \\ (100)^2 = & \underline{10{,}000} \\ \text{Total} = & 15{,}800 \end{array}$$

Clearly, the greater the differences between the numbers and the mean, the greater the squares of these differences, and so the greater the sum of these squares.

However, our problem of finding a single number to summarize the degree of dispersion of a set of numbers about their mean has not yet been solved. By simply summing the squares of the differences, we run the risk that the sum may be large, not because the numbers are widely dispersed about their mean, but because there are many numbers. Suppose we have a set of 1,000 numbers, 500 of which are equal to 1 and 500 of which are equal to 3. Their mean is then 2. Each number is only one unit away from the mean, and we would say that the numbers were closely clustered about their mean, yet the sum of the squared differences is equal to 1,000, i.e., $500 \times (-1)^2 + 500 \times (1)^2$. What we need is some measure of the "average" difference, i.e., some way of allowing for the number of values involved. This is done by dividing by the number of values. In this example we would divide by 1,000; in the previous example we would divide by 3. Hence, we have arrived at a procedure for finding a number that summarizes the extent to which a set of numbers are dispersed about their mean. This number is called the variance, and it is defined by the formula:

$$\text{Variance} = \Sigma^2 = \frac{1}{n} \sum_{i=1}^{n} (x_i - \bar{x})^2$$

where x_i is the ith number, $\bar{x}$ is the mean, and n is the number of values, x_1, $x_2 \ldots x_n$. This formula says succinctly: Calculate the difference between each number and the mean; square these differences; sum these squared differences; divide this sum by the number of numbers, i.e., by n. The greater the dispersion of the numbers about their mean, the greater will be the differences between each and the mean, and so the greater the value of the variance.

To illustrate how we might use the variance in practical situations, suppose we were told that two companies had each, over the past 10 years, paid out on the average a DIVIDEND of 10 percent—i.e., the mean dividend was 10 percent, but that the variance of dividend payments of one company was four times that of the other (i.e., the dividend payments of one were much more dispersed about the average than the other, being in some years much higher but in other years much lower). Then, if we attach importance to consistency or stability of dividends, we should choose the share with the lower variance. Examples of the applications of the variance to all fields that involve numerical data and its analysis are numerous.

One slight problem that occurs when an attempt is made to give a variance an everyday interpretation is that, since it involves the squares of numbers, it must be expressed in terms of the squares of the units in which those numbers are measured. If we were calculating the variance of a set of weights measured in pounds, then the variance would be measured in "pounds squared" or "square pounds." However, this problem can easily be overcome by defining the STANDARD DEVIATION as the square root of the variance.

Vector. A set of numbers arranged in a row or column. For example, we have the row vector: (3 2 0); and the column vector:

$$\begin{pmatrix} 3 \\ 2 \\ 0 \end{pmatrix}$$

These vectors are three-dimensional, because they have three components, the three numbers 3, 2, 0. If we let $a_1, a_2, a_3, \ldots a_n$ stand for any n numbers, then we can define the n-dimensional row vector: $(a_1\ a_2\ a_3\ \ldots\ a_n)$; and the n-dimensional column vector:

$$\begin{matrix} a_1 \\ a_2 \\ a_3 \\ \cdot \\ \cdot \\ \cdot \\ a_n \end{matrix}$$

where n can be any positive number greater than 1. Just as basic elementary operations of addition, subtraction and multiplication have been defined for ordinary numbers, so mathematicians have framed rules for carrying out these operations with vectors. Much of economic theory, and particularly GENERAL EQUILIBRIUM theory, can be translated into terms of vectors and a related concept, the MATRIX. Such a translation permits considerable simplification and clarification. In addition, the development of the mathematical theory of vectors and matrices has stimulated some extremely important innovations in economics, most notably INPUT-OUTPUT ANALYSIS, which is based entirely on the algebra of matrices and vectors.

Velocity of circulation. ⇛ INCOME VELOCITY OF CIRCULATION

Venture capital. ⇛ RISK CAPITAL

Vertical integration. The undertaking by a single firm of successive stages in the process of production of a particular good. The oil industry is a good example of a vertically integrated industry. The major firms undertake exploration, drilling and extraction; transport of crude oil to refineries; refining into gasoline, fuel oils, etc.; transport to distribution outlets (gas stations and garages); and ownership of those outlets. There are several advantages arising from vertical integration, the extent of these varying from industry to industry and presumably determining the degree of vertical integration. There may be technical advantages to be gained from physical proximity of successive processes, e.g., iron-ore smelting and the production of steel and steel products. Important advantages may arise out of greater security and stability, and improvements in coordination between stages of production, which come about if control is centralized. In addition, a firm may be able to eliminate excessive PROFITS of a seller or buyer, or carry out the relevant operation more efficiently, by itself taking over the operation. Or the firm may have to integrate vertically from sheer necessity—there may be no other firm capable of supplying the raw material, component or service efficiently enough and to the required specifications. Finally, vertical integration may simply represent a very profitable INVESTMENT, particularly if the product is sold to other buyers. (⇛ MERGER).

Vertical merger. ⇛ MERGER; VERTICAL INTEGRATION

Viner, Jacob (1892–1970). ⇛ CUSTOMS UNION

Visible balance. The BALANCE OF PAYMENTS in VISIBLE TRADE, i.e., IMPORTS and EXPORTS.

Visible trade. INTERNATIONAL TRADE in merchandise, IMPORTS and EXPORTS. (⇒⇒ INVISIBLES).

Voting shares. EQUITY shares entitling holders to vote in the election of directors of a company. Normally all COMMON STOCKS are voting shares, but sometimes a company may create a class of nonvoting stocks if the existing stockholders wish to raise more equity capital but exclude the possibility of losing control of the business. PREFERRED STOCKS do not normally carry voting power (except for certain limited statutory voting rights) nor do corporate BONDS.

W

Wage and price guidelines. ⇛ PRICES AND INCOMES POLICY

Wage drift. The tendency for wage earnings to exceed wage rates gives rise to wage drift, measured as the difference between wage earnings and rates. This difference will consist of overtime earnings and special bonuses not provided for in the general agreement that establishes the wage rates for a particular class of workers. Since wage earnings are, on the one hand, what determines the spending power of a large group of consumers, and, on the other, the costs of producing goods and services, it is these rather than wage rates that influence the rate of INFLATION. The significance of wage drift therefore lies in the fact that, to the extent that it exists, control of inflation through restraint on wage rates is ineffective. In general, government control can only really be exercised over wage rates: Overtime working, special bonuses, etc., tend to be determined at the place of work and hence are very difficult to supervise. The extent of wage drift therefore shows the degree of failure of a policy of wage freeze (⇛ PRICES AND INCOMES POLICY). However, some economists would argue that wage drift is a desirable thing. If wage rates are pegged at particular levels, then they are not able to fulfill their functions as PRICES in indicating situations of scarcity and eradicating these by rising and attracting more LABOR. If the extent of wage drift does, in fact, measure the degree of labor scarcity at particular places, then wage earnings will be fulfilling their role as prices, and this is desirable from the point of view of market efficiency. It would not necessarily be desirable to eliminate wage drift entirely.

Wage fund theory. ADAM SMITH took over from the PHYSIOCRATS the idea that wages are advanced to the workers in anticipation of the sale of their output. Wages could not be increased unless the CAPITAL destined to pay them was increased. Capital, in turn, was determined by SAVINGS. The CLASSICAL SCHOOL developed its theory of wages around these ideas. In the short run there was a given number of workers and a given amount of savings to pay their wages. The two together determined the average wage. In the long run the supply of LABOR was related to the minimum of subsistence needed to sustain the labor force. (This subsistence level was not simply physiological; it was related to a standard of living accepted by custom.) If the wage rate rose above this, the population increased; if it fell below, it contracted. In the long run the level of the demand for labor was determined by the size of the wages fund, and this, in turn, by the level of savings. This meant that, as JOHN STUART MILL put it, "the demand for COMMODITIES is not the demand for labor." If you increased CONSUMPTION, you reduced savings and therefore the wage fund. PRODUCTIVITY did not influence REAL WAGES; what mattered was the level of PROFITS, for savings depended on profits. The argument assumed that savings flowed into fixed capital and variable (wage) capital in equal proportions, so that what KARL MARX called the organic composition of capital remained constant. DAVID RICARDO worried about this point in his analysis of the effect of machinery on employment. Investment bypassed the wages fund, and the demand for labor was reduced. W.T. Thornton criticized the wages fund doctrine on the grounds that wages were determined by SUPPLY and DEMAND in the market. J.S. Mill accepted some of Thornton's points and admitted that the wages fund idea might be more appropriate in the context of a discontinuous production process (akin to seed-time to harvest) rather than a continuous flow of output, which was the true state of affairs. There was some popular confusion at the time, because it was thought the economists meant there existed a definite fund available for wages, so that there was no hope of workers obtaining higher average earnings.

Wagner Act. An Act of Congress (1935) that guaranteed the right of workers to elect a bargaining unit, by secret ballot, based on majority vote. (⇛ TAFT-HARTLEY ACT).

Wall Street. The name given to the New York STOCK EXCHANGE because of its location in that city.

Walras, Marie Esprit Leon (1834–1910). A mining engineer by training, he accepted the offer of a newly created Chair of Economics in the Faculty of Law at Lausanne in 1870. He held this post until he was succeeded by VILFREDO FEDERICO DAMASO PARETO upon his retirement in 1892. His publications include *Elements d'economie Politique Pure* (1874–77), *Etudes d'economie Sociale* (1896) and *Etudes d'economie Politique Appliquee* (1898). One of the three economists to propound a MARGINAL UTILITY theory in the 1870s, he set out the theory of diminishing marginal utility and showed how PRICES at which COMMODITIES exchanged are determined by the relative marginal utilities as perceived by the people taking part in the transaction. (⇛⇛ GOSSEN, HERMANN HEINRICH; JEVONS, WILLIAM STANLEY; MENGER, CARL). He also constructed a mathematical model of general equilibrium as a system of simultaneous equations in which he tried to show that all prices and quantities are uniquely determined. This is regarded as one of the foremost achievements in mathematical economics, of which Walras is considered the founder.

Wasting assets. ASSETS with strictly limited, though not necessarily determinate, lives, e.g., a mine, timber lands or a property on lease. Wasting assets have many of the characteristics of current assets, but they are normally included under fixed assets.

Watering stock. The issue of the nominal capital of a company in return for less than its money value, thus overstating the capital of the company and reducing its apparent return on capital. (⇛ RATE OF RETURN).

Wealth. The wealth of an individual is his total stock of tangible or intangible possessions that have a market value. This implies that they must be capable of being exchanged for MONEY or other goods—i.e., the ownership in them must be capable of being transferred. It also implies that we not only include the individual's physical possessions—such as a house, STOCKS and SHARES, bank accounts, etc.—but also his business and professional connections, together with the value of particular skills that he may possess. These latter

Y

Yaounde Convention. ⇛ LOME CONVENTION

Yield. The INCOME from a SECURITY (⇛ SECURITIES) as a proportion of its current market price. Because prices fluctuate, the yield will not, except by accident, be the same as the nominal or "coupon" rate of interest on a BOND. The *redemption yield* is normally applied only to bonds and is the interest payment over the remaining life of the security, plus or minus the difference between the purchase price and the redemption value—i.e., it is the earnings yield adjusted to take account of any CAPITAL GAIN or loss to redemption. An IRREDEEMABLE SECURITY in the form of a government bond having a flat yield of 3 percent with a PAR VALUE of $100, but a market price of $50, provides an earnings yield of 6 percent. The yield will fluctuate with the price of the security, rising as security prices fall, and vice-versa.

Z

Zero-sum game. A type of game, analyzed extensively in the theory of games (⇛ GAMES, THEORY OF), in which the gains and losses of the "players" sum to zero for every possible choice of STRATEGIES (⇛ STRATEGY). For example, suppose there are only two players, Firm A and Firm B, which between them control 100 percent of the MARKET for a particular product. Whatever increase in market share Firm A might gain will be exactly equal to the loss suffered by Firm B. The importance of this type of game is that the players are in *pure conflict.* There is no scope for joint action to increase the total sum of payoffs. (⇛⇛ MAXIMIN STRATEGY).

forms of wealth have a MARKET value in the sense that they can be exchanged in the relevant market. If it is desired to distinguish between the tangible and intangible types of wealth, the terms *human wealth* and *nonhuman wealth* are often used (⇛ CAPITAL; HUMAN CAPITAL). A basic property of wealth is that it is a means of generating INCOME—i.e., income is often regarded as the return on wealth. It follows that the value of a stock of wealth is given by the PRESENT VALUE of the flow of income it generates.

Weighted average. A form of arithmetic mean (⇛⇛ AVERAGE) constructed by first multiplying each number by a number designed to reflect its relative importance, summing the resulting products and then dividing by the sum of the numbers used as weights. The object of "weighting" the numbers is simply to obtain an overall average that correctly reflects the differing relative importances of the constituent items. For example, suppose that we want a number that shows the average change in the cost of providing a family with the basic necessities of life between now and some past period. One method would be to choose the set of items that we take to be the basic necessities, find by how much their PRICES have changed and calculate a straightforward arithmetic mean. Assume that there are three goods involved, and the current prices as percentages of the earlier prices are 120, 115 and 125, respectively. The simple mean of these is

$$\frac{120 + 115 + 125}{3} = 120.$$

However, if we want our average to give an accurate representation of the change in the family's cost of living, we should take into account differences in the relative importance of the goods. For example, if they spend most of their income on the second good, whose current price is only 115 percent of its earlier price, their cost of living has obviously risen by less than if they spent most of their income on the third good, whose price is 125 percent of its former value. In fact, taking a straightforward unweighted average implicitly assumes that each item has exactly equal importance or, in this example, that one-third of income is spent on each good. Instead, suppose that 30 percent of income is spent on the first good, 60 percent on the second and only 10 percent on the third. It seems natural, then, to weight each percentage by its share of total expenditure and to obtain the weighted average as:

$$\frac{\left(\frac{30}{100}\right) \times 120 + \left(\frac{60}{100}\right) \times 115 + \left(\frac{10}{100}\right) \times 125}{\frac{30}{100} + \frac{60}{100} + \frac{10}{100}} = \frac{36 + 69 + 12.5}{1} = 117.5$$

This is lower than the previous value, because the smallest price rise has the largest weight, and vice versa. Where the weights to be used are expressed as percentages or proportions, the denominator in the calculation will generally be equal to one, and this can be used to simplify calculations. This need not always happen, however. Suppose we thought that the relative importance of the three percentages could best be expressed by the weights 3, 12 and 1. That is, we regard the first percentage as three times more important than the third, and the second as four times more important than the first. Then we would construct our weighted average as:

$$\frac{3 \times 120 + 12 \times 115 + 125}{3 + 12 + 1} = \frac{360 + 1380 + 125}{16} = \frac{1865}{16} = 117$$

Clearly, the greater the differences in the values of the items, the greater the sensitivity of the final average value to choice of particular weights. (⇛ CONSUMER PRICE INDEX; INDEX NUMBER; INDEX-NUMBER PROBLEM).

Weights. ⇛ WEIGHTED AVERAGE

Welfare economics. That branch of economics concerned, first, with defining ECONOMIC EFFICIENCY; second, with evaluating the economic efficiency of particular systems of RESOURCE ALLOCATION; and finally, with analyzing the conditions under which economic policies may be said to have improved (⇛ SOCIAL WELFARE FUNCTION). The first two sets of problems are approached by defining the conditions that are necessary for a maximum of economic efficiency to be achieved and then by examining the degree to which actual systems—e.g., the PRICE SYSTEM—fulfill these conditions. The third set of problems is approached by defining tests or criteria that may be applied to proposed changes to decide if they represent improvements in welfare or not. (⇛⇛ COMPENSATION PRINCIPLE; COST-BENEFIT ANALYSIS; PIGOU, ARTHUR CECIL).

Wharton model. An econometric (⇛ ECONOMETRICS) model developed at the Wharton School of Business, University of Pennsylvania, used chiefly for short-run economic forecasting. (⇛ KLEIN, LAWRENCE ROBERT).

Wicksell effect, price. In discussing the derivation of factor (⇛ FACTORS OF PRODUCTION) prices from the value of MARGINAL PRODUCTS, KNUT WICKSELL pointed out that, in equilibrium, the RATE OF INTEREST would be greater than the value of the marginal product of capital. This is because the whole of the existing stock of capital is revalued when rates of interest change. (⇛ CAPITAL RESWITCHING).

Wicksell, Knut (1851–1926). Educated at Uppsala University in Sweden, where he studied mathematics and philosophy, he was appointed to the Chair of Economics at Lund in 1904, a post he held until 1916. His major publications include *Uber Wert, Kapital und Rente* (1893), *Finanz theoretische Untersuchungen* (1895) and *Geldzins und Guterpreise* (1898). A synthesis of his work was published in 1901 and 1906 with the English title of *Lectures on Political Economy*. He assimilated the GENERAL EQUILIBRIUM analysis of MARIE ESPRIT LEON WALRAS with the work of EUGEN VON BOHM-BAWERK and worked out a theory of distribution (⇛ DISTRIBUTION, THEORY OF) based on the new MARGINAL ANALYSIS of WILLIAM STANLEY JEVONS, Walras and CARL MENGER. In addition, he had a significant influence on monetary theory. He pointed out that high RATES OF INTEREST often coincided with high prices, which was contrary to what current theory predicted. He drew attention to the significance of the relative level of interest rates rather than their absolute level. Prices were related to the difference between changes in the real or natural rate of interest (which was determined by the expected rate of PROFITS) and the money rate. The CENTRAL BANK had an important influence over the price level through its operations on the DISCOUNT RATE. These theories were incorporated into his theory of the TRADE CYCLE. (⇛ INTEREST, NATURAL RATE OF; WICKSELL EFFECT, PRICE).

Wieser, Friedrich von (1851–1926). He succeeded CARL MENGER to the Chair of Economics at Vienna University in 1903 after a period at Prague University. His most important works include *Uber den Ursprung und die Hauptgesetze des Wirtschaftlichen Wertes* (1884), *Der Naturliche Wert* (1889) and *Theorie der gesellschaftlichen Wirtschaft* (1914). He developed a law of costs that became known later as the principle of opportunity COST. FACTORS OF PRODUCTION will be distributed by competition such that, in EQUILIBRIUM, the value of their marginal outputs will be equal. The costs of production of any COMMODITY reflect the competing claims in other uses for the services of the factors needed to produce it. The law became an important element in the theory of RESOURCE allocation. (⇛⇛ ECONOMIC EFFICIENCY).

Williams Commission. The presidential commission on INTERNATIONAL TRADE and investment policy that reported in 1971, following a wide-ranging review in congressional hearings and inquiries into U.S. overseas economic policy. The commission's report, entitled *International Economic Policy in an Interdependent World,* was published a few months before the conclusion of the SMITHSONIAN AGREEMENT.

Williamson, Oliver. ⇛ FIRM, THEORY OF

Windfall-profits tax. An extraordinary and usually temporary tax on corporate profits or corporate profits in excess of some long-run average level of profits. For example, a rapid rise in the price of oil has the potential (for producers still producing oil from low-cost wells) to create large increases in profits. Governments may feel it is legitimate to tax these windfall profits or RENTS using a special tax.

With the decontrol of crude oil prices in 1979–80, oil companies earned extremely large profits, leading to the establishment of special taxes on oil revenues. Producers would pay a tax of between 50 percent and 70 percent on what they earn above a base price for oil that had already been discovered. That tax is considerably lower for oil discovered after 1978.

Working capital. The surplus of current ASSETS over current LIABILITIES (where positive). It is financed from long-term funds. (⇛ CURRENT RATIO).

World Bank. ⇛ INTERNATIONAL BANK FOR RECONSTRUCTION AND DEVELOPMENT

X

X-efficiency. The term used to denote general managerial and technological efficiency. That is, the efficiency with which a firm uses INPUTS, solves its organizational problems and undertakes all its activities at minimum cost. In economic theory it is usually argued, as a corollary of PROFIT maximization, that firms will operate with the maximum x-efficiency. More recently, however, it has been pointed out that, when firms are insulated from competition, this may not be the case. (⇛ ECONOMIC EFFICIENCY; FIRM, THEORY OF; MONOPOLY; OLIGOPOLY).

Y

Yaounde Convention. ⇛ LOME CONVENTION

Yield. The INCOME from a SECURITY (⇛ SECURITIES) as a proportion of its current market price. Because prices fluctuate, the yield will not, except by accident, be the same as the nominal or "coupon" rate of interest on a BOND. The *redemption yield* is normally applied only to bonds and is the interest payment over the remaining life of the security, plus or minus the difference between the purchase price and the redemption value—i.e., it is the earnings yield adjusted to take account of any CAPITAL GAIN or loss to redemption. An IRREDEEMABLE SECURITY in the form of a government bond having a flat yield of 3 percent with a PAR VALUE of $100, but a market price of $50, provides an earnings yield of 6 percent. The yield will fluctuate with the price of the security, rising as security prices fall, and vice-versa.

Z

Zero-sum game. A type of game, analyzed extensively in the theory of games (⇛ GAMES, THEORY OF), in which the gains and losses of the "players" sum to zero for every possible choice of STRATEGIES (⇛ STRATEGY). For example, suppose there are only two players, Firm A and Firm B, which between them control 100 percent of the MARKET for a particular product. Whatever increase in market share Firm A might gain will be exactly equal to the loss suffered by Firm B. The importance of this type of game is that the players are in *pure conflict.* There is no scope for joint action to increase the total sum of payoffs. (⇛⇛ MAXIMIN STRATEGY).